TO MISHA, LAURENS AND KERS

GIBRALTAR
SPAIN
FRANCE
ITALY
CROATIA
ALBANIA
GREECE
CYPRUS
TURKEY
SYRIA
LEBANON
ISRAEL/
WEST BANK & GAZA
EGYPT
LIBYA
TUNISIA
ALGERIA
MOROCCO

SO BLUE *SO BLUE*

EDGES OF THE MEDITERRANEAN **AD VAN DENDEREN** STEIDLMACK

I

Globalization is a broad concept that encapsulates processes of change of an economic, cultural, political, ecological and military nature which, propelled by sometimes dizzying technological 'advances', play out on a local, regional, national and international level. These processes leave virtually no place on earth untouched. This justifies the use of the term when we try to grasp developments with a supranational character. The disadvantage, however, is the implication that the intended changes are the same all over the world. In this sense the term is not productive, and could even be called misleading. After all, we can only truly understand the effects of globalization when we take the specific character of local and regional societies, cultures and economies as our starting point, without forgetting the historical perspective.

This all sounds very abstract, but let us imagine, for example, that 'globalization' suggests a process of neutral unification, behind which the demise of eurocentrism lurks. The fact that Europe resists or 'defends' itself against this becomes clear when we look more closely at developments in the Mediterranean region. After all, following the so-called postcolonial period of mock guilt and penance came a period in which Europe shamelessly bid farewell to the African continent. It did this by erecting an impenetrable border that cut through the middle of the Mediterranean Sea. The inclination to carve up the Mediterranean is just as understandable as the call for unity, as recently made by an (over?) ambitious French president in a plea for a Mediterranean Union.[1] Europe, Africa and the Middle East meet each other in this region. Cultures, relgions, ideals and ideologies clash as strongly as rich and poor. Research institutes must make clear how relationships that have developed historically can be made visible, comprehensible and effective on a geopolitical level.[2] But for most Europeans, the region consists merely of attractive holiday destinations on the northern edge of an azure sea, from Gibraltar to South Turkey (with the exception of parts of Morocco and Tunisia). This coastline has developed into one long *aquapolis*, where around 200 million second homes will be built in the coming 20 years.[3]

'Everyone pretends it's so beautiful,' complains Predag Matvejevic, a Croatian writer, Mediterranean expert and chairman of the Comité Scientifique International of the Fondation Laboratorio Mediterraneo.[4] And beauty blinds: behind the sparkling waves lurk numerous problems that no one sees, let alone deals with. There is no perspective, no vision, no common *image* that would provide a starting point for a meaningful discussion about the Mediterranean.

Indeed, the region suffers under different processes of perception. For the average tourist – who, according to surveys regularly conducted on television, is unable to indicate even vaguely on a map of Europe where they are currently on holiday – there are no conflicts or cultural clashes. No one remembers the *Achillo Lauro* anymore.[5] The continuous stream of refugees to the island of Lampedusa is kept out of view of the sun worshippers as much as possible. Business as usual. The Mediterranean is an idyll – Multiplicity, a collective of artists, architects and photographers, has shown how keen local authorities are to keep the fairytale alive.[6] The Mediterranean is also a myth – the myth that European history books call the cradle of Western civilization, from 'Ancient Egypt' to 'the Greeks' and the 'Roman Empire'. But who still knows where Carthage, Knossos or Troy were located? The long history and current geopolitical situation make the process of forming an image of this region complex and indistinct. In 1966, the French historian Fernand Braudel published his extensive cultural history of the Mediterranean in the 16th century under the title *La Mediterranée*, the first and, to this day, the only historiography that treated the region as a unity. In the book, Braudel introduced his three-layered division of historical time,

1] NICOLAS SARKOZY IN HIS VICTORY SPEECH AFTER THE PRESIDENTIAL ELECTIONS, ON 6 MAY 2007 (WWW.LIBERATION.FR/ACTUALITE/POLITIQUES/ ELECTIONS2007/252080.FR.PHP)

2] SEE WWW.MEDOBS.NET

3] SEE THE UNITED NATIONS ENVIRONMENT PROGRAMME'S BLUE PLAN REPORT (WWW.UNEP.ORG/DOCUMENTS. MULTILINGUAL/DEFAULT.ASP?DOCUMENTID=475&ARTICLEID= 5248&1=EN)

4] DIJKGRAAF, M, 'WAT EEN KOLOSSALE VERGISSING! DE OPEN BRIEVEN VAN PEDRAG MATVEJEVIC' ('WHAT A COLOSSAL MISTAKE! PEDRAG MATVEJEVIC'S OPEN LETTERS'), IN: *NRC HANDELSBLAD* (CULTURAL SUPPLEMENT), 22 JUNE 2007, P.20.

5] CRUISE SHIP THAT WAS HIJACKED BY PALESTINIANS OFF THE COAST OF EGYPT IN 1985. ONE KIDNAPPED PASSENGER DIED.

6] IN THE DOCUMENTARY VIDEO INSTALLATION *SOLID SEA* (2003), MULTIPLICITY REVEALED HOW THE ITALIAN AUTHORITIES HAD COVERED UP THE FACT THAT A SHIP CARRYING ILLEGAL IMMIGRANTS HAD SUNK OFF THE COAST OF SICILY. SEE WWW.MULTIPLICITY.IT.

which has since become famous among historians: the slow, almost unchanging progression, the slow movement of medium-term duration and the quick succession of short duration. At what historical speed is the Mediterranean region developing today?

The size and complexity of the region make it difficult to regard it as a unity. There are undoubtedly parties who, as a result of political or economic interests, benefit from this fragmented perception. *So Blue, So Blue – Edges of the Mediterranean* is an attempt by Dutch photographer Ad van Denderen to view the Mediterranean as a connected territory, within which a certain cohesion rules, despite the evident contrasts and paradoxes. Or where, at the very least, relationships can be determined between developments that may be geographically, culturally or otherwise far removed from each other, but which are insufficiently explained by the word 'globalization'. Van Denderen's odyssey not only has a political necessity, but also – and this is certainly no less important – a crucial new photojournalistic form.

II

For nearly 20 years, Ad van Denderen – winner of the prestigious Visa d'Or in 2001 – worked for the politically left-leaning weekly *Vrij Nederland*, which since the middle of the 70s has enjoyed a certain reputation in the Netherlands in the area of engaged photojournalism. He did photo journalistic reports on the most diverse news items. His book published in 1991, entitled *Welkom in South Africa,* about a small community in post-apartheid South Africa, bestowed on him a certain degree of authority in Dutch photojournalism circles with regard to the events that were playing themselves out in the former Dutch colony. His great interest in conflict zones also took him to the Middle East and the enduring Israeli–Palestinian war. This led to numerous reportages and the publication of *Peace in the Holy Land* (1997), in which he sketched a much more finely nuanced picture of daily life in the two camps than the rather cynical title would these days lead one to suppose. Characteristic of his way of working was his willingness to look behind the immediate news, to stay longer, sometimes for months in a row in a region, in order to record what, according to him, future generations should be able to *see.* He learned his craft from the

Hungarian immigrant Ata Kando, and that undoubtedly helped him to earn a place in the best tradition of Dutch documentary photography, alongside contemporaries such as Bertien van Manen and Koen Wessing, distinguished by powerful politico-social engagement, a strongly developed sense of form and a preference for contrast-rich, dramatic black-and-white.

Even though his direct reason for doing so was perhaps quite prosaic, Van Denderen's recent departure from *Vrij Nederland* is understandable within a broader, international development in which the traditional podia for photojournalism are slowly making way for new ones. This is a process that has been taking place for some time; but through both the rise of new image production and image dissemination technologies and a changing market for the news and the stories behind it, this process has become more rapid.

The shift from the printed magazine to the exhibition platform has not only an economic cause. Among an increasing number of photojournalists and documentary photographers, the realization has grown that the exhibition brings with it a fundamentally different way of looking and observing, one which lends itself well to an intelligent edit of images on the wall (format, order, location in the space), but which above all offers resistance to the leveling of journalism in the mass media. On the one hand, there is room here for immersion and reflection; on the other hand, the opportunity to slow down one's look. To an increasing extent, old and new media such as the photo book, the website and the weblog also offer these photographers diverse ways of escaping the whim of editors who have bet their cards on infotainment, citizen journalism or emotion-focused reporting.

III

Van Denderen's growing need to approach things differently received a crucial boost at two moments over the past few years. One of them was a portrait sitting with a Palestinian suicide bomber in Hebron who, on the evening before he blew himself up, allowed himself be photographed as a proud father in a child's bedroom with his two young children on his arm. After his deadly act, the photo was circulated in the Western media. In an attempt to grasp the event,

Van Denderen said that he 'looked into the children's eyes for a very long time.'[7] His changed insight into the psychology of the lingering conflict led him to photograph posters of Palestinian suicide bombers in the West Bank. These pamphlets, which portray the suicide bombers as martyrs, are distributed immediately after a suicide attack, and just as quickly removed by Palestinians who are dragged from their beds by Israeli soldiers. This is why these posters, which according to the photographer can be regarded as devotional cards, are rarely seen in the Western media.

As a regular visitor to the West Bank, Van Denderen was acquainted with this phenomenon. In an apparently paradoxical step, he decided to return to one of the primary functions of photography, which is rooted in the creation of a faithful reproduction of reality.[8] He photographed these posters in colour wherever and whenever he saw them and in as *matter-of-fact* a way as possible, disregarding himself as author. The initiative that resulted in the *Martyrs* series was a crucial step, even though the impulse for a new way of working had occurred several years previously. At the time, Van Denderen was working on a series about a diverse group of immigrants attempting to penetrate 'Fort Europe'. He recounts an experience in 2001, which cast a different light on illegal immigration, a phenomenon he had been photographing since 1986. Hidden early one morning in the dunes of Punta Paloma in the south of Spain, he waited for the arrival of the illegal immigrants who were being brought over the sea from Morocco by human traffickers. Within no time, the small rubber boats had unloaded their cargo and just as quickly the immigrants had disappeared into the dunes. Van Denderen was able to catch several of them on film. What made the experience really distressing was the fact that a few hours later unwitting tourists, keen to spend a day in the sun, spread out their towels on the same spot.

He came to the realization that there was no opportunity in his work to reproduce these kinds of contrasts and experiences. By focusing on concrete events, the larger connections and relationships between apparently incompatible, but fundamentally connected, situations remain out of sight. He decided a different approach was needed. By converting this photo series, which appeared under the title *Go No Go – The Frontiers of Europe* (2003), into a book and exhibition, he took the first steps.[9] At various points in the book he and his fellow editors inserted colour photos from travel brochures, related to the places and countries from which the migrants came.[10] The stark contrast with Van Denderen's black-and-white reportage images had a disturbing effect on the flow of the journalistic story. In the exhibition, the second perspective was introduced by combining the projected photos with *Britanya* (2003), a commissioned four-part film production made by Marjoleine Boonstra with illegal immigrants who had tried to enter Great Britain from the French town of Sangatte.[11] They were the first interesting, if cautious, attempts to break loose from the respected, but by that time outdated, tradition of documentary photography, by utilizing simple interventions to break through the authority of the single perspective.

His decision, at the start of a new project dealing with the 17 countries on the Mediterranean, to swap his 35mm camera loaded with black-and-white film for a medium format camera with colour film was of a more fundamental nature. The transition from a negative format with image proportions of 2:3 to one of 6:7 also implied the transition to a radically new (journalistic) way of working.[12] The medium-format camera is not only a very different object, in the physical sense, but it needs to be handled differently. The image proportions force the photographer to look at and compose pictures differently, leaving behind the nervousness and speed associated with a 35mm camera in favour of a slower, more concentrated way of *observing*. In a certain sense, the change meant a departure from the role

7] SEE 'AD VAN DENDEREN', IN: GIERSTBERG, F *ET AL.* (EDS), *DOCUMENTARY NOW! CONTEMPORARY STRATEGIES IN PHOTOGRAPHY, FILM AND VISUAL ARTS*, ROTTERDAM (NAI PUBLISHERS) 2005, PP.76-80.
8] THE SERIES *MARTYRS* WAS PUBLISHED IN USEFUL PHOTOGRAPHY NO. 4, 2004, AND EXHIBITED AT THE NEDERLANDS FOTOMUSEUM IN ROTTERDAM THE SAME YEAR.
9] SEE WWW.GO-NO-GO.NL. THE PROJECT WAS SHOWN AT THE FOTOMUSEUM AMSTERDAM (FOAM) IN 2003.
10] *GO NO GO* WAS EDITED BY AD VAN DENDEREN, HANS AARSMAN AND GRAPHIC DESIGNER ROELOF MULDER.
11] *BRITANYA* (2003) WAS COMMISSIONED BY PARADOX (PRODUCER OF *GO NO GO*) AND BASED ON AN IDEA BY JEROEN DE VRIES (EXHIBITION DESIGNER) AND EXECUTIVE PRODUCER BAS VROEGE.
12] AS A RESULT OF CROPPING, THE PHOTOGRAPHS IN THE BOOK HAVE DIFFERENT PROPORTIONS. THIS DECISION WAS MADE BECAUSE THEY WOULD HAVE A MORE POWERFUL IMPACT IN THE MEDIUM OF A BOOK. IN THE EXHIBITION, THE PROPORTIONS OF THE NEGATIVE FORMAT HAVE BEEN RETAINED IN THE PRINTS.

of reporter of news events, of the proverbial fly on the wall, of the 'decisive moment'. Van Denderen noticed that he started to see things he had not seen before. He began to pay more attention to surroundings and context, to 'indecisive moments' and *signs* – things or situations that openly point to a web of causes and effects, of developments and results, of connections and parallels – and to aspects that at first glance appear to have no meaning, but are just *there*. Instead of the messenger, he was now the onlooker, without prejudice, judgements or even concrete ideas about what he photographed. More an informed finder than a purposeful seeker. *So Blue, So Blue – Edges of the Mediterranean* is witness to this new way of working, which can still be called journalistic because at its core it is focused on investigating, informing and showing a concrete reality within a social framework (more specifically: that of a well-functioning democracy, for which journalism's informational and opinionated roles are of vital importance).

This journalistic approach has signed a pact with slowness, however (hence the term *Slow Journalism*), and on two fronts: first, it distances itself emphatically from the daily stream of news facts that are beamed around the globe via the 'fast' media such as newspapers, television and the internet. Second, the basic principle of this way of working requires a long-lasting commitment from the photographer to his subject. This slowness is ultimately critical to the intensity of the result. The term 'intensity' is more suitable in this instance than the obvious 'quality', because it relates to the act of looking. Only by investing more time can a certain amount of concentrated looking be developed; only then can the photographer leave behind first impressions, distance himself from the cursory glance of the day tripper, the confirmation-seeking glance of the tourist, the exoticizing glance of the traveller.

When we accept that Van Denderen's documentary photos are documents of experience, then we can see that they are the experiences of an informed photographer.[13] The concentrated observation and the extent to which the look is informed are deeply ingrained in the images in *So Blue, So Blue*. As a result, the images cannot hide their subjectivity. But it is also clear that they offer a fundamentally alternative consciousness and insight that is missing in a photo reportage. In other words, it is about a fundamentally different *image language*, one which can be called both personal and documentary. And which, as can be expected, constructively disrupts the usual perceptions of the Mediterranean.

Frits Gierstberg (b. 1959) studied Art History and Archaeology at the University of Leiden. He is currently Head of Exhibitions at the Nederlands Fotomuseum, and Extraordinary Professor of Photography at Erasmus University, Rotterdam, specializing in the socio-historical and documentary aspects of photography.

13] AFTER THE DEFINITION BY JEAN-FRANÇOIS CHEVRIER, ACCORDING TO WHOM A PHOTOGRAPHIC DOCUMENT DOES NOT RECORD REALITY BUT IS A DOCUMENT OF EXPERIENCE.

Gibraltar is the smallest territory in the Mediterranean. It falls under the sovereignty of the British Crown, having been ceded by the Spanish in 1713. As such, it is probably the most visible remnant of the centuries-long struggle around the Mediterranean. Until 1914, the Ottoman Empire extended along the eastern end of the sea, while North Africa was occupied by France, Italy, Spain and Great Britain. It is almost impossible to compare this map with one from the 1960s, by which time the countries of North Africa and the Middle East were independent.

While Europe's ragged borders were the result of centuries of war and arranged marriages between royal houses, Africa's borders were determined very differently. The geographic divisions of the present-day African states were drawn with a ruler during the Congress of Berlin in 1878.

Sea battles have not been fought in the Mediterranean since the Second World War. The region is, however, responsible for a long list of internal conflicts and wars between neighbouring countries. Gibraltar has not been completely free of conflict either. From 1969 to 1982, the border between Gibraltar and Spain was closed. Relations with Spain are still strained. Spain has never given up its claim over Gibraltar and views the United Kingdom as a colonial power. Gibraltar's political parties, on the contrary, are pro-sovereignty. No one wants to become part of Spain.

10. **GIBRALTAR**

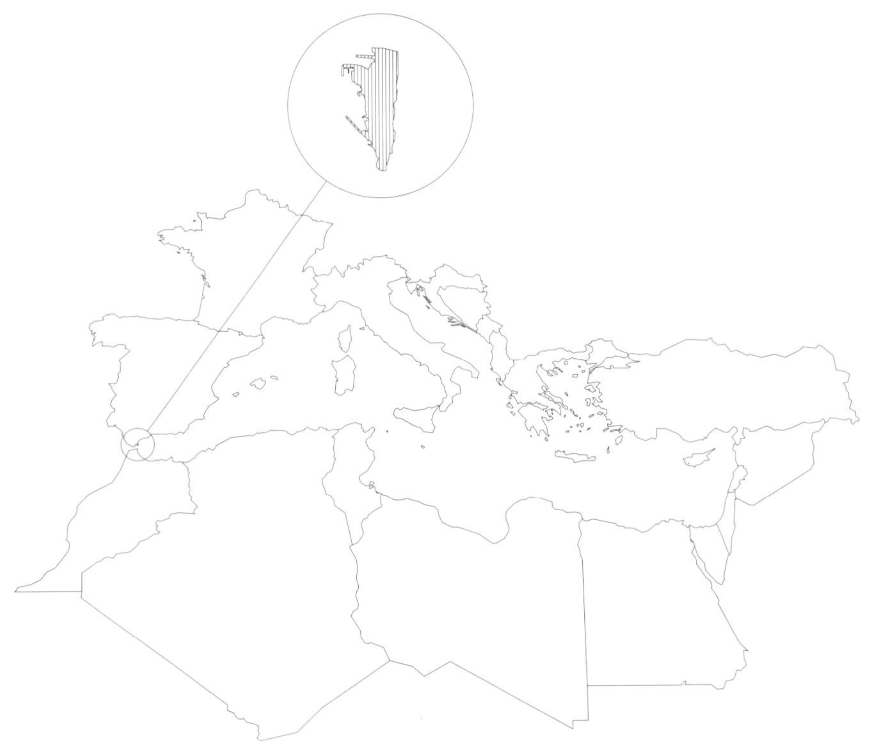

12. GIBRALTAR

Gibraltar is also known as 'The Rock'. It is a British enclave of Moroccans, Spaniards, Brits and a considerable Jewish community. Perhaps the most striking feature is the airport's runway, which crosses Gibraltar's main road.

14. GIBRALTAR

It wouldn't surprise me if Gibraltar cost the British money. It used to be an unbelievably strategic piece of land. Morocco is visible to the naked eye on the other side of the Strait.

16. GIBRALTAR

A mosque is located on Gibraltar's southern-most point. This is a Saudi Arabian-funded prestige project. Moroccan immigrants feel shut out in Gibraltar. They pay taxes but are not eligible to make use of social services when they retire.

SURFACE/AREA

IN KM²

GIBRALTAR	6.5	
SPAIN	504,782	
FRANCE	643,427	
ITALY	301,230	
CROATIA	56,542	
ALBANIA	28,748	
GREECE	131,940	
CYPRUS	9,250	
TURKEY	780,580	
SYRIA	185,180	
LEBANON	10,400	
ISRAEL	20,770	
W.B.& GAZA	6,220	
EGYPT	1,001,450	
LIBYA	1,759,540	
TUNISIA	163,610	
ALGERIA	2,381,740	
MOROCCO	446,550	

SOURCE : THE CIA WORLD FACTBOOK 2008

12.

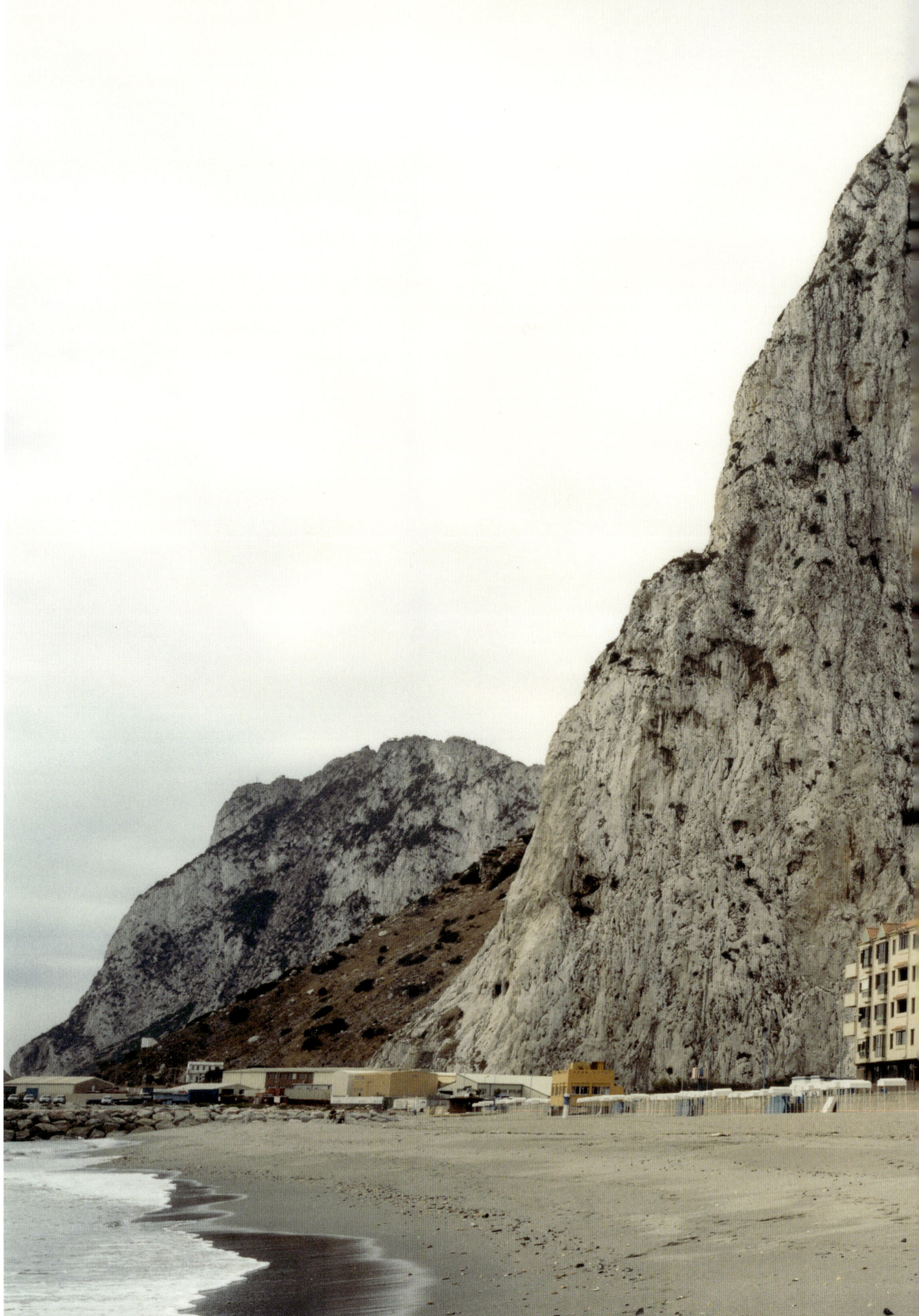

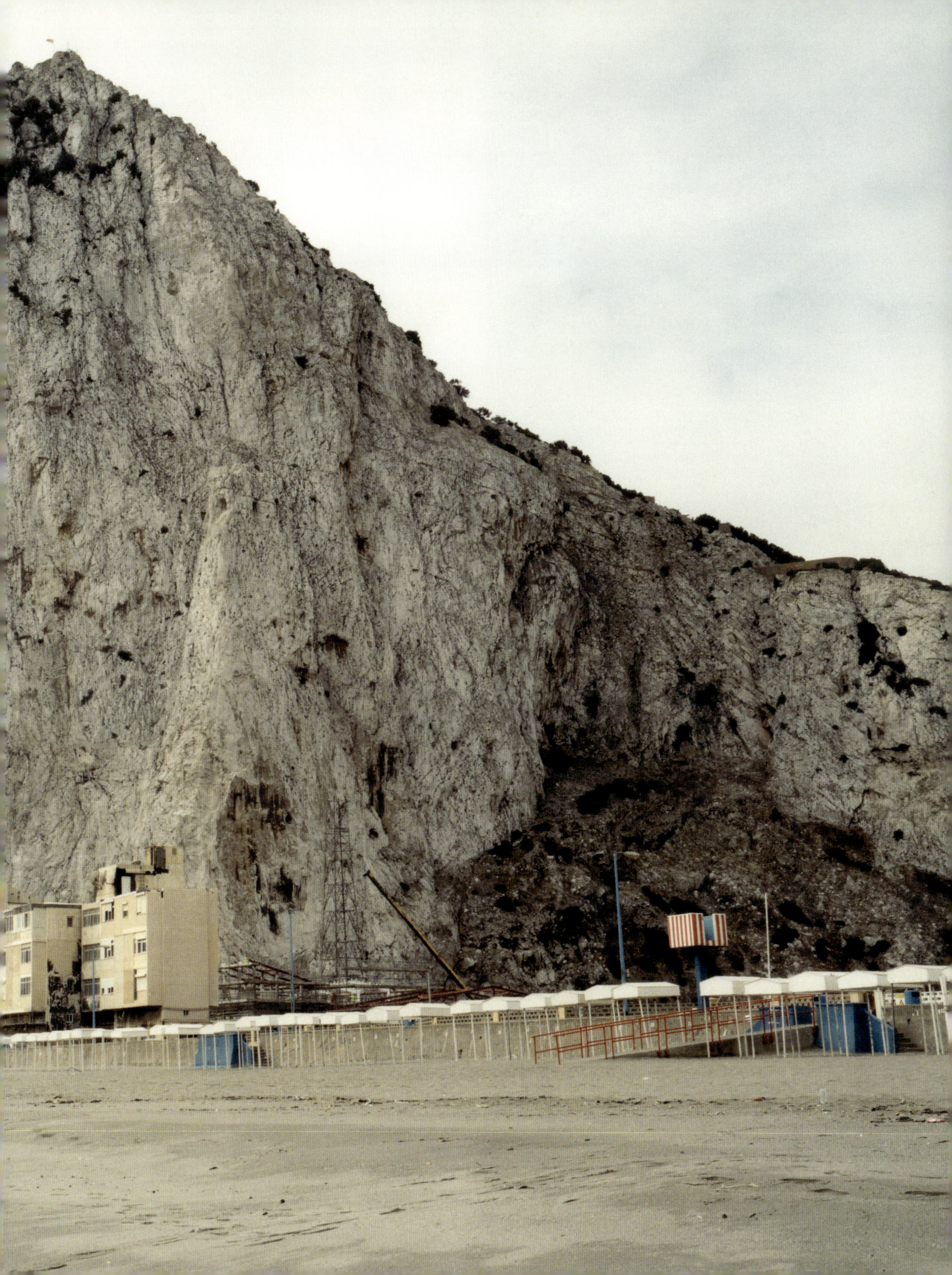

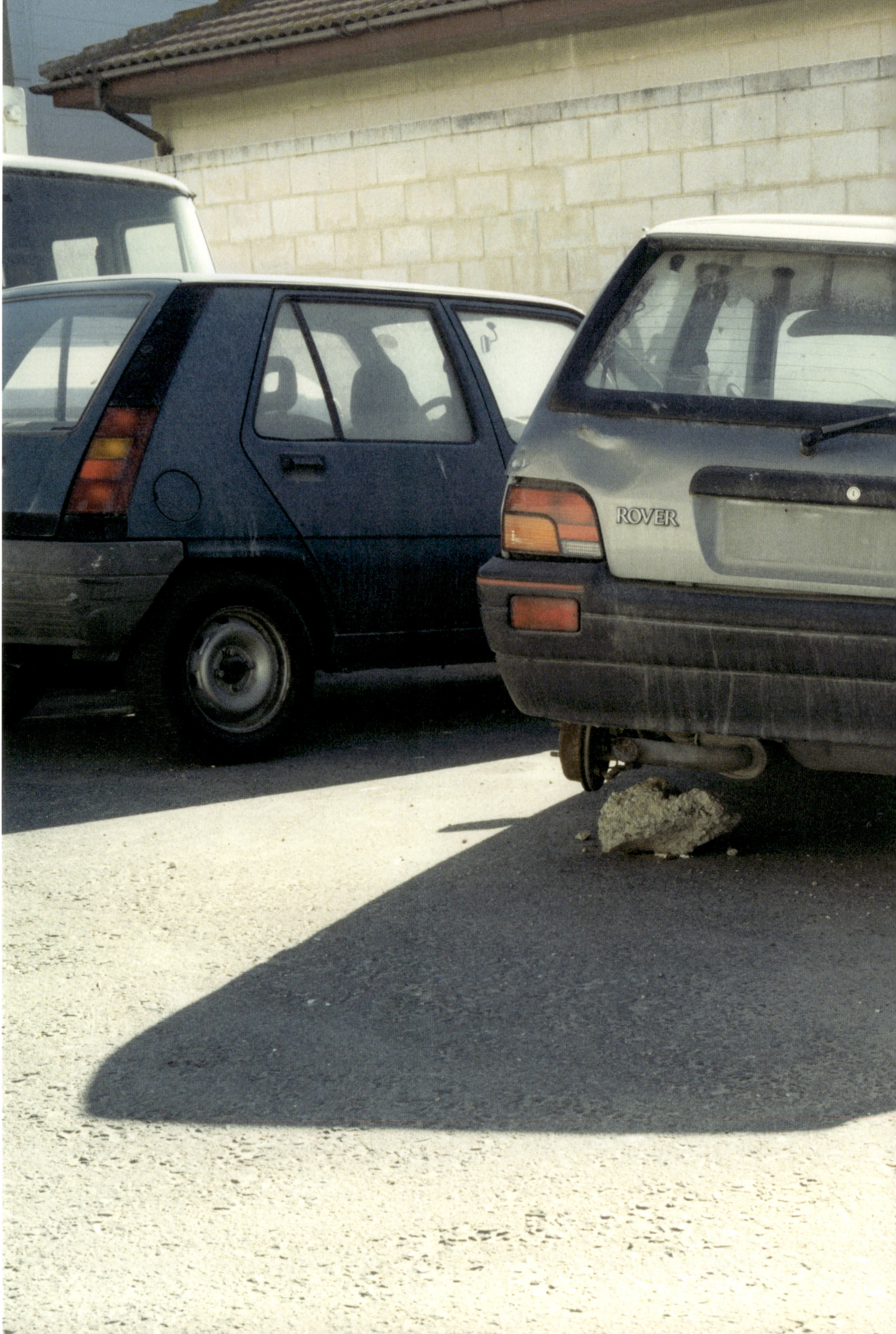
ROVER

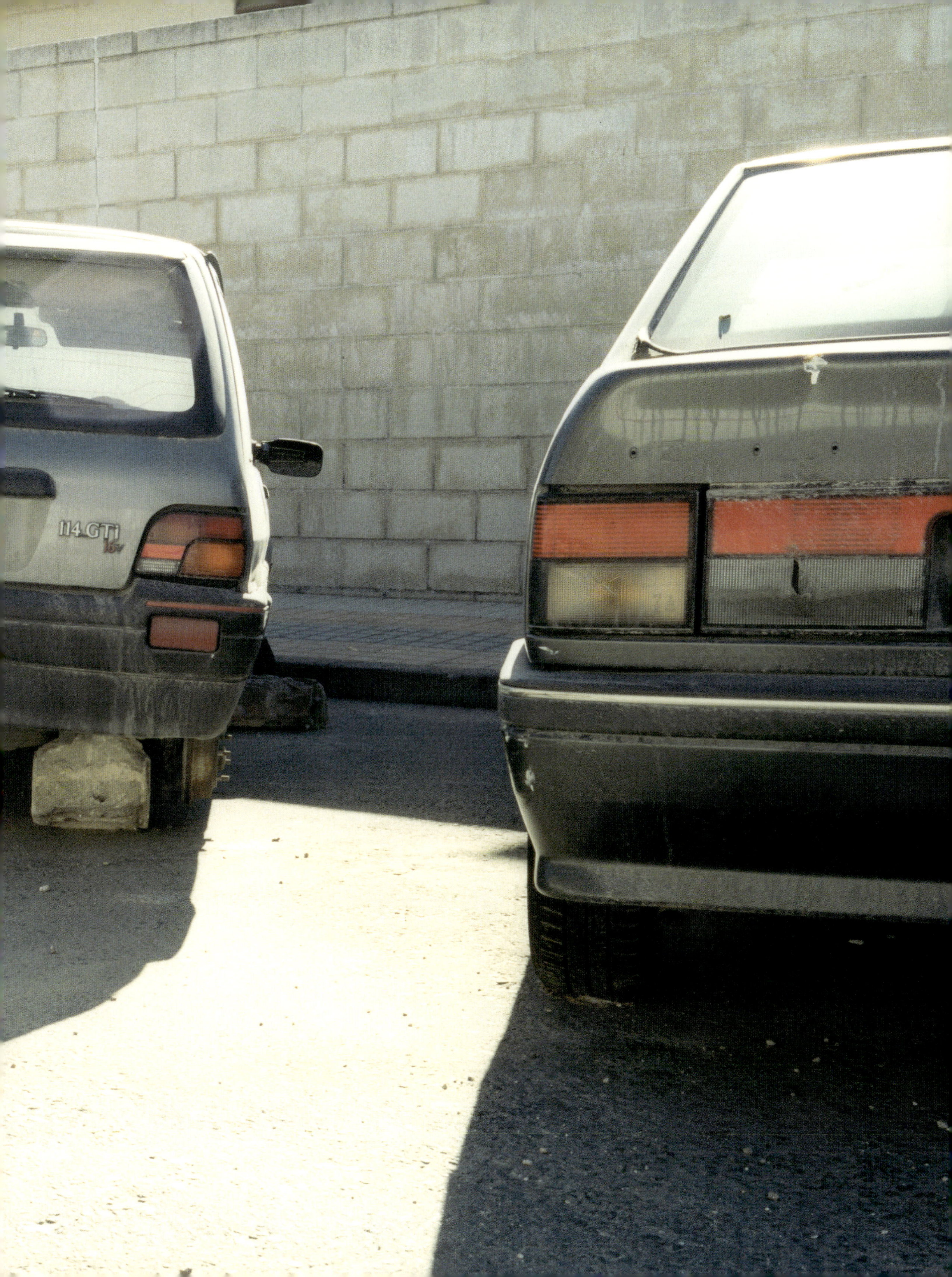
114 GTi

16.

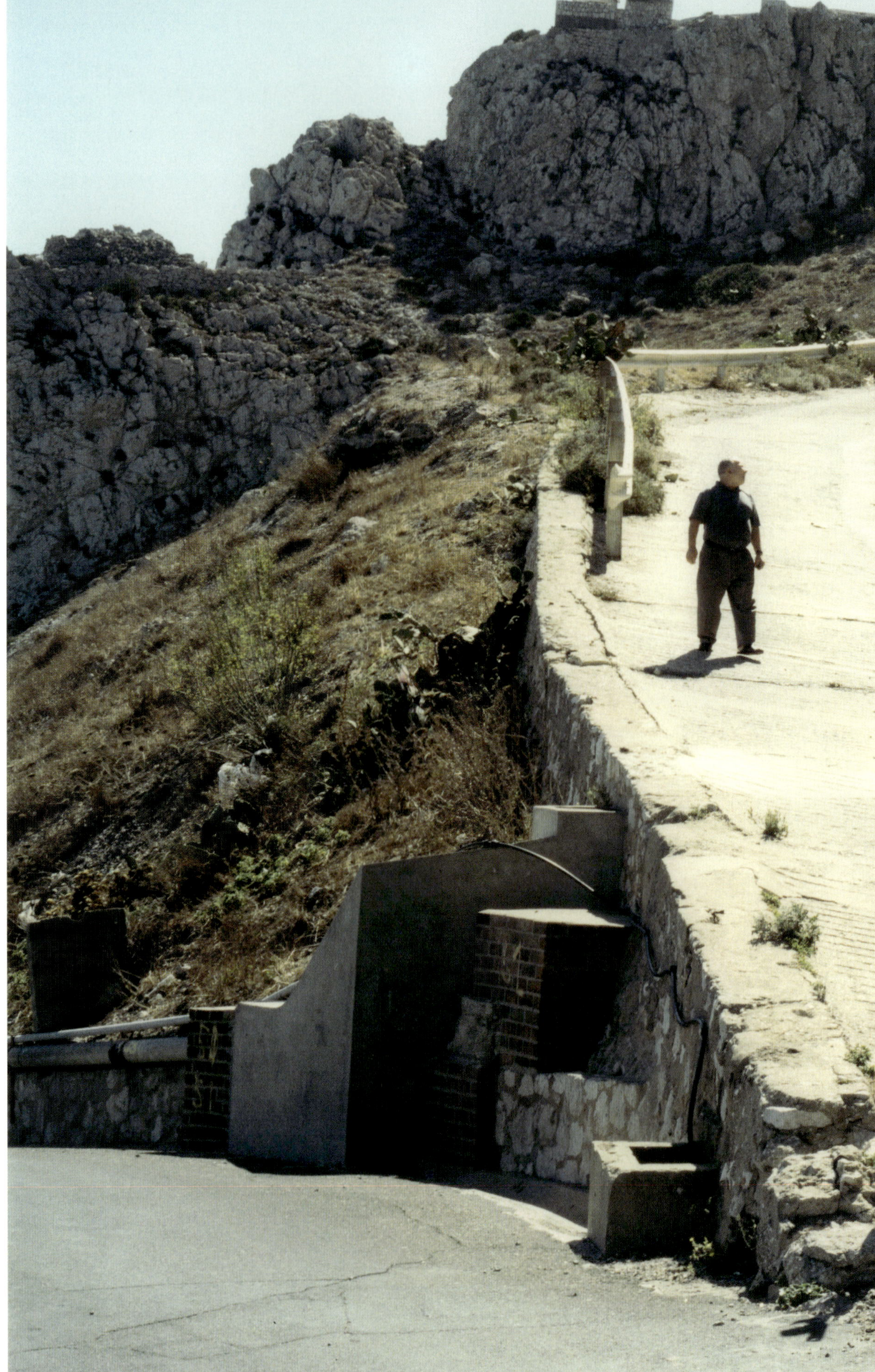

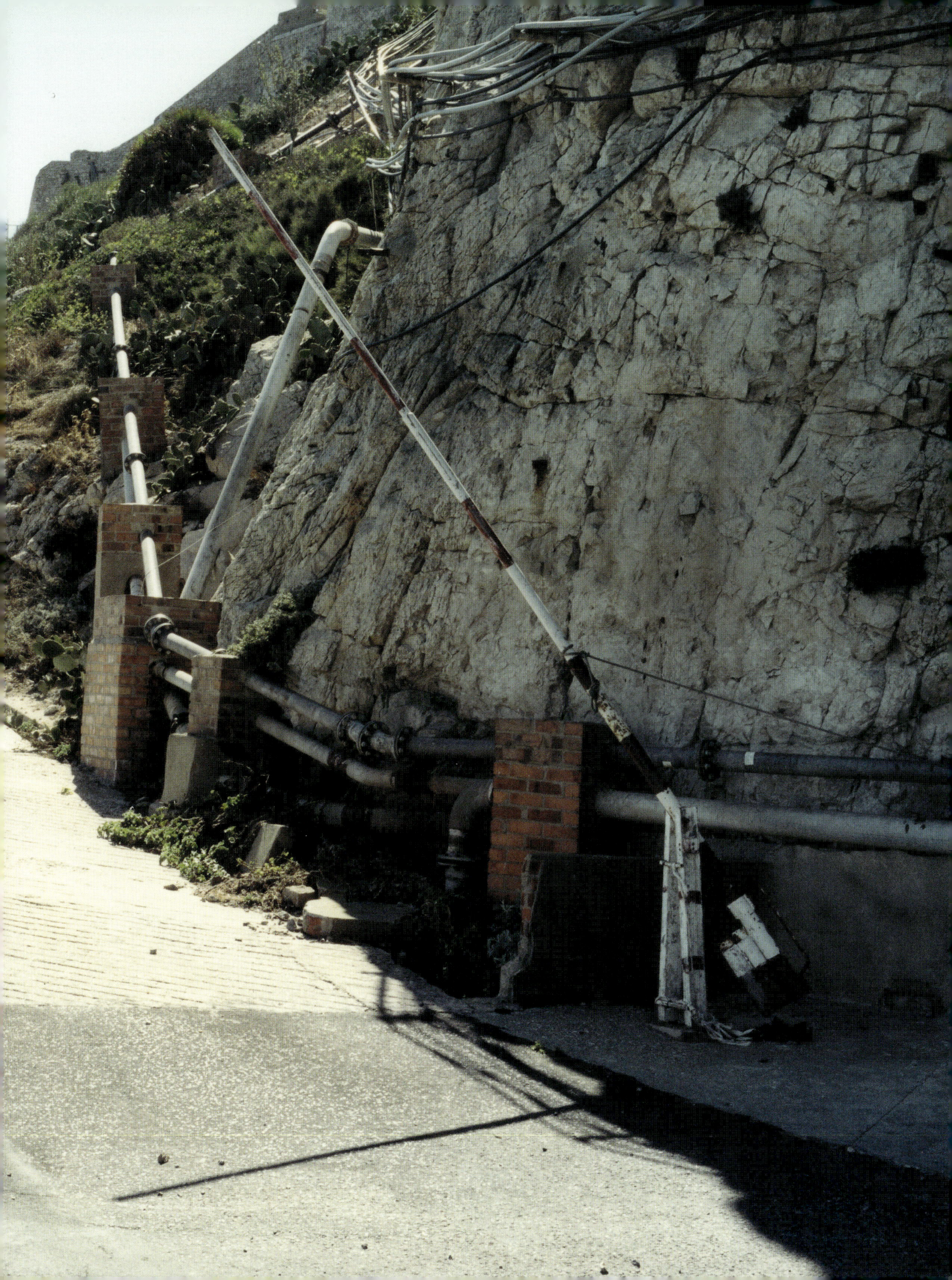

The Spanish 'Costas' are among the most popular holiday destinations for Northern Europeans. This is clearly visible, from Gibraltar to Eastern Turkey and increasingly in North Africa. The United Nations Environment Programme's *Plan Bleu* of 2006 predicts that, in 2025, 50% of the coastal area around the Mediterranean Sea will be built up. At present, 427 million people already live in the countries bordering the Mediterranean and 175 million tourists visit this coast every year. This will soon be 525 and 312 million respectively. Most of the areas around the sea are as dry as tinder, and the water shortage in many areas is dire. In order to counter this, water rationing has been imposed on inhabitants, entrepreneurs and farmers. At the same time, in response to the increasing budget tourism in countries such as Turkey and Tunisia, around 90 golf courses will be built in Spain. These will be in addition to the existing one hundred water-guzzling courses: irrigating just one of these golf courses requires as much water per year as a town of 12,000 inhabitants.

All the countries of the Mediterranean have a water problem, not just Spain. The country does lead the development of large-scale plants to extract drinking and irrigation water from the Mediterranean's salt water. However, there are fears for the effect this highly polluting desalination process will have on what is already the most polluted sea on earth.

18. **SPAIN**

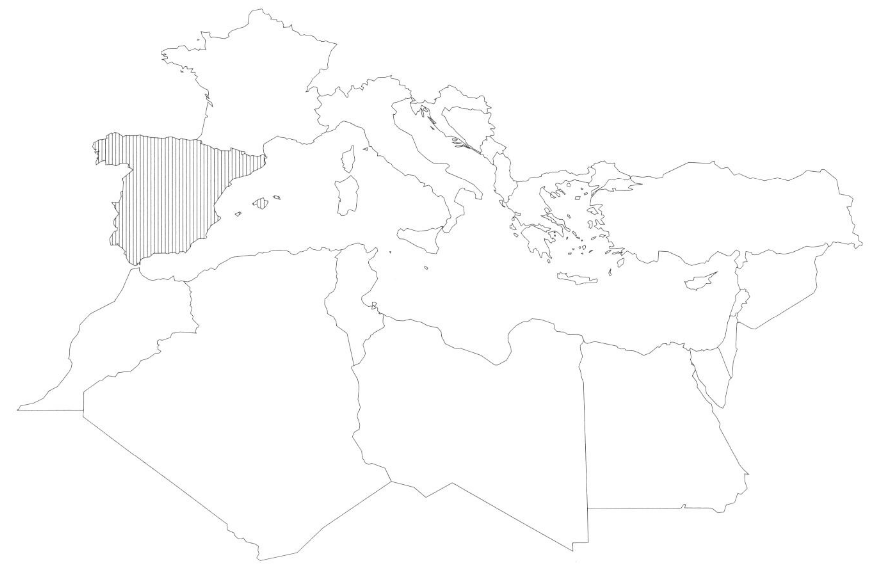

WATER CONSUMPTION

M³/CAPITA

GIBRALTAR	38.6	
SPAIN	**867**	
FRANCE	675	
ITALY	766	
CROATIA	NA	
ALBANIA	534	
GREECE	830	
CYPRUS	300	
TURKEY	567	
SYRIA	1202	
LEBANON	311	
ISRAEL	319	
W.B. & GAZA	90	
EGYPT	NA	
LIBYA	891	
TUNISIA	281	
ALGERIA	197	
MOROCCO	437	

SOURCE : GIBRALTAR GOVERMENT, FOOD AND AGRICULTURE ORGANIZATION OF THE UNITED NATIONS & ORGANIZATION FOR ECONOMIC CO-OPERATION AND DEVELOPMENT

NA : NOT AVAILABLE

20. ALICANTE

French Algerians wait for the ferry to Oran. At the Red Cross tent on the quay, food and water are distributed.

22. BENIDORM

A new, 18-hole golf course. The soil is removed in order to lay drainage pipes. The golf green is brewing under the green cover. The golf courses are laid in order to dramatically increase the value of the surrounding houses.

25. ALICANTE

Wait, watch, lie, stand and keep on waiting. Every day some boats leave for Algeria. Newcomers have to join the back of the queue. It is absolute chaos.

26. MAGALLUF

Magalluf is little more than an English colony on Mallorca. During their two-week stay, tourists rarely leave their all-inclusive hotel or apartment complexes.

28. PEAJE, BETWEEN MARBELLA AND TORREMOLINOS

Property developers buy a mountain. Development prospects are sold 'off-plan', directly from the drawing board, as long as you can pay in advance. I came across just one traditional village along the entire Spanish coast. The whole country is being plundered.

30. ARENAL

Mallorca is divided into segments. The English occupy one part, the Germans another, the Dutch yet another. More than 40,000 people spend the winter here. The locals have named the next street along the 'Bierstrasse'.

33. EL EJIDO

El Ejido is the largest greenhouse-cultivation area on earth. Most of the work is carried out by immigrants, including many illegal workers from Eastern Europe and Africa.

34. ARENAL

This is what the first sighting of Europe must be like for many immigrants, in a boat that floats just above the waves with a view of the tourist coast.

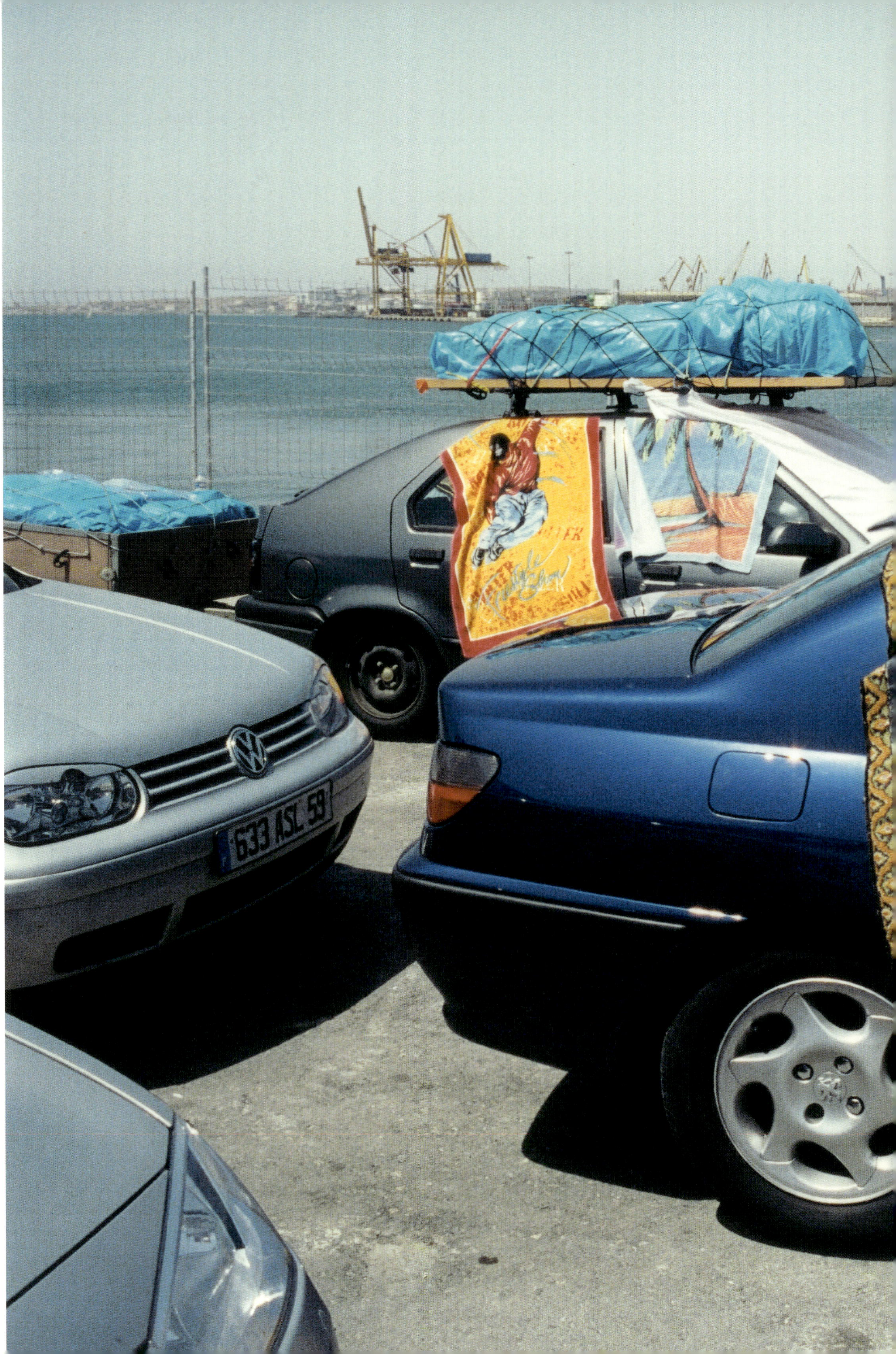

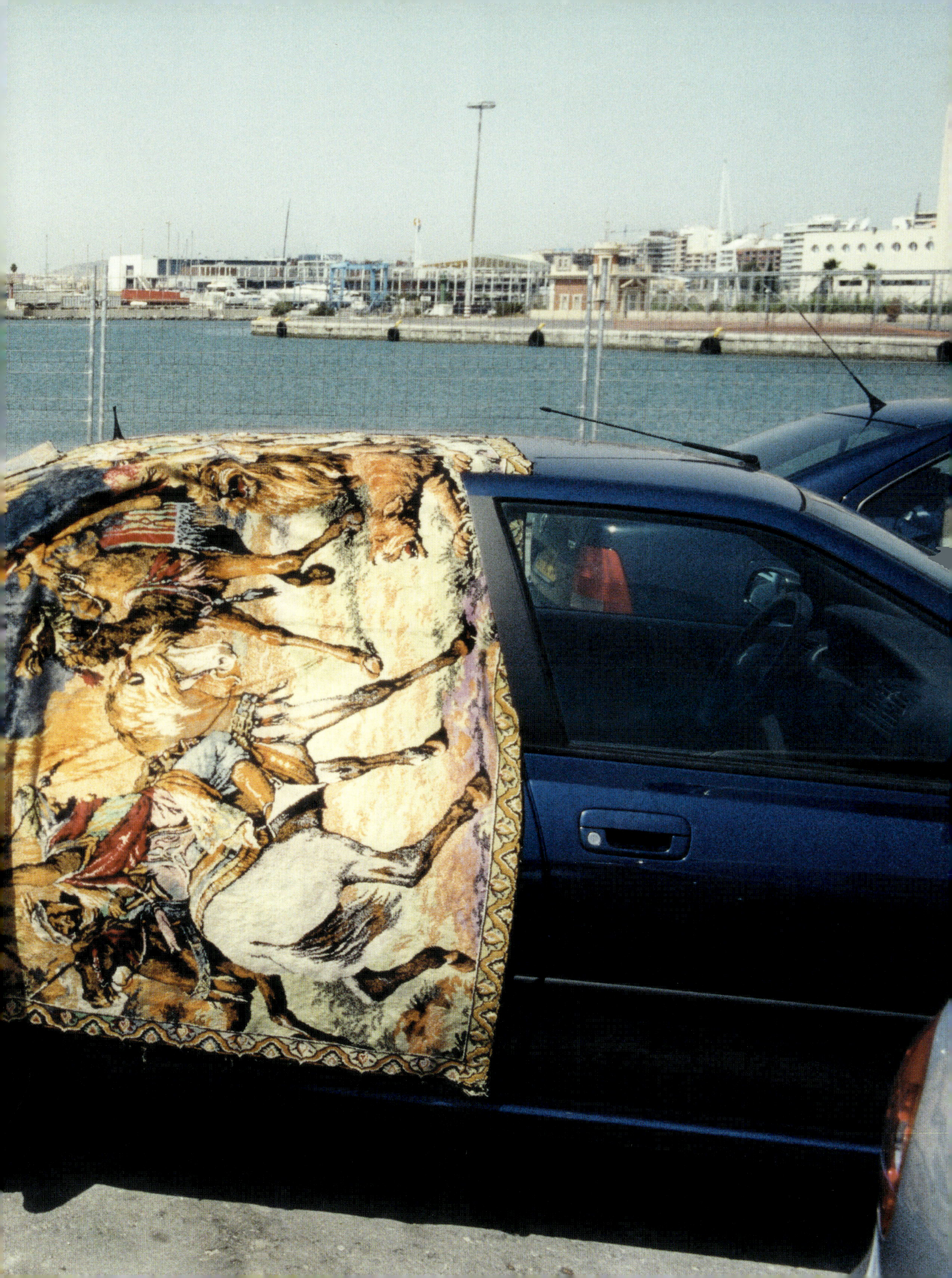

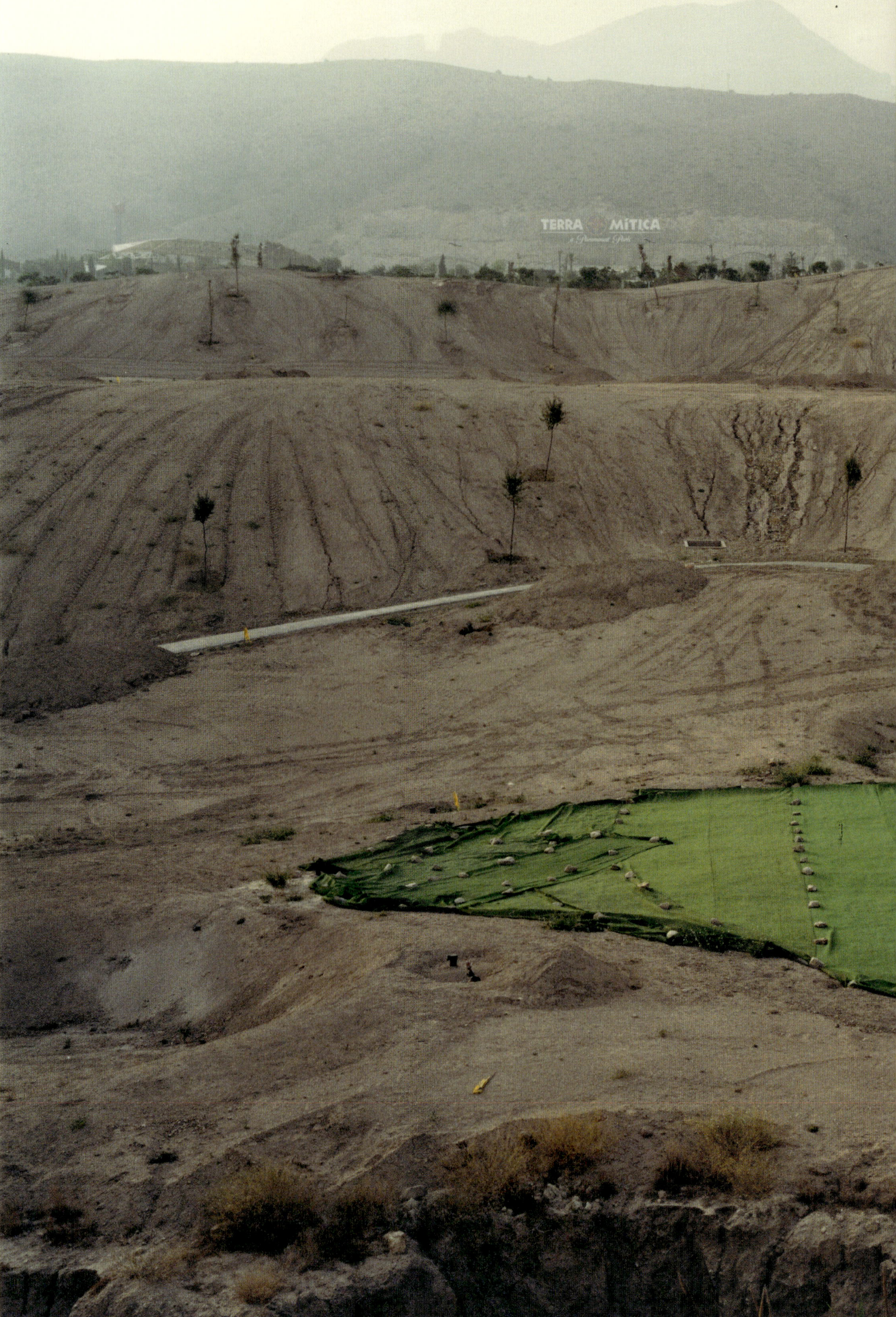

TERRA MITICA
a Paramount Park

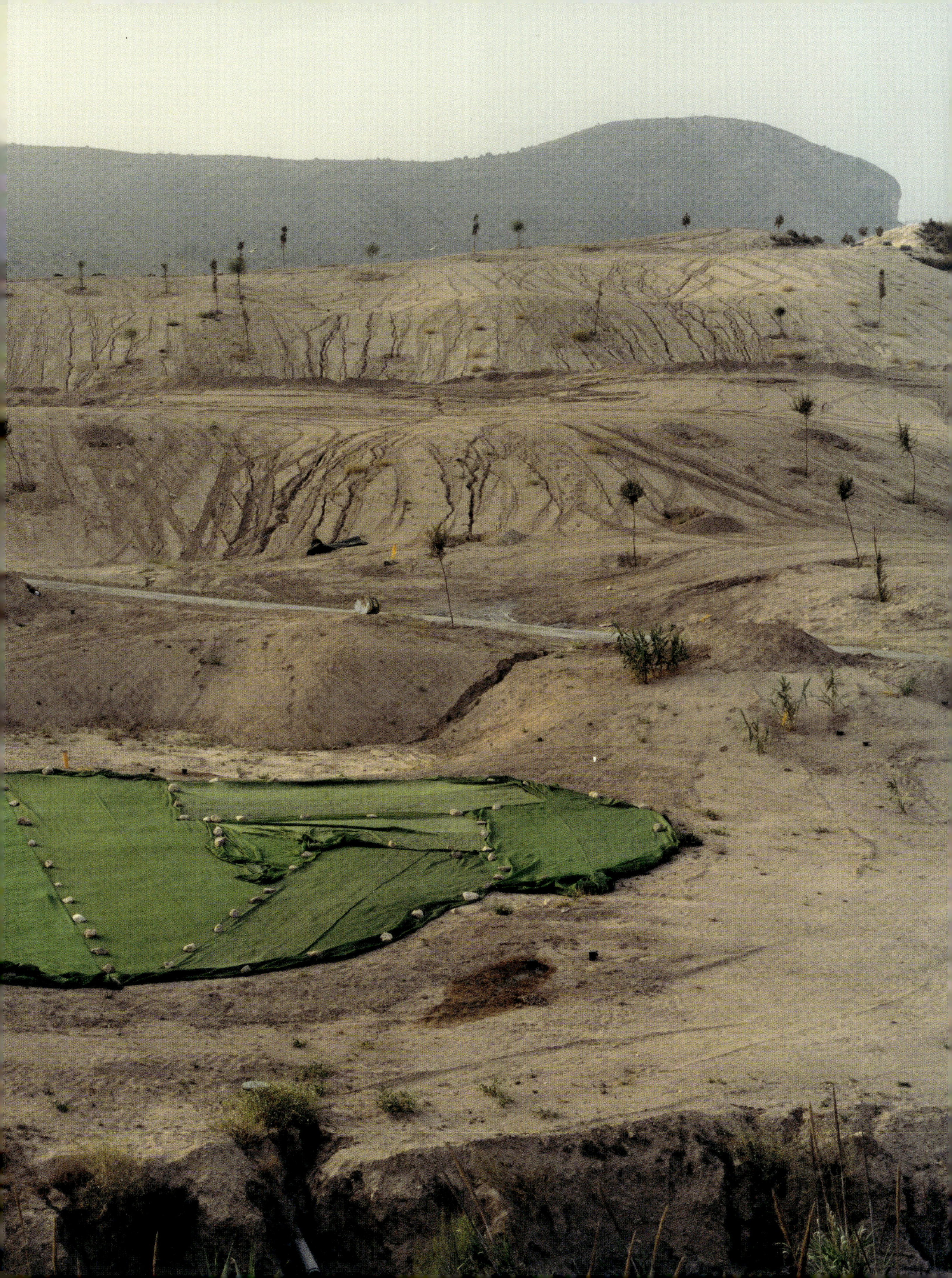

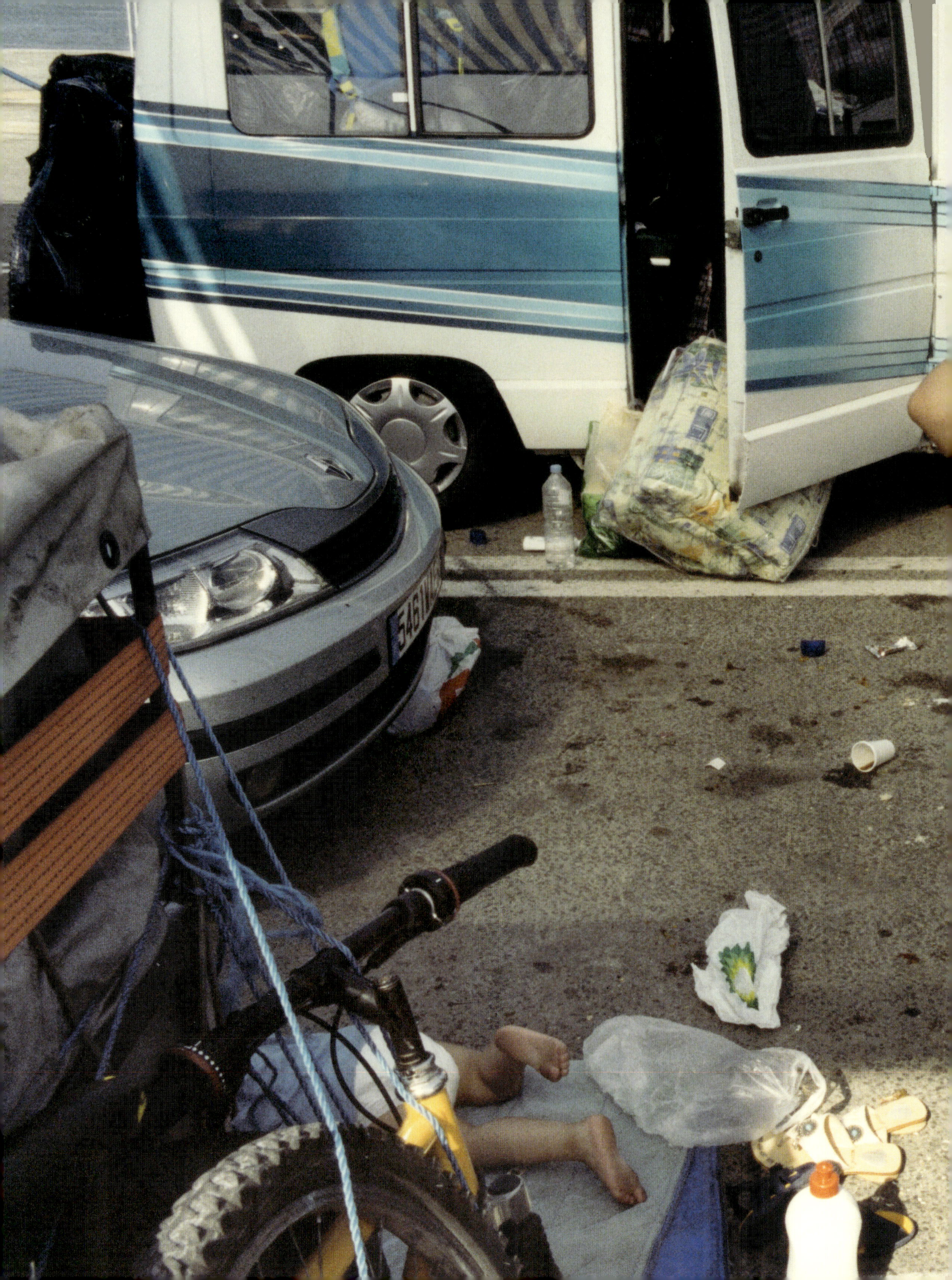

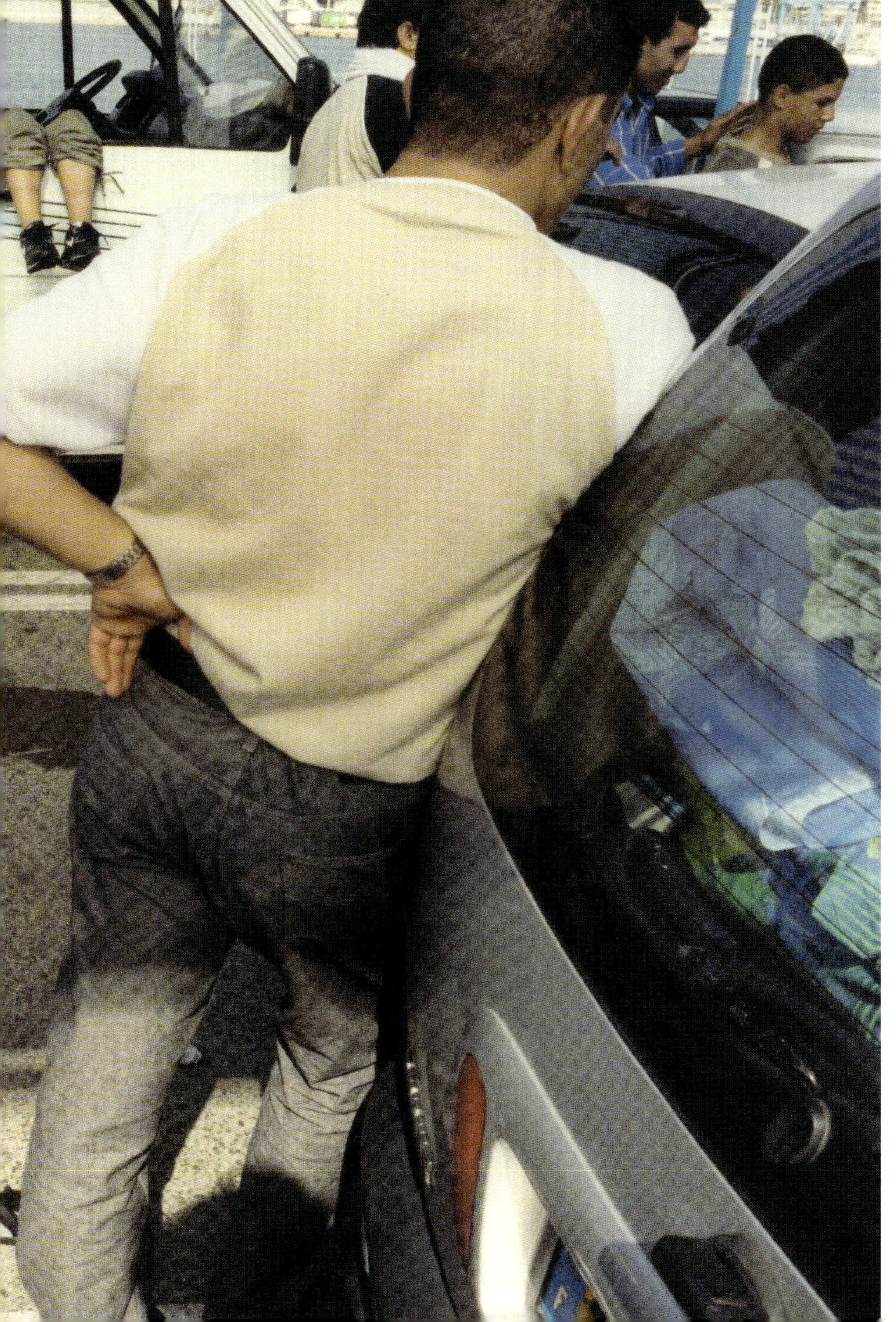

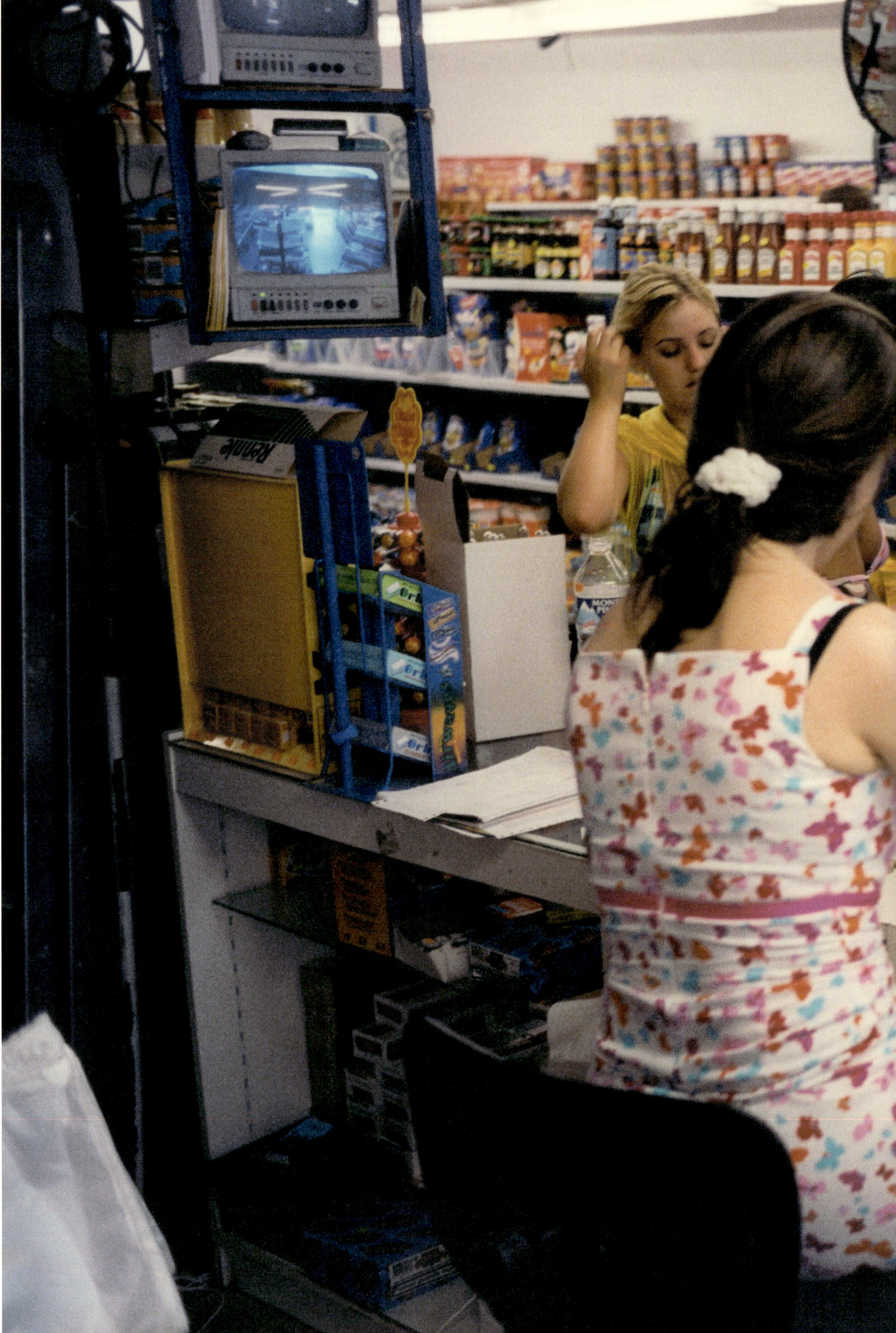

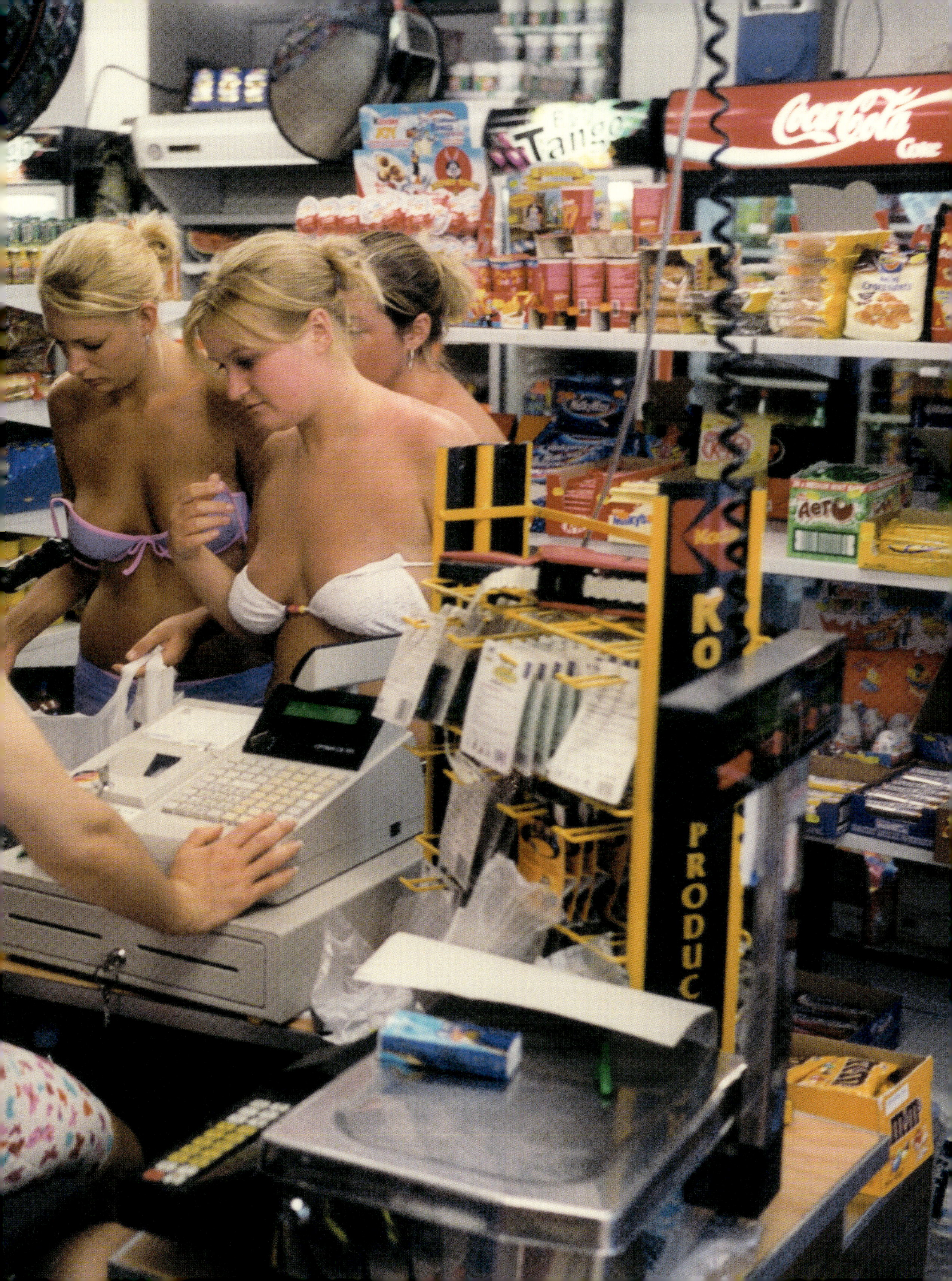

Tango
Coca-Cola
Coke
KitKat
Milky Bar
Aero
PRODUC
KO

28.

Your home on the Golf C
Los
Arqueros
Golf & Country
Tel: 952 78 58 88

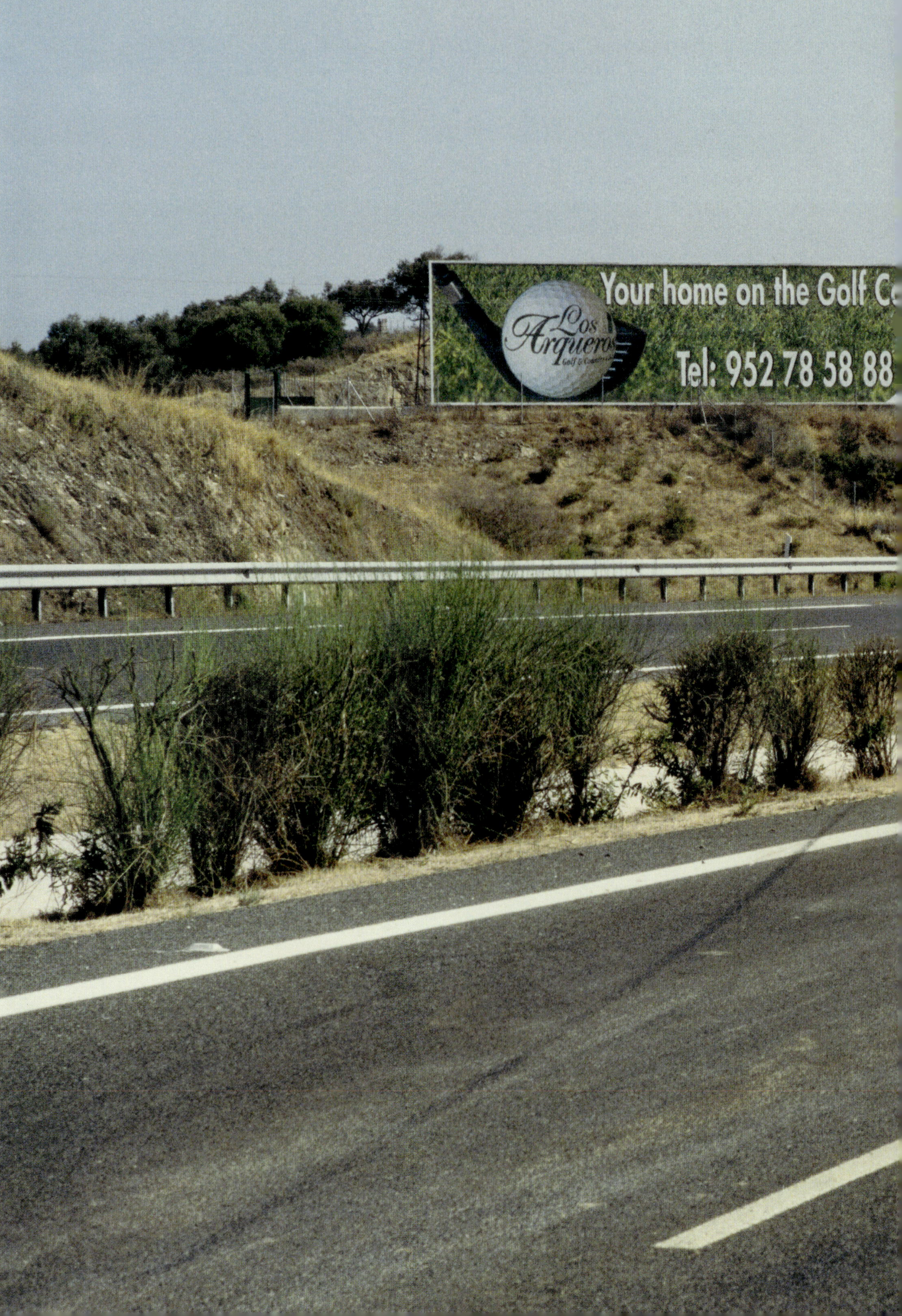

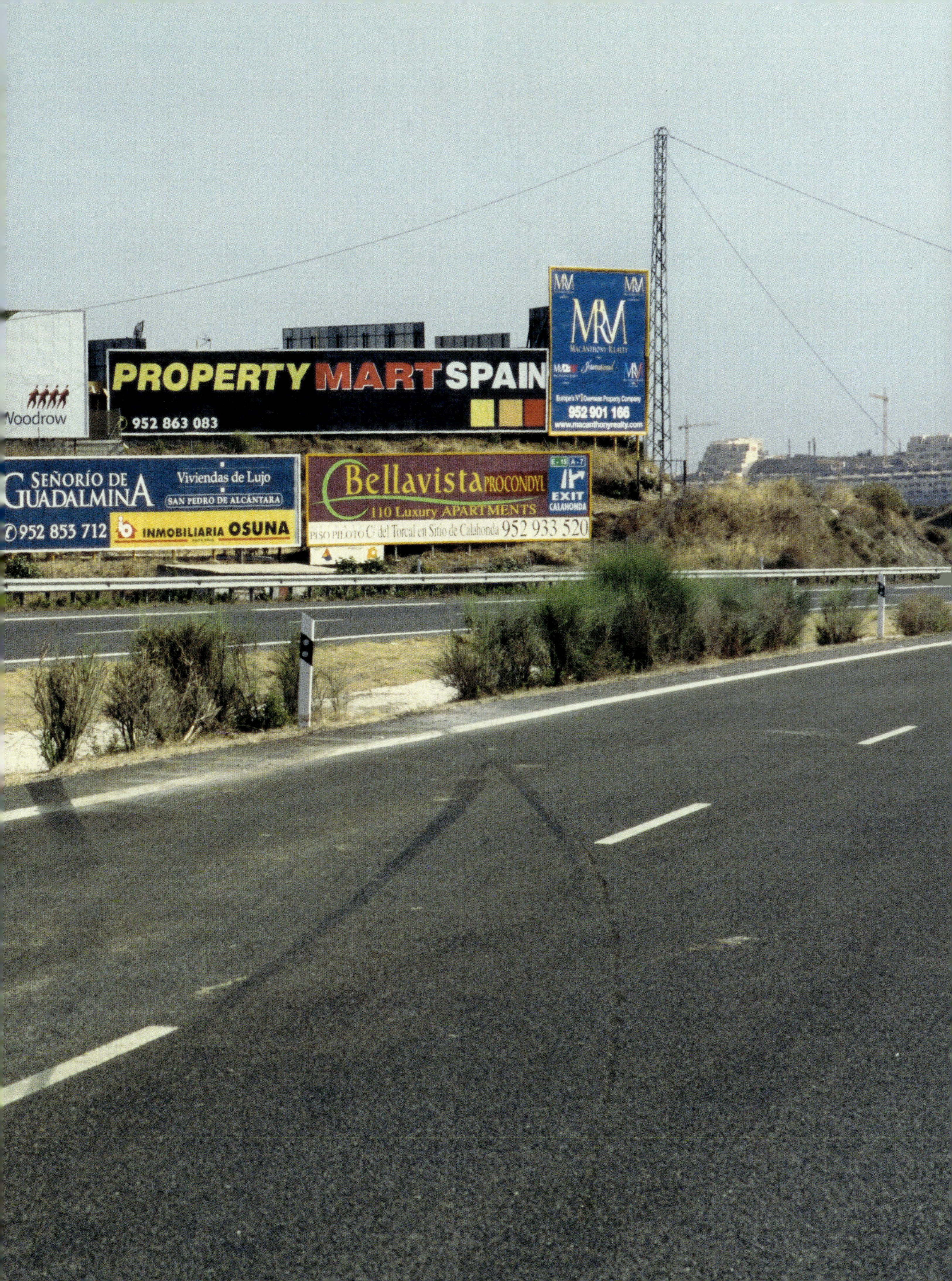
Woodrow
PROPERTY MART SPAIN
952 863 083
MRM
MacAnthony Realty
Europe's Nº1 Overseas Property Company
952 901 166
www.macanthonyrealty.com
SEÑORÍO DE GUADALMINA
Viviendas de Lujo
SAN PEDRO DE ALCÁNTARA
952 853 712
INMOBILIARIA OSUNA
Bellavista PROCONDYL
110 Luxury APARTMENTS
PISO PILOTO C/ del Torcal en Sitio de Calahonda 952 933 520
E-15 A-7
EXIT
CALAHONDA

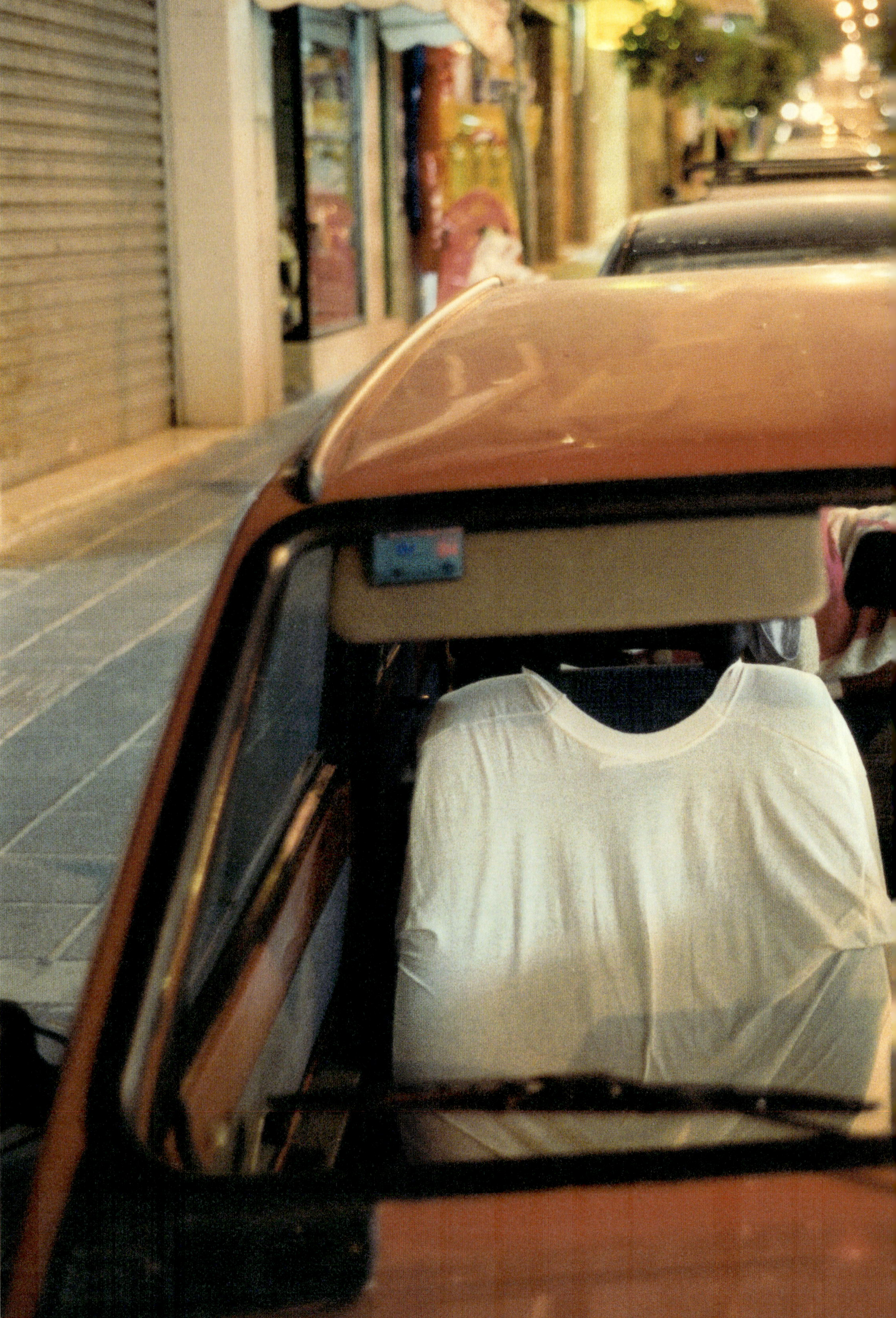

30.

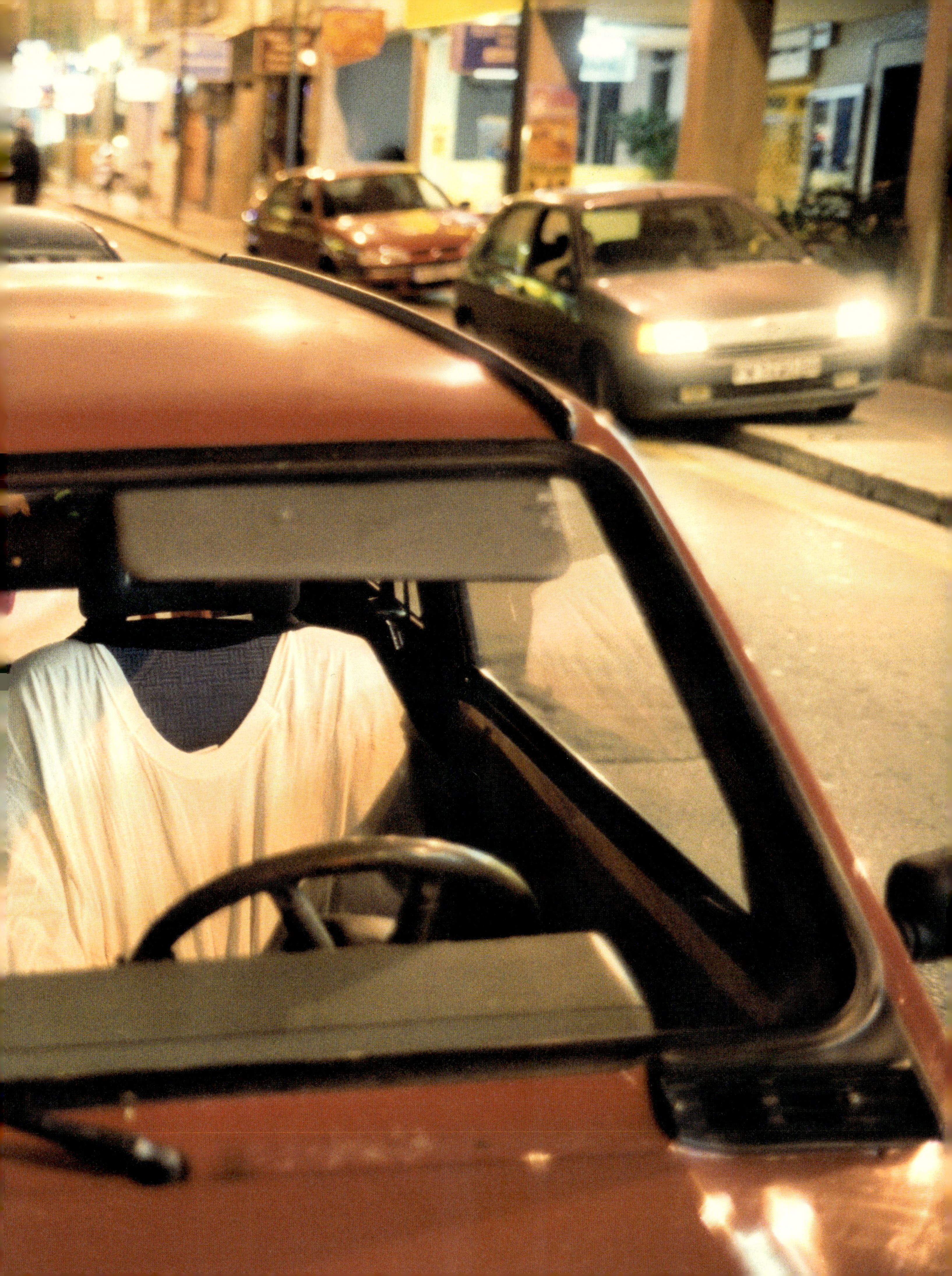

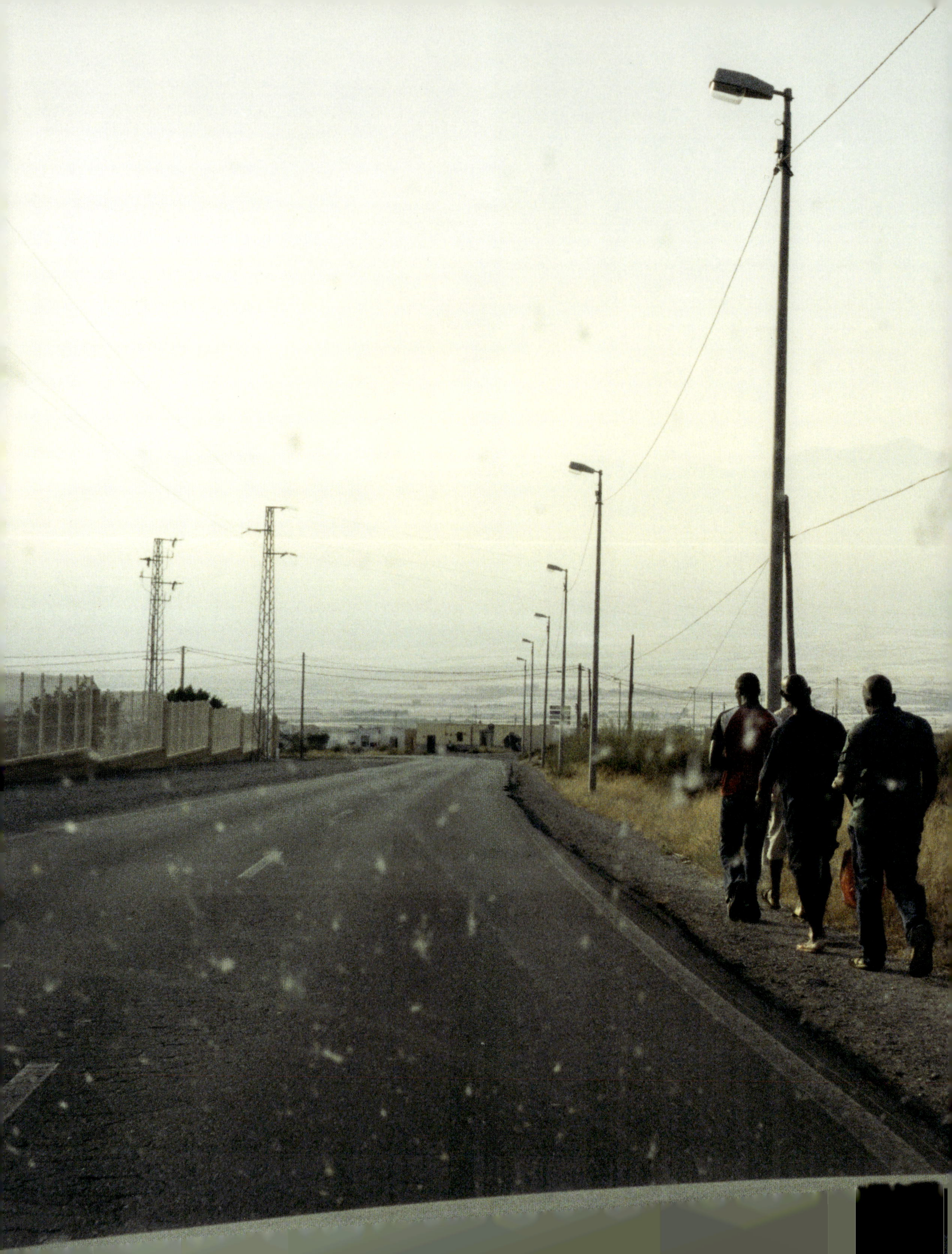

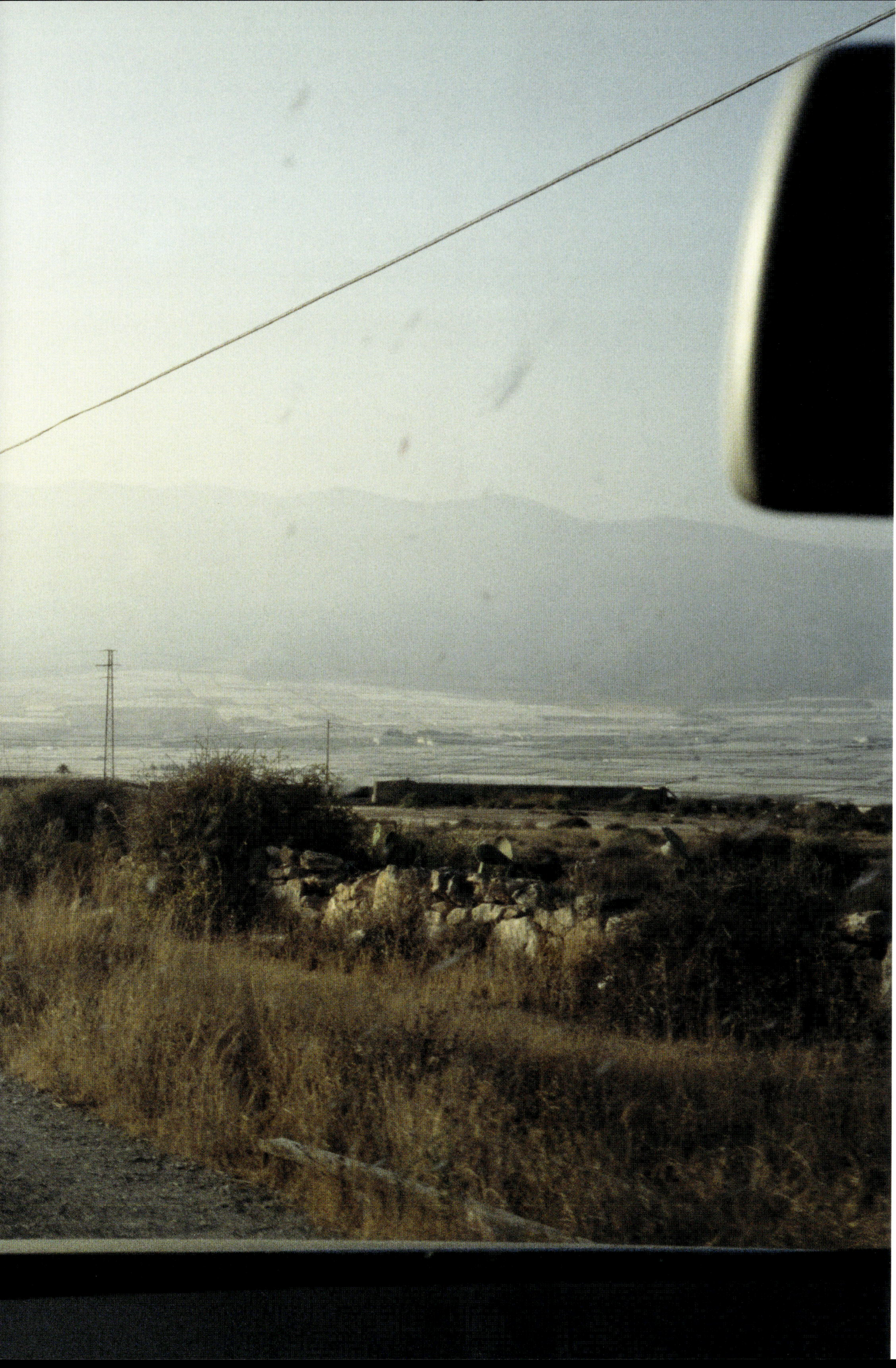

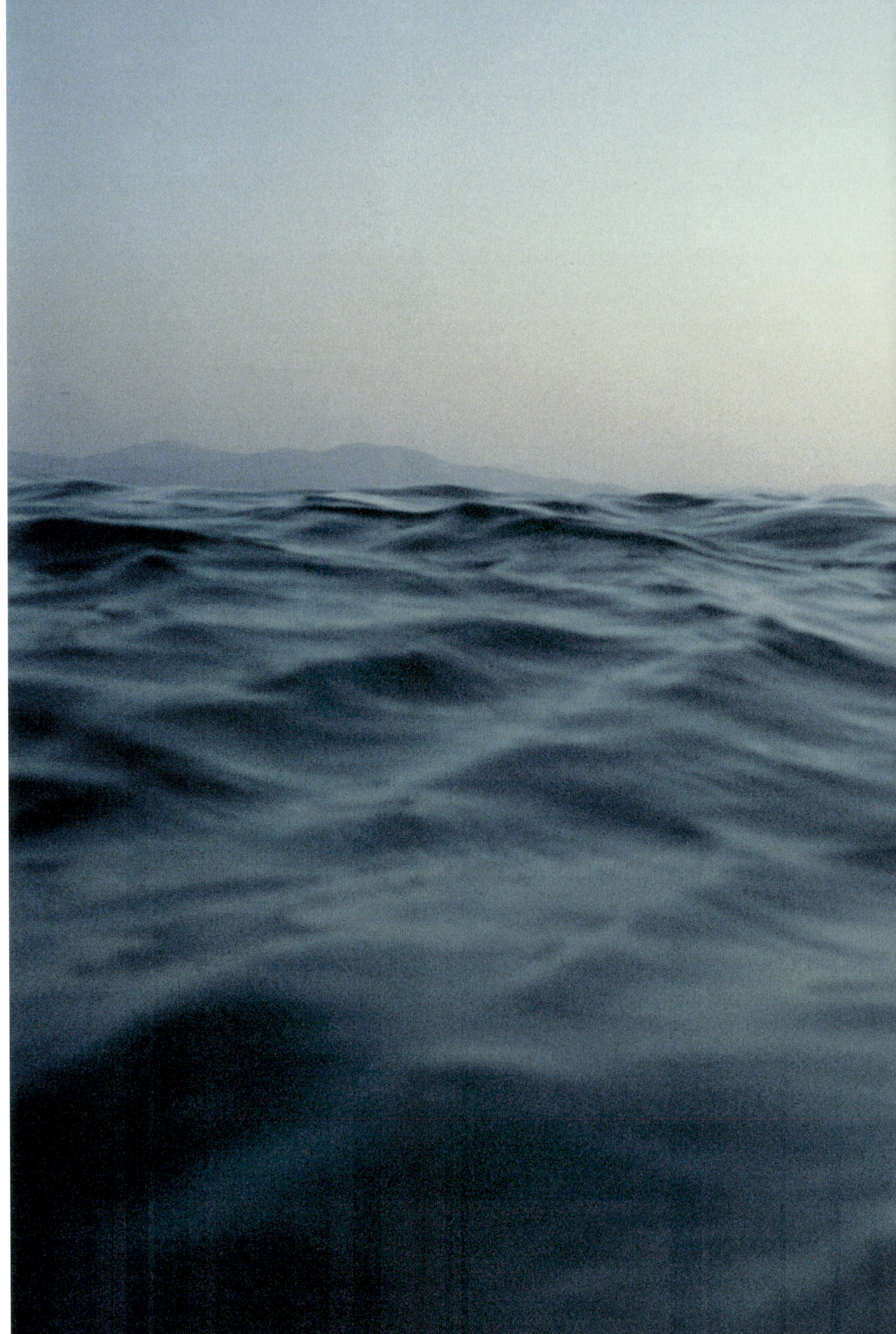

34.

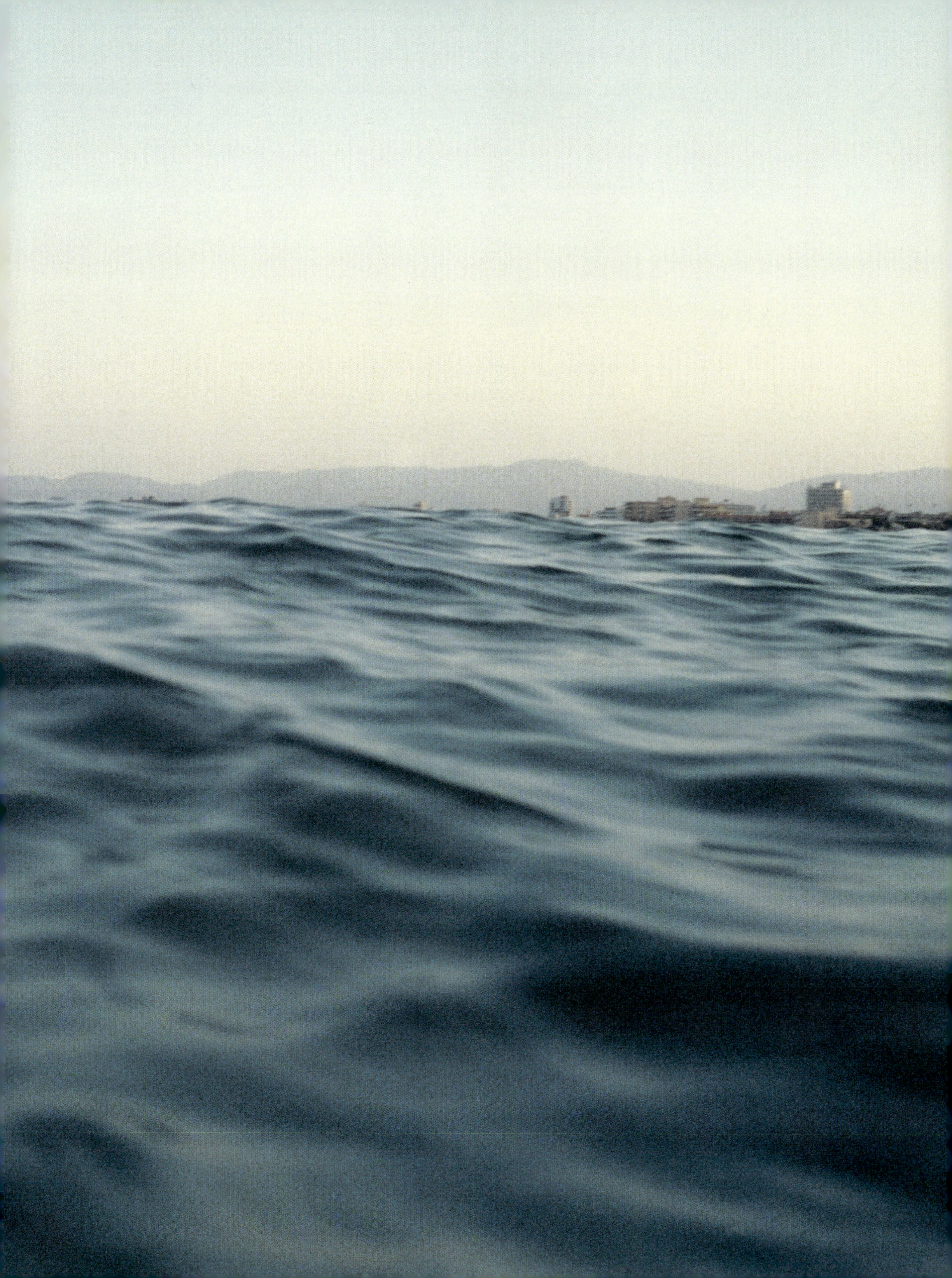

Every year, at the end of July and the beginning of August, tourists stream into France. No other country on earth receives so many foreign tourists. On the country's so-called Black Saturdays, traffic jams of up to 700 kilometres long block the motorways heading south. For the Brits, Germans, Belgians, Dutch and Italians, France is the most accessible holiday destination and highly desirable as a result of its pleasant climate and varied landscape.

The rise in low-budget flights in Europe has resulted in a shift in favour of destinations farther afield. Countries such as Tunisia, Turkey and Egypt are attempting to lure tourists away from traditional holiday destinations to their all-inclusive resorts. Charter flights shuttle the tourists back and forth.

Even so, tourist figures from Turkey, the largest newcomer, do not compare with those of the 'big three', Spain, Italy and France. An important reason is the unstable situation in many of these new tourist destinations. Every attack in Turkey, Israel or Egypt results in an immediate dip in bookings to these places. The attacks in the USA on September 11 2001 resulted in a dramatic decrease in the number of tourists visiting Islamic countries. Compare this with the terrorist attacks on the trains in Madrid in 2003. Only Madrid itself saw a brief decline in tourist numbers; it was not long before the Spanish tourism sector returned to business as usual.

FRANCE

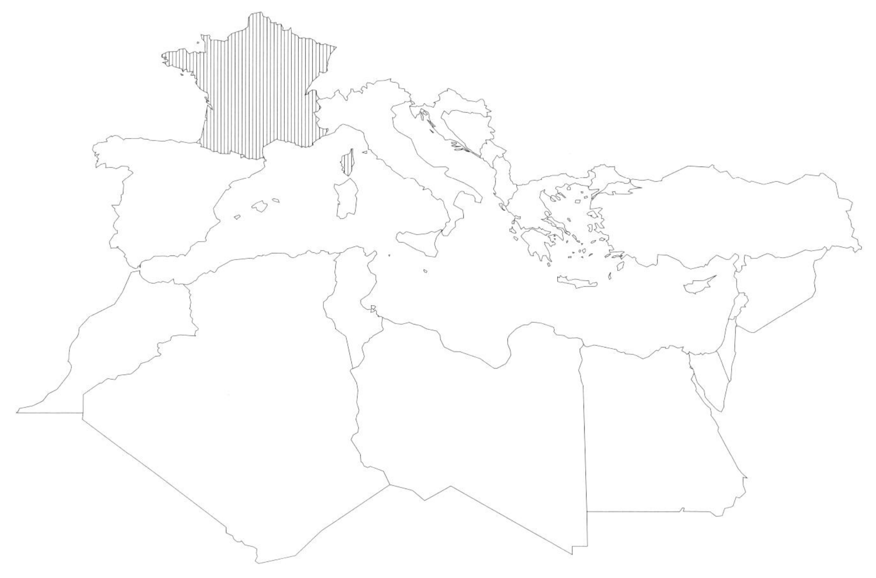

ANNUAL NUMBER OF TOURISTS

GIBRALTAR	236,000
SPAIN	58,914,000
FRANCE	**79,083,000**
ITALY	41,058,000
CROATIA	8,659,000
ALBANIA	645,409
GREECE	15,449,133
CYPRUS	2,401,000
TURKEY	18,916,000
SYRIA	3,777,000
LEBANON	1,063,000
ISRAEL	1,825,000
W.B. & GAZA	NA
EGYPT	8,646,000
LIBYA	125,480
TUNISIA	6,550,000
ALGERIA	1,233,719
MOROCCO	6,558,000

39. BEAUNE

One week after Black Saturday, the busiest day on France's roads. The A7, better known as the *Autoroute du Soleil* (*Highway to the Sun*) is one of the two trunk roads through France to the south. In July and August the motorway is a world in itself. Activities for children are organized at every service area.

40. VARENNES-LE-GRAND

Everyone is on the move. You meet very few people on the long journey south. In the past, holidaymakers camped and cooked along the route.

42. DIJON

The service areas along the French motorways can hardly be called French anymore. The food is international and fast. Only two kilometres from the road, the food becomes French again and the world smells of herbs instead of petrol.

44. VIDAUBAN

You sit in permanent traffic jams in the Côte d'Azur. People are drawn to each other. In Saint-Tropez, you walk along the yacht harbours as if you were glued together. The coastal strip is virtually unaffordable. Further inland, more and more buildings are going up. In other parts of southern France, almost entire villages are bought up by foreigners, pricing the local population out of its own housing market.

46. DIJON

A lonely, rouged woman at an 'Aire'. Whether you are driving through Germany or France, service areas all look the same.

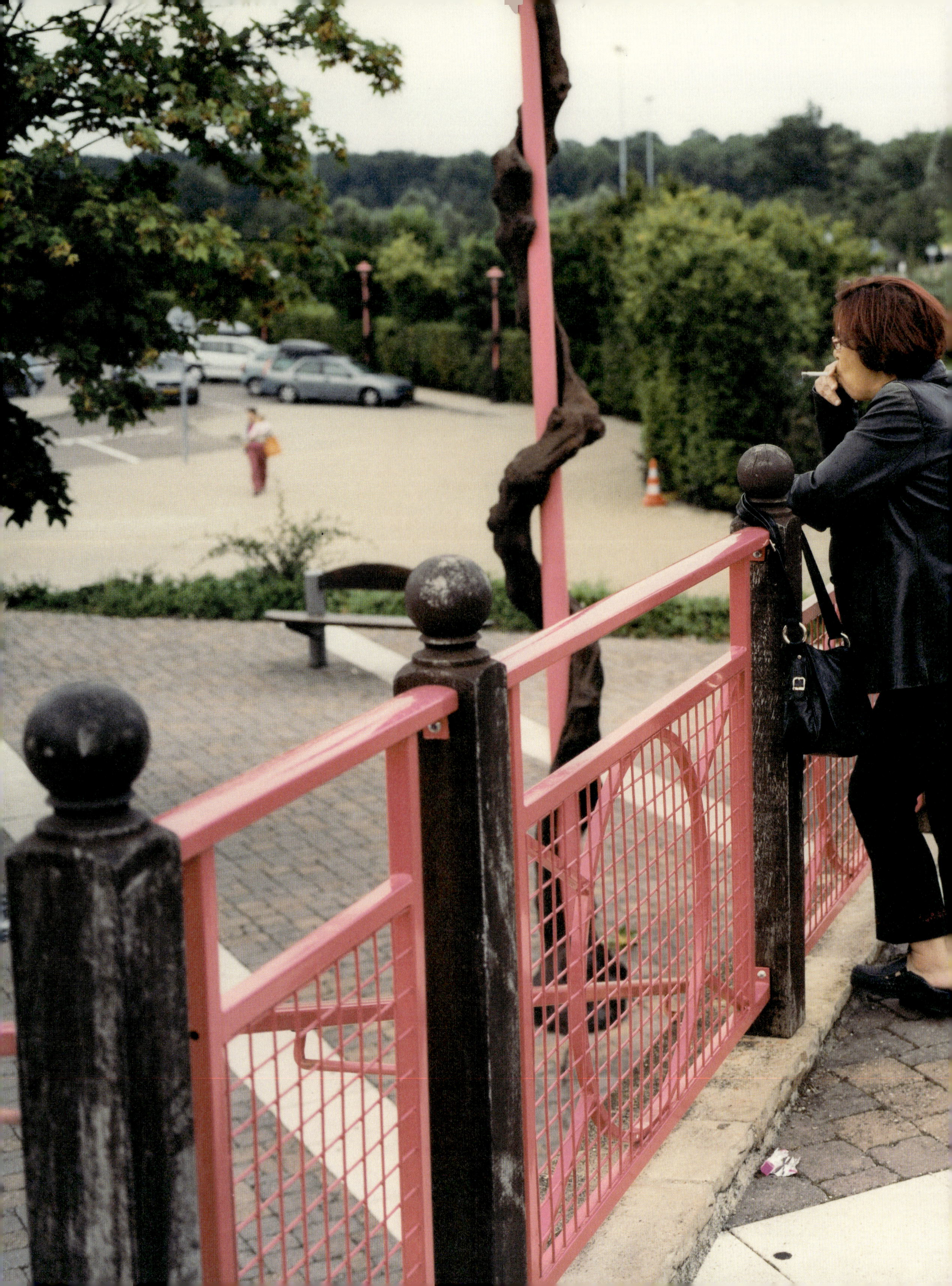

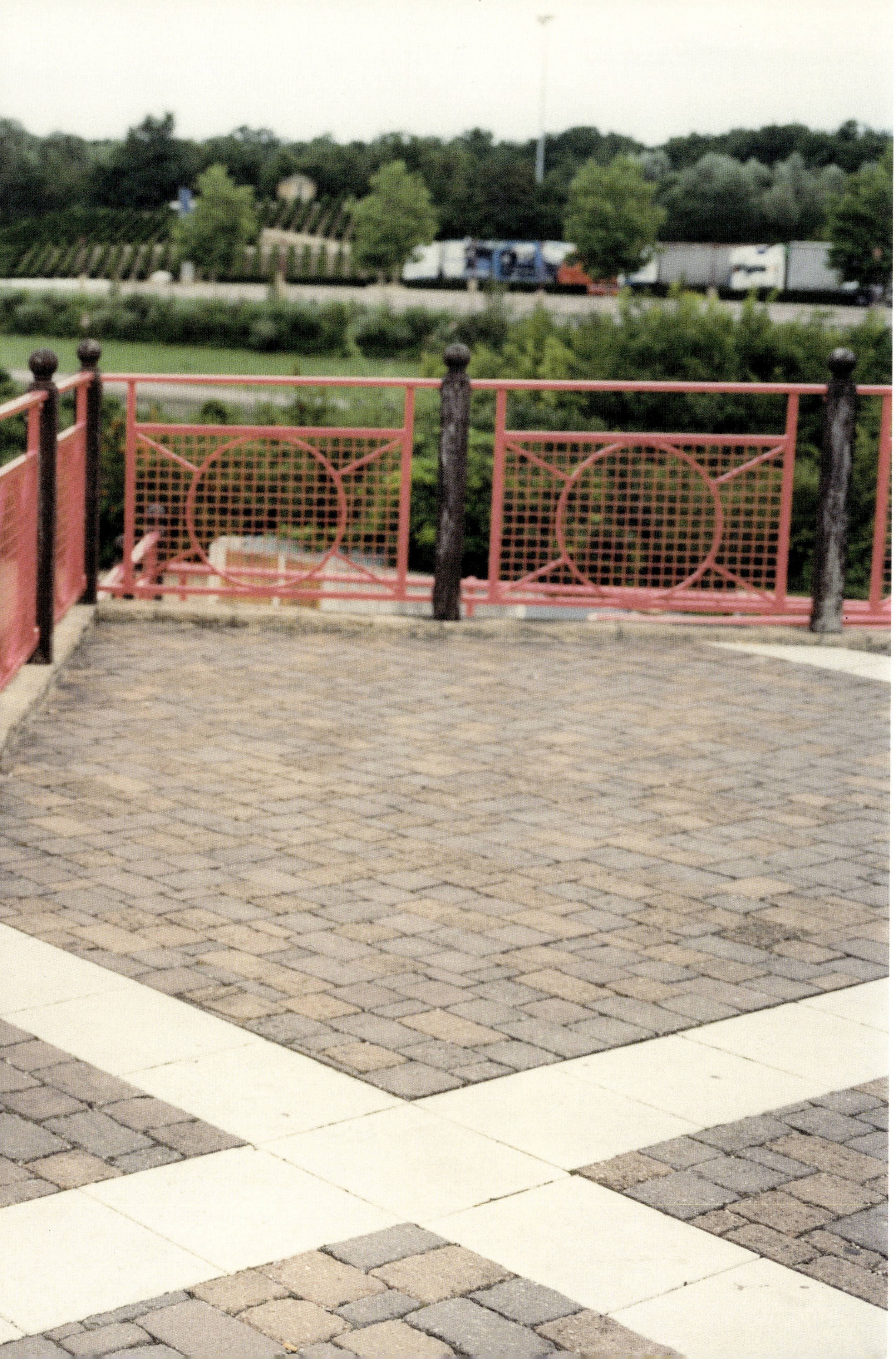

39.

40.

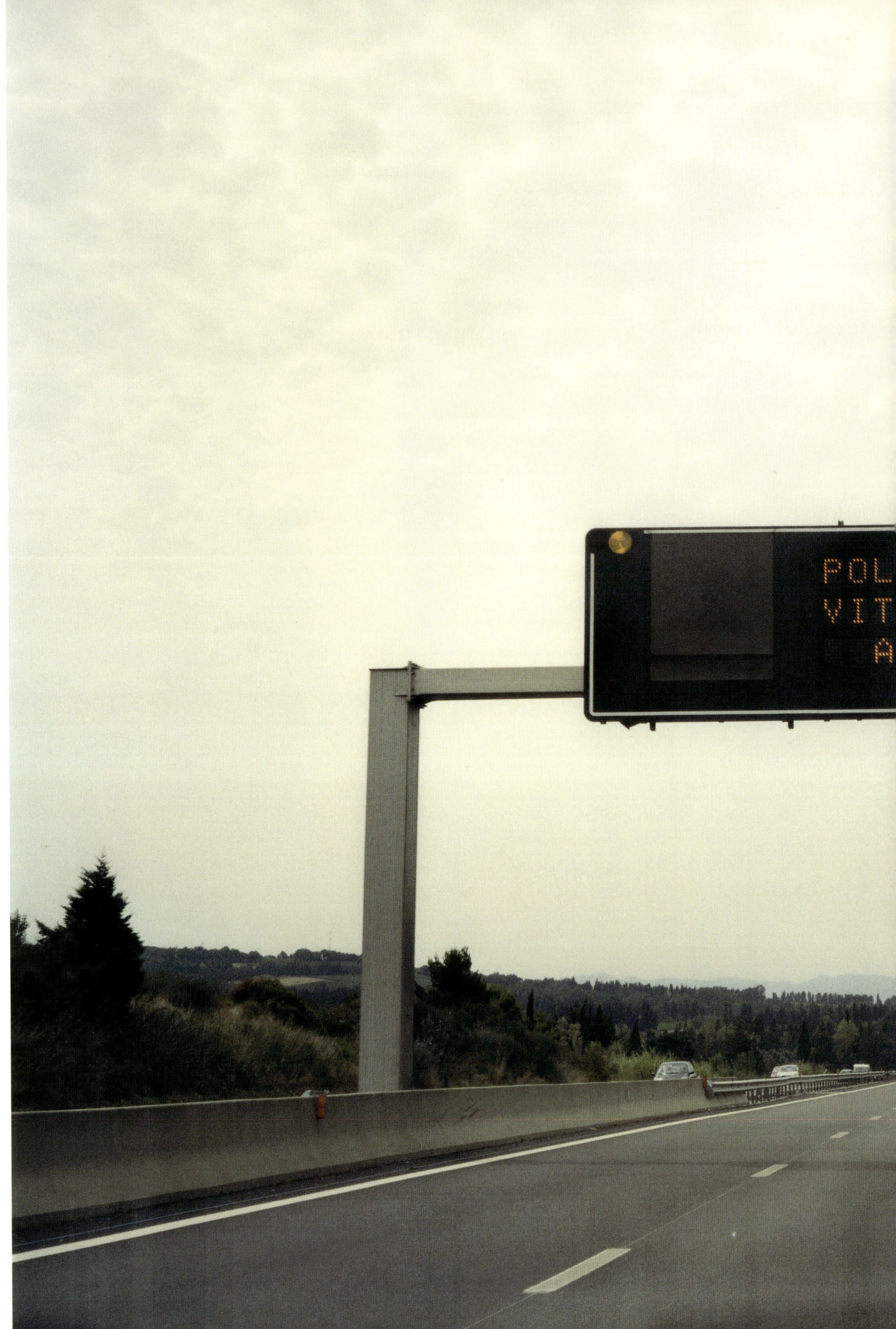
POL
VIT
A

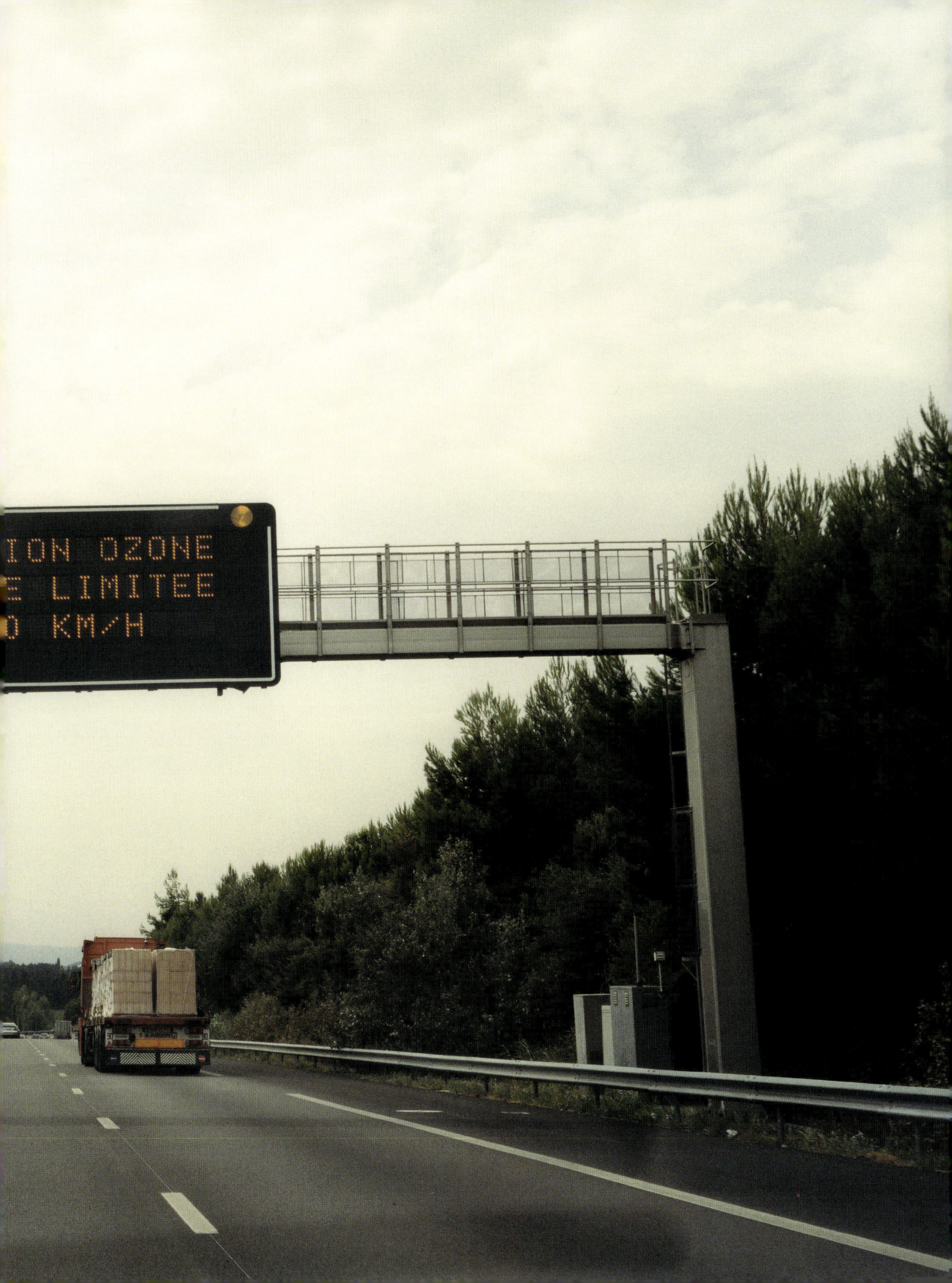
ION OZONE
E LIMITEE
0 KM/H

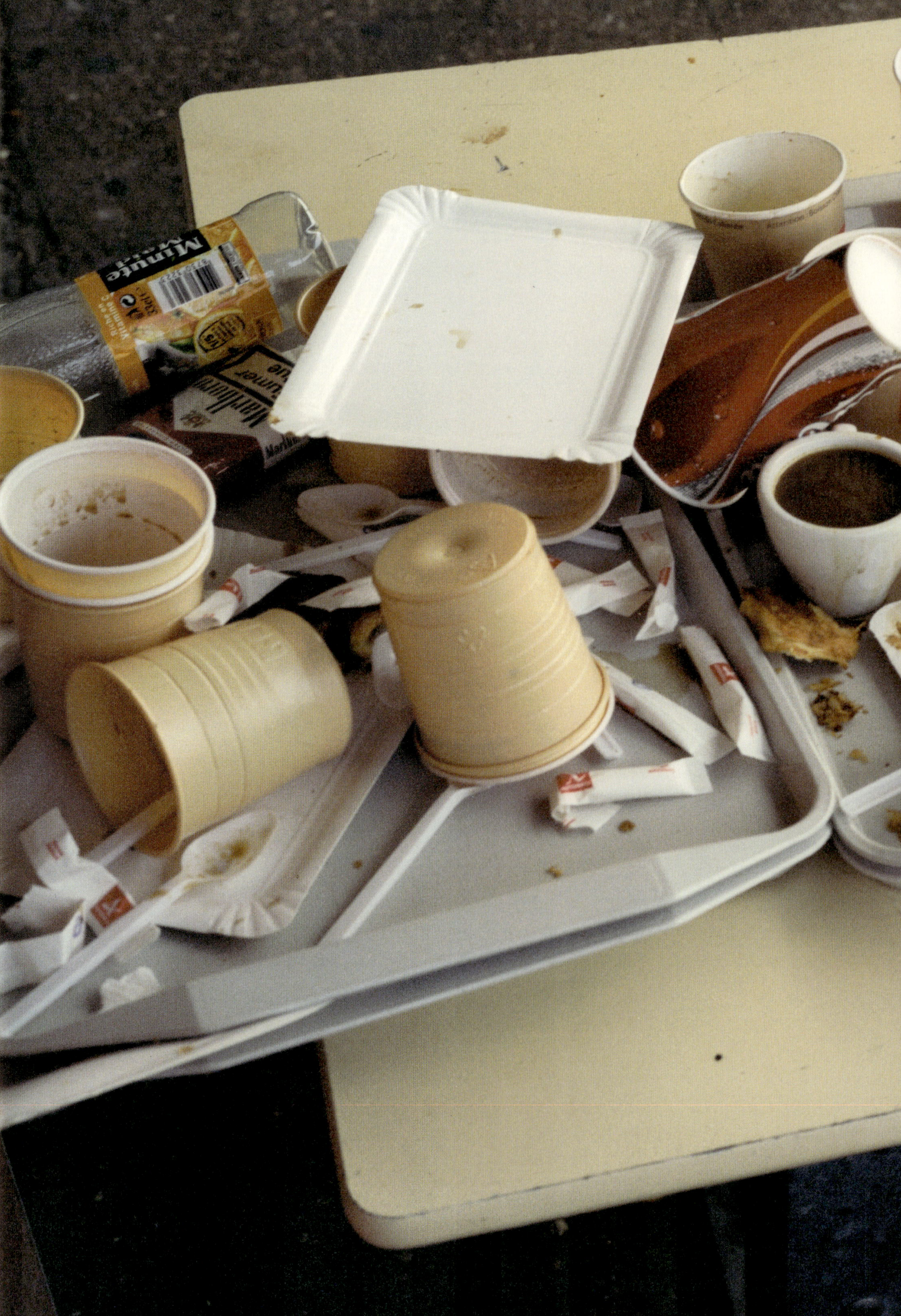

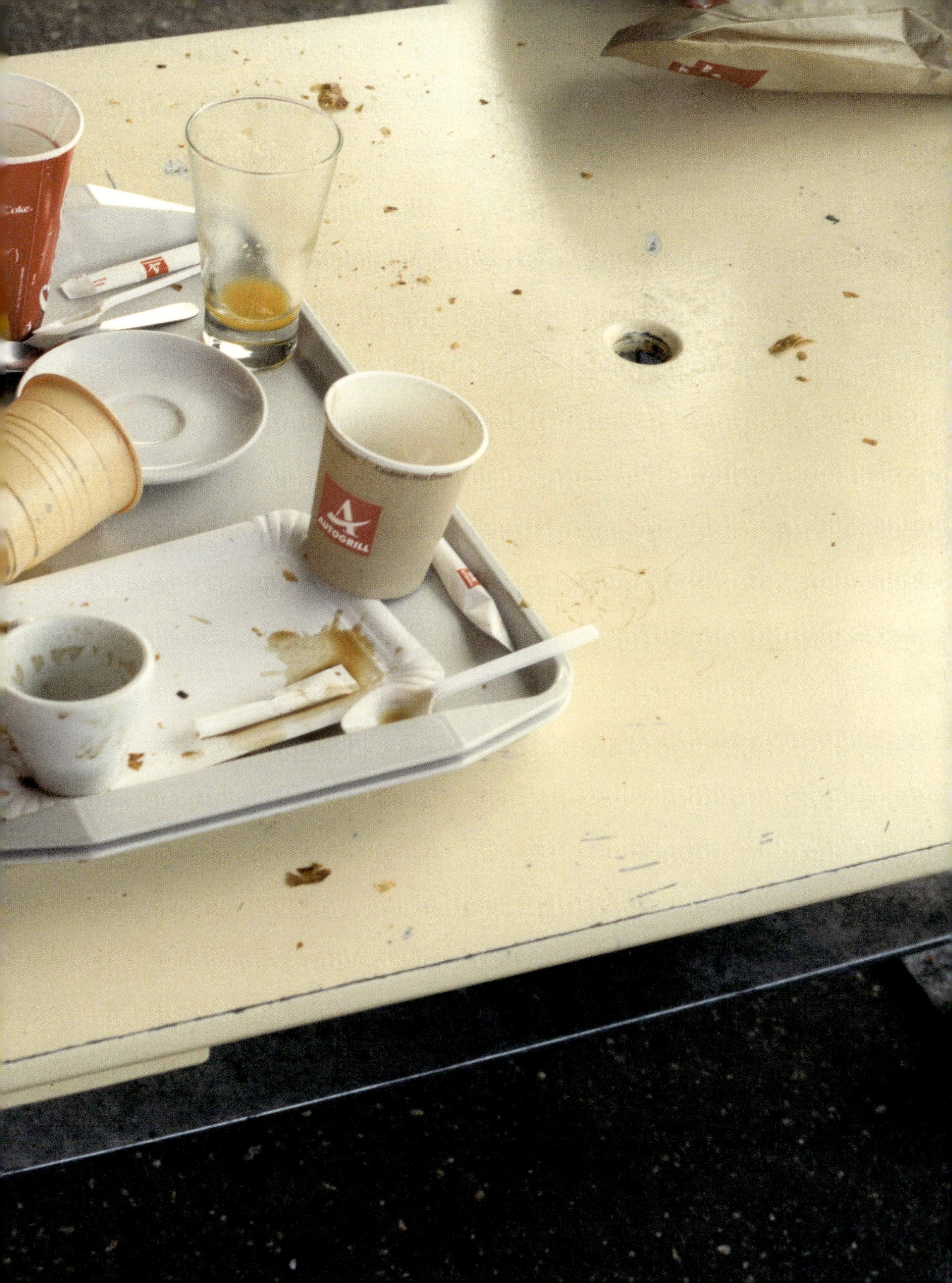

AUTOGRILL
Coke.

44.

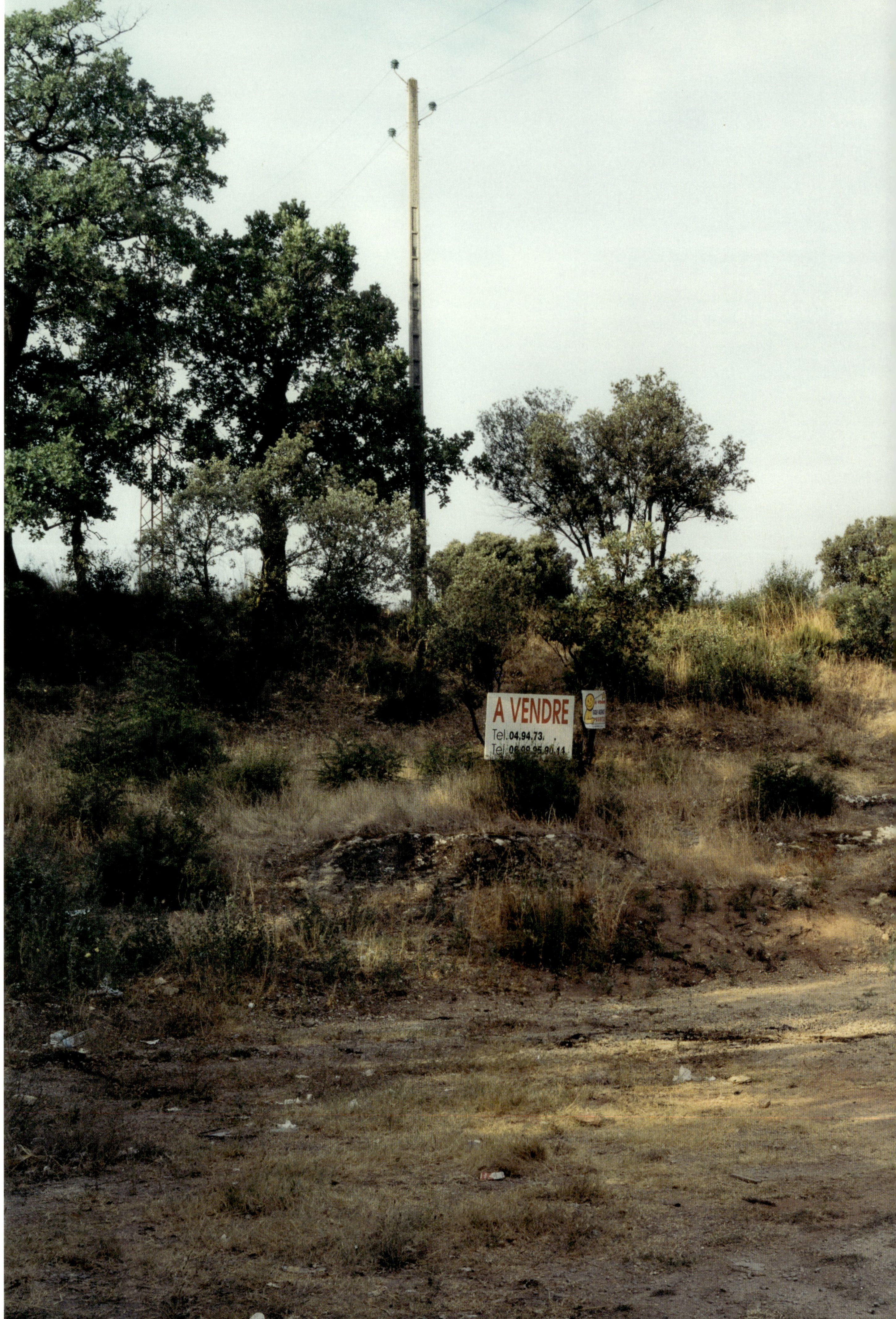

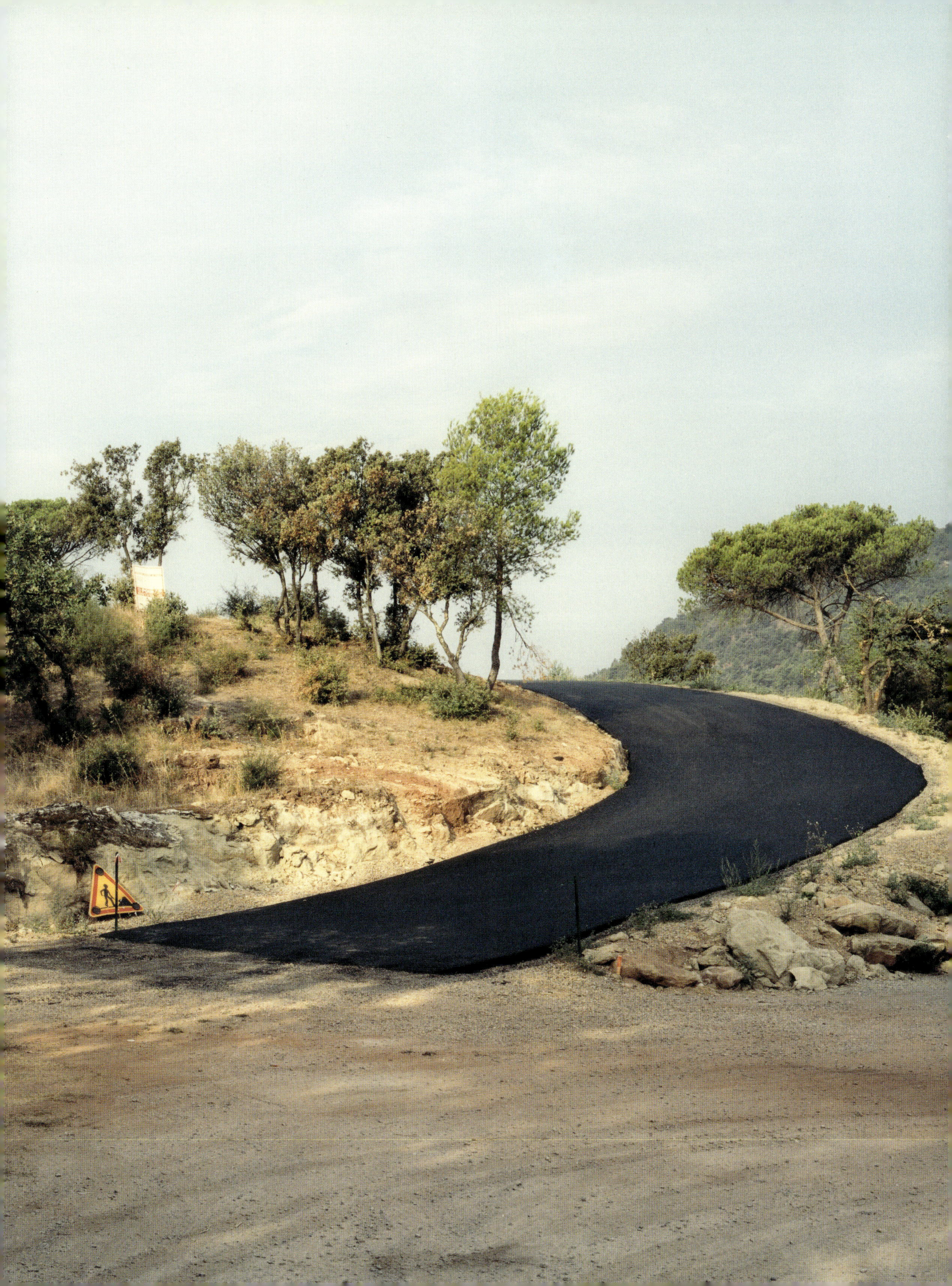

46.

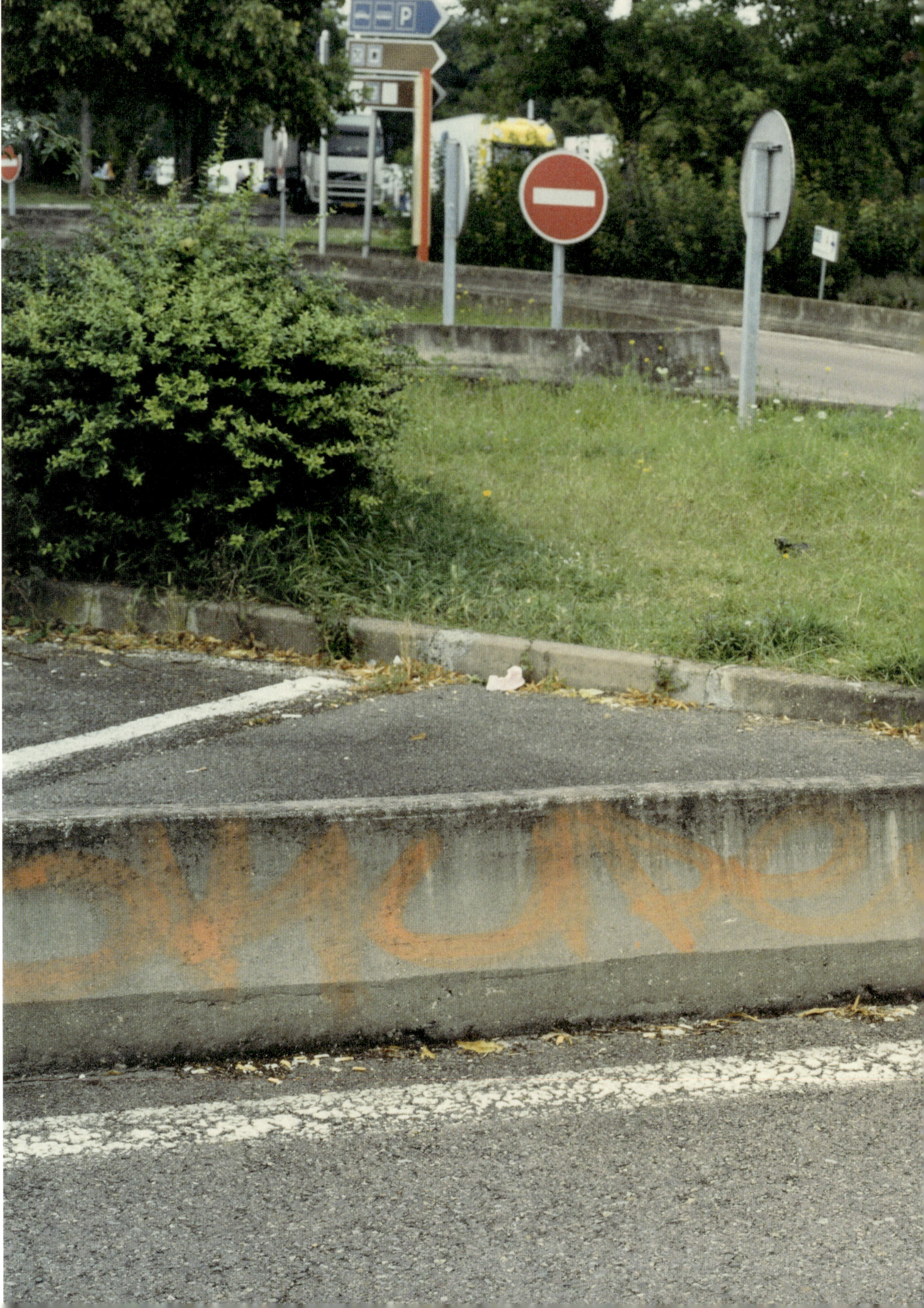

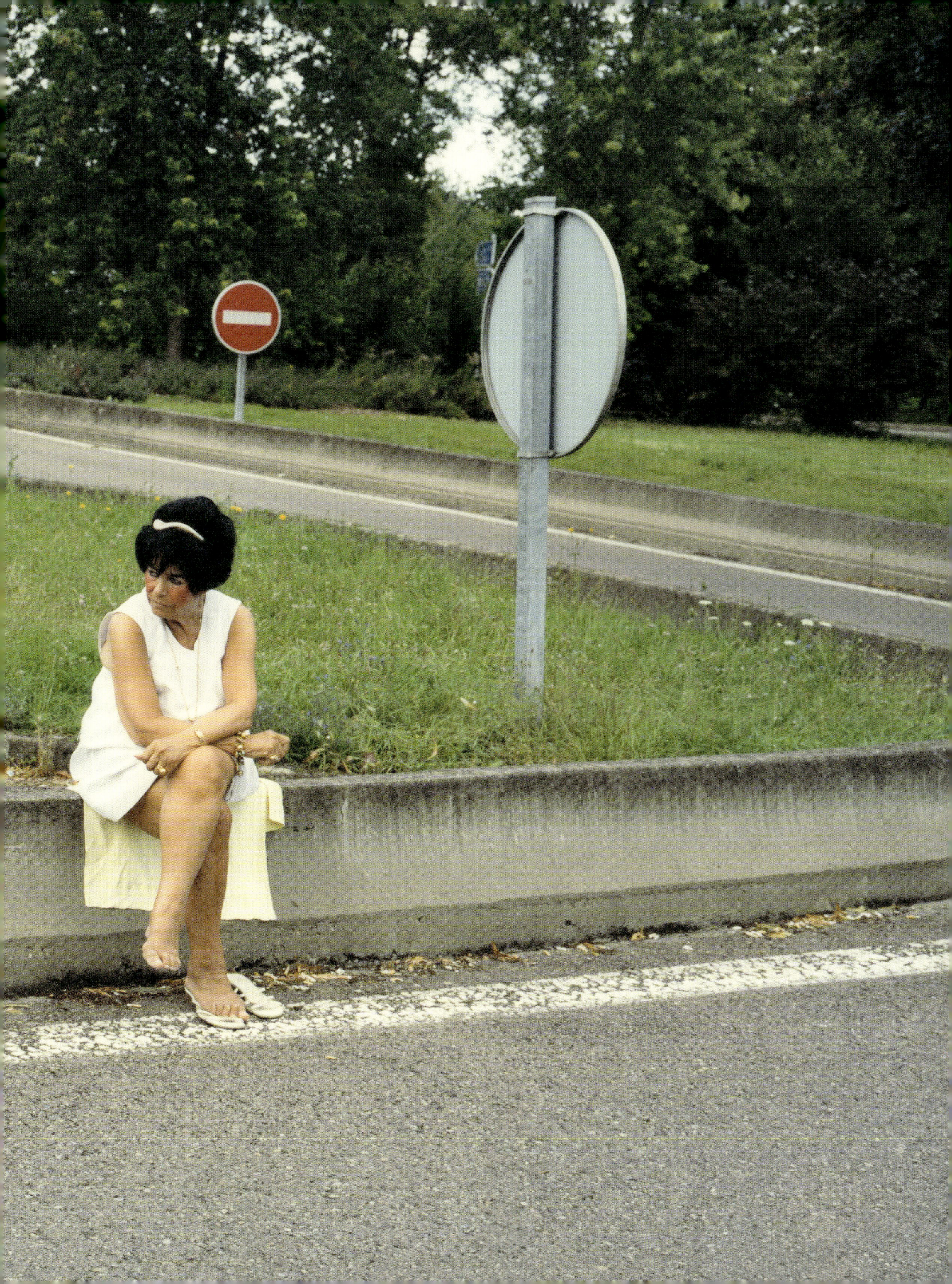

With its 7,600 kilometres of coastline, Italy is an important immigration point for many fortune hunters from the Balkan Peninsula and Africa, and, together with Spain, France and Greece, it forms the southern border of 'Fort Europe'. When Italy's neighbours tightened their immigration policy, Italy instantly felt the effects. The stream of immigrants increased immediately.

The history of illegal immigration is one with many victims and is made up of dramatic stories of boats that have capsized on the Mediterranean's rough waters. Over the last 10 years, the trek through the Sahara to Libya alone has already cost around one thousand people their lives. The total number of people who did reach Europe in boats last year was around 50,000. These are the people who have been counted – fished out of the water, caught, or registered on arrival. Those that die – according to an Italian action group, more than a thousand last year – are not counted, just like those who arrive and 'disappear' anonymously into society. It is estimated that between 500,000 and 800,000 illegal immigrants live in Italy.

Through cooperation with African countries, Italy has tried in recent years to send illegal immigrants back to their country of origin. This has attracted much criticism from human rights organizations. They worry that, in the wake of economic refugees, political refugees may also be sent home too quickly. Many African migrants are economic refugees – last year, only 300 people requested asylum in Spain, even though that same year 32,000 people arrived on the Canary Islands alone.

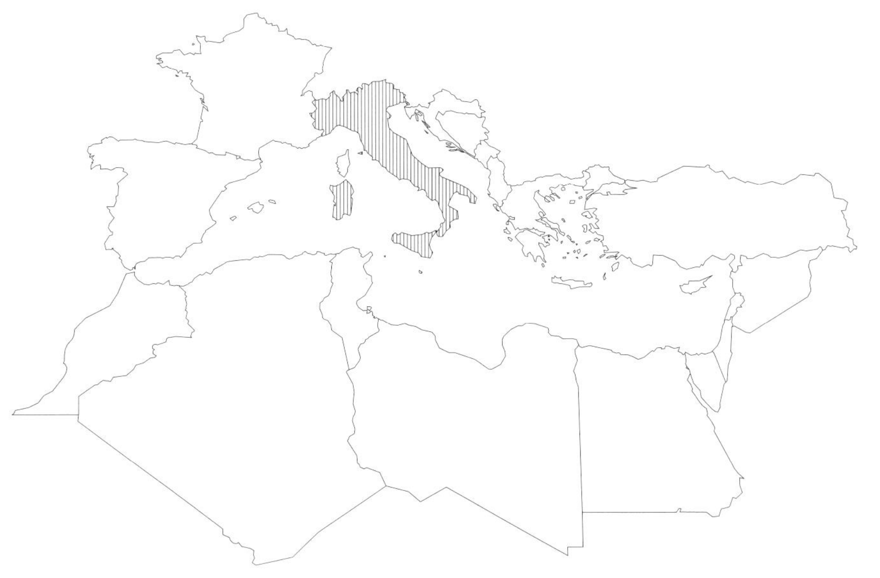

NET MIGRATION
MIGRANTS/1,000 POPULATION

		-5.0	0.0	5.0
GIBRALTAR	0			
SPAIN	0.99			
FRANCE	0.66			
ITALY	**2.07**			
CROATIA	1.58			
ALBANIA	-4.54			
GREECE	2.34			
CYPRUS	0.42			
TURKEY	0			
SYRIA	0			
LEBANON	0			
ISRAEL	0			
W.B.& GAZA	NA			
EGYPT	-0.21			
LIBYA	0			
TUNISIA	-0.47			
ALGERIA	-0.33			
MOROCCO	-0.82			

SOURCE : WWW.MIGRATIONINFORMATION.ORG, CIA WORLD FACTBOOK

50. NAPLES
Caserta lies about 20 kilometres to the north of Naples. This is where southern Italy begins. Motorists suddenly drive differently and the rubbish is no longer cleared up.

53. NAPLES
Campania's governor visits Naples. Security personnel are everywhere. The street in front of Parliament Square is immediately packed. At these sorts of occasions, Members of Parliament come to show their faces.

55. SORRENTO
Italy's west coast is predominantly visited by Italian tourists. Sorrento and Capri are the two big exceptions. If you drive through the small villages here, curtains twitch. People want to know who is passing by.

56. NAPLES
Immigrants display their junk on the street. Naples is in the stranglehold of the mafia. At 7% of the Gross National Product it is the biggest industry in Italy. They control almost all the trade. Hell often breaks loose if you take a photo here.

59. NAPLES
Naples is Italy's only real metropolis. It is the filthiest, most problematic and chaotic city in the country. At the same time, this is what makes it so interesting.

61. SENIGALLIA
The entire village takes to the streets on Sunday afternoon. Babies are shown off and the latest gossip makes the rounds. Climbing frames are put up for the children.

62. ROME
The demand for fake Prada bags is high. It seems as if no other brands are sold here. It must be an enormous industry.

65. ROME
On Sunday afternoon, every family cruises the streets for an hour and half in cars or on scooters. After that, the streets are deserted again.

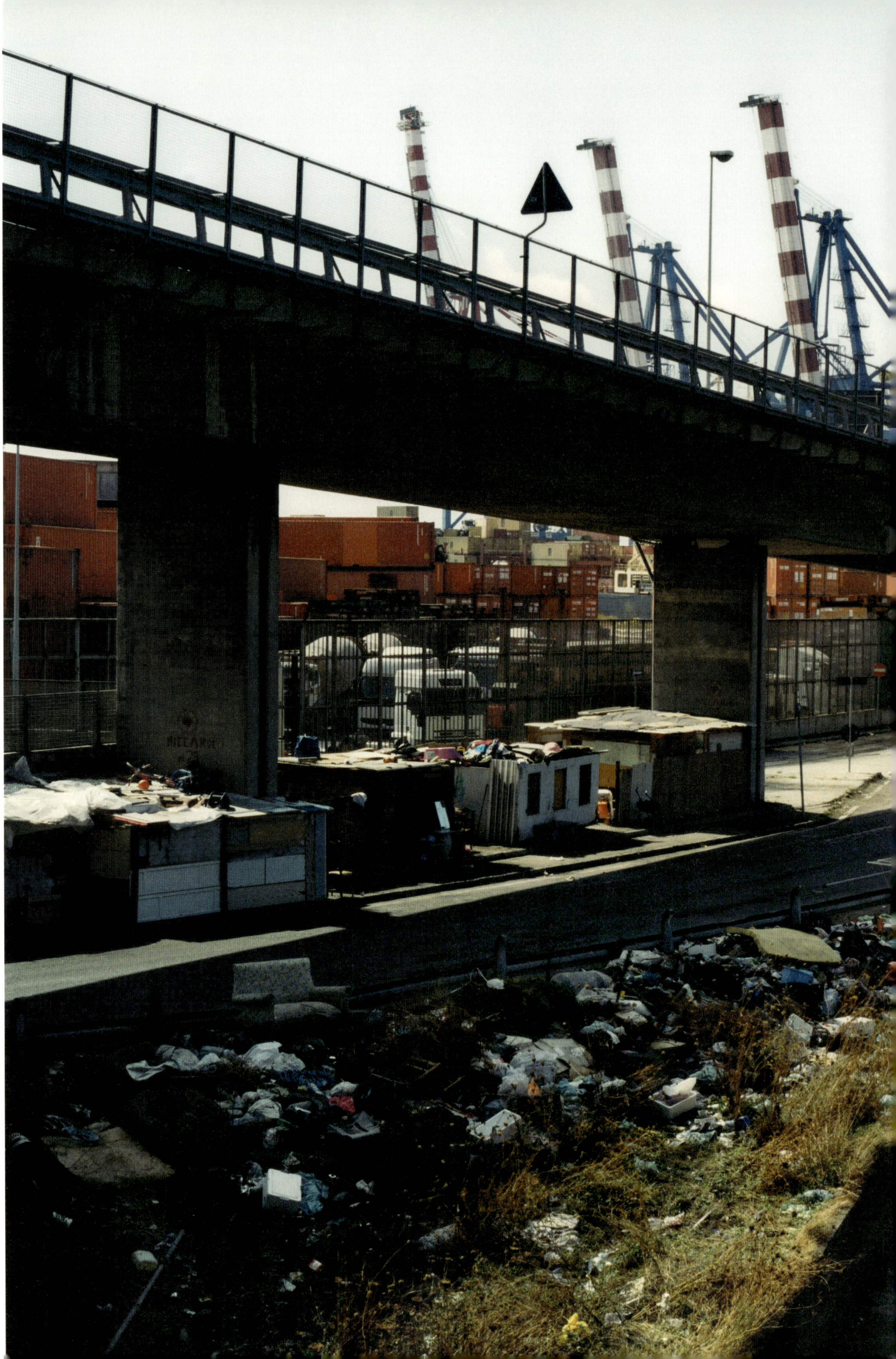

50.

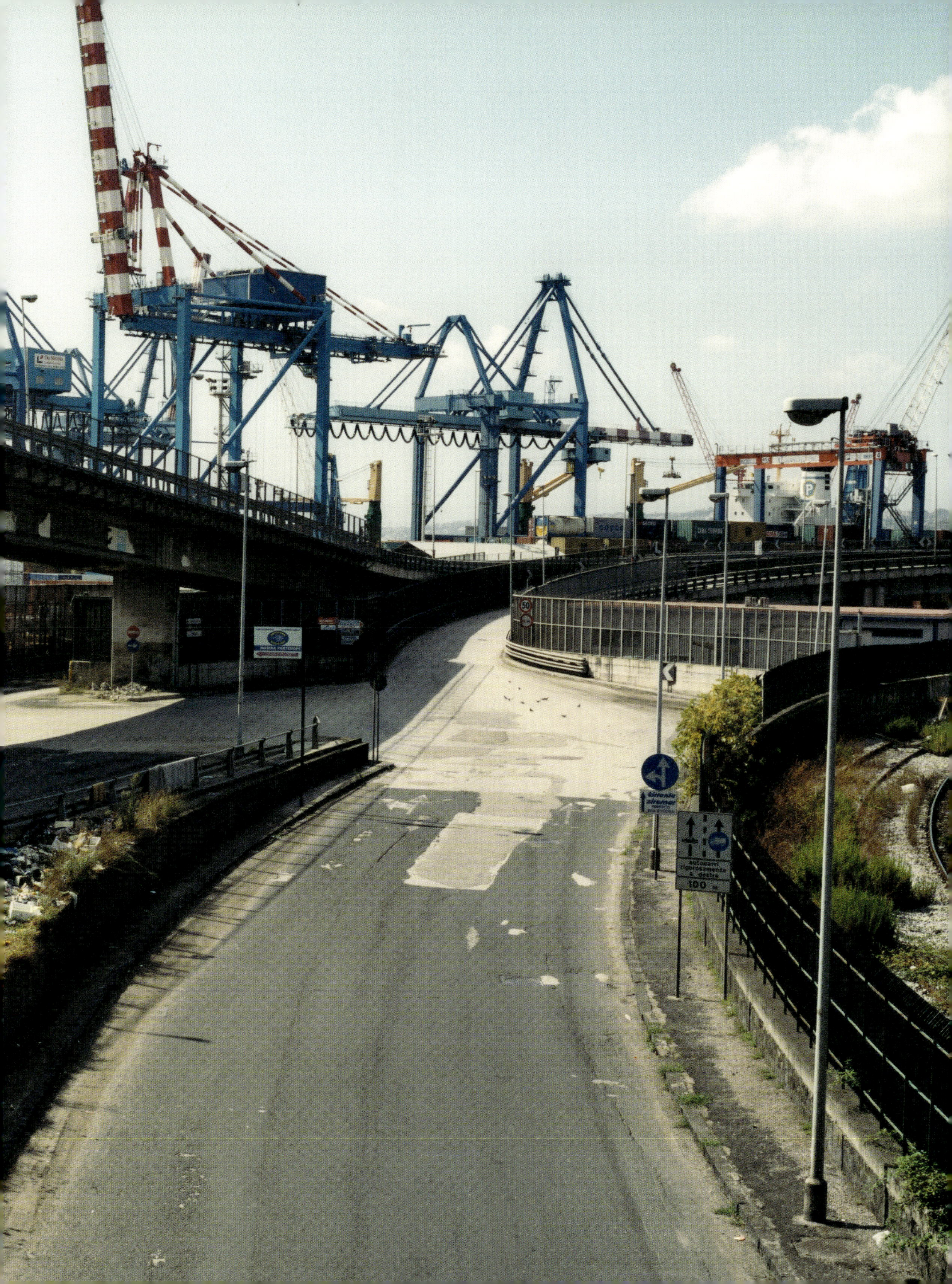

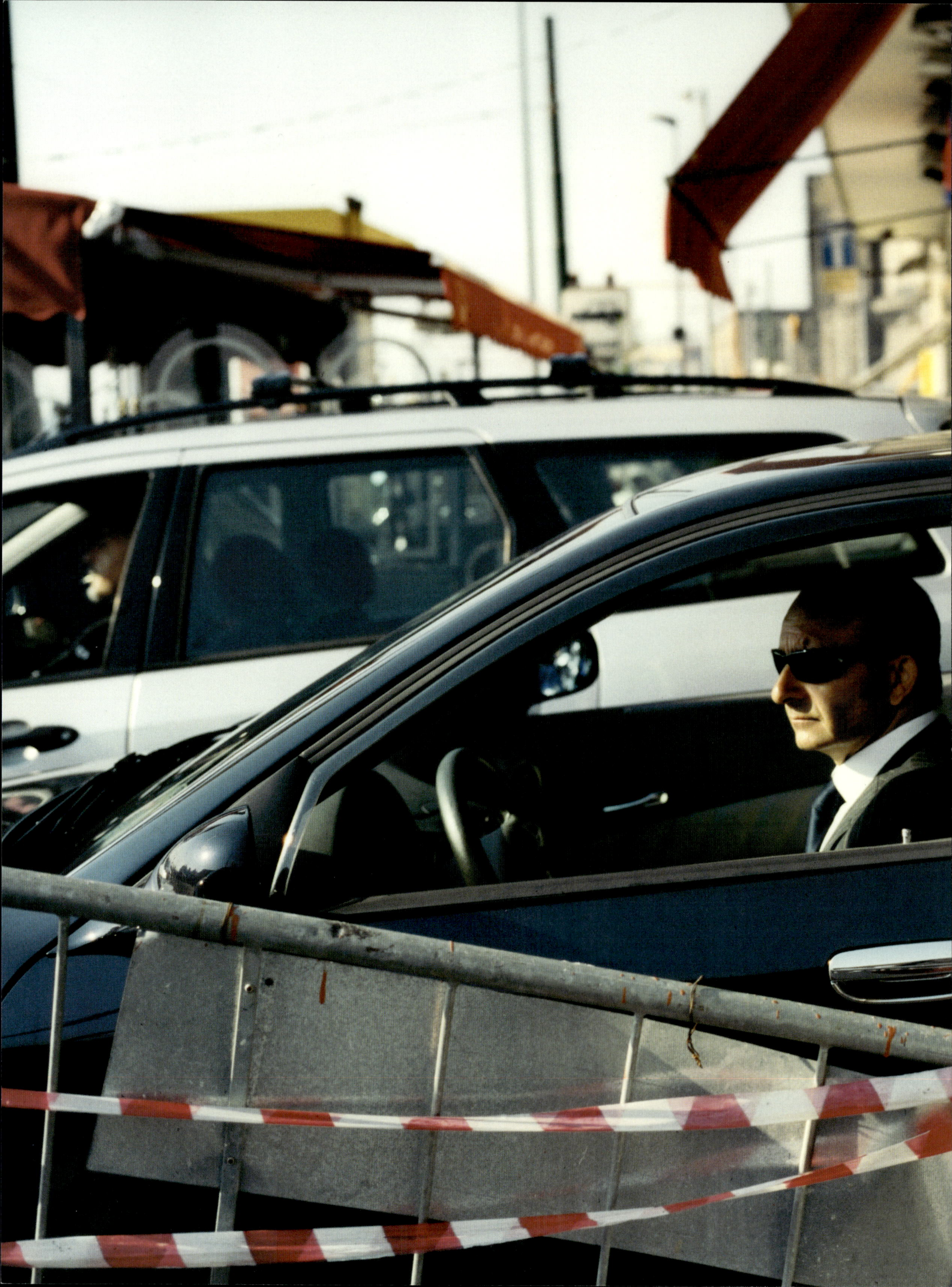

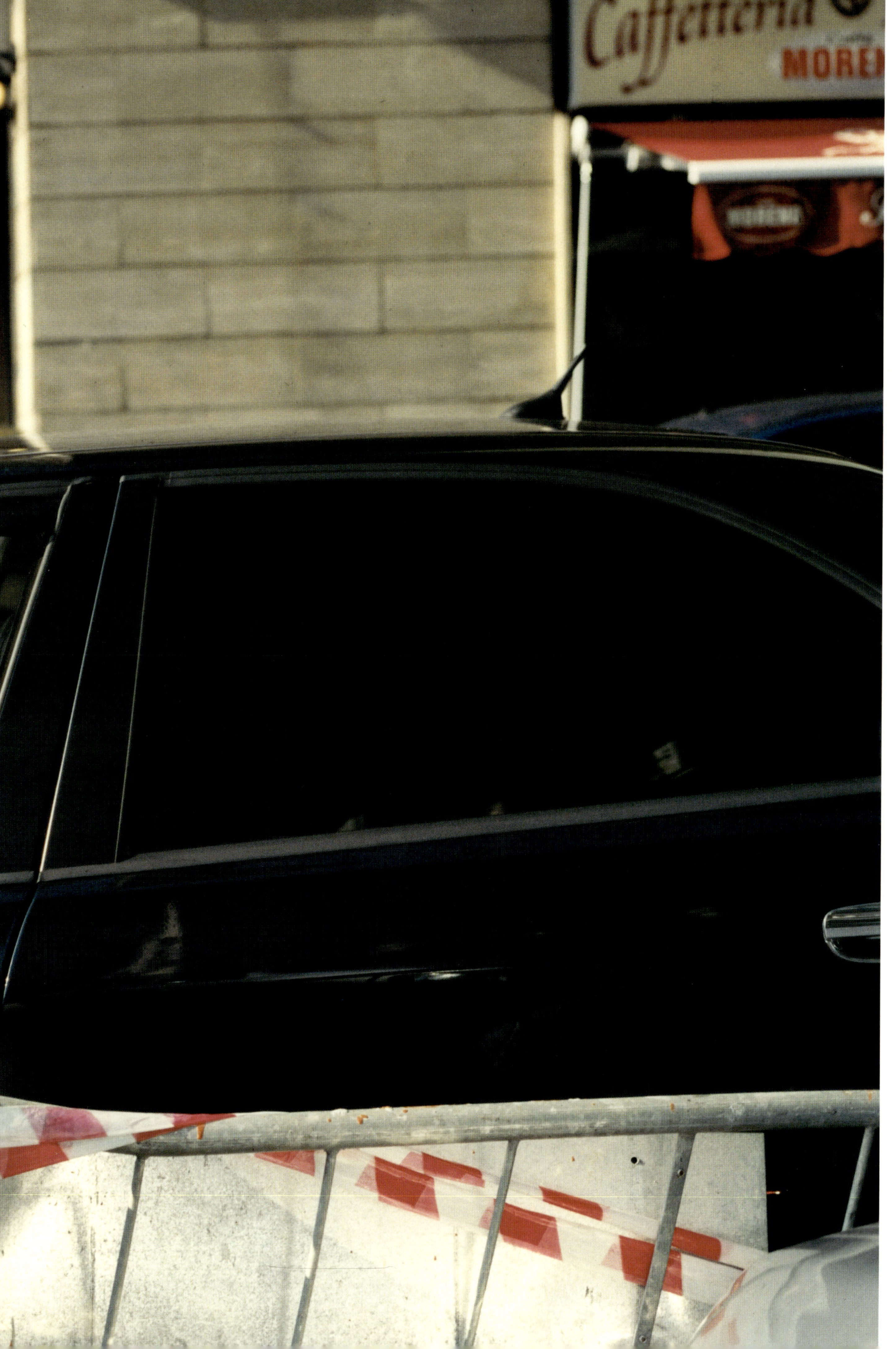

53.

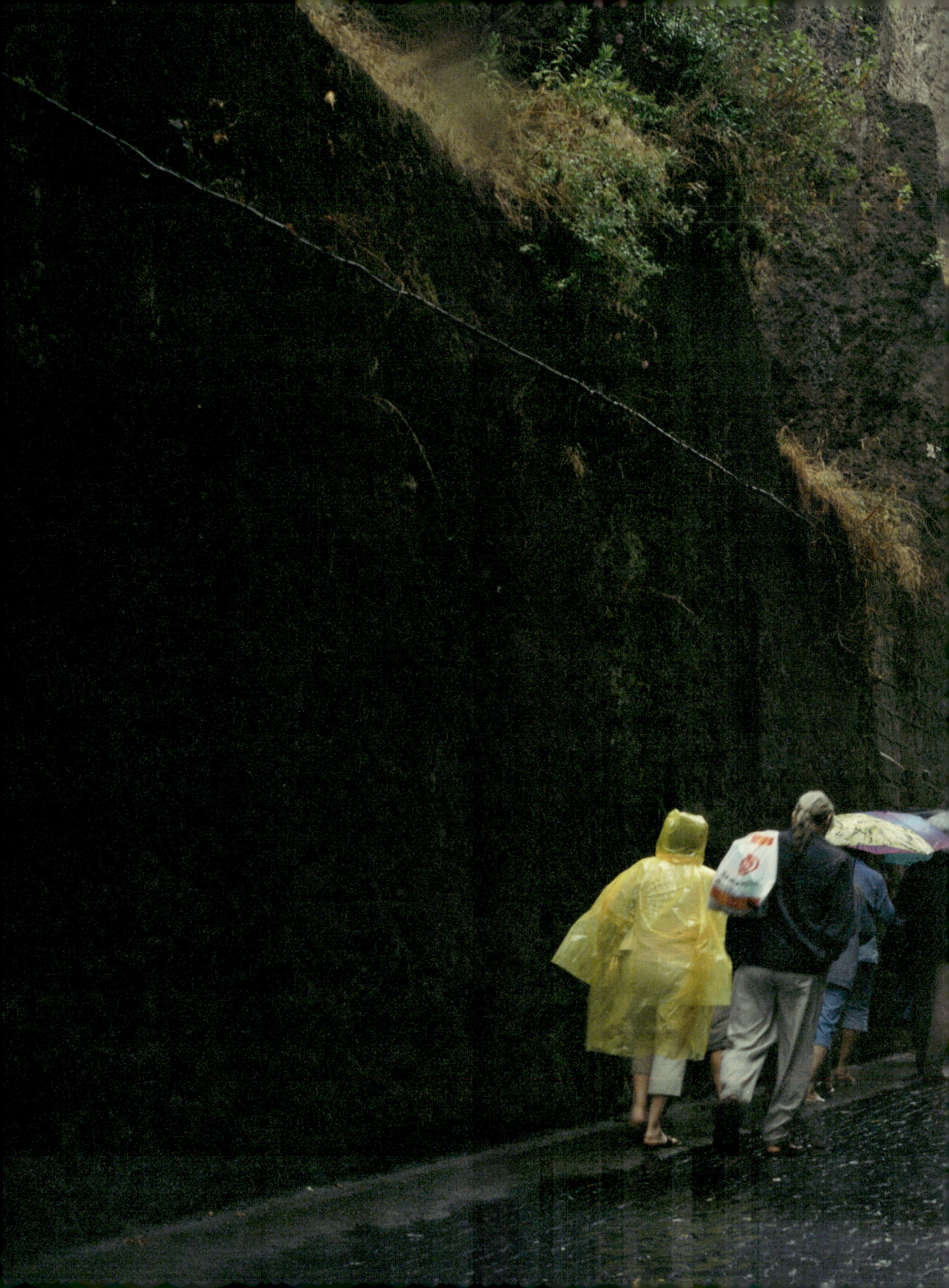

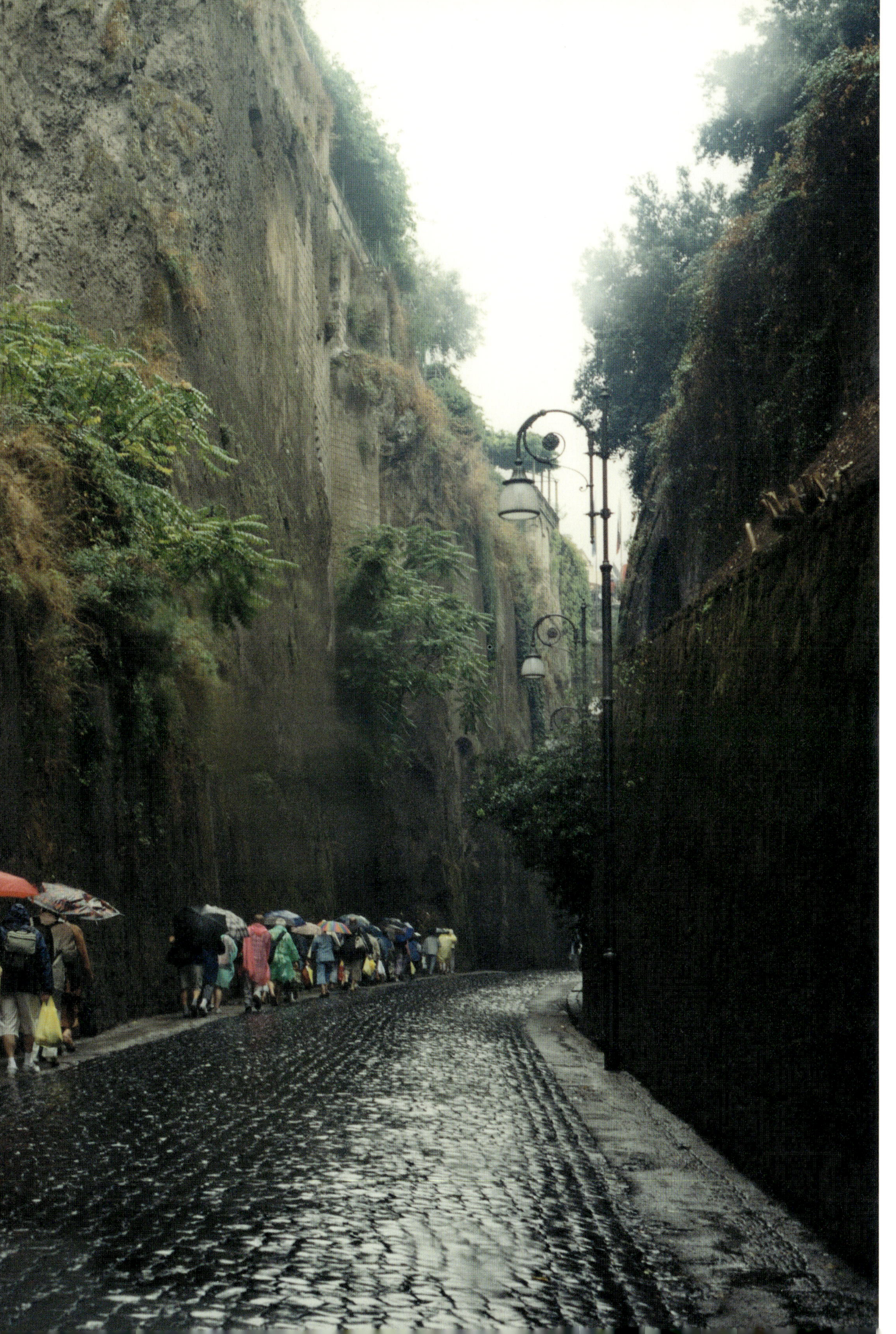

55.

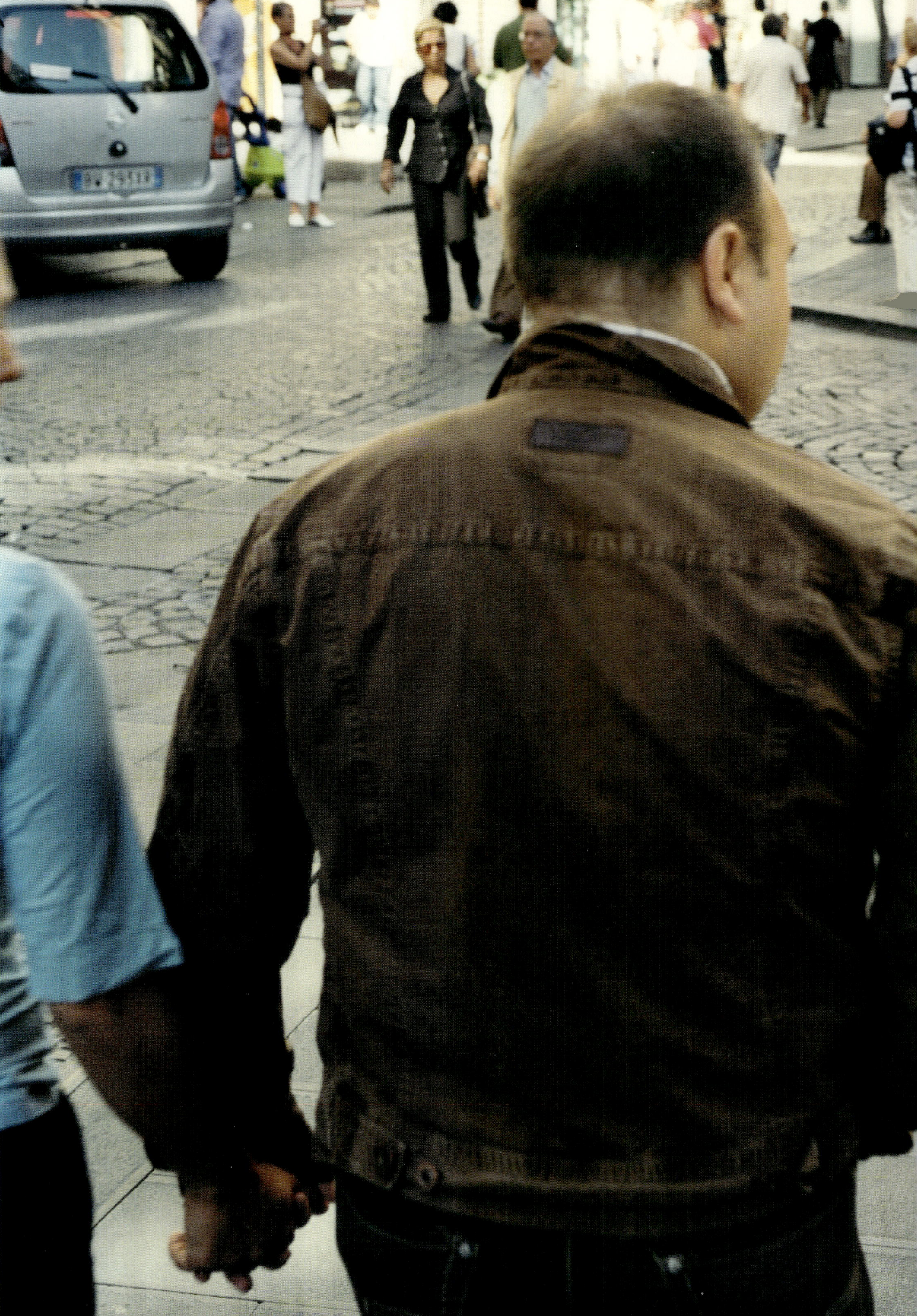

56.

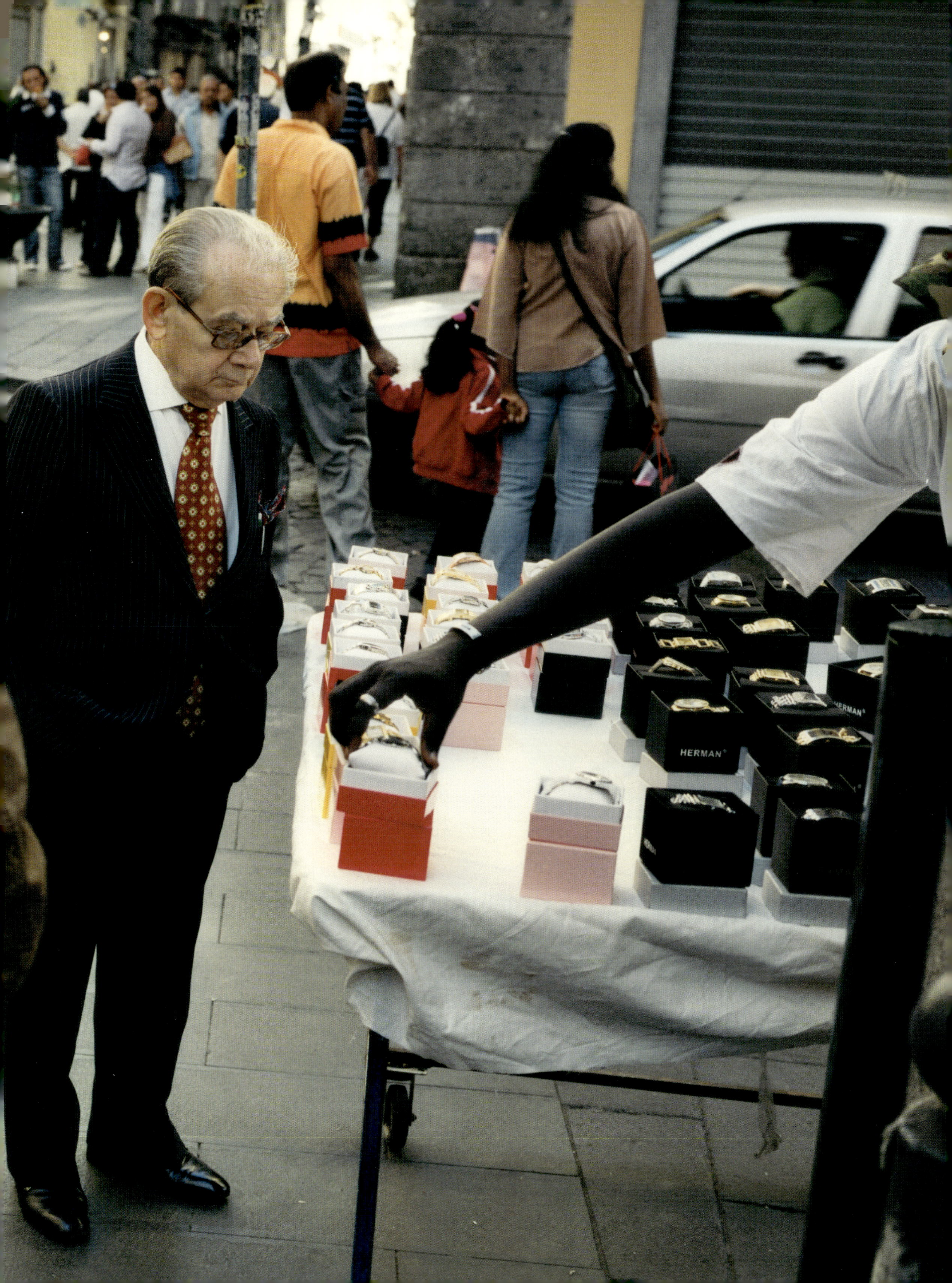

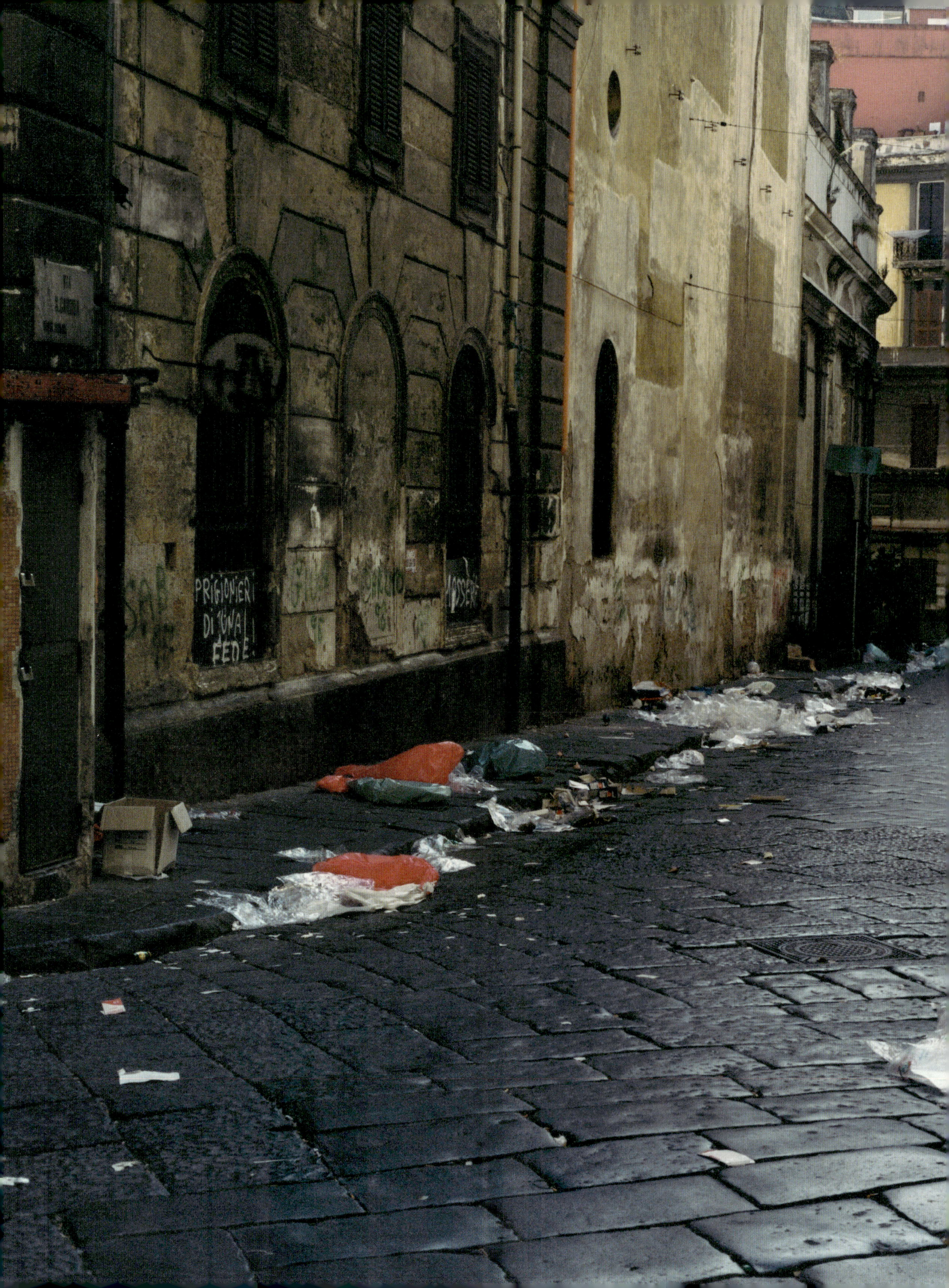

PRIGIONIERI
DI UNA
FEDE!

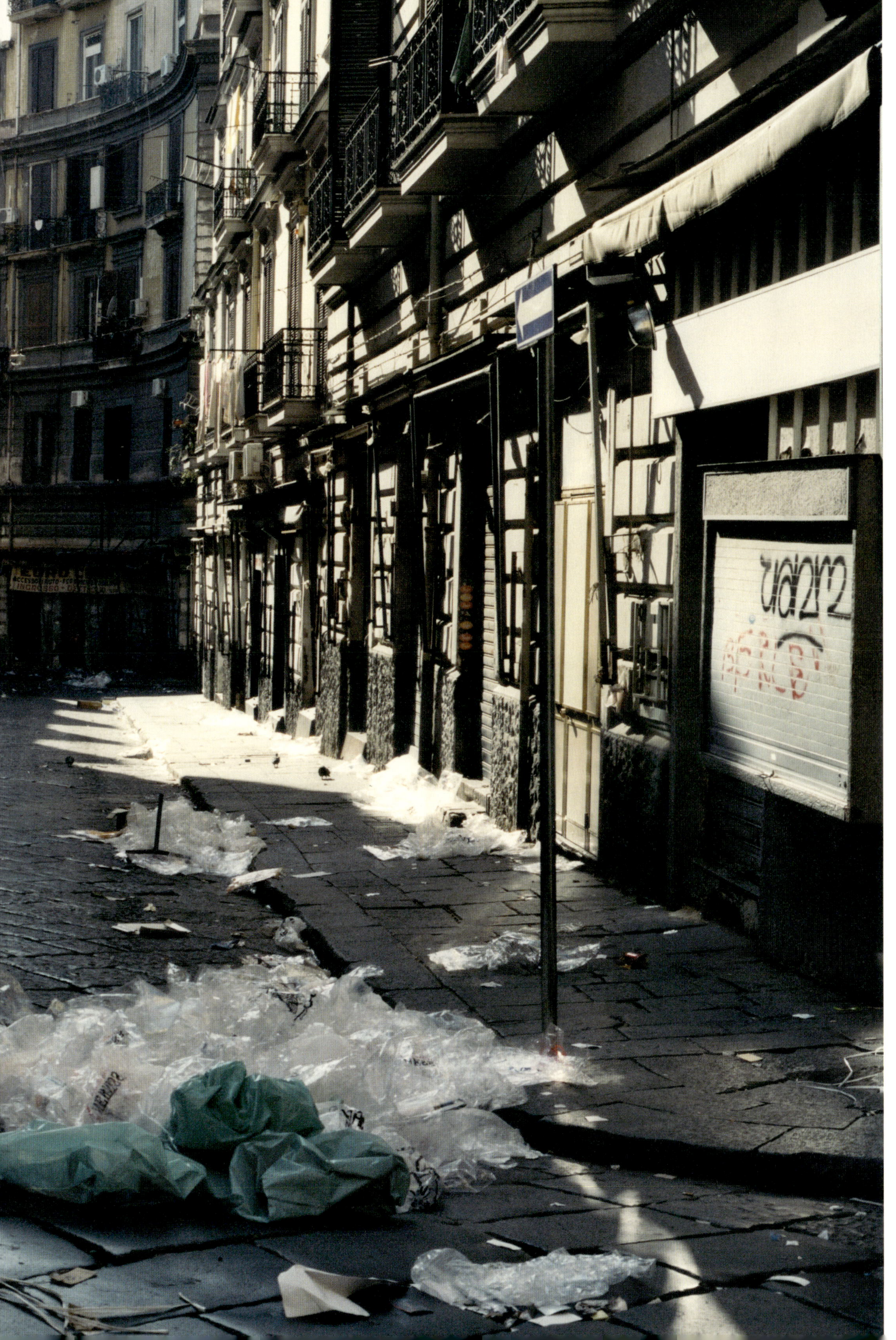

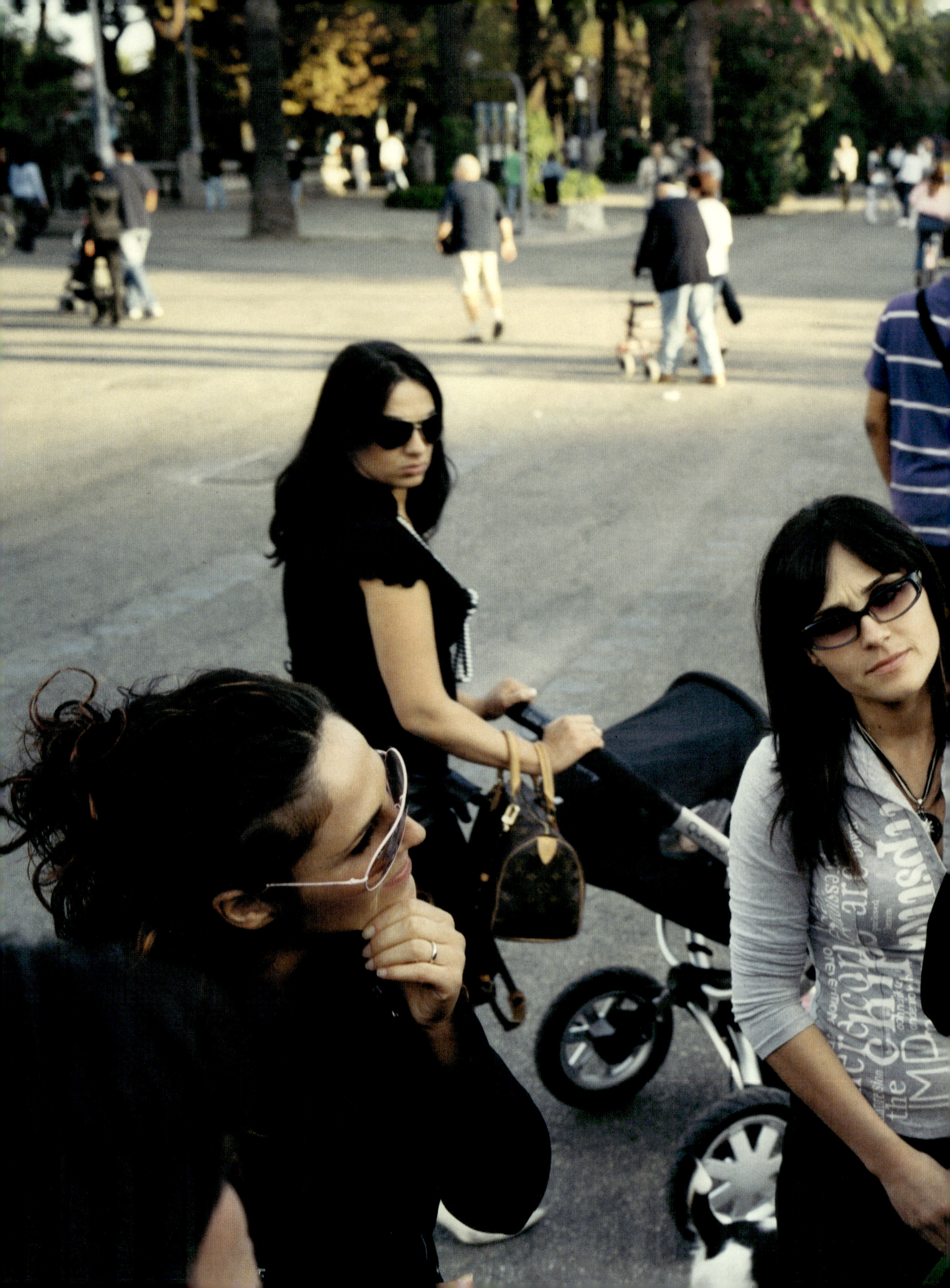

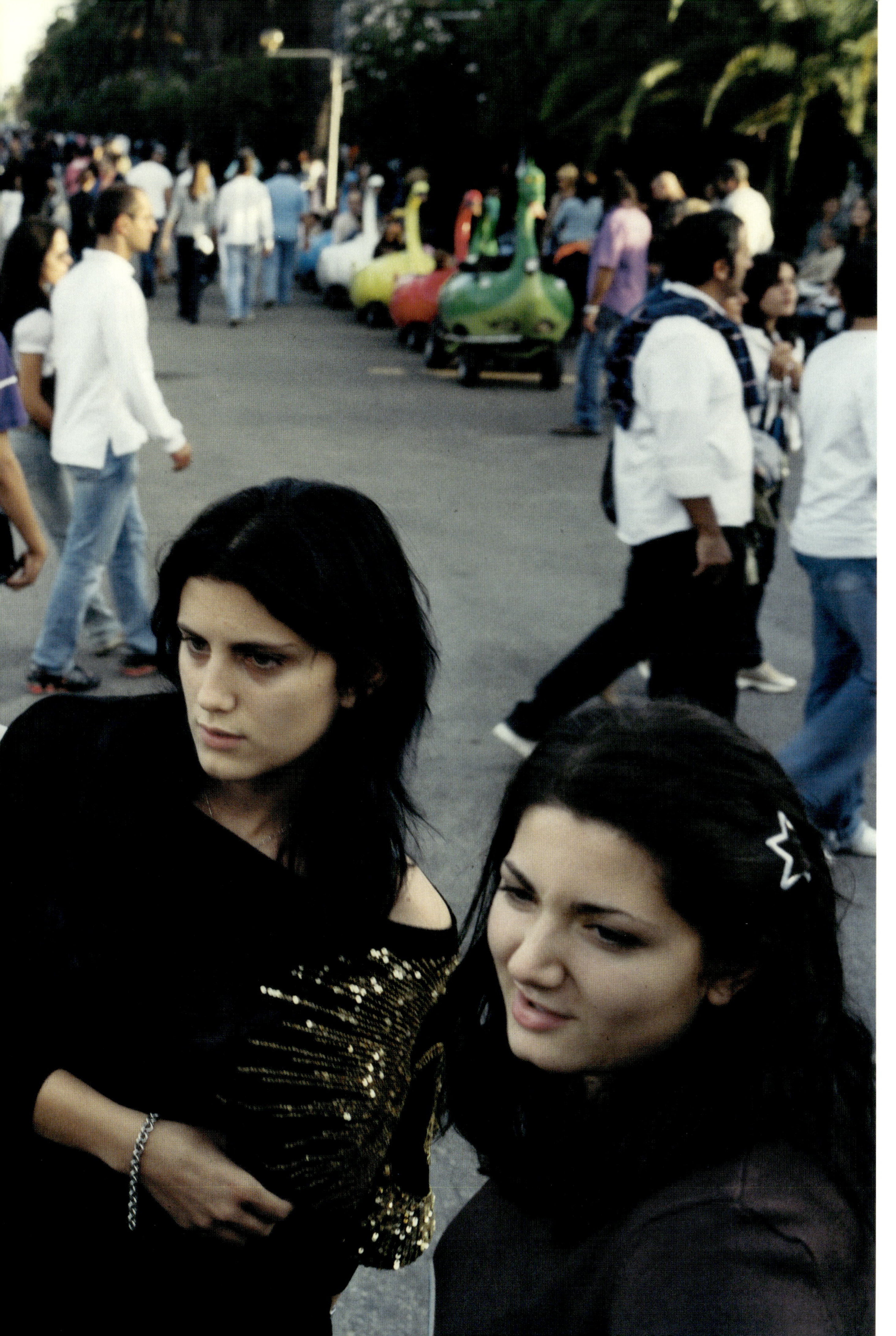

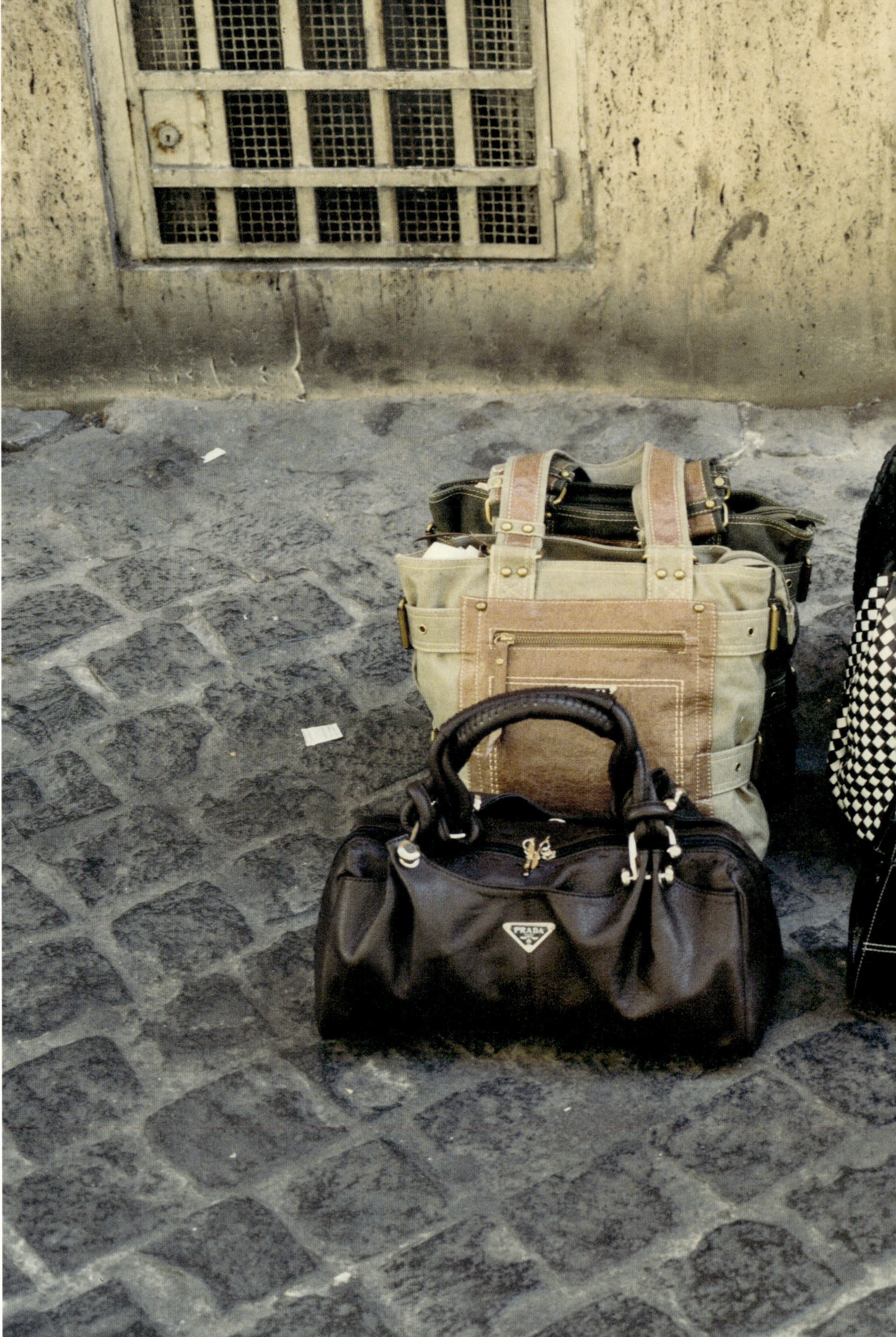

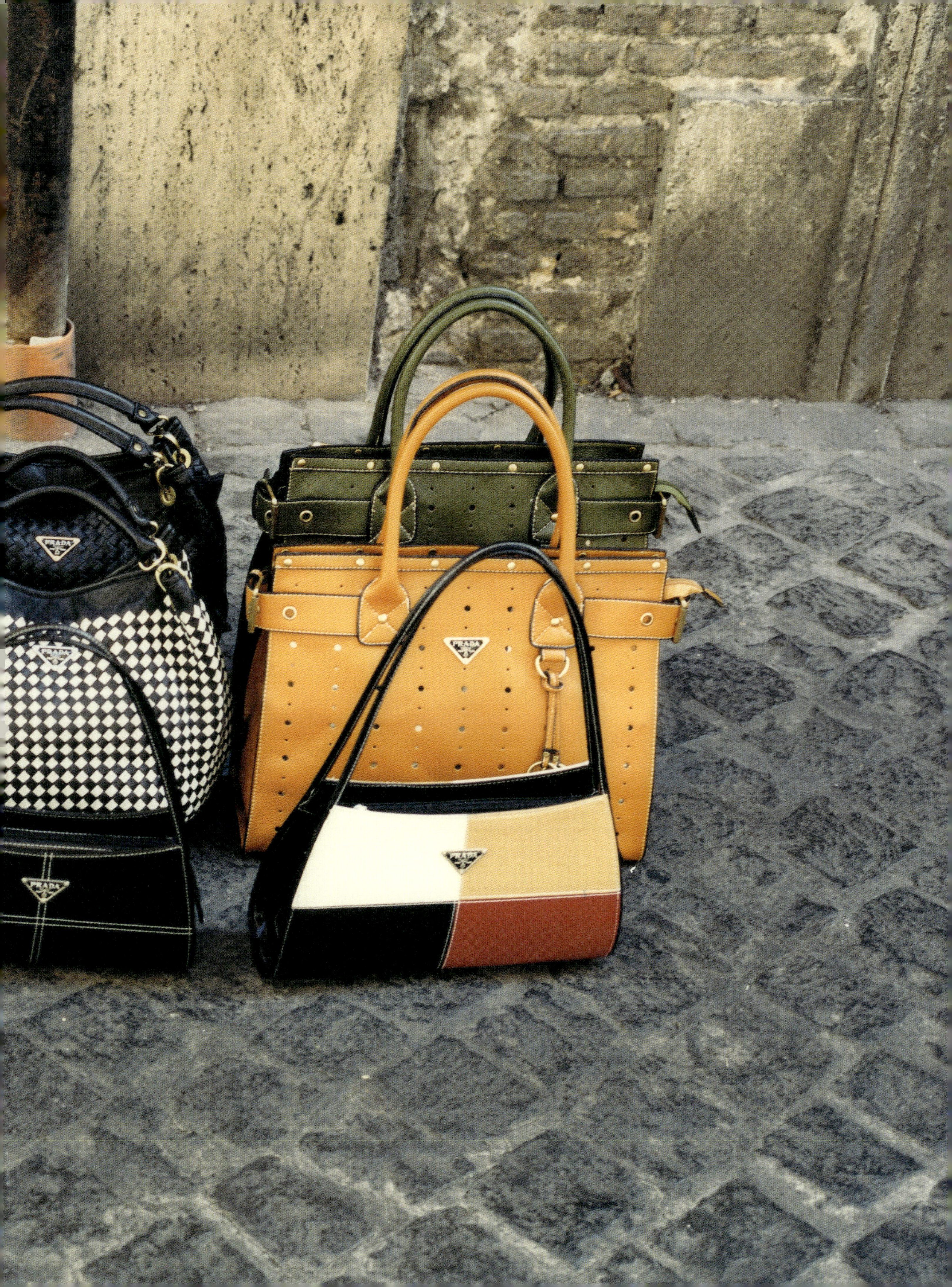

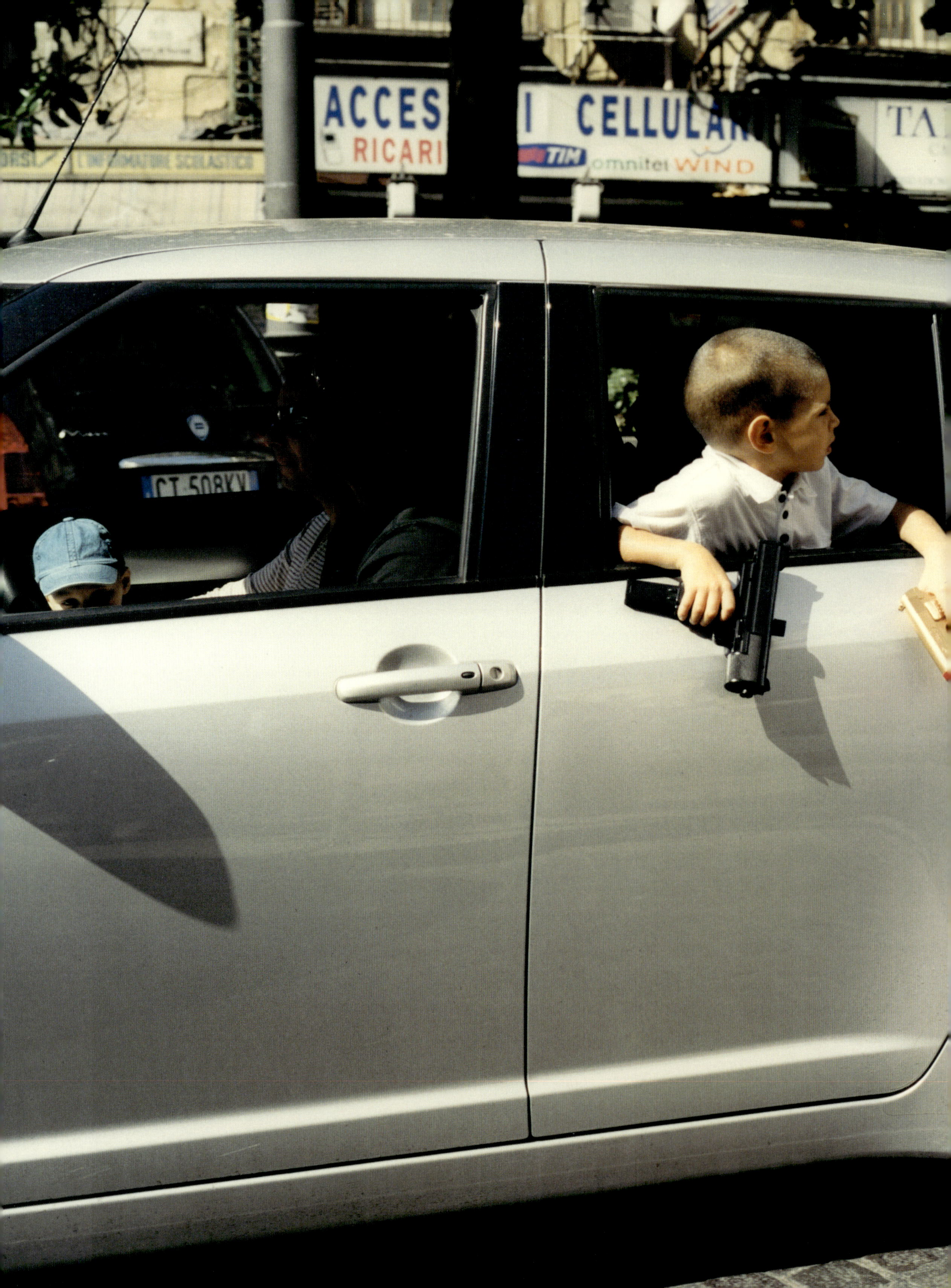

ACCES
RICARI
I CELLULA
TIM   omnitel WIND
TA
CT 508 YV

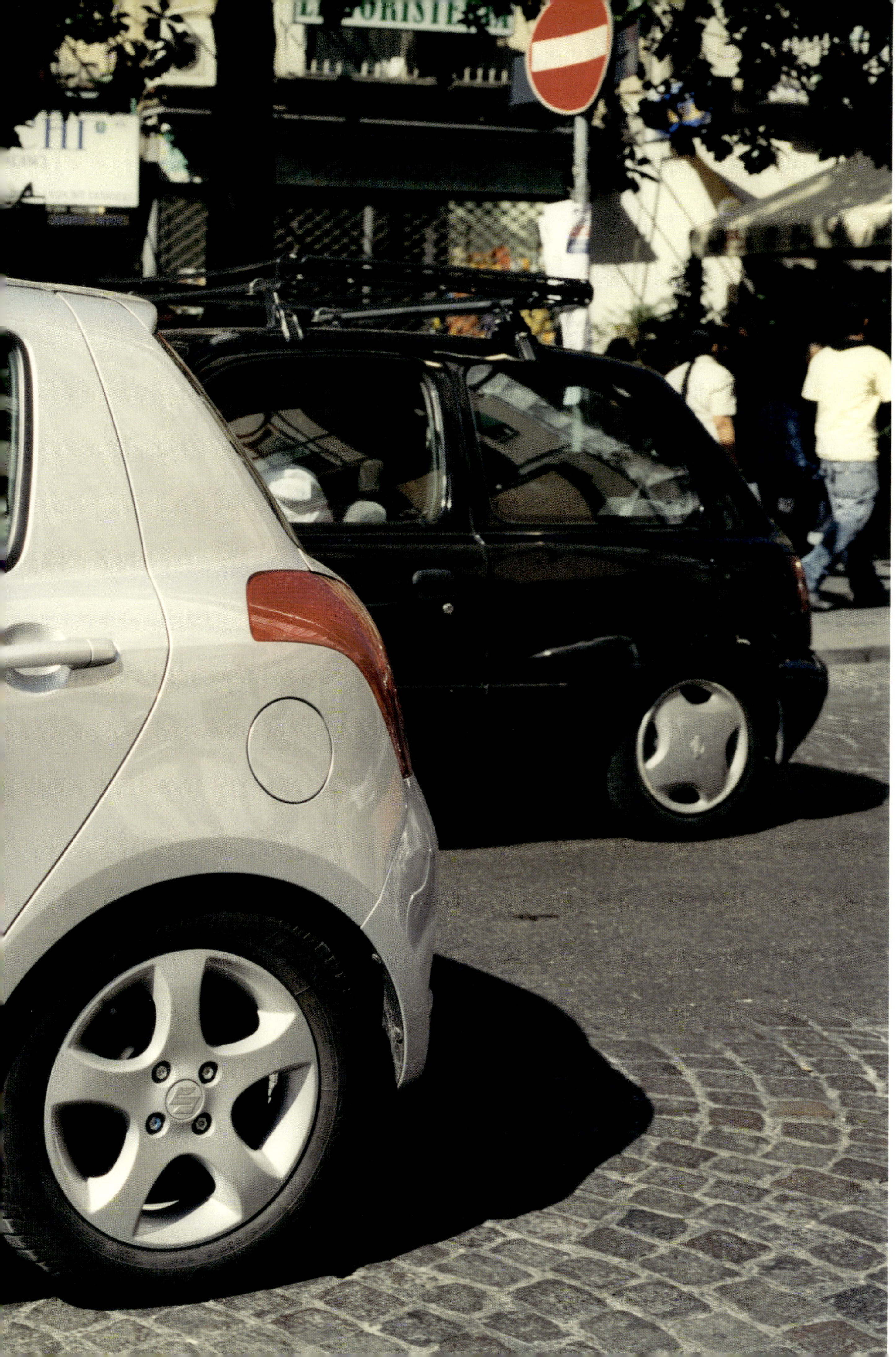

Croatia has a low crime rate, if one is to believe the statistics. In 2000, 678 offences per 100,000 inhabitants were committed in Croatia, compared for example with 4,123 in France. This low crime rate is widely cited in government travel advice. The question is: when is an 'offence' included in the statistics? After it has been committed? When it has been reported to the police? According to criminologists, most offences are neither reported nor registered.

The offence on page 79 should have been number 679. But the victim found it impossible to report the attack, which took place on a beach near Split, to the police. The Czech Republic, Hungary, Austria and France have now insisted that their own police officers be allowed to work in Croatia during the holiday season, in order to assist their countrymen in the event that they have to report a crime.

     CROATIA

The statistics suggest that Western European countries are considerably more dangerous than the less democratic countries to the east and south of the Mediterranean Sea. Israel is the exception that proves the rule. Could the crime rate have something to do with the form of government? There appears to be a parallel between the democracy index figures on page 97 and the crime rate.

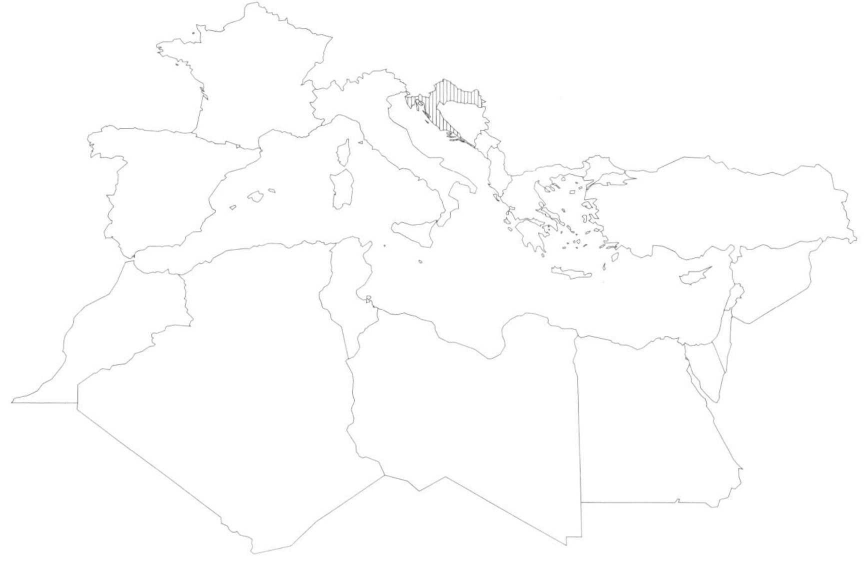

CRIME RATE
CRIMINAL OFFENCES/100,000 POPULATION

GIBRALTAR	5,638.10	
SPAIN	2,308.40	
FRANCE	4,434.51	
ITALY	4,123.00	
CROATIA	**678.01**	
ALBANIA	148.90	
GREECE	742.56	
CYPRUS	574.70	
TURKEY	711.50	
SYRIA	28.96	
LEBANON	237.10	
ISRAEL	6,276.00	
W.B. & GAZA	NA	
EGYPT	37.00	
LIBYA	343.84	
TUNISIA	520.96	
ALGERIA	259.76	
MOROCCO	877.00	

SOURCE : COMPARATIVE CRIMINOLOGY WEBSITE (CCW)

69. VERUDA
At the end of a long day, beachgoers walk back to their cars through the woods.

71. OPATIJA
Opatija resembles the Monte Carlo of the 1920s, although the beach here has been covered with cement. The Croatian women and children bathe, while the men play cards and drink beer.

73. MEDULIN
The most unbelievable palaces sprang up along the coast. These were the spas of the Austro-Hungarian nobility.

75. SPLIT
On the beach of one of Split's dismal suburbs. The coast here is packed with cheap flats. This man sports a tattoo of Ante Gotovina, the war general who is currently living out his days in a prison in The Hague.

77. MEDULIN
Lunch in the Hotel Belvedere. Every morning, groups of boys in shorts and matching shirts run outside. The hotel has the aura of one of the former socialist pioneer camps.

79. SPLIT
I took this photo of myself out of pure anger. I was aware that the camera bag was still lying on the beach; and that I had to take the photo with a short shutter speed because I was shaking violently. The police never dealt with the report of the attack on me.

80. OPATIJA
Tea dance in a hotel. One girl sings, while another sits at the keyboard. This is part of Croatia. A brooding feeling pervades everything. I have never found it so hard to make contact with people as I did in Croatia.

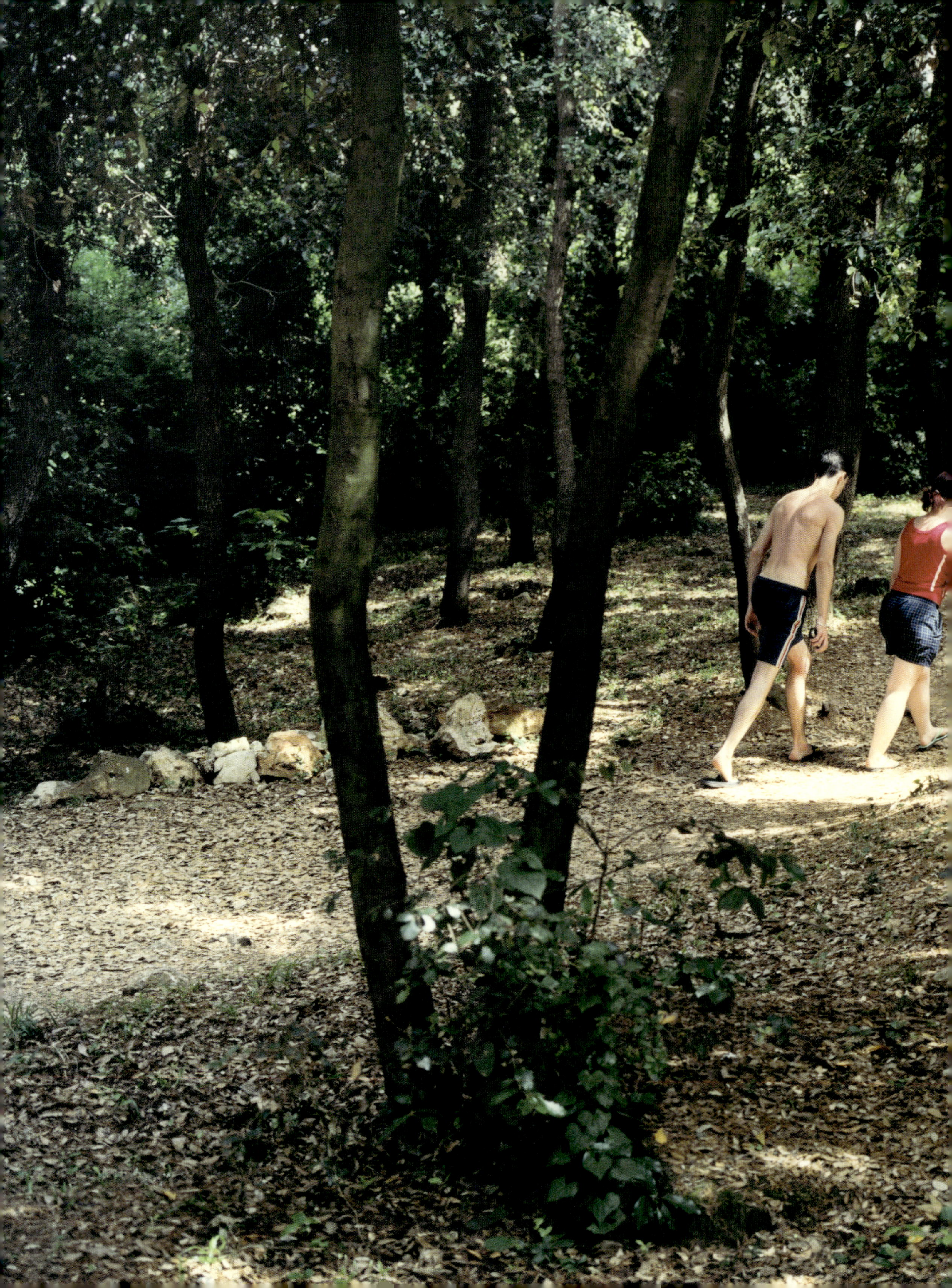

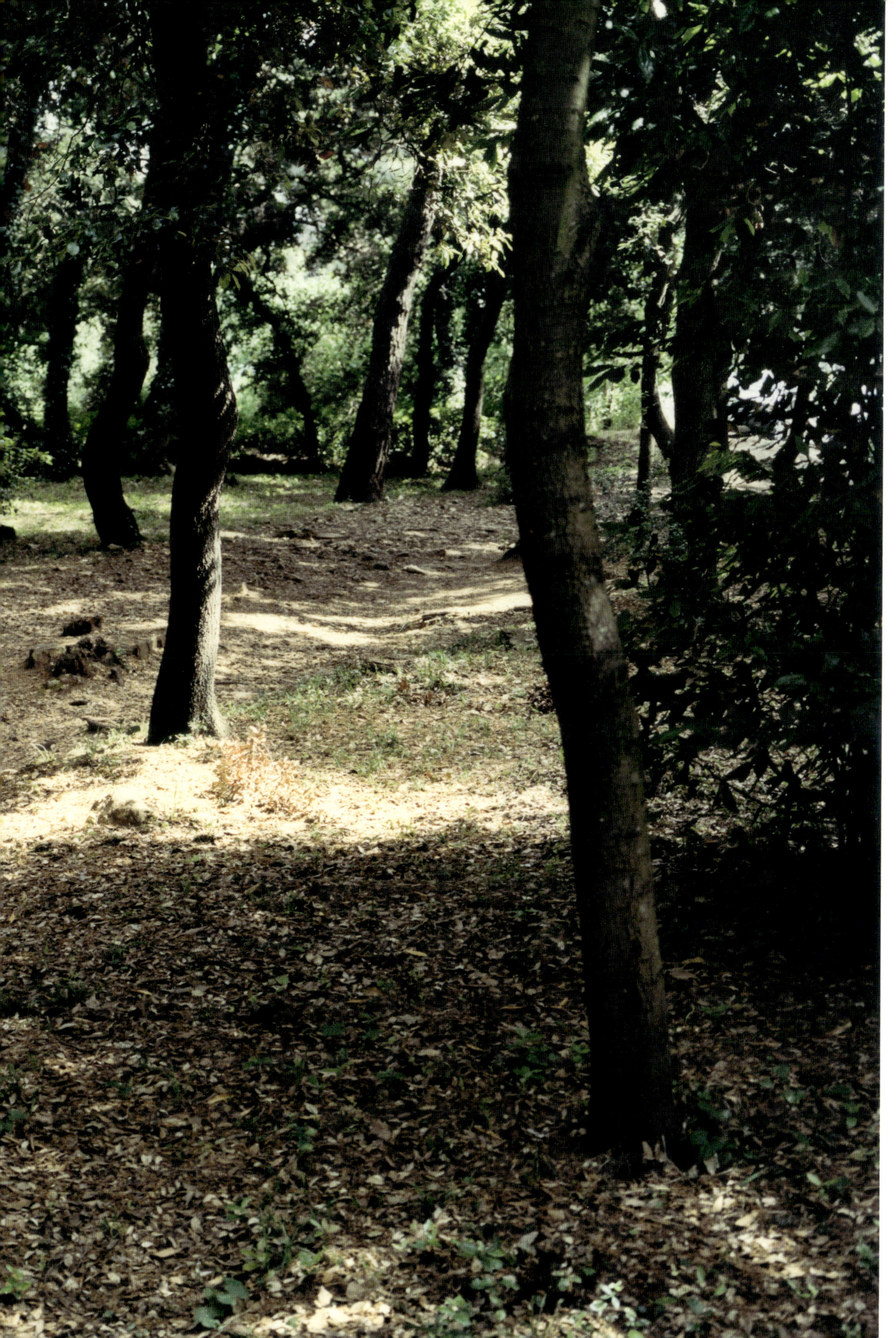

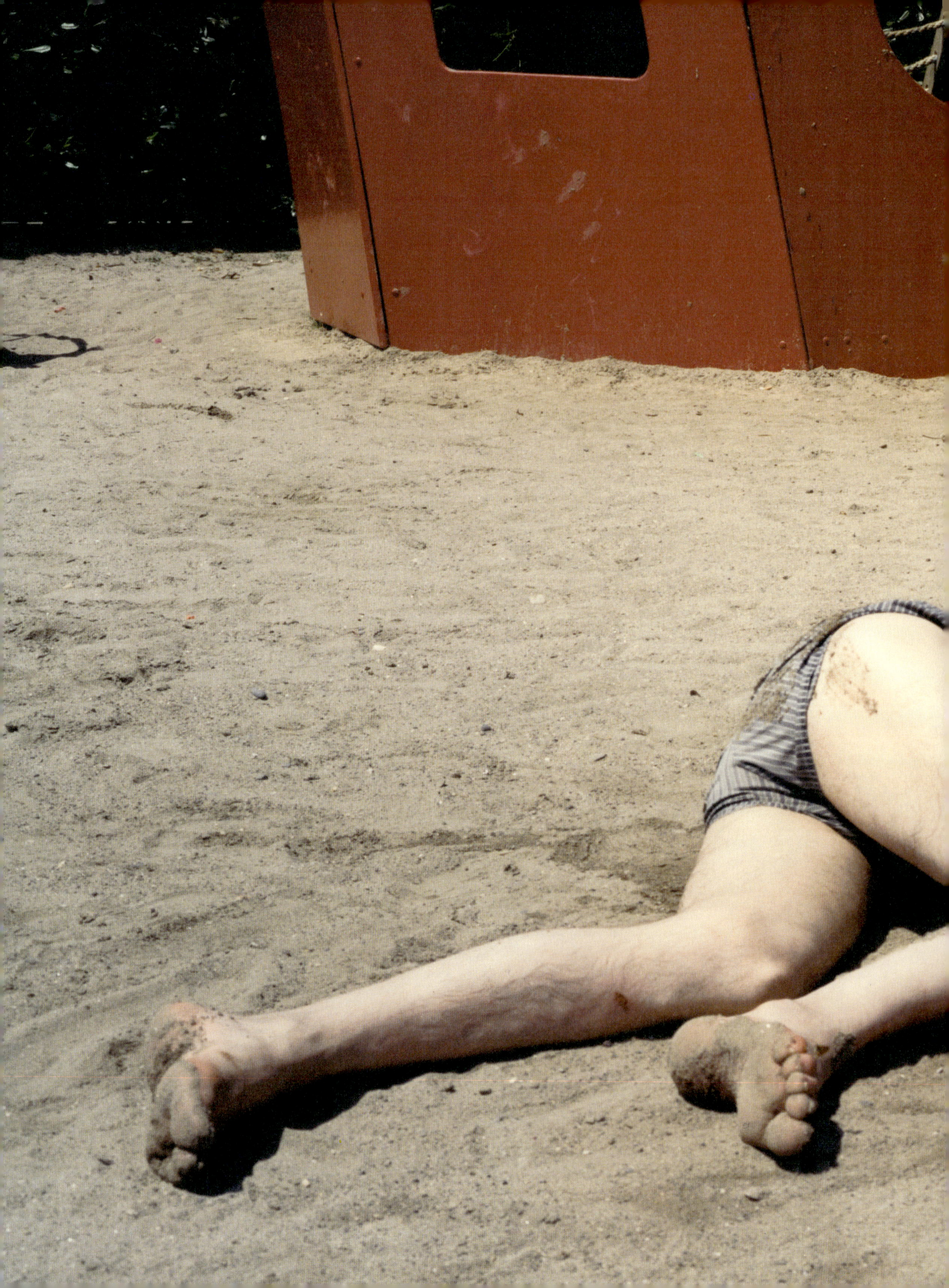

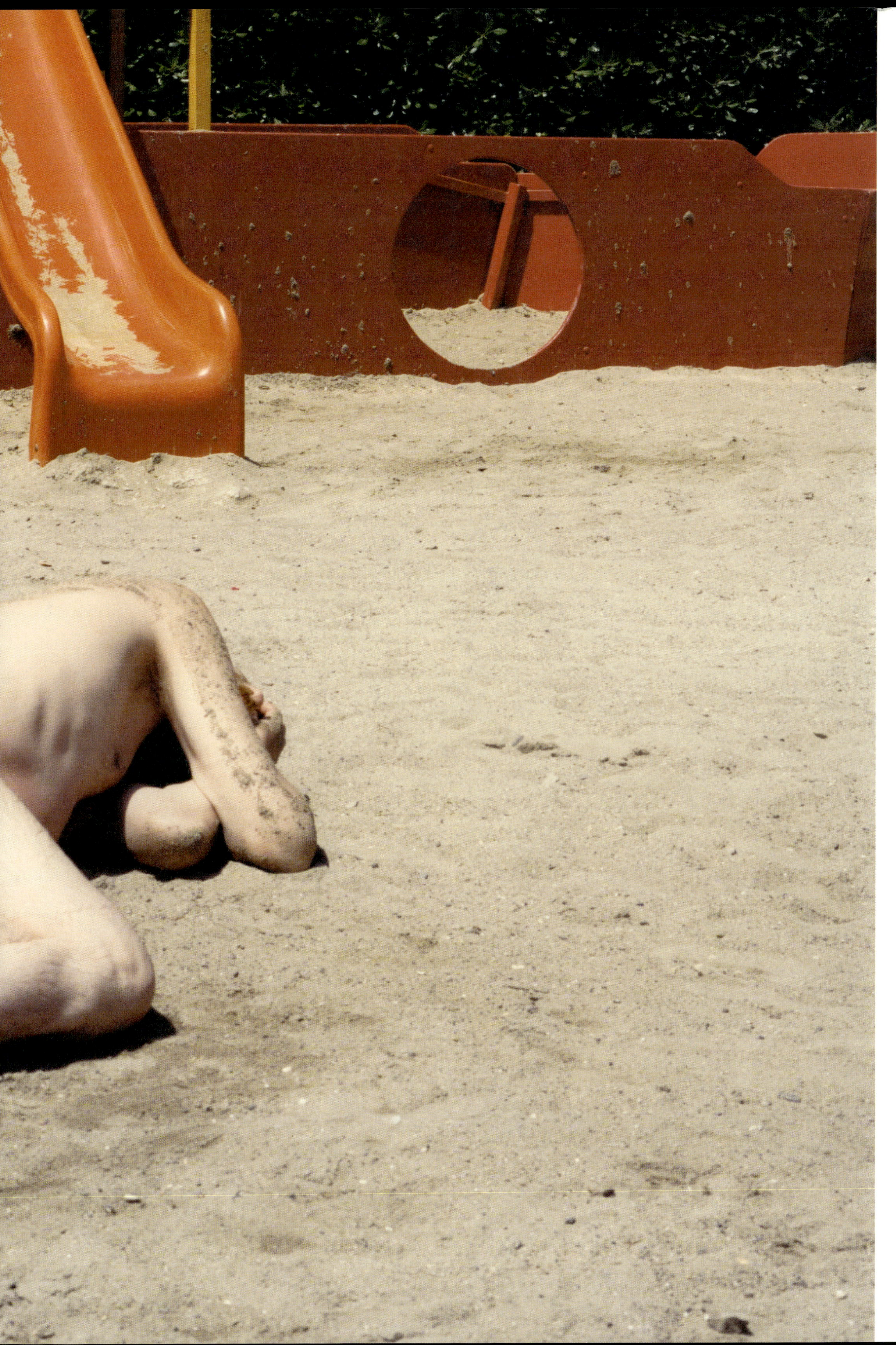

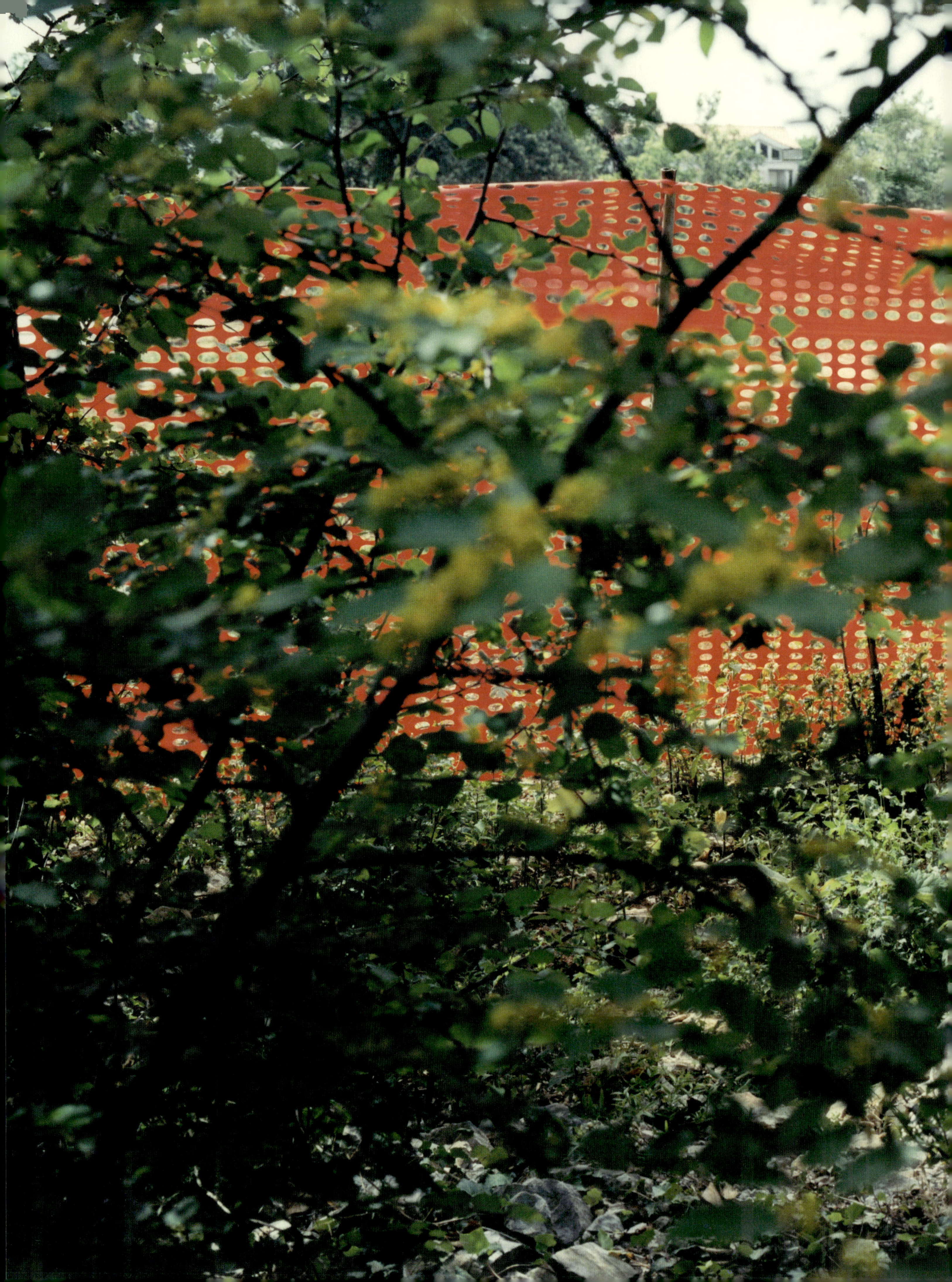

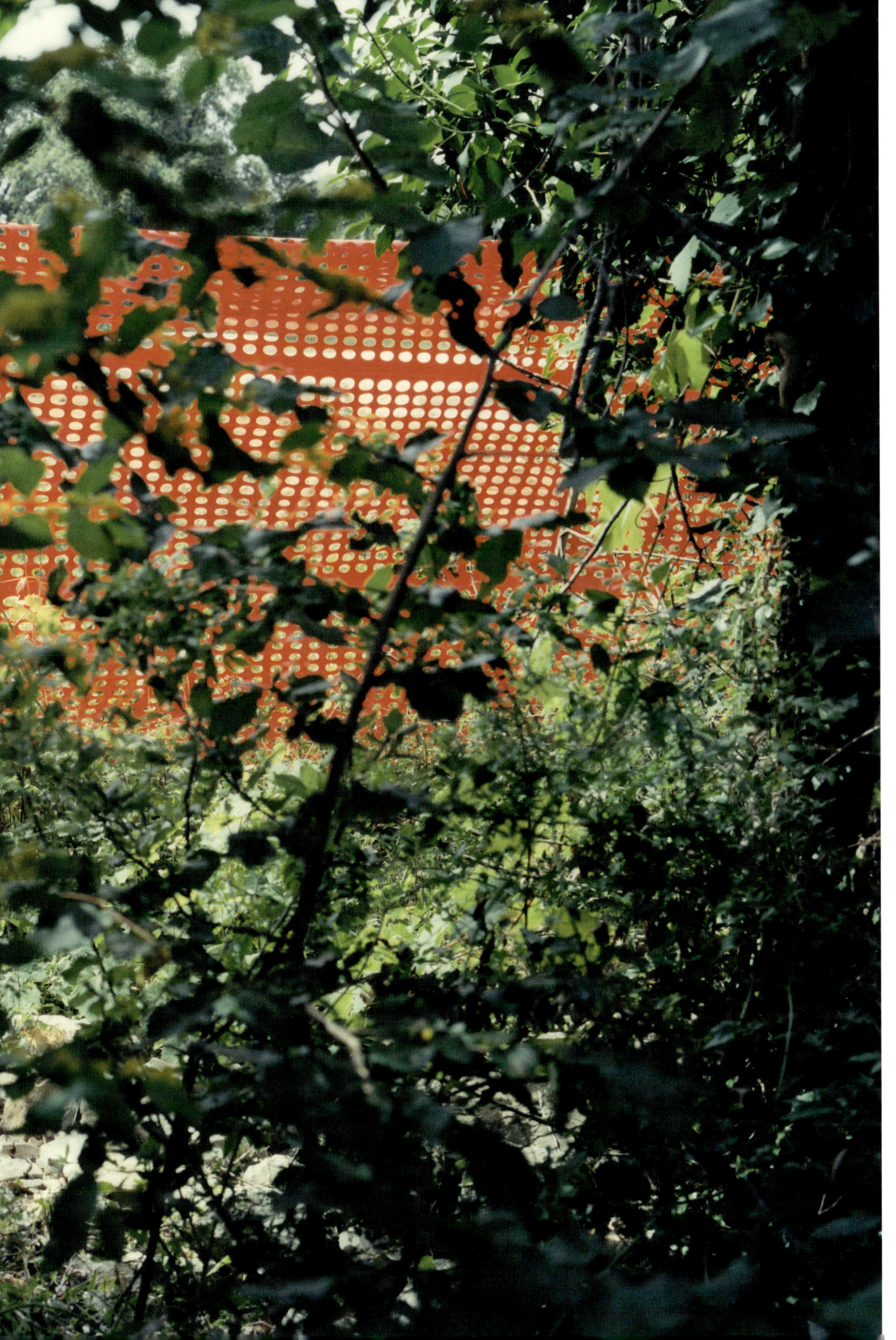

73.

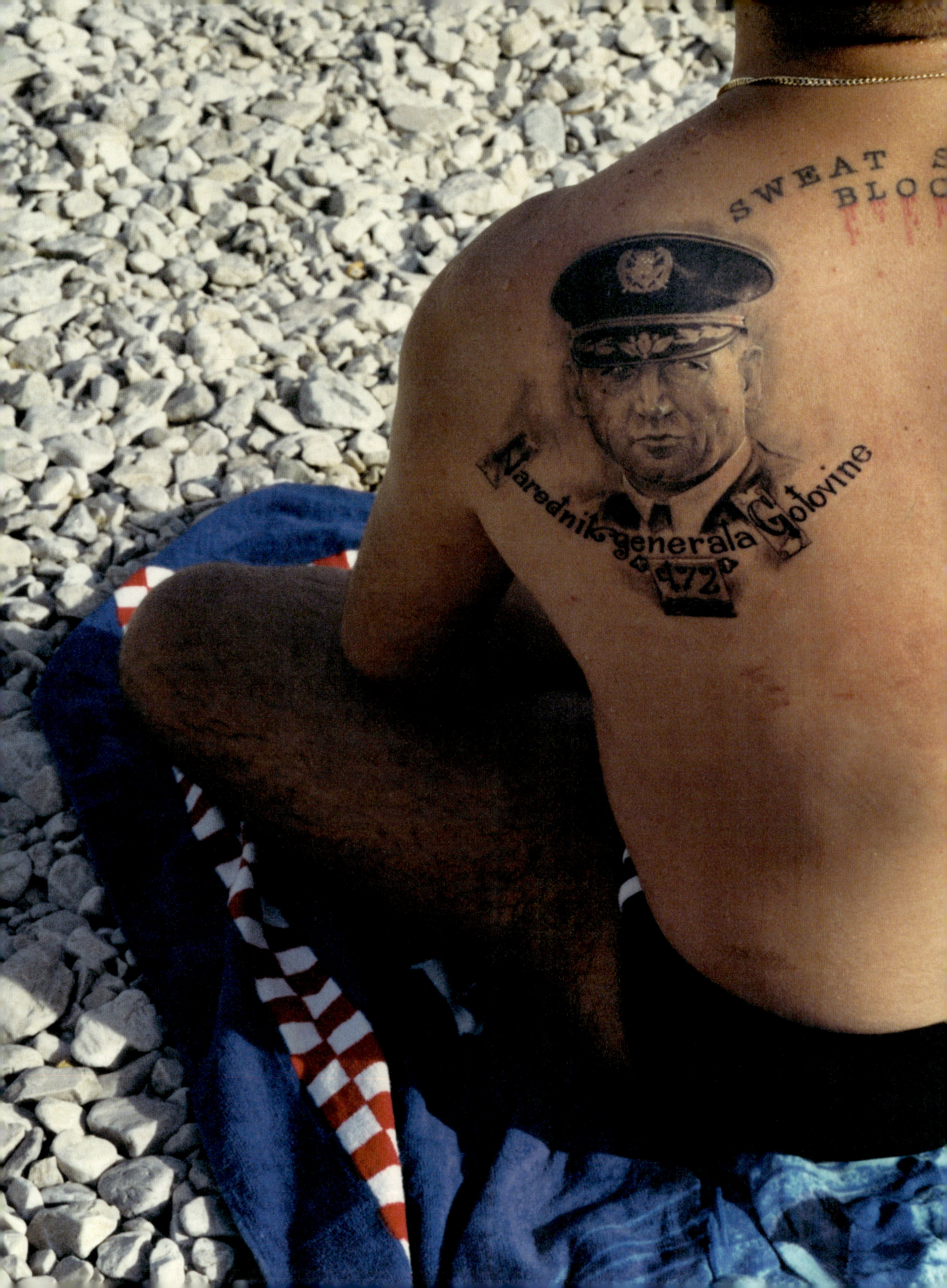
SWEAT S
BLOO
Narednik generala Golovine
472

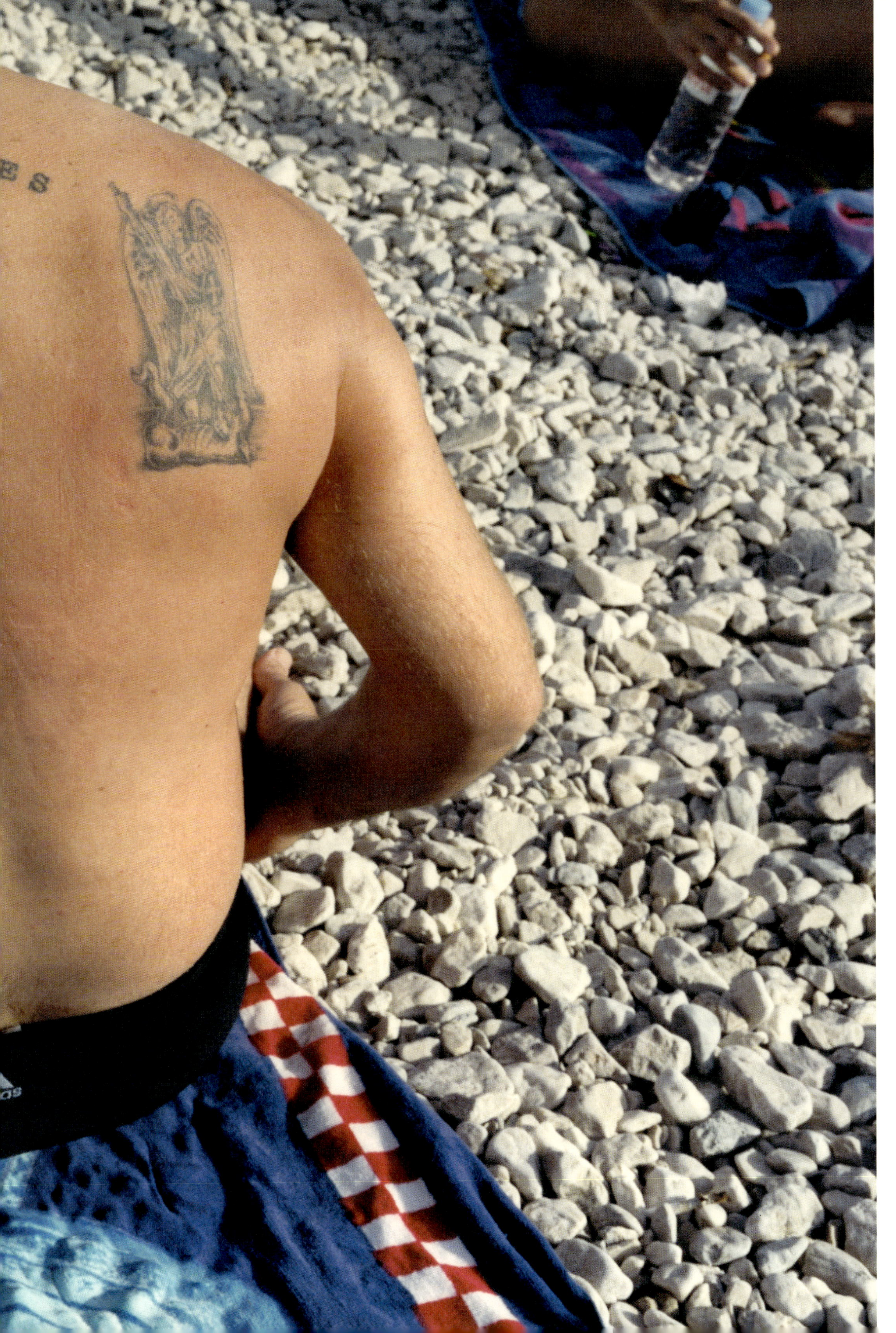

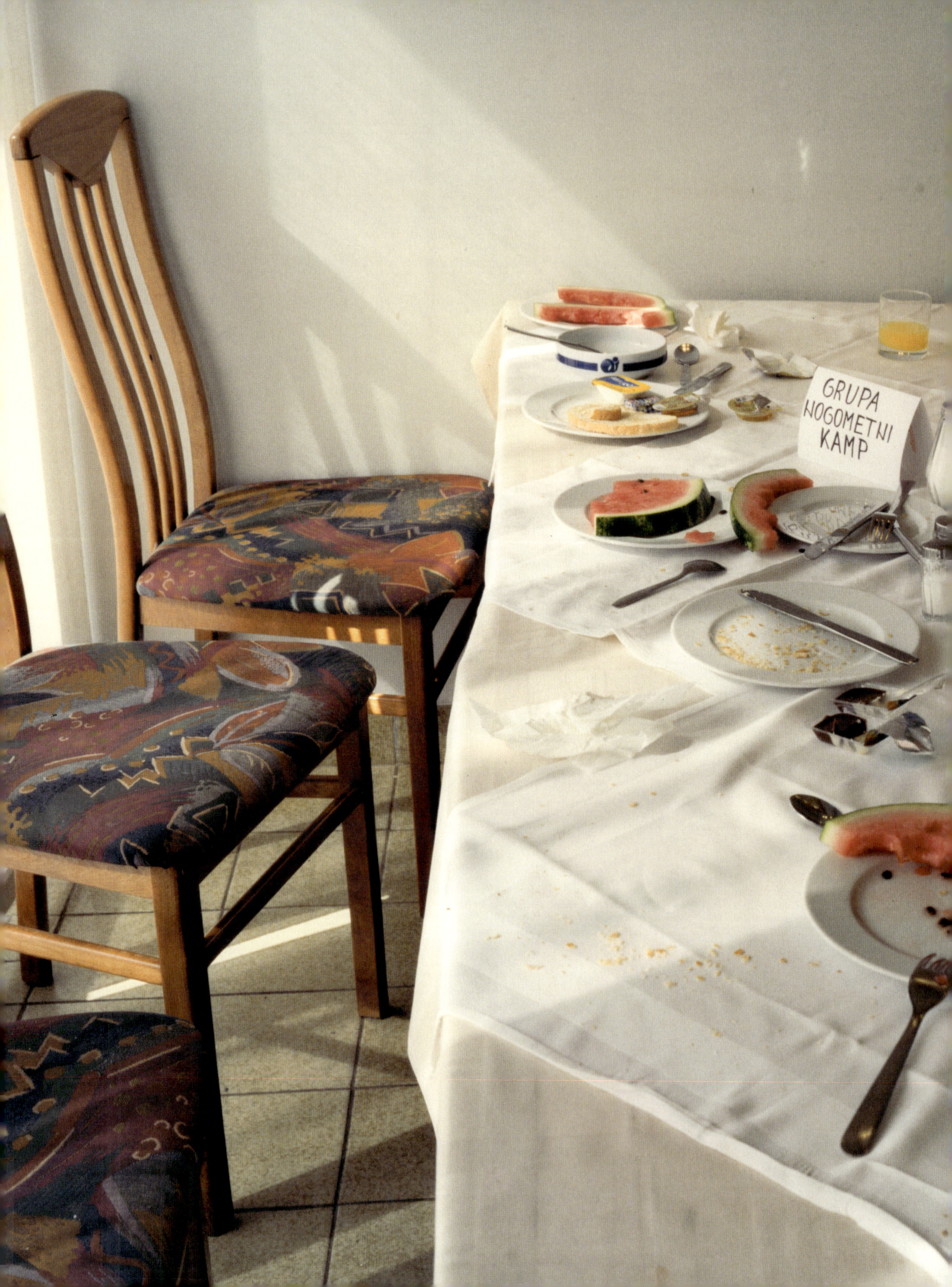
GRUPA
NOGOMETNI
KAMP

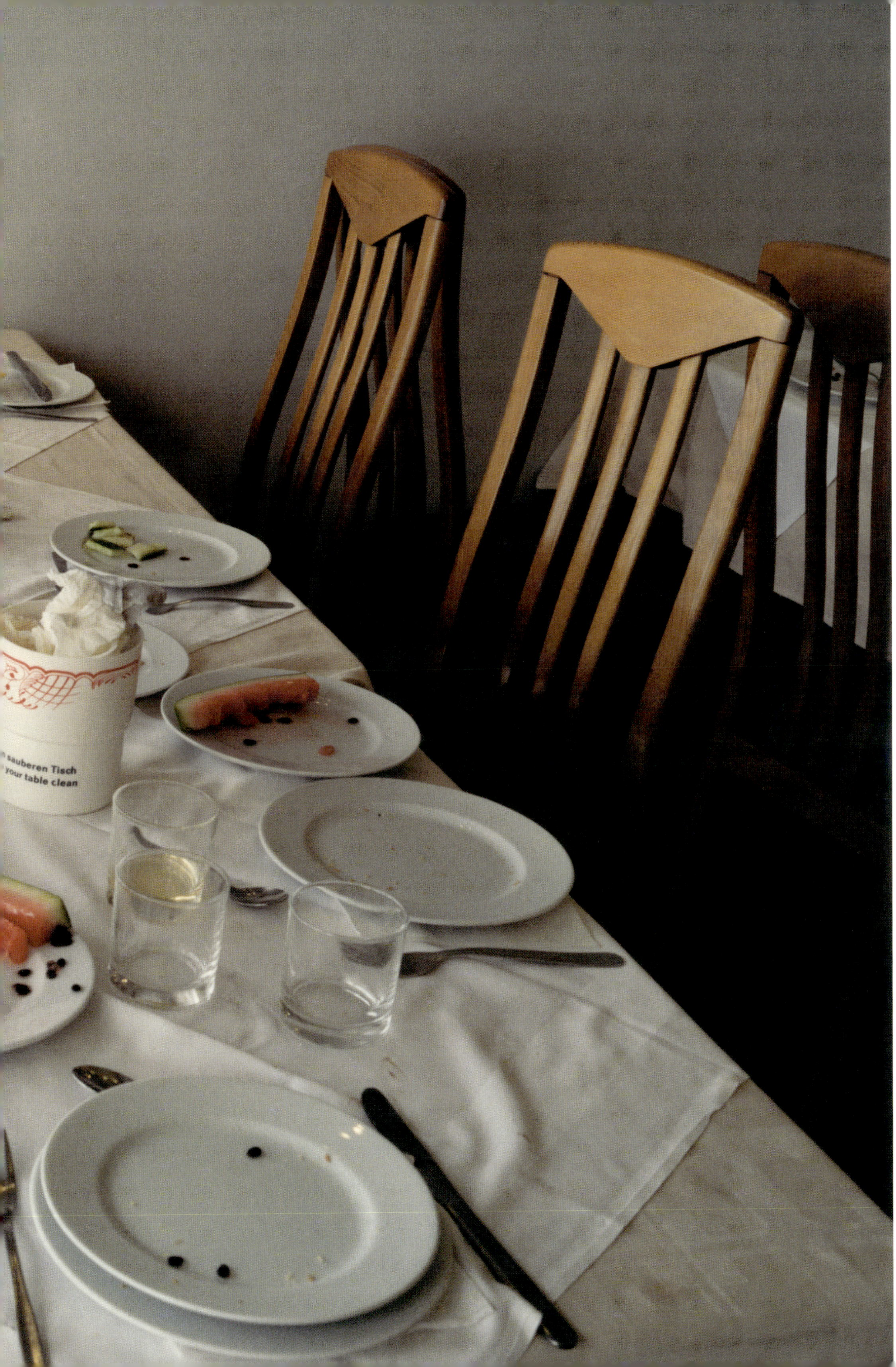

sauberen Tisch
your table clean

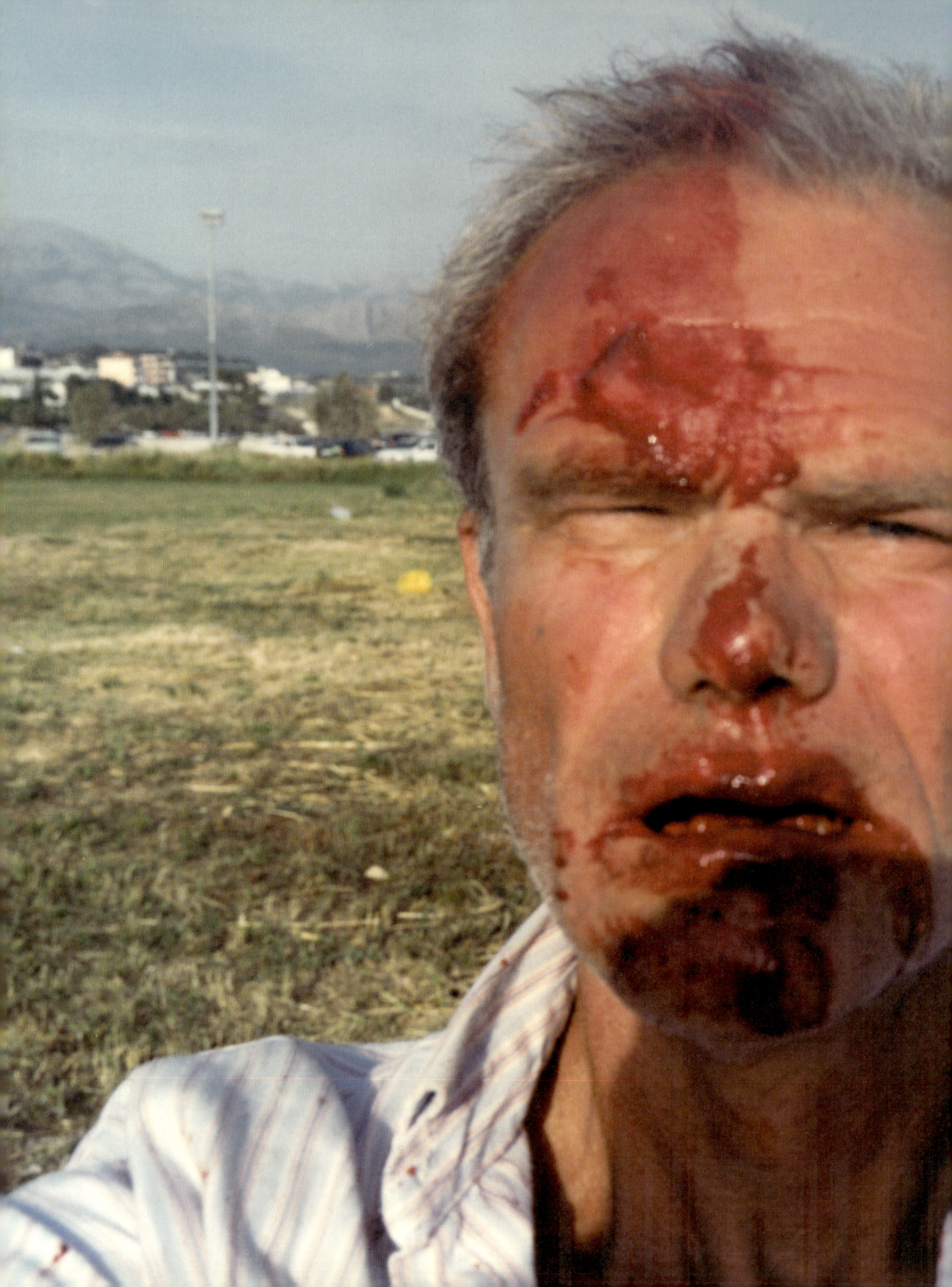

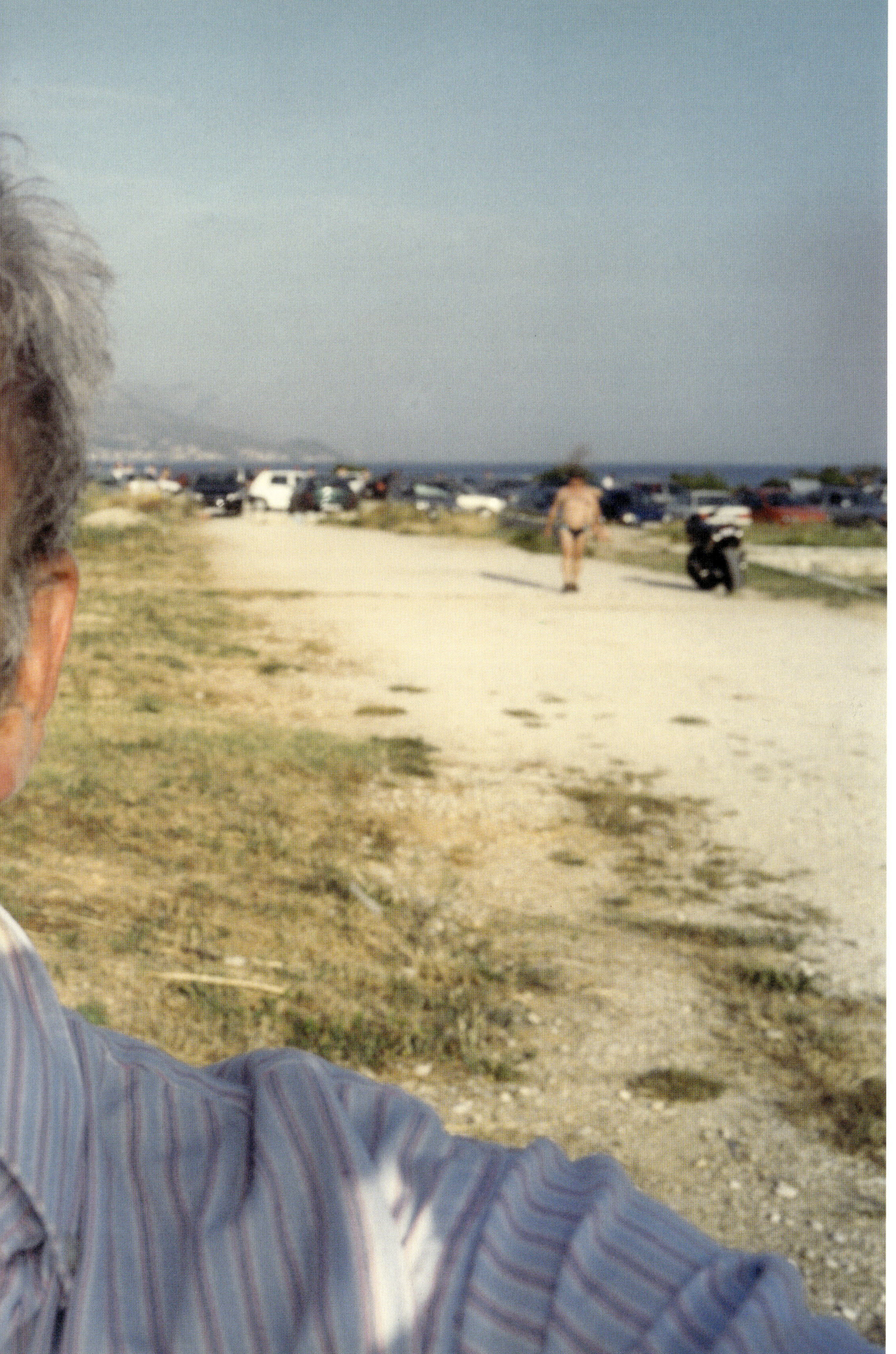

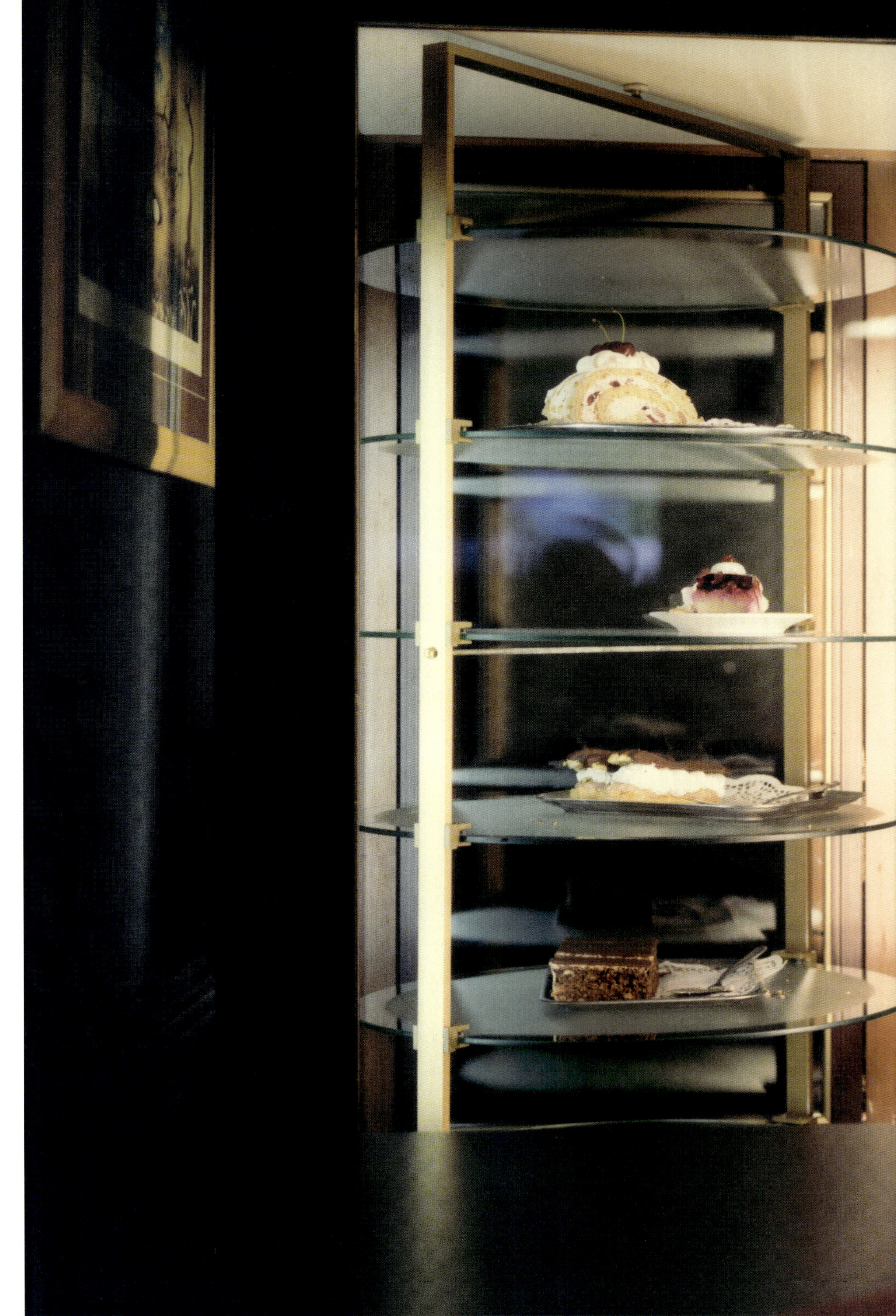

80.

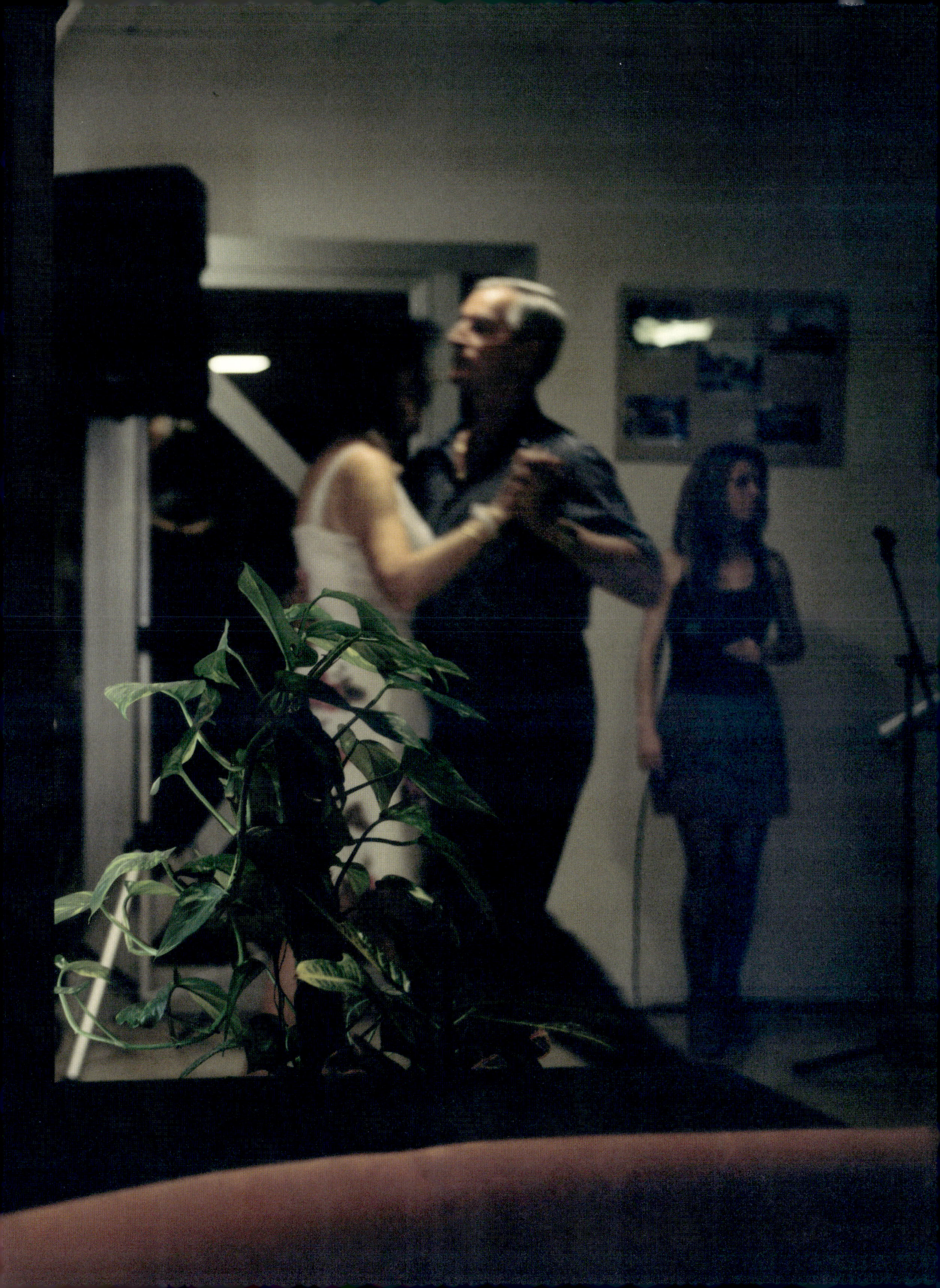

Until the fall of Enver Hoxha's communist regime in 1991, Albania was the most isolated country on earth. The figures indicate that it has not yet recovered from this period. Anyone analysing the statistics without knowing which country they related to would probably think they were for an African country. Nearly all the numbers – the widespread illiteracy, the negative migration figure, the fact that 15% of GDP comes from money transfers made by emigrants – show more similarities with countries on the southern coast of the Mediterranean than on the northern coast.

But the most conspicuous of the country's ills is its rampant corruption. Albania is thus an exception among the countries on the north of the Mediterranean, nearly all of which rank low on the corruption list. No international company or national enterprise can function unhindered here, as a result of the disruptive criminal practices that have seeped into every pore of society. In Albania, 71% of the population says that it pays bribes every year. A doctor will only treat or operate on a patient if he first receives money 'under the table' and – on a larger scale – houses can only be built after a string of government officials have been paid off.

82.   **ALBANIA**

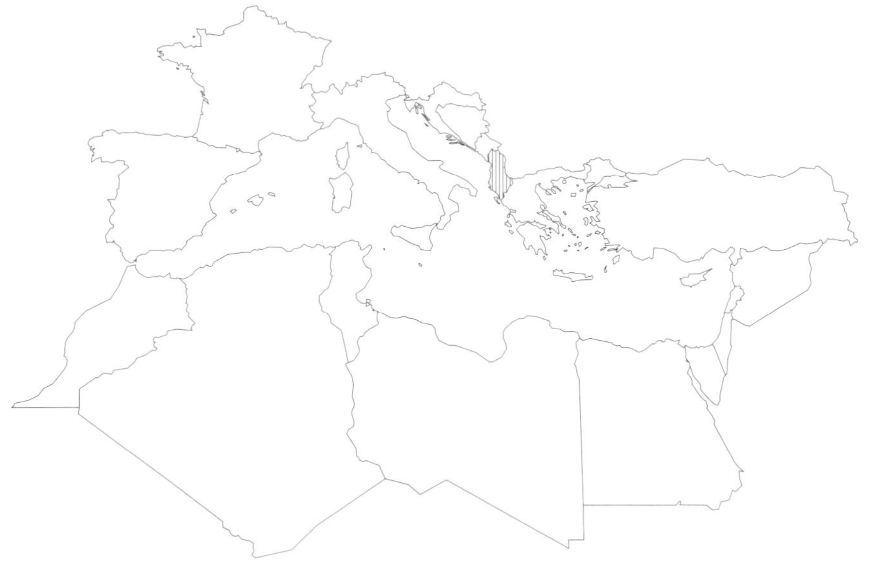

CORRUPTION INDEX
1 TO 10

GIBRALTAR	NA	
SPAIN	6.8	
FRANCE	7.4	
ITALY	4.9	
CROATIA	3.4	
ALBANIA	**2.6**	
GREECE	4.4	
CYPRUS	5.6	
TURKEY	3.8	
SYRIA	2.9	
LEBANON	3.6	
ISRAEL	5.9	
W.B. & GAZA	NA	
EGYPT	3.3	
LIBYA	2.7	
TUNISIA	4.6	
ALGERIA	3.1	
MOROCCO	3.2	

SOURCE : TRANSPARENCY INTERNATIONAL, GLOBAL CORRUPTION BAROMETER 2006

85. DURRËS
At the beginning of the 90s, a trip to Albania was like travelling back in time to the 15th century. You could blindly step into the street because there was no traffic. These days, Albania is being developed with money from the thousands of emigrants who have gone to Western Europe.

87. DURRËS
A mother and her daughters on the beach. After the fall of the communist regime, her husband left for Italy in a small, rickety boat. He comes back every summer. The daughter wearing the black bikini wants to be a film star.

89. VLORES
In 2000, this beach was the departure point for many emigrants. The expensive villas on the beach were owned by human traffickers. Passing policemen were shot at. In 2004, the police dismantled the whole operation. These days, most of the human trafficking to Italy takes place from Croatia.

90. DURRËS
Every holiday, the men who have emigrated come back to build a new floor on their houses. It can take years before a house is finished.

93. TIRANA
Nazerne has kept her eyes lowered for her entire wedding day. This is expected from the bride and is a sign of devotion and modesty. Afterwords she is only allowed to visit her parents' house with the permission of her husband Korab.

94. TIRANA
Under communism, only the party cadres were allowed to own a car. They now have the highest number of Mercedes per capita in the world. In 2000, the minister of public safety was apprehended during a state visit to Greece. The car he was in turned out to be stolen.

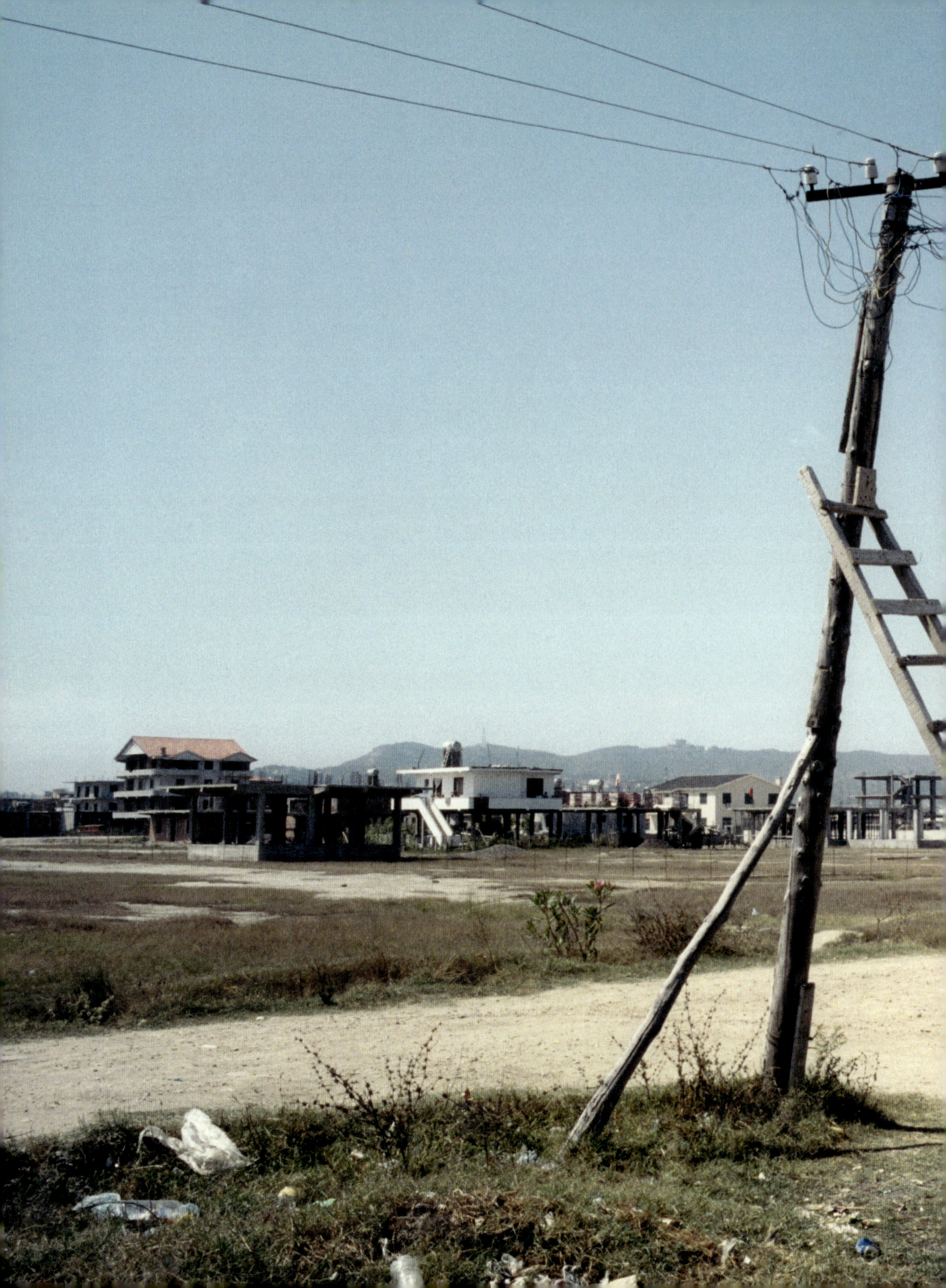

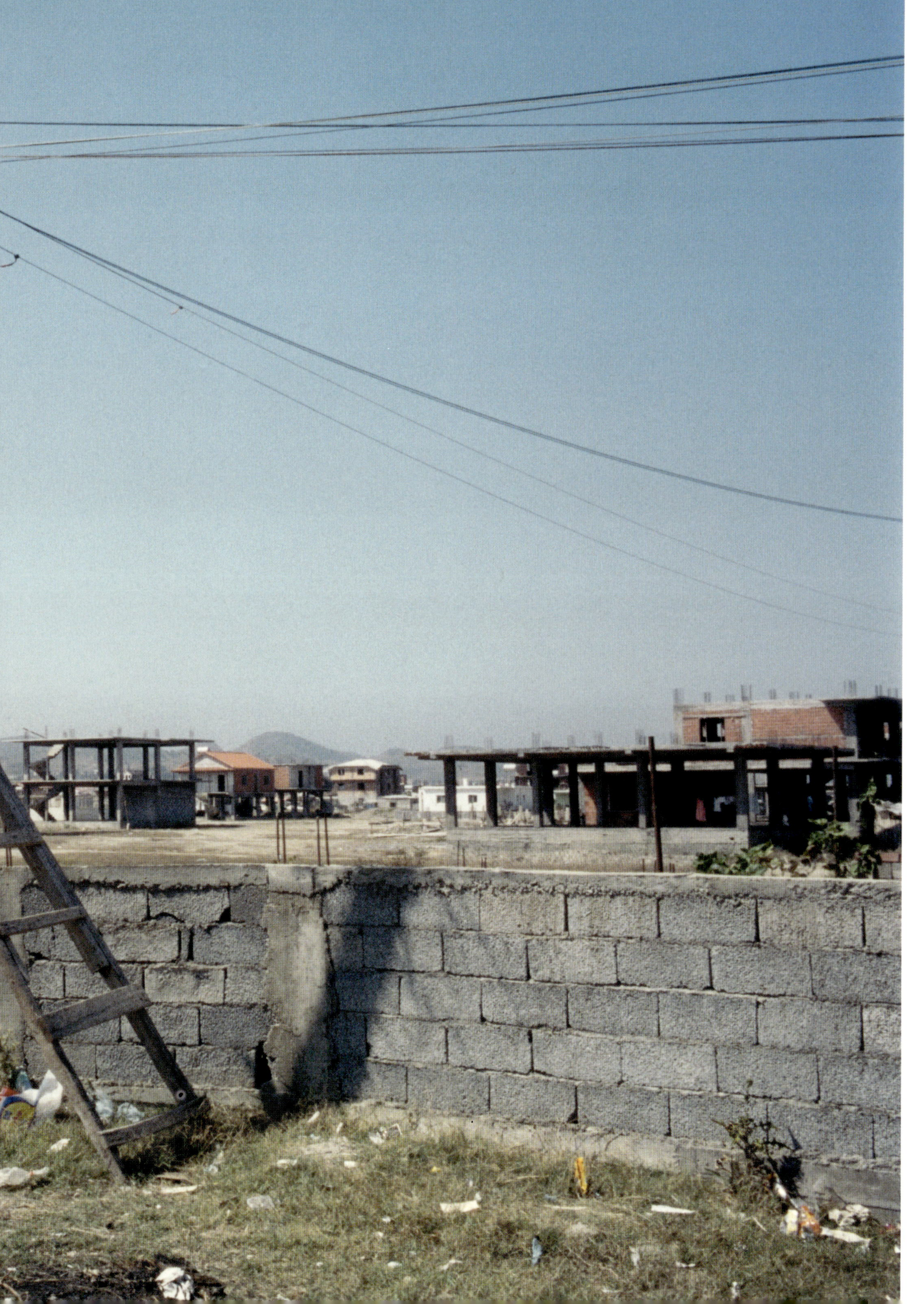

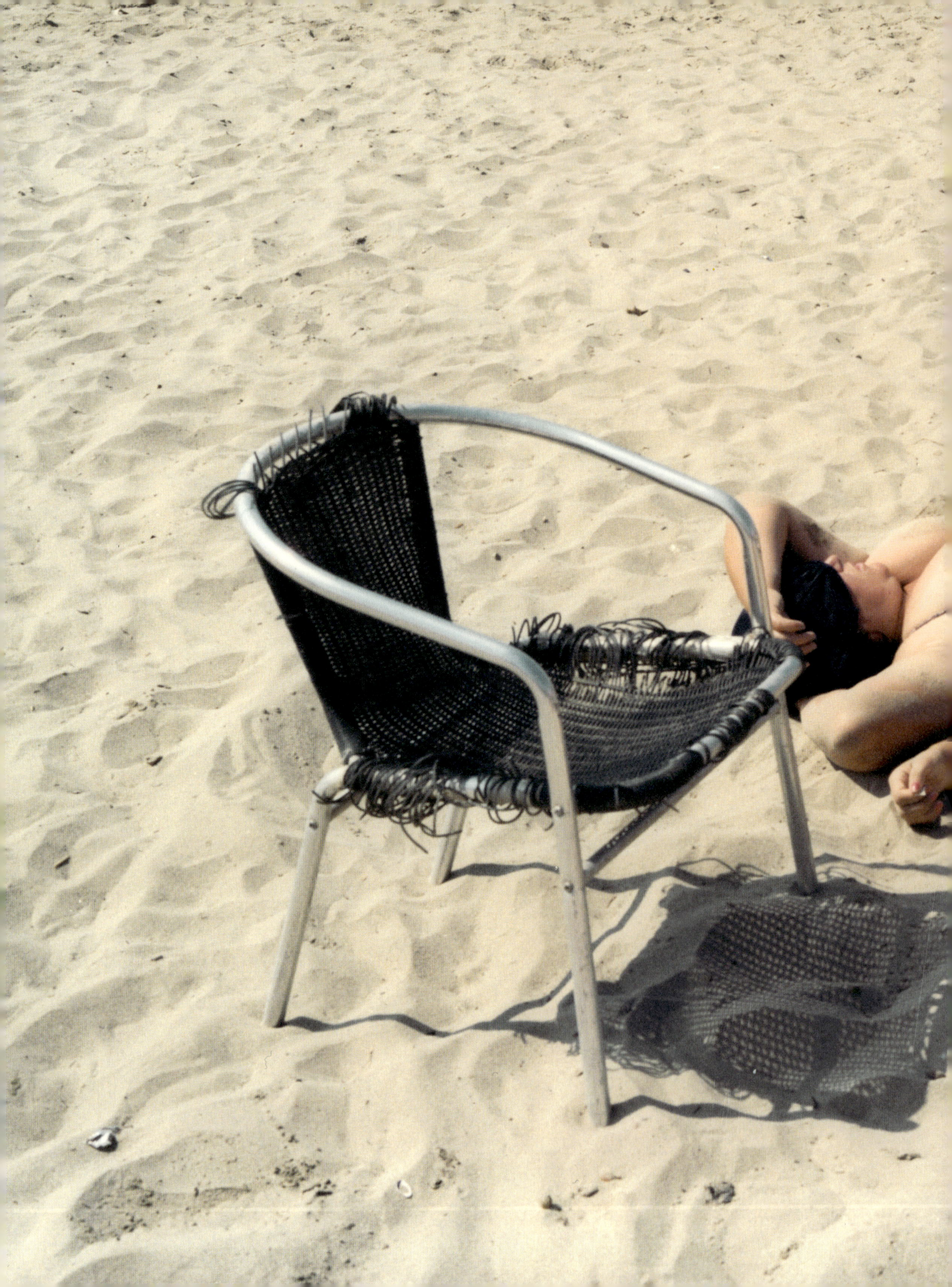

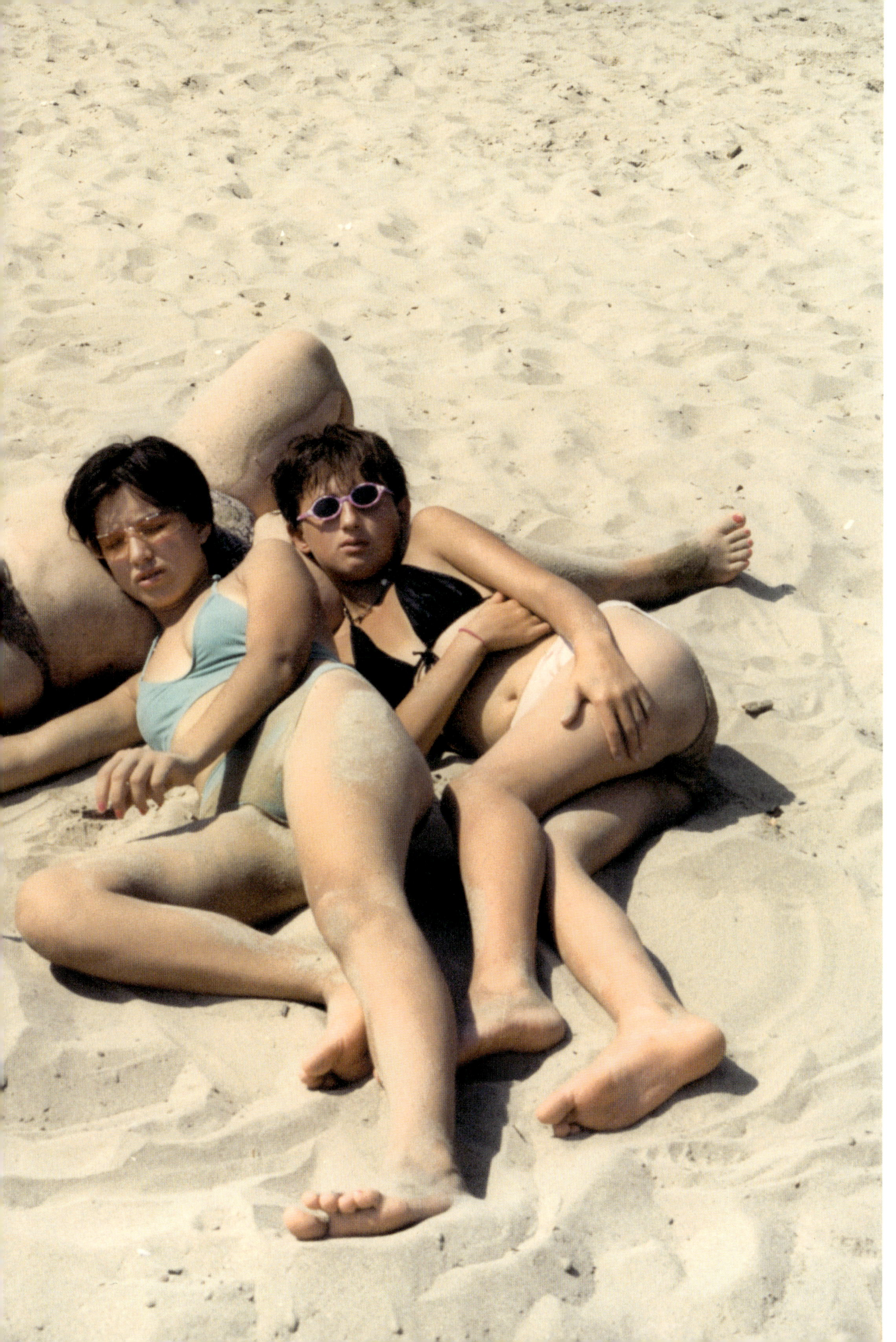

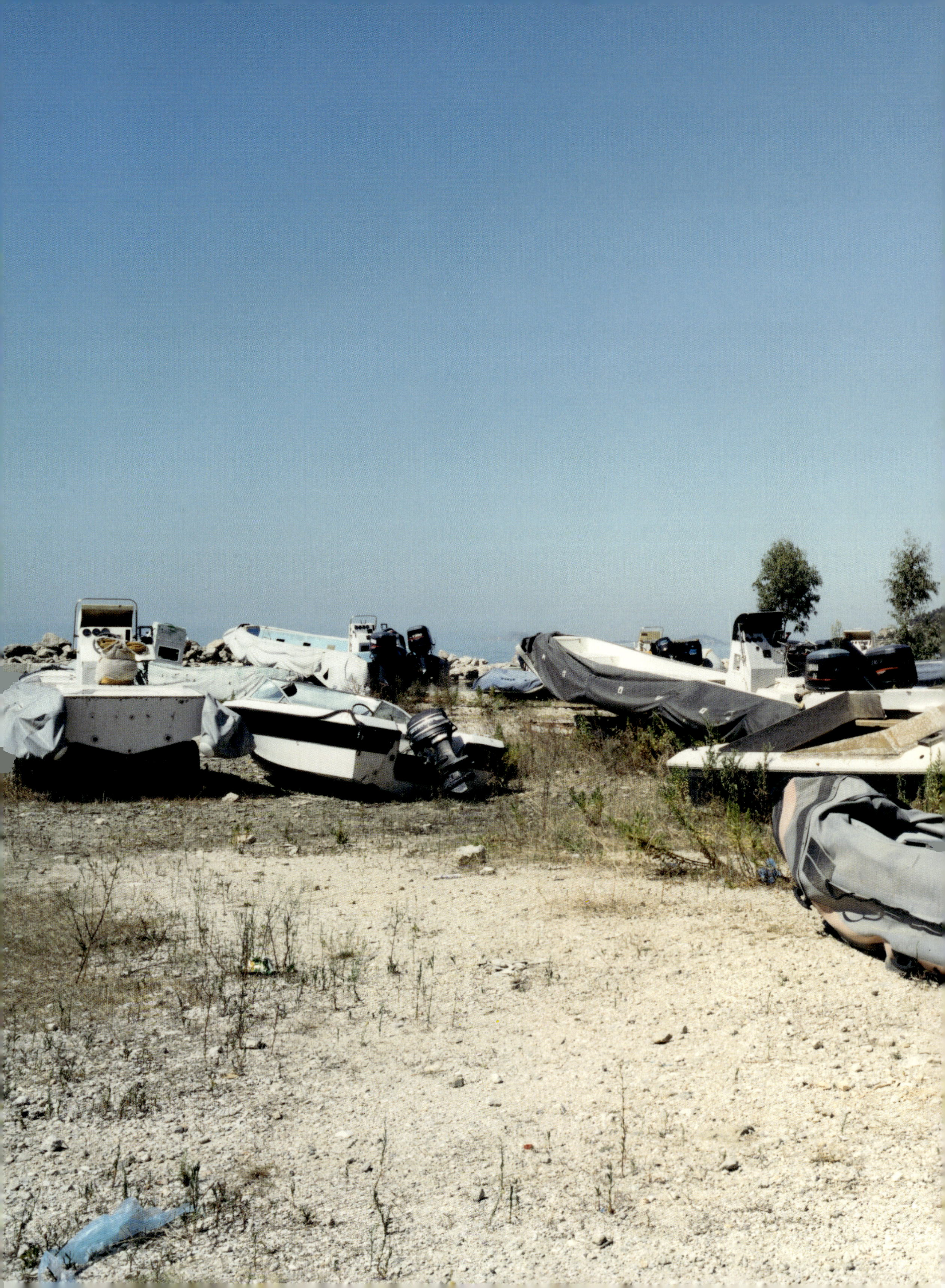

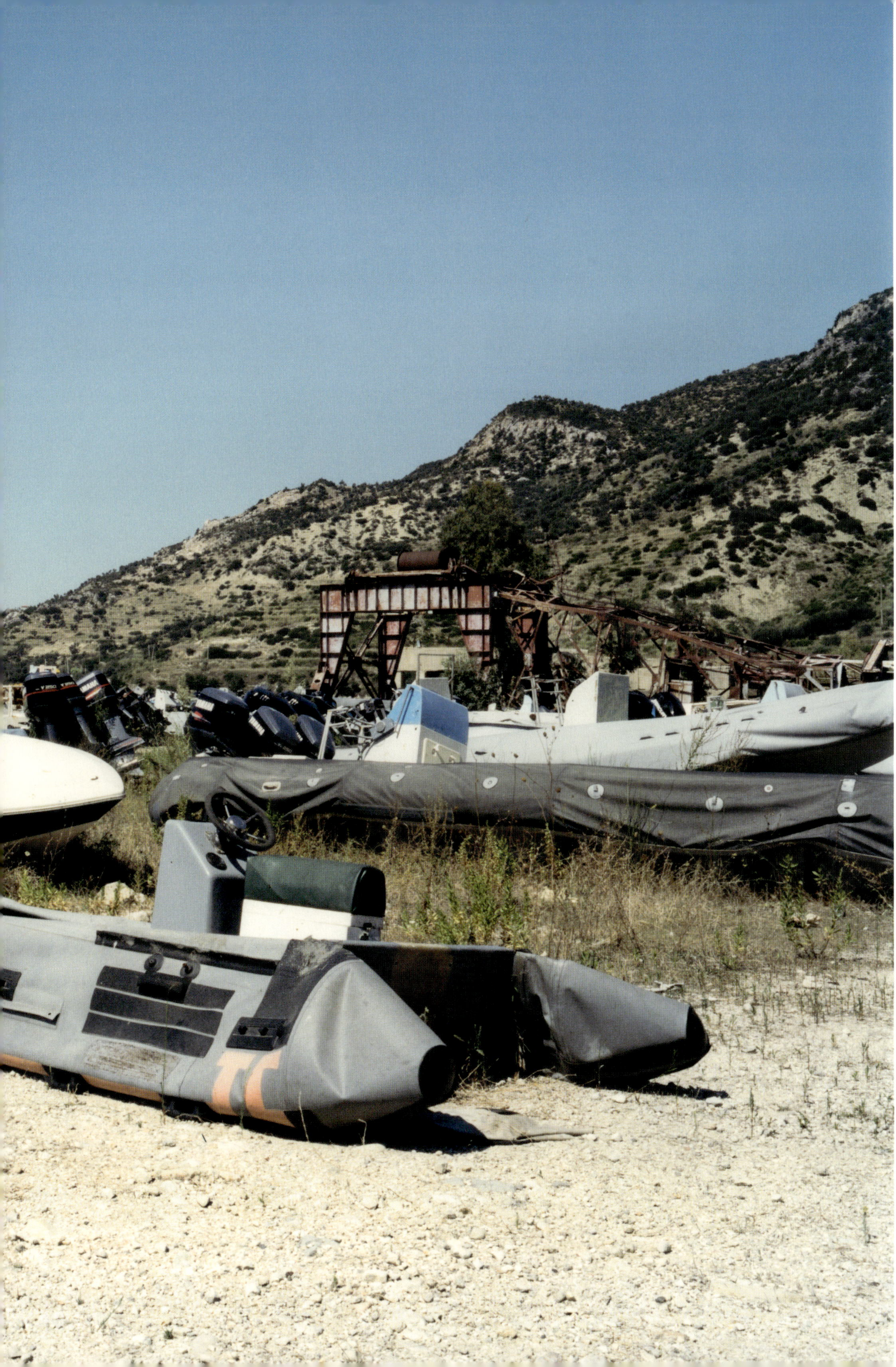

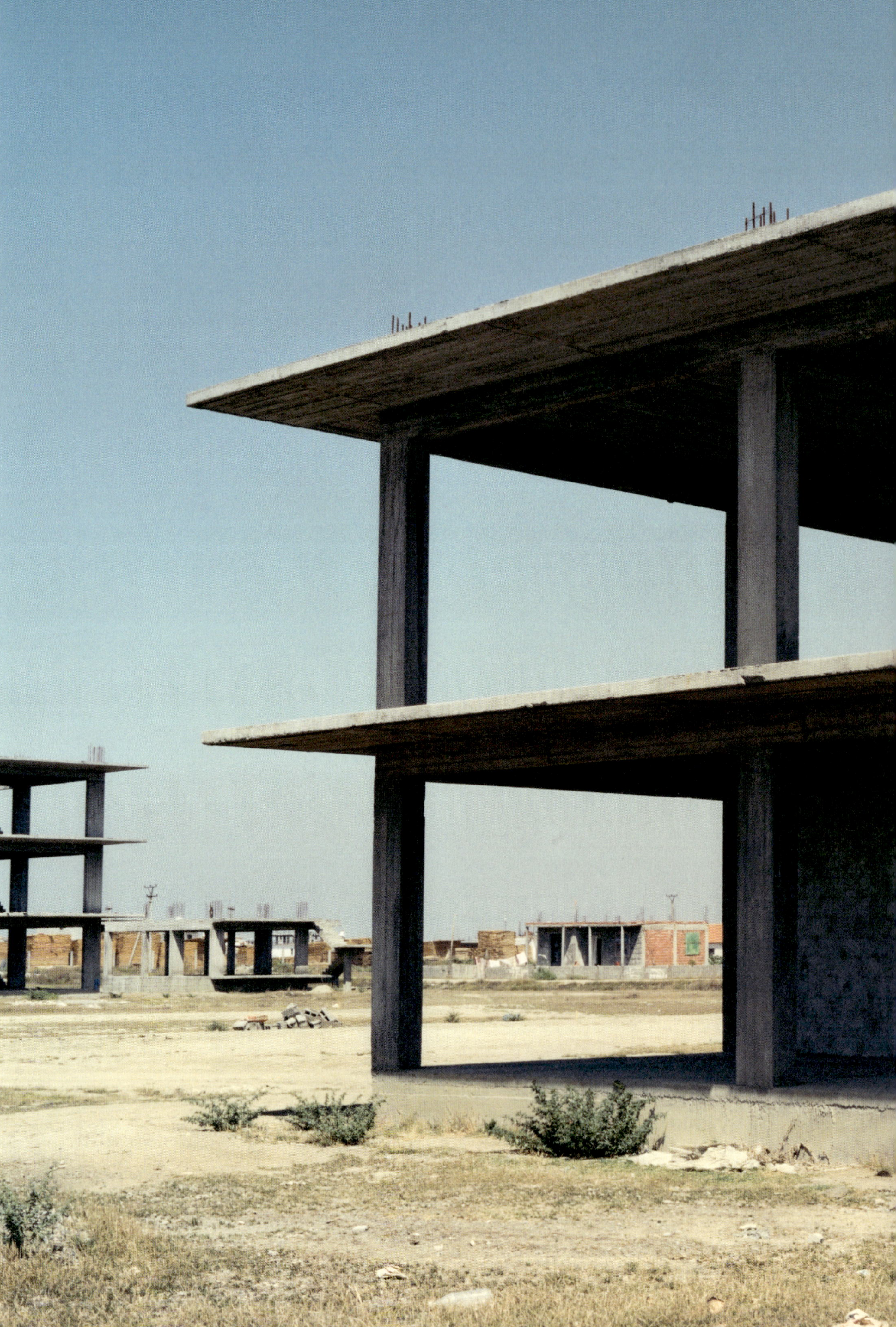

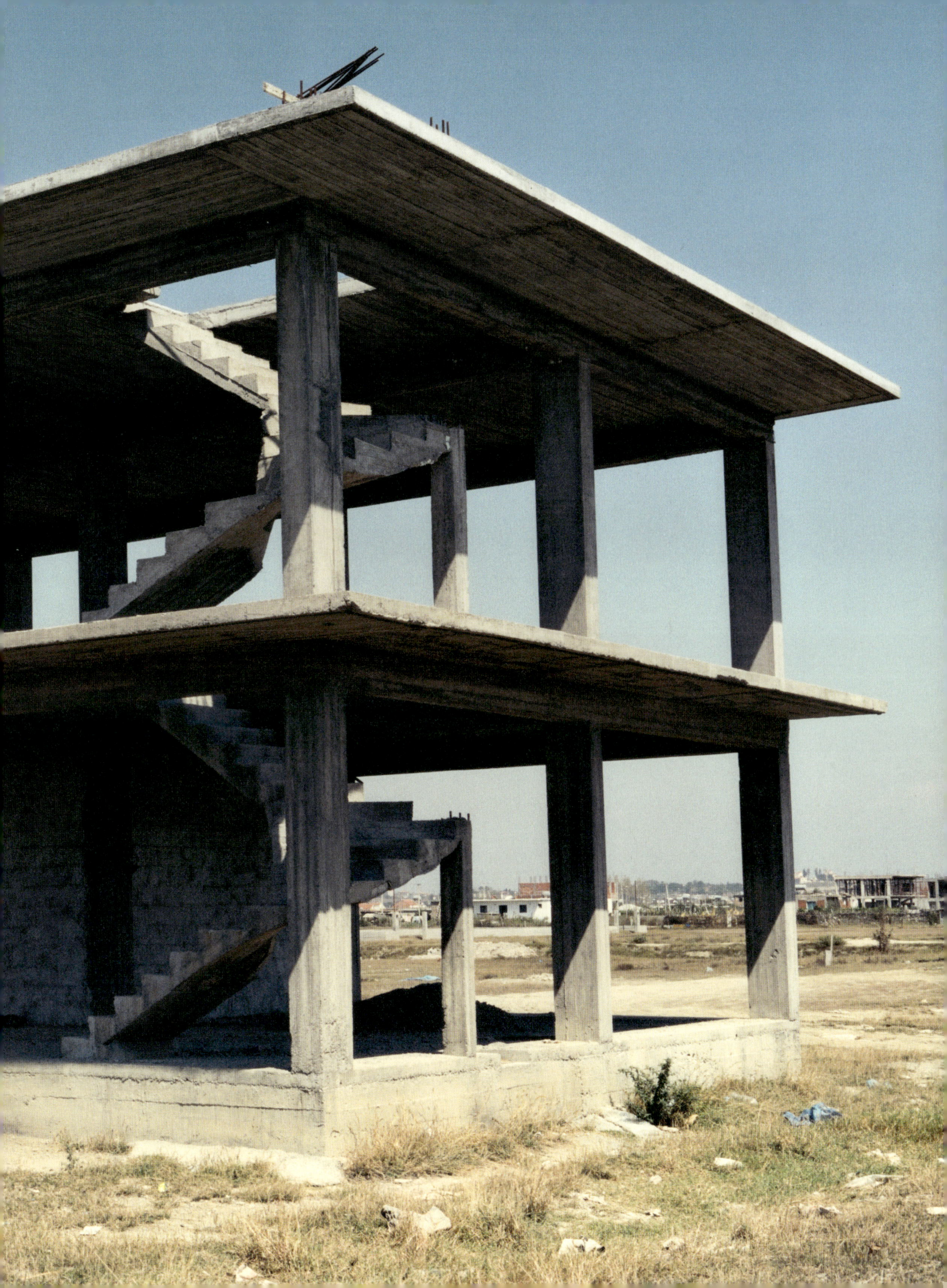

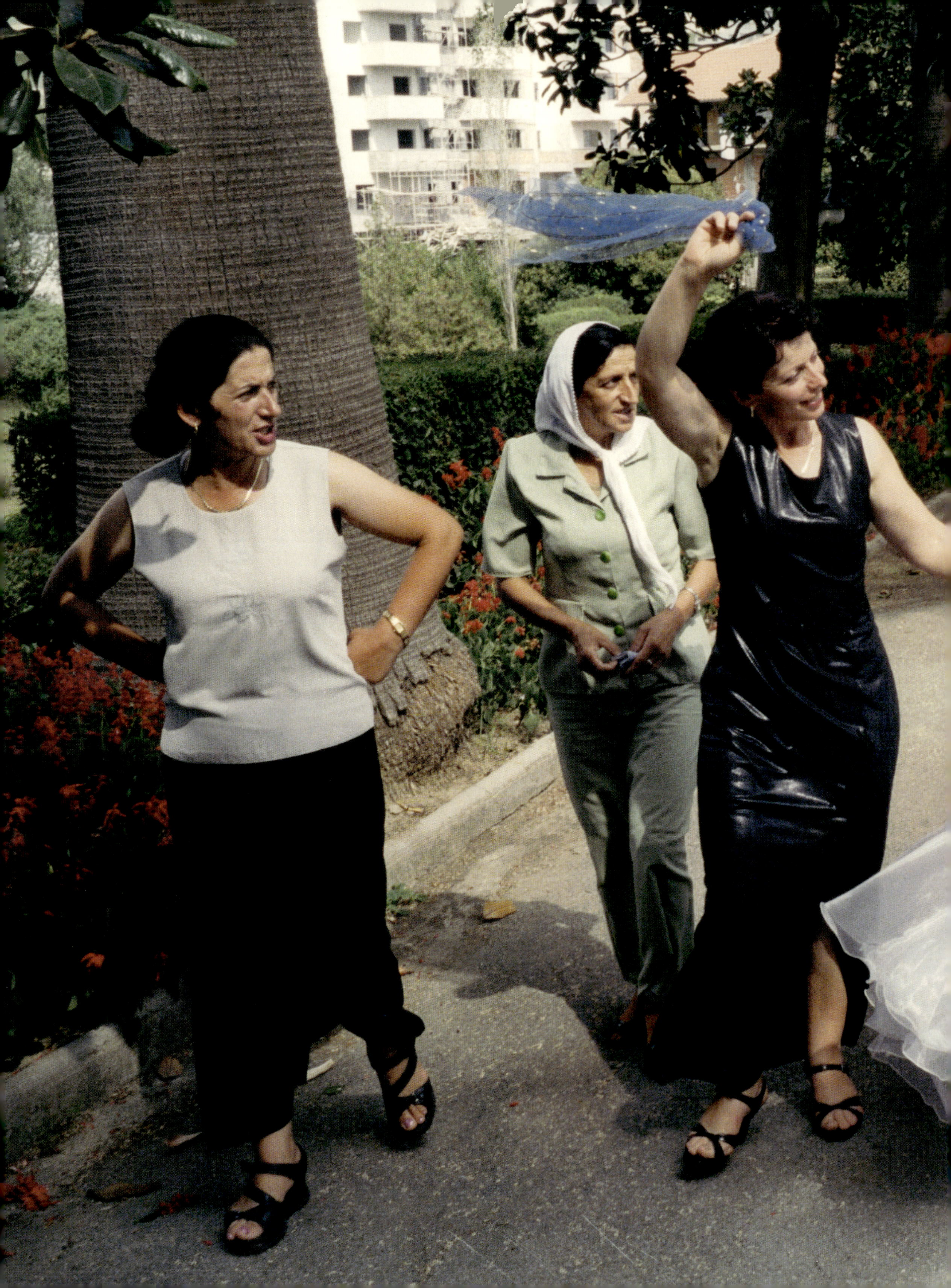

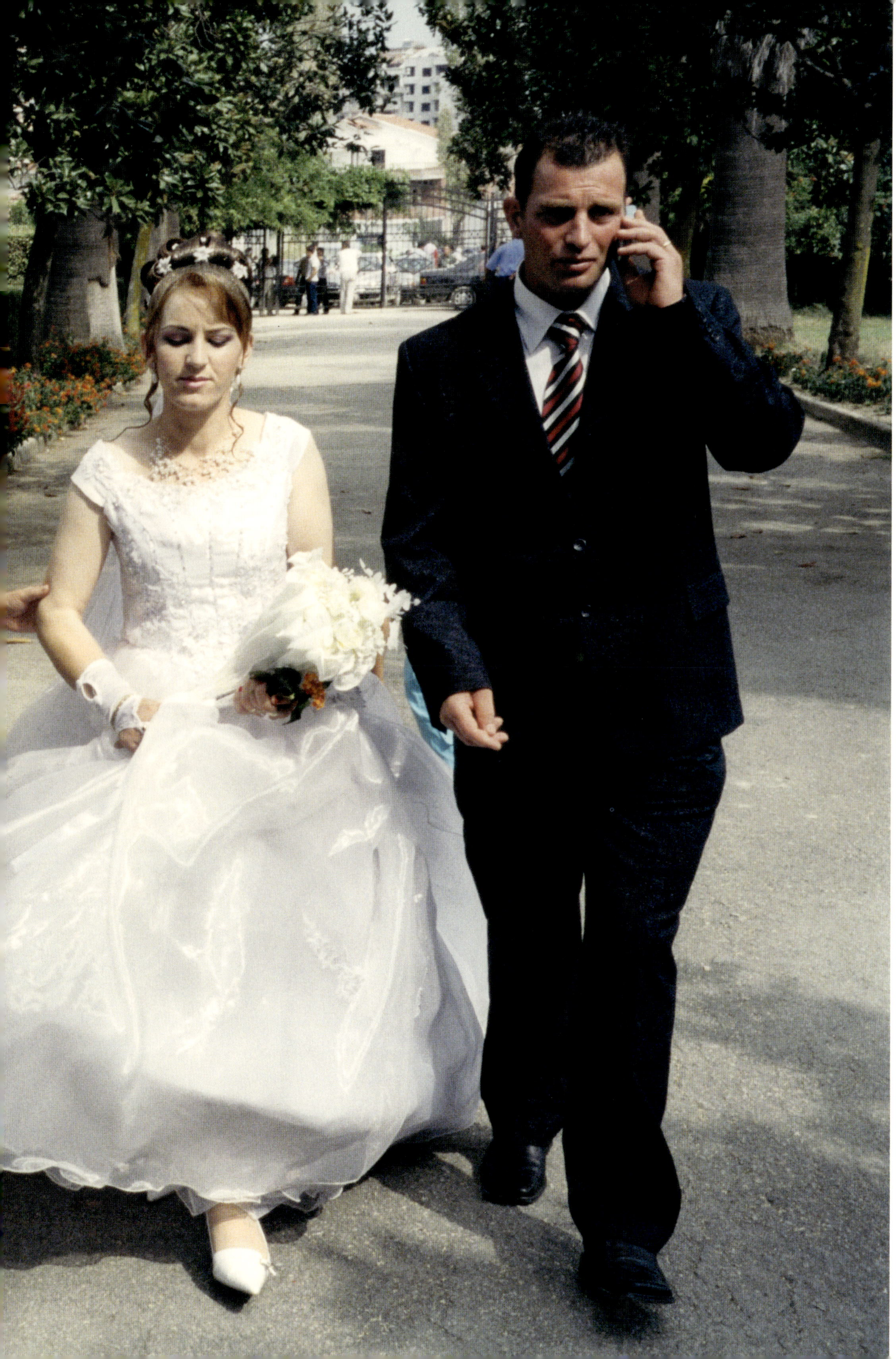

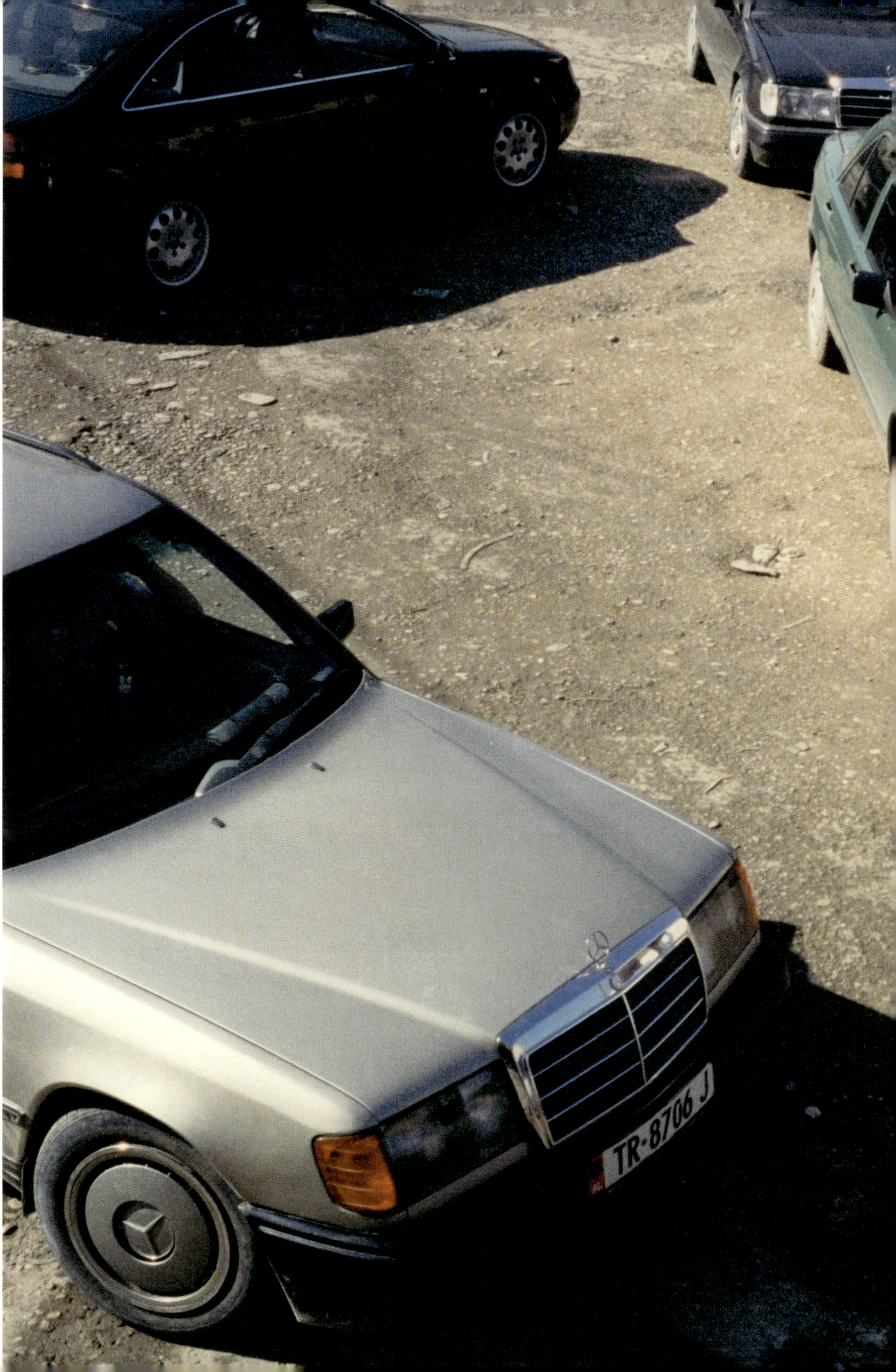

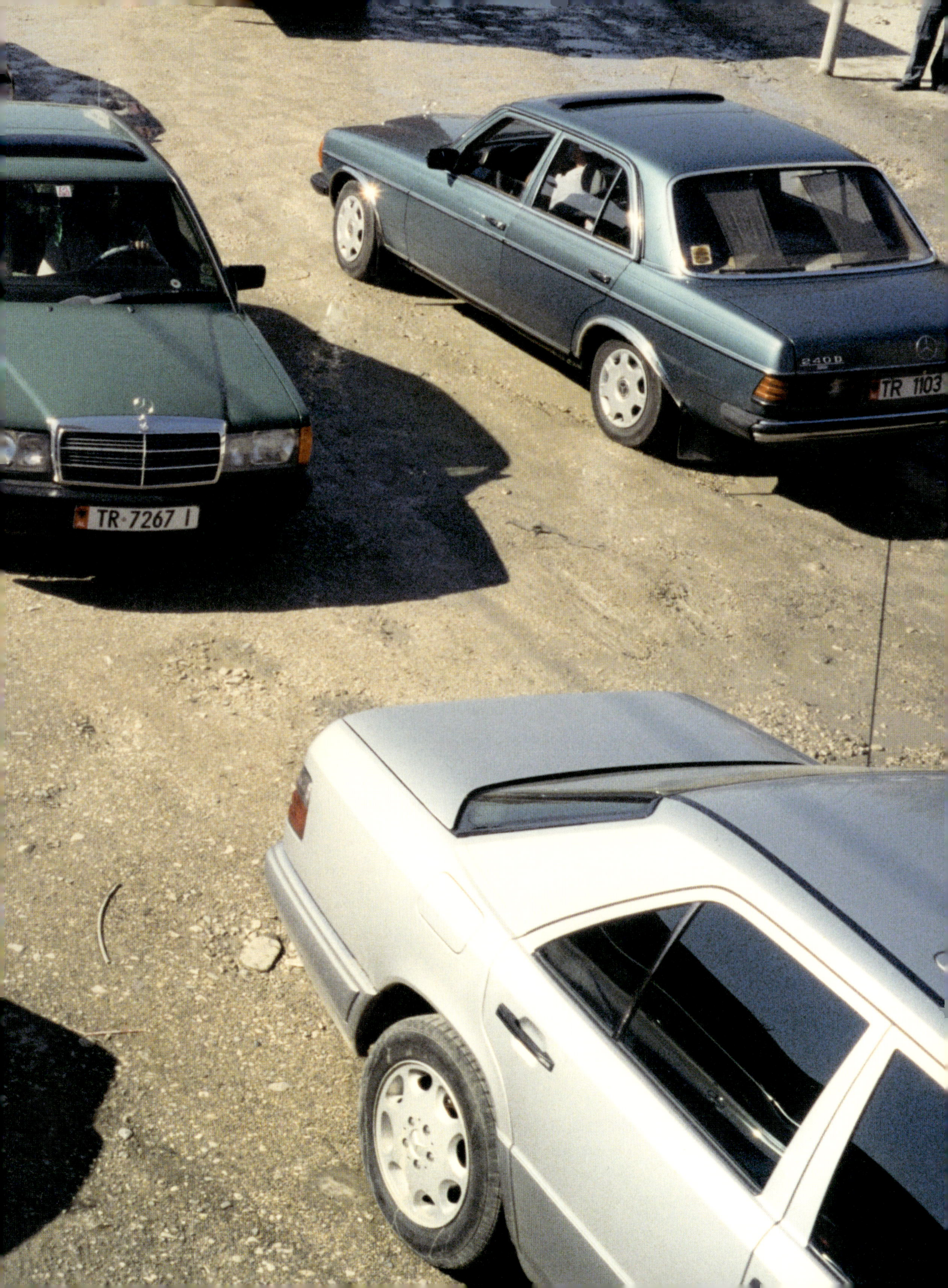

Even though Greece is widely regarded as the cradle of democracy, in the 20th century the country suffered for a long time under an autocratic regime and military coups. It was only after the Second World War and the start of European cooperation that democracy became a self-evident factor in northwest Europe, while the Portuguese Carnation Revolution in 1974 seems to have been the catalyst for the democratic upheaval in southern Europe. In 1975, the colonels' regime in Greece was overthrown; three years later, generalissimo Franco's dictatorship in Spain collapsed.

With the fall of the communist dictatorships in Eastern Europe at the beginning of the 90s, and the subsequent expansion of the European Union, the spread of democracy became an important factor in Western countries' international politics.

The dictator-led countries in North Africa and the Middle East largely interpret the concept of democracy more broadly than in Europe. For example, the current democratically elected president of Tunisia has now been in office for four terms, instead of the original, constitutional maximum of two. Countries such as Egypt, Syria and Morocco have mostly made cosmetic changes, and languish with the proud-to-be-Libyan dictator Gadaffi at the bottom of the list of democracies. In Algeria, the first democratic elections resulted in 1991 in victory for the Islamists. The army intervened with force, seizing control of the country until 2004. The French government lent its support to the new regime, because Algeria had been saved from the 'Islamic threat'. Many Westerners believed that, despite the undemocratic actions of the army, Algeria's democracy had been rescued. The Muslim world was shocked by this Western expression of double standards.

GREECE

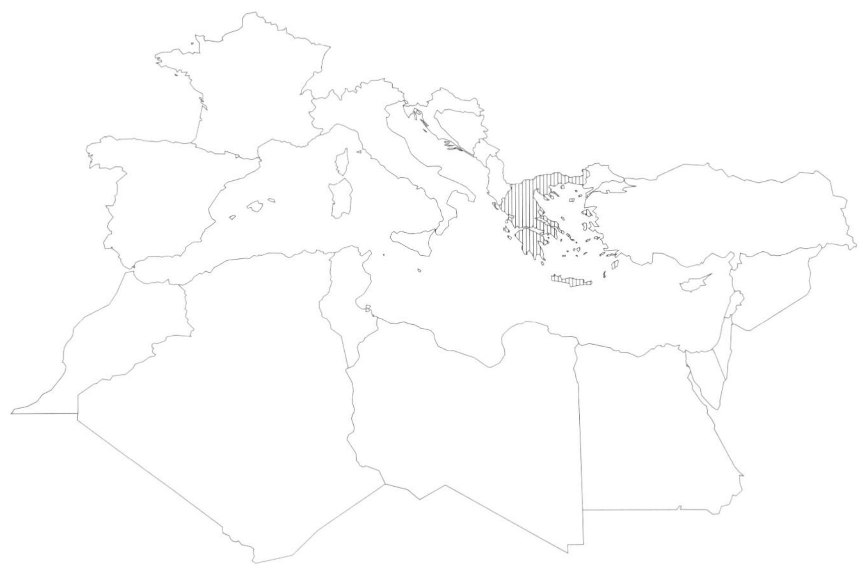

98. PLATOMONAS

The girl didn't want to eat anything. In fact, she didn't want to be there at all. On Greece's mainland, you see Greek holidaymakers almost exclusively and no foreigners. On the islands, it is the exact opposite.

101. MALIA

Charter flights offload hordes of tourists on Crete. They spend their holiday drinking and driving recklessly around the island. It is hard to find anything authentically Greek here.

103. FERRY PIRAEUS - CRETE

Almost everything is transported by boat here. This is hardly surprising with so many islands. Only urgent freight is transported by air.

105. MALIA

People walk half-naked between tourism's gravestones. You can only eat 'globalized' food here, just like in all the other tourist haunts along the coast of Crete.

107. FALIRAKI

A water park on Rhodes. You can spend the whole day here with the family, following a pre-determined programme.

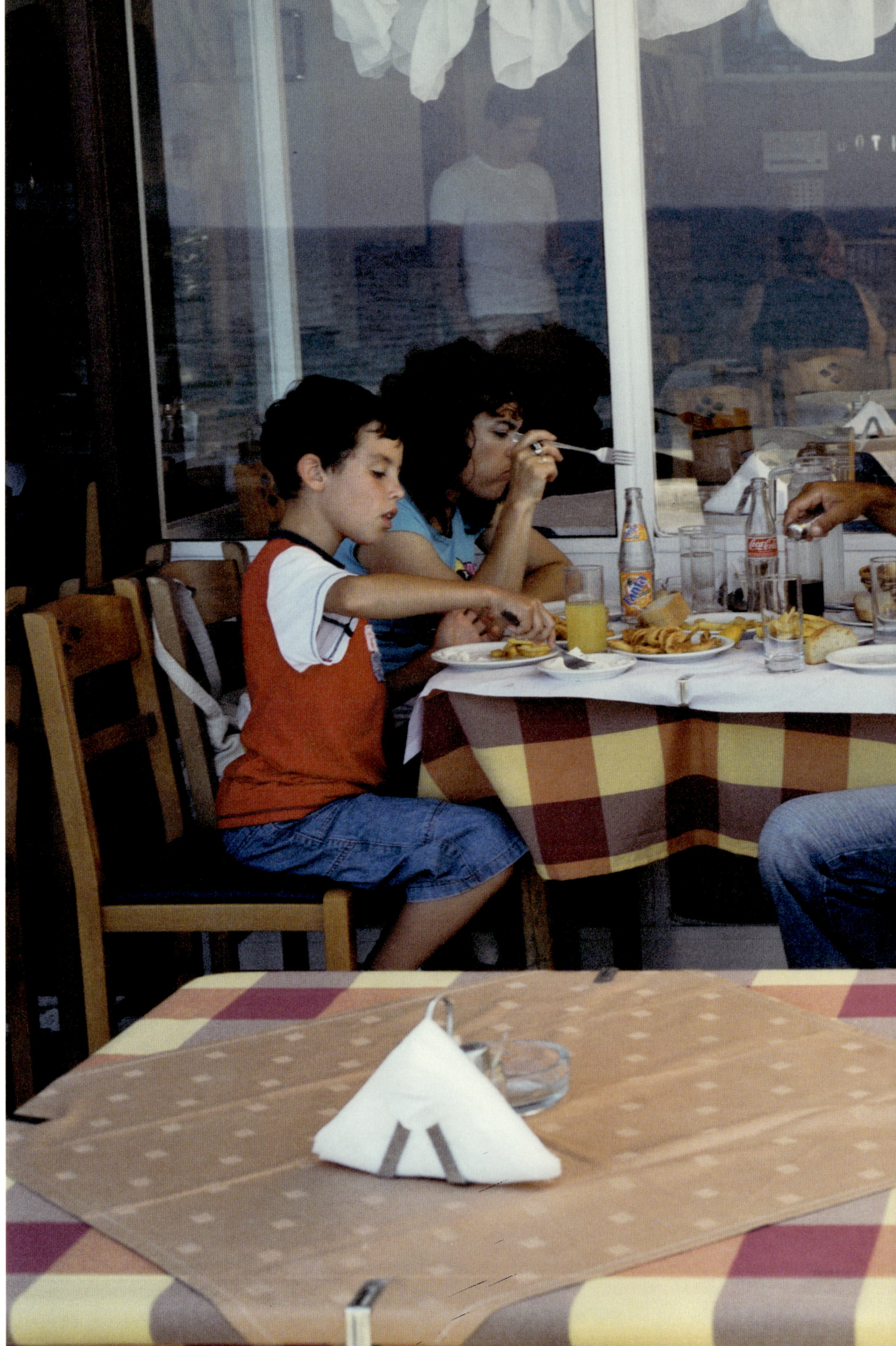

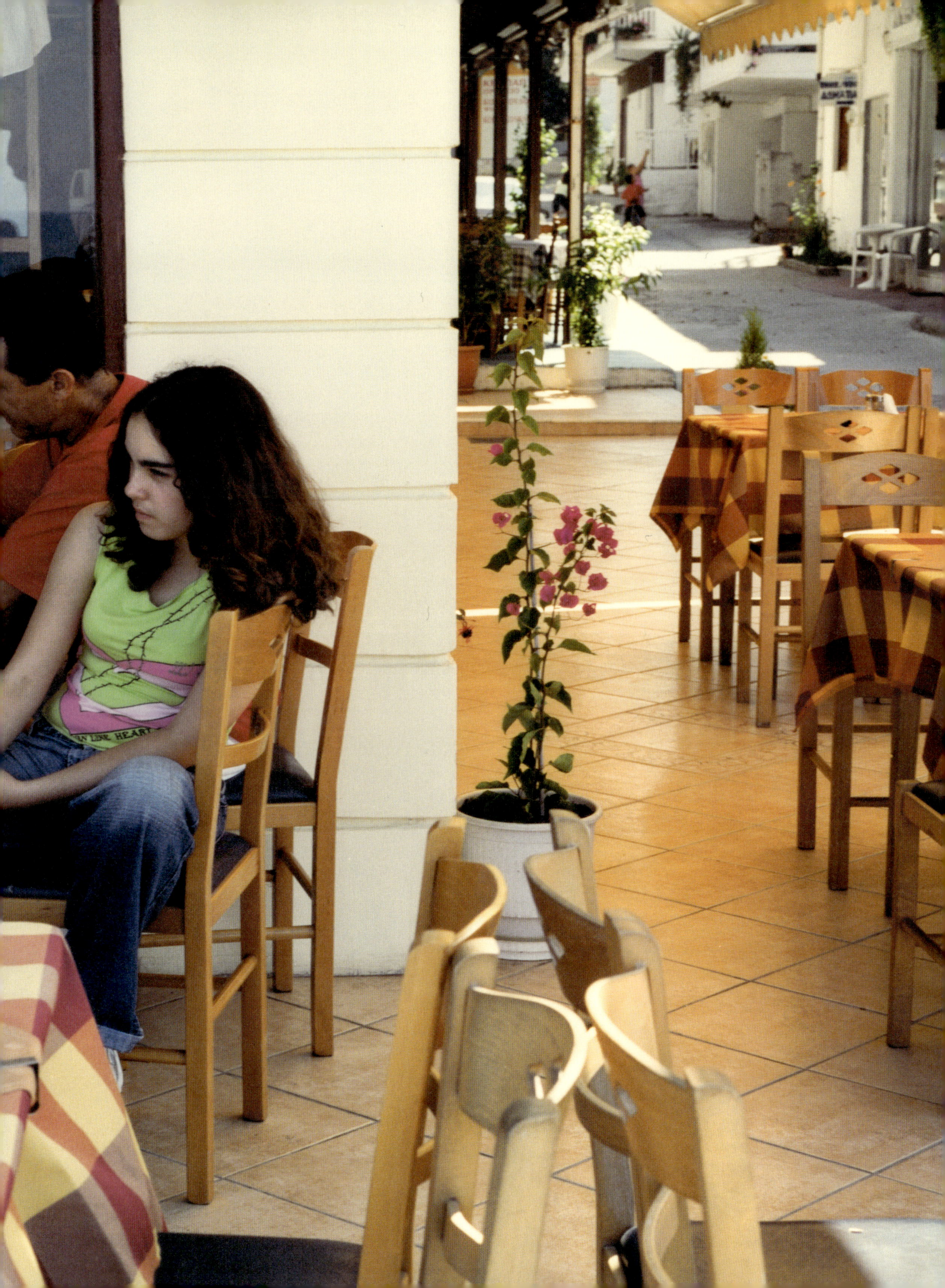

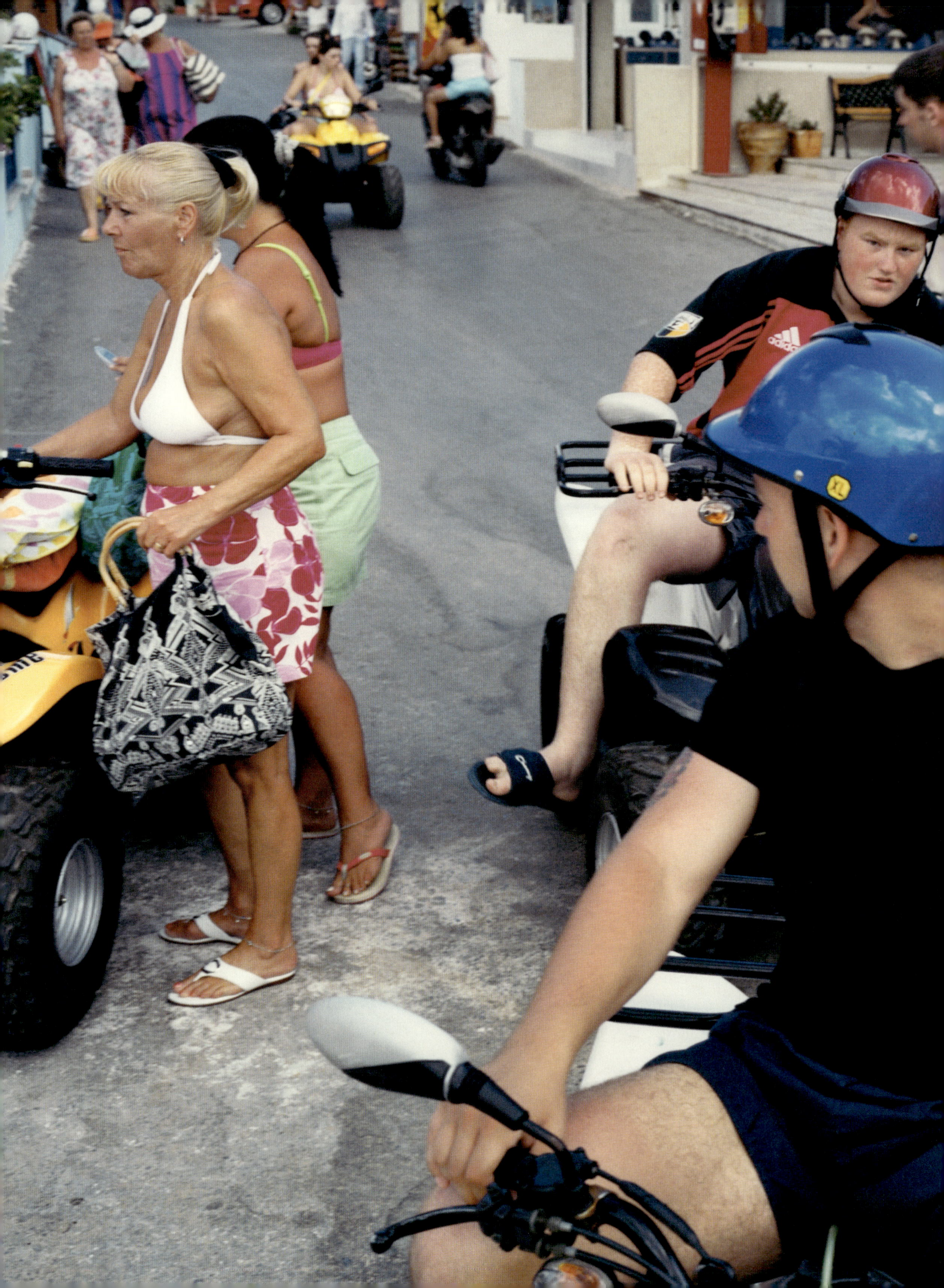

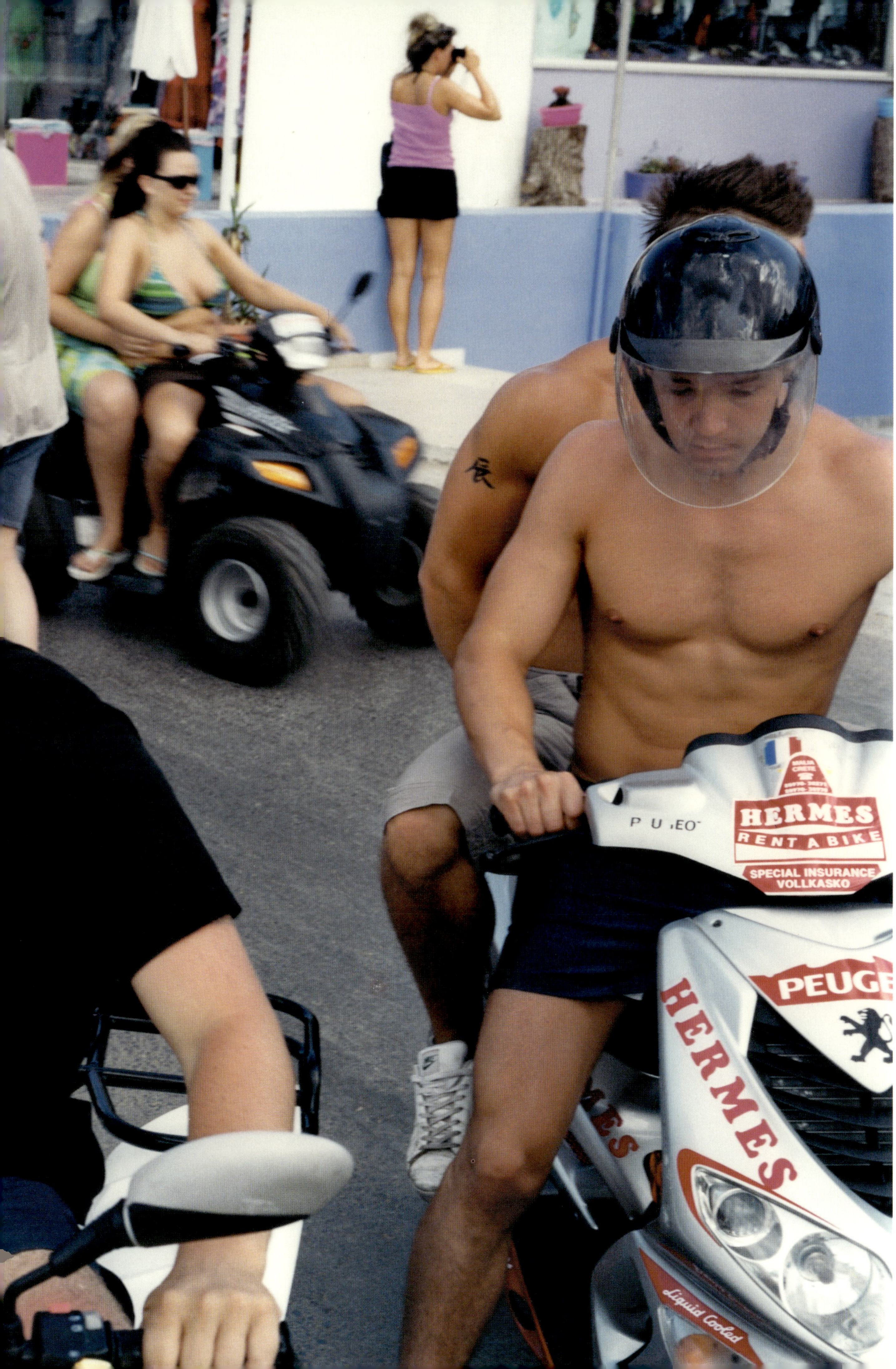

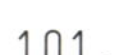

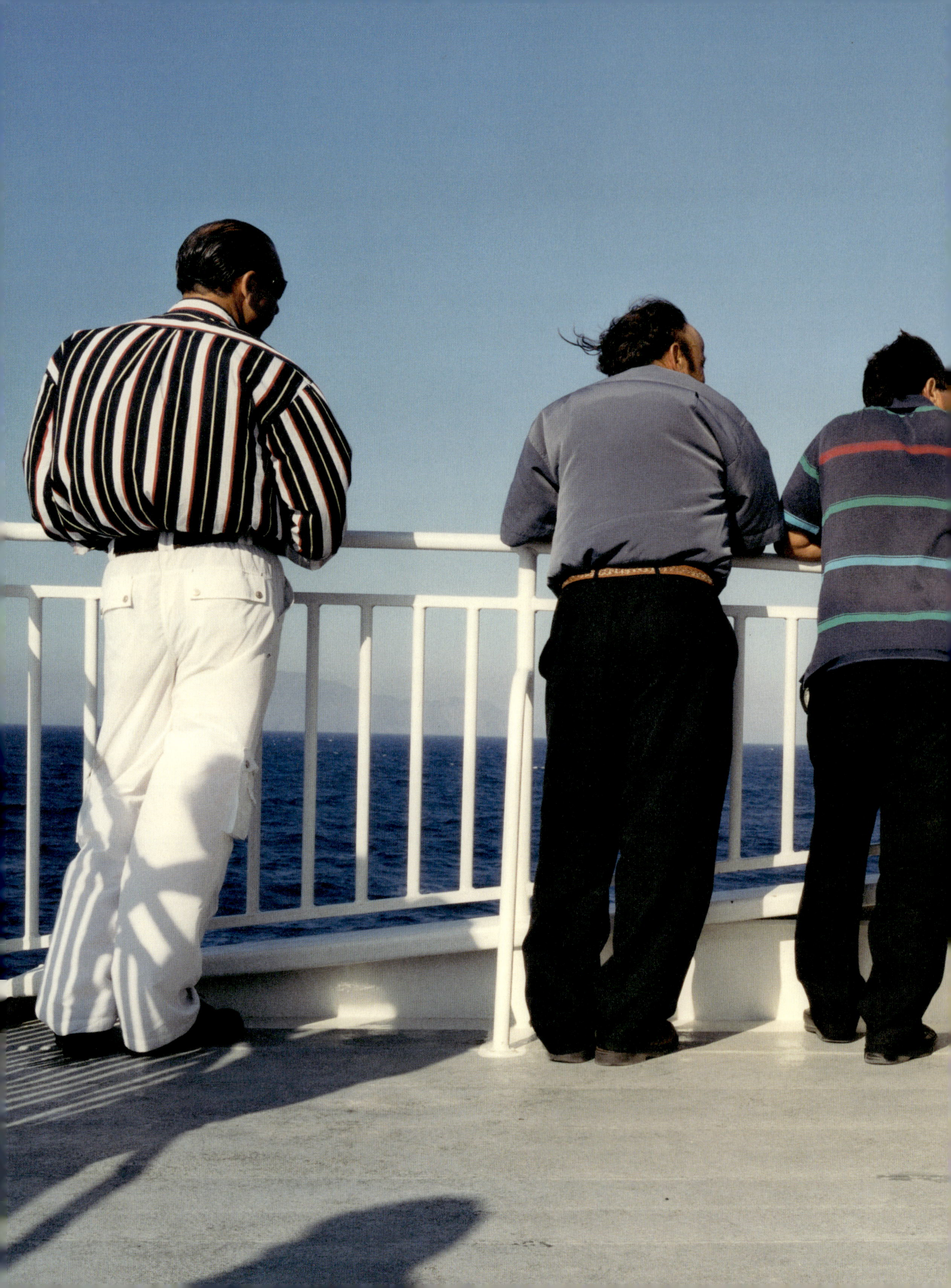

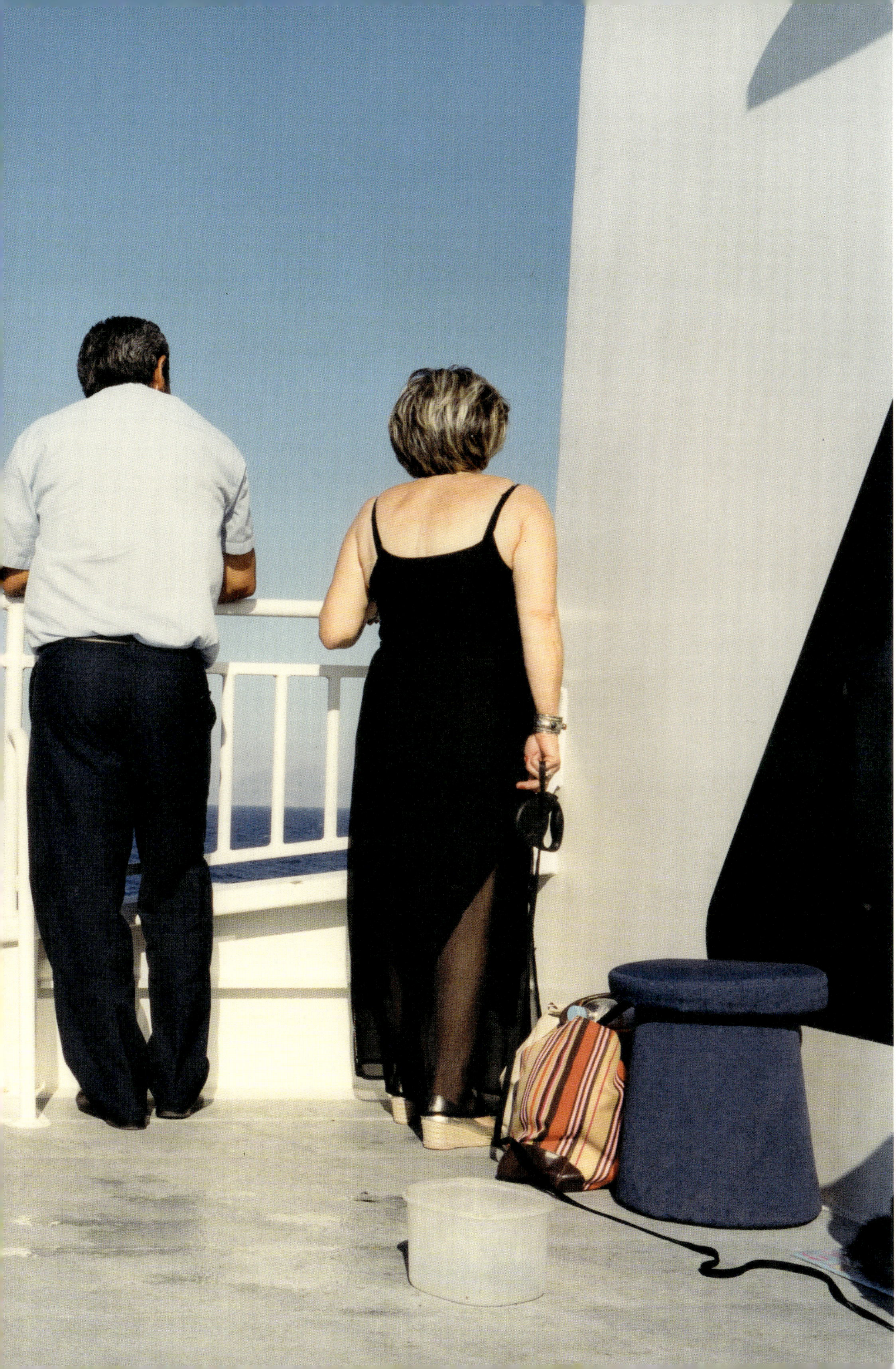

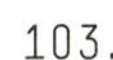

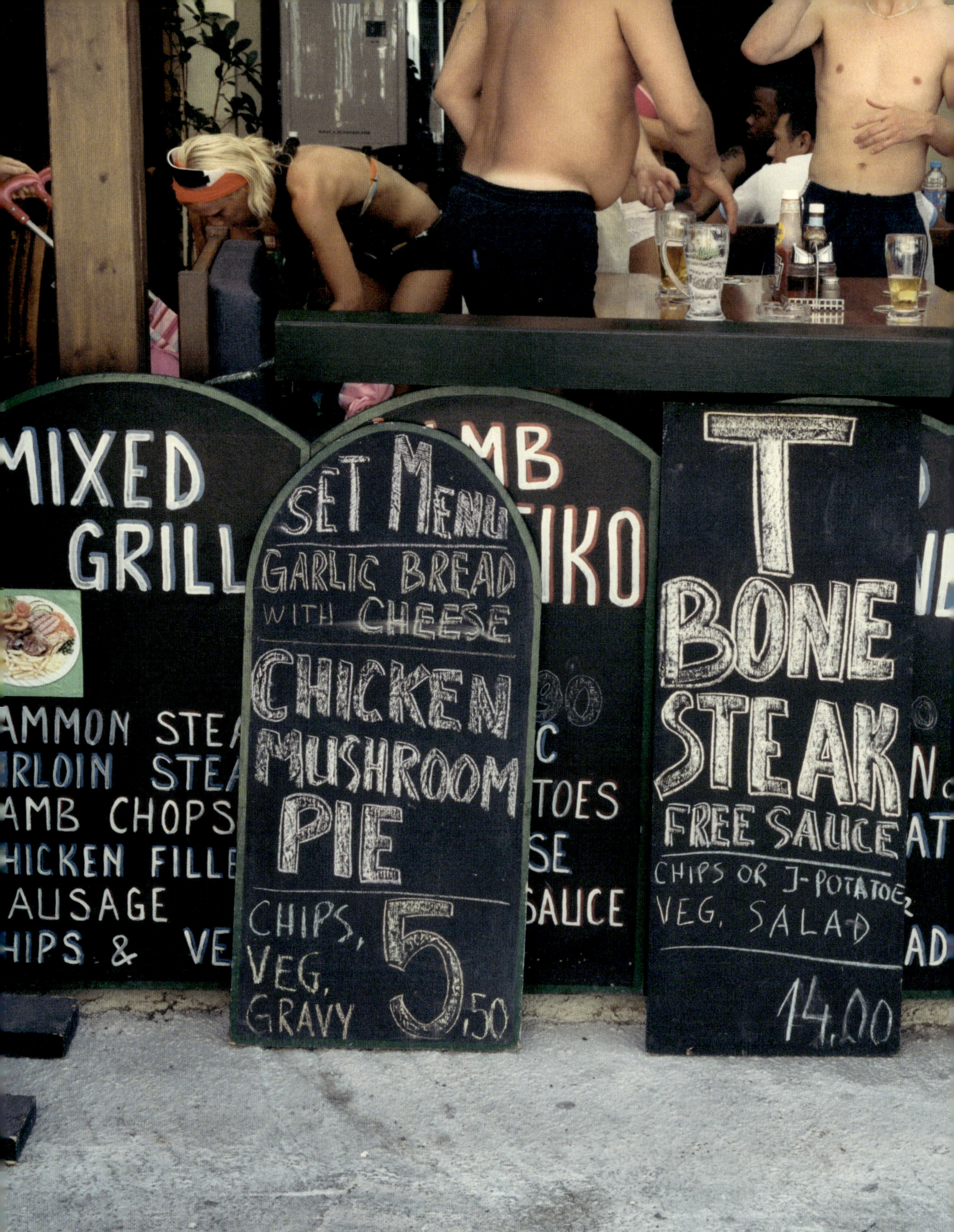
MIXED
GRILL
AMMON STEA
IRLOIN STEA
AMB CHOPS
HICKEN FILLE
AUSAGE
HIPS & VE
SET MENU
GARLIC BREAD
WITH CHEESE
CHICKEN
MUSHROOM
PIE
CHIPS,
VEG,
GRAVY
5.50
AMB
FIKO
TOES
SAUCE
T
BONE
STEAK
FREE SAUCE
CHIPS OR J-POTATOEZ
VEG. SALAD
14.00

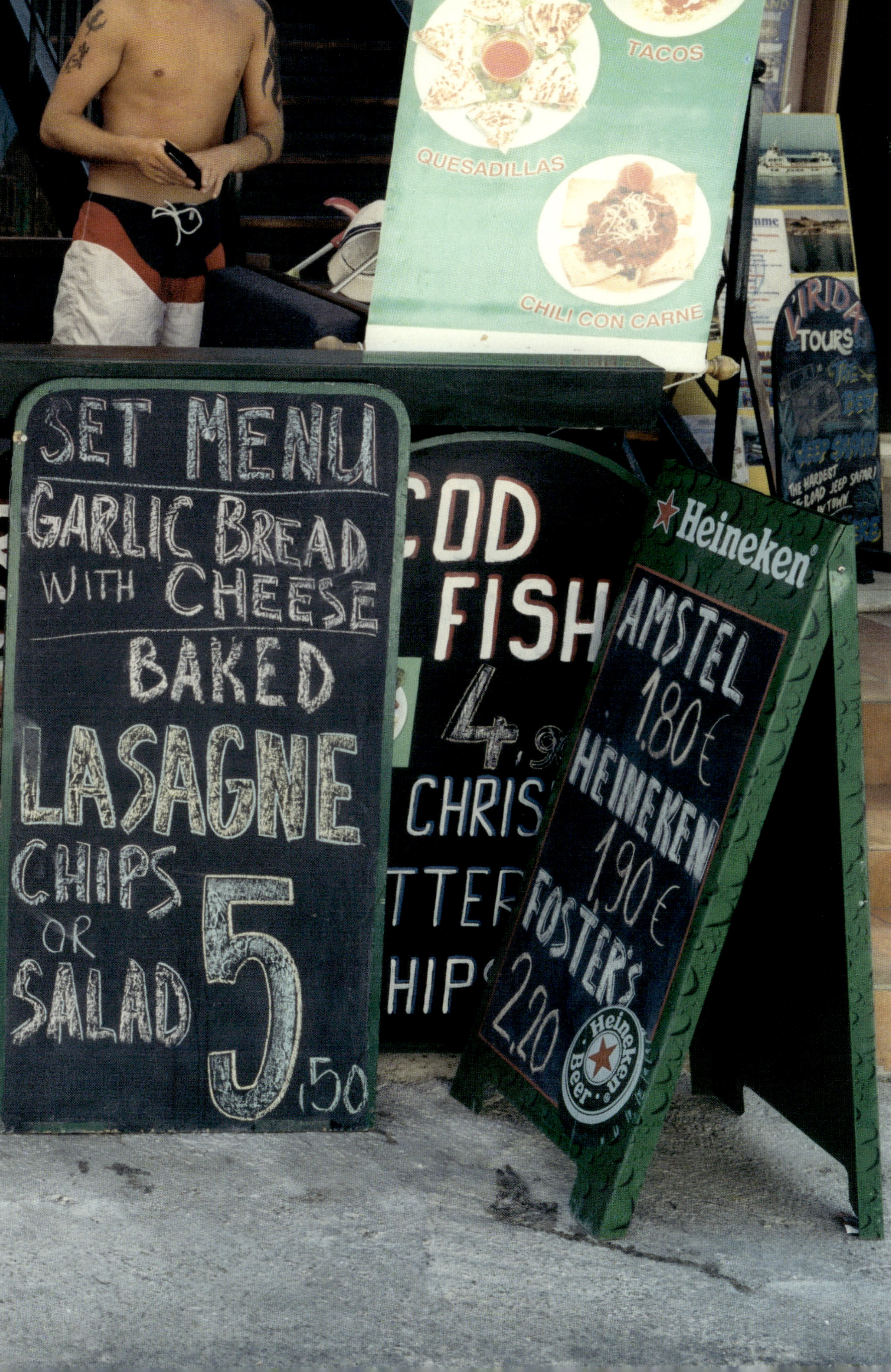
TACOS
QUESADILLAS
CHILI CON CARNE
L'IRIDA TOURS
THE BEST
JEEP SAFARI
THE HARDEST
ROAD JEEP SAFARI
IN TOWN
SET MENU
GARLIC BREAD
WITH CHEESE
BAKED
LASAGNE
CHIPS
OR
SALAD
5.50
COD
FISH
4.90
CHRIS
TTER
HIPS
Heineken
AMSTEL
1.80 €
HEINEKEN
1.90 €
FOSTER'S
2.20
Heineken
Beer

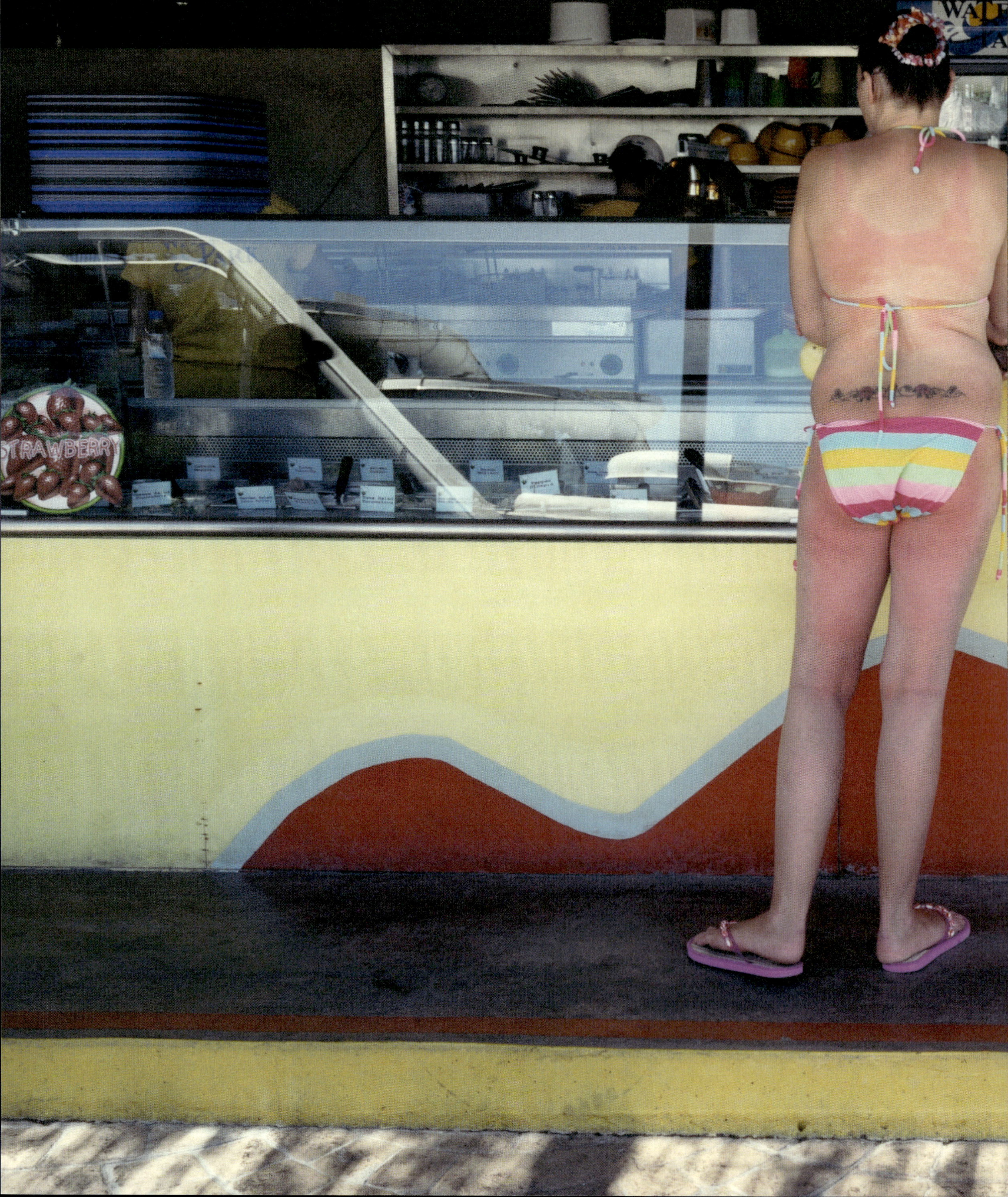
STRAWBERRY

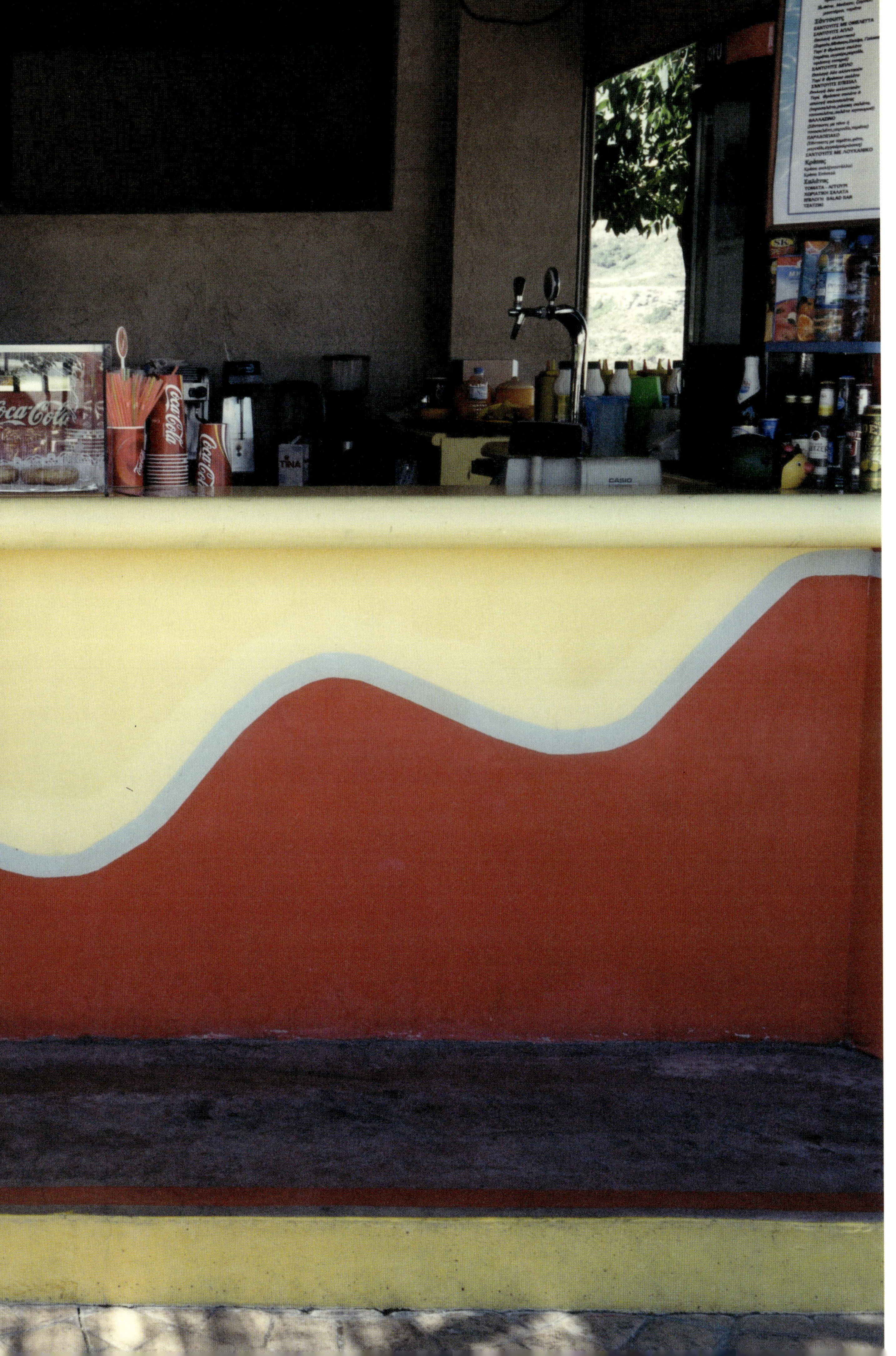

Since the war in 1974, a fragile ceasefire has been in place between the Greeks on the western side of Cyprus and the Turks in the northeast. The conflict appears to be slowly resolving itself. The western part has joined the European Union, while in 2008, Ledra Street in the mediaeval centre of the divided capital Nicosia was reopened. Until recently, this famous street functioned as a border between the two halves of the island. Since the conflict began, there has never been this much hope that the island will reunite.

That would at least be one less conflict in the Mediterranean region. The sea is literally surrounded by conflicts: Basque activism in Spain, Corsican separatism in France, the Polisario struggle for independence from Morocco in the Western Sahara, the ongoing conflict between Israel and the Palestinians; Islamic terrorism in Algeria and Kurdish separatism in Turkey.

Many countries are still shaken by terrorist attacks or threats on a weekly basis. The statistics reveal no more than a glimpse of the reality, if only because figures about the victims of terrorist attacks are by definition the most unreliable in the world. Governments often release low figures in order to paint a rosier picture of their country.

The world is divided over exactly what terrorism is. Globally, at least 109 definitions of terrorism are in use. The statistics that accompany them come from the American Ministry of Foreign Affairs: a relatively subjective source, as attacks in Libya and Syria are not included because both entire states are regarded as terrorist. Other countries consider Israel a terrorist state, due to its rocket attacks on residential areas and its bulldozing of refugee camps.

110. NICOSIA

The no-man's-land between the Turkish and Greek halves of the island. Sometimes the border area is narrow, sometimes quite wide. After the war in 1974, this airstrip at Nicosia's airport was closed down. Everything is covered with dust.

112. NICOSIA

In a carpenter's workshop hang photos of family members and acquaintances who were killed or disappeared during the conflict between 1964 and 1974.

115. NICOSIA

In the mornings, a procession of Turkish Cypriots enters the Greek half of the island to work. The border sometimes reminds you of the Berlin Wall. In this no-man's-land stand streets of empty houses. Occasionally, a United Nations patrol drives through them.

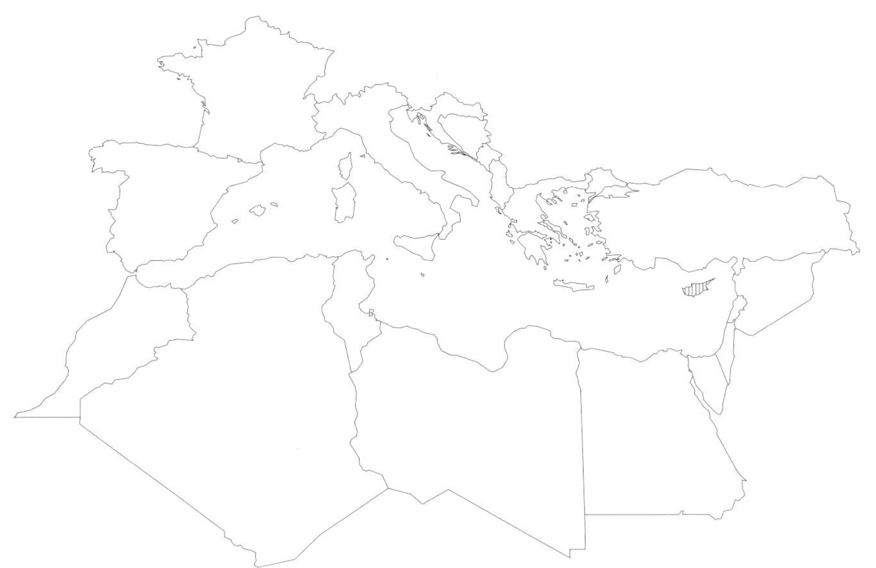

VICTIMS OF TERRORIST ATTACKS

ESTIMATE IN THE YEARS BETWEEN 2000 AND 2006

GIBRALTAR	0
SPAIN	250
FRANCE	21
ITALY	0
CROATIA	0
ALBANIA	0
GREECE	2
CYPRUS	**0**
TURKEY	793
SYRIA *	1
LEBANON	40
ISRAEL **	525
W.B. & GAZA	NA
EGYPT	133
LIBYA *	0
TUNISIA	20
ALGERIA ***	357
MOROCCO	45

SOURCE : US STATE MINISTRY PATTERNS OF GLOBAL TERRORISM; COUNTRY REPORTS ON TERRORISM

*   : SYRIA AND LIBYA ARE SO-CALLED 'STATE SPONSORS OF TERRORISM', AND ARE THEREFORE VIEWED IN THE REPORT AS BREEDING GROUNDS FOR GLOBAL TERRORISM.

**   : ISRAEL, THE WEST BANK AND GAZA. THE NUMBER OF VICTIMS COULD EASILY BE IN THE HUNDREDS, ACCORDING TO THE REPORT.

*** : THE NUMBER OF VICTIMS COULD EASILY BE HUNDREDS MORE THAN STATED, DUE TO THE DISPARITY BETWEEN OFFICIAL AND UNOFFICIAL FIGURES.

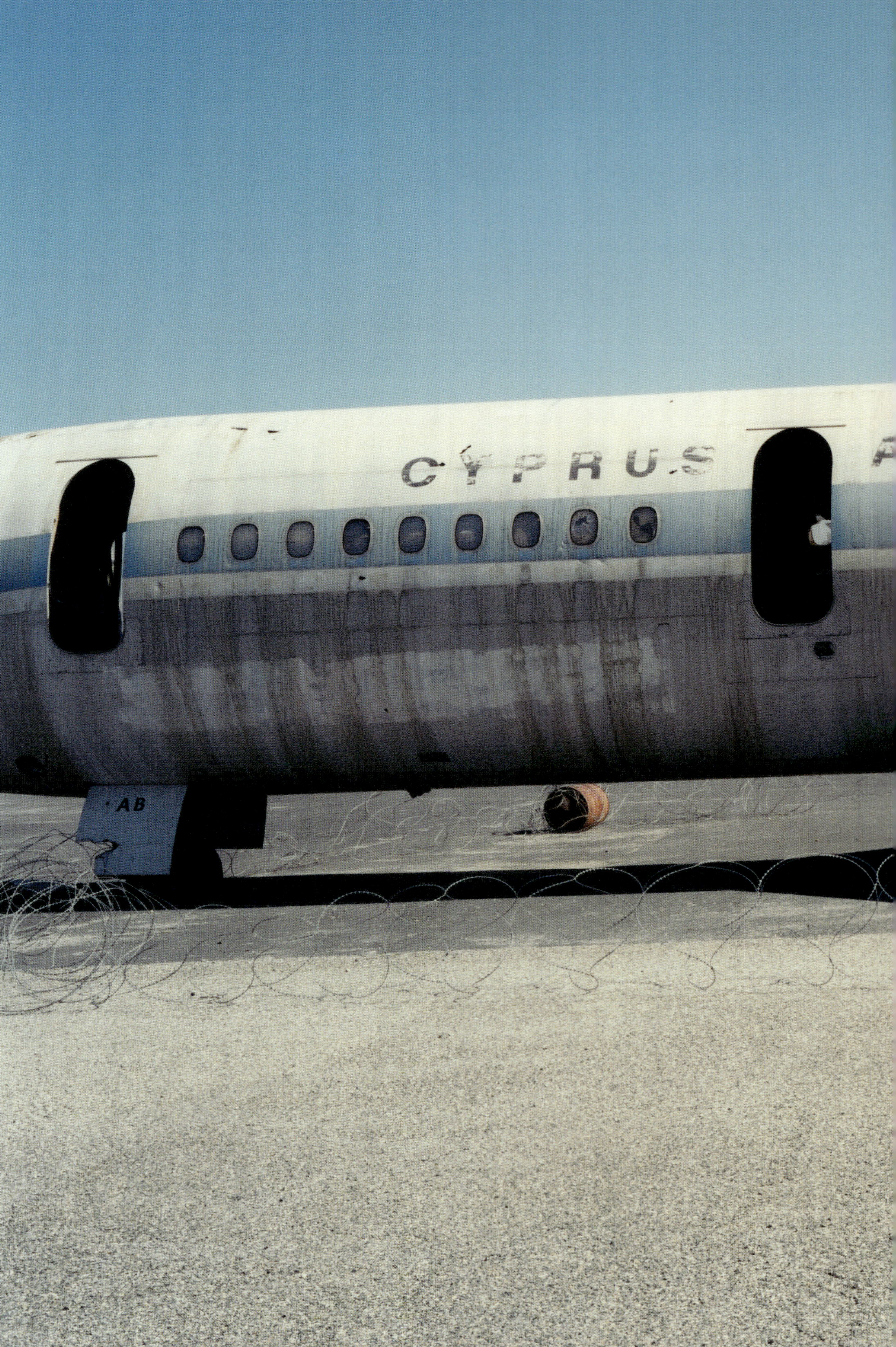
CYPRUS
AB

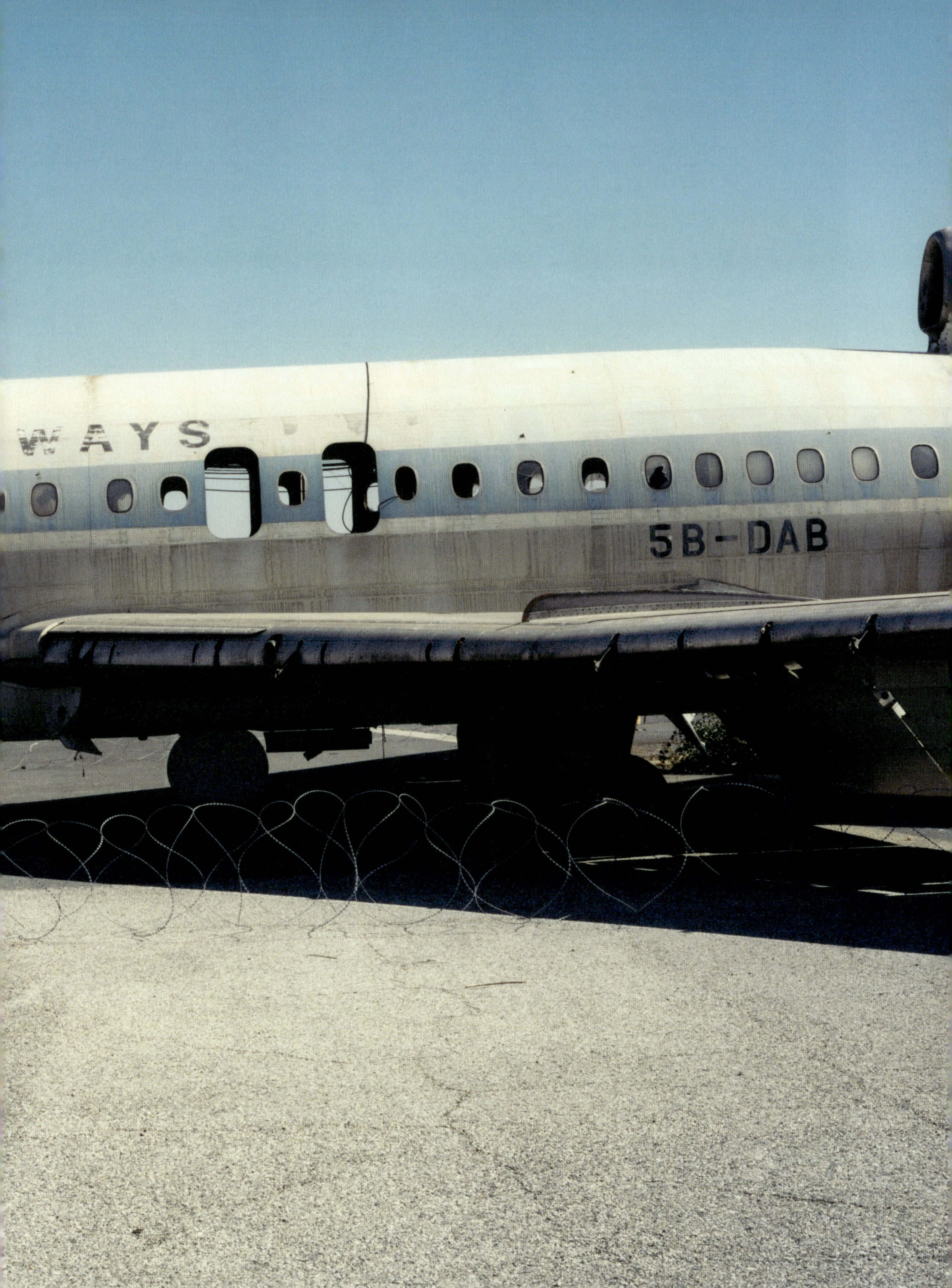
WAYS
5B-DAB

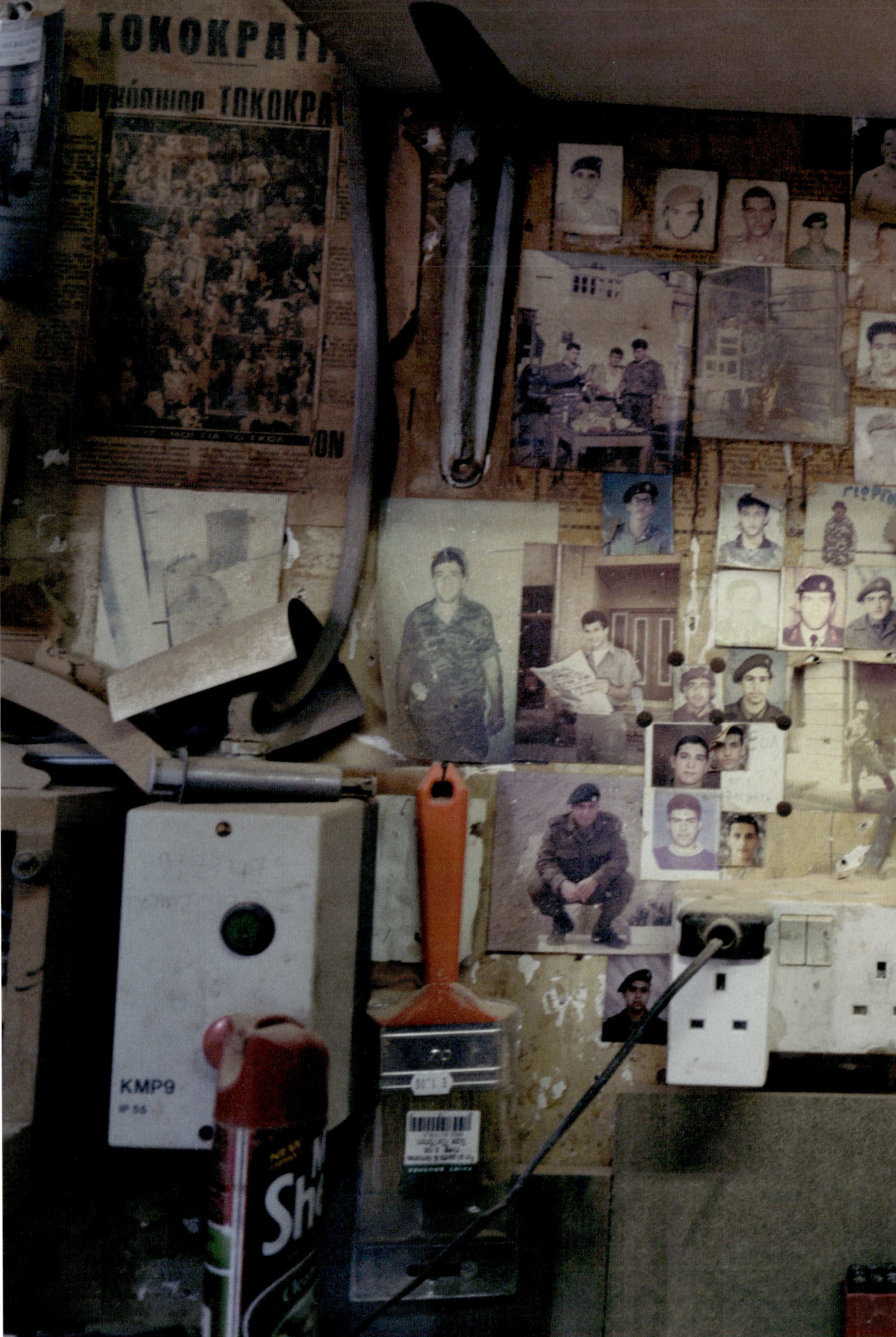

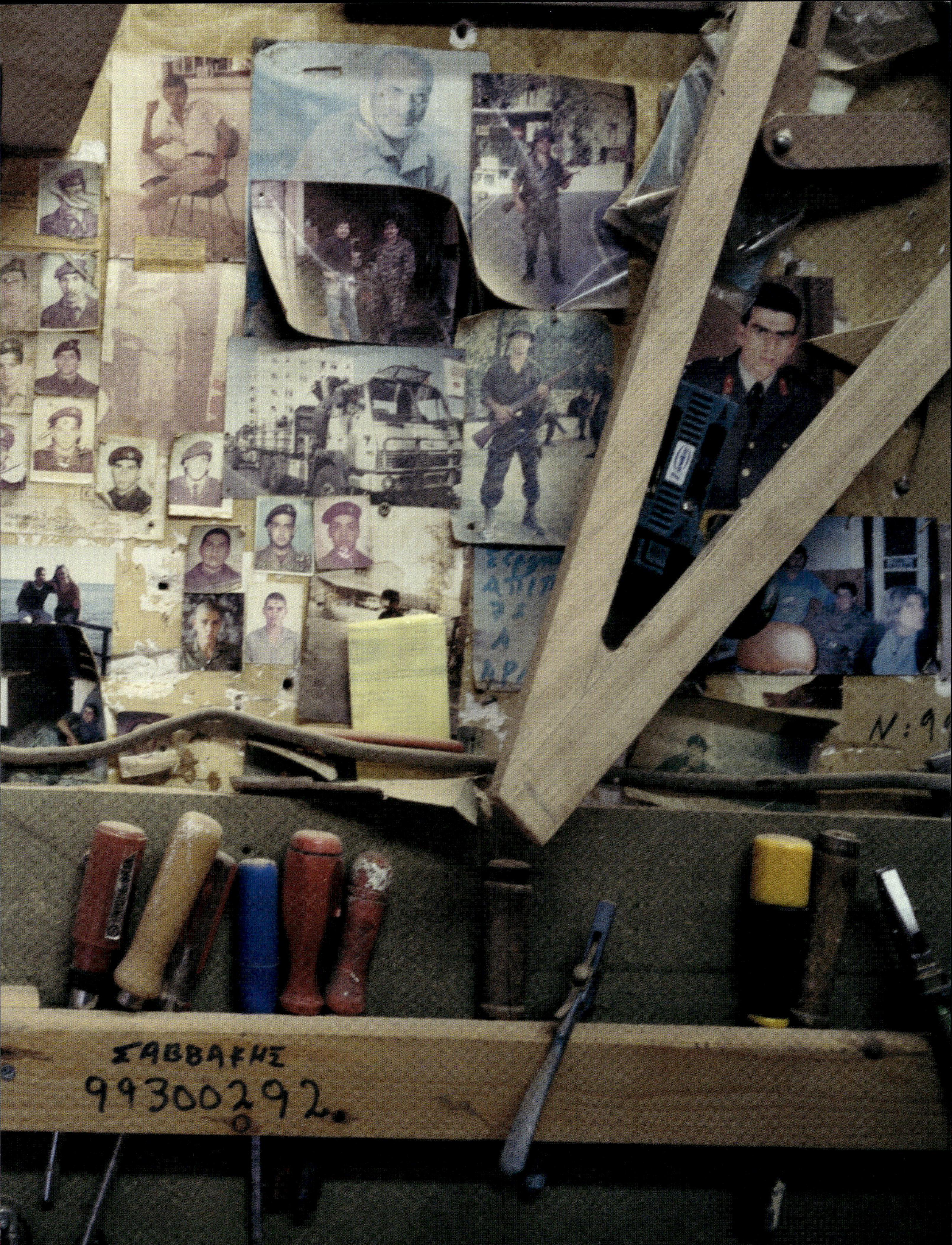
N:9
ΣΑΒΒΑΚΗΣ
99300292

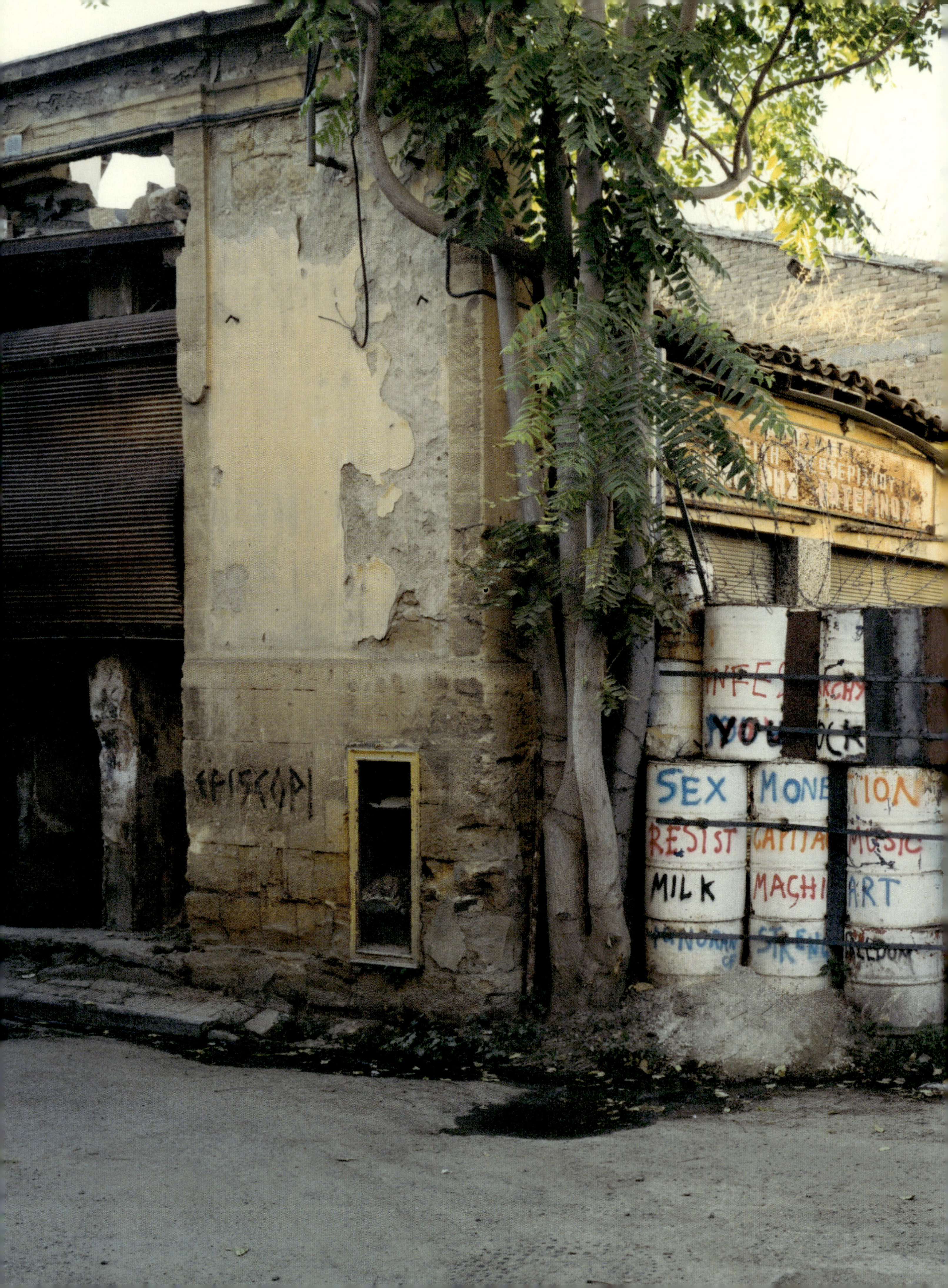
EPISCOPI
SEX
RESIST
MILK
MONE
CAPITA
MACHI
TION
MUSIC
ART

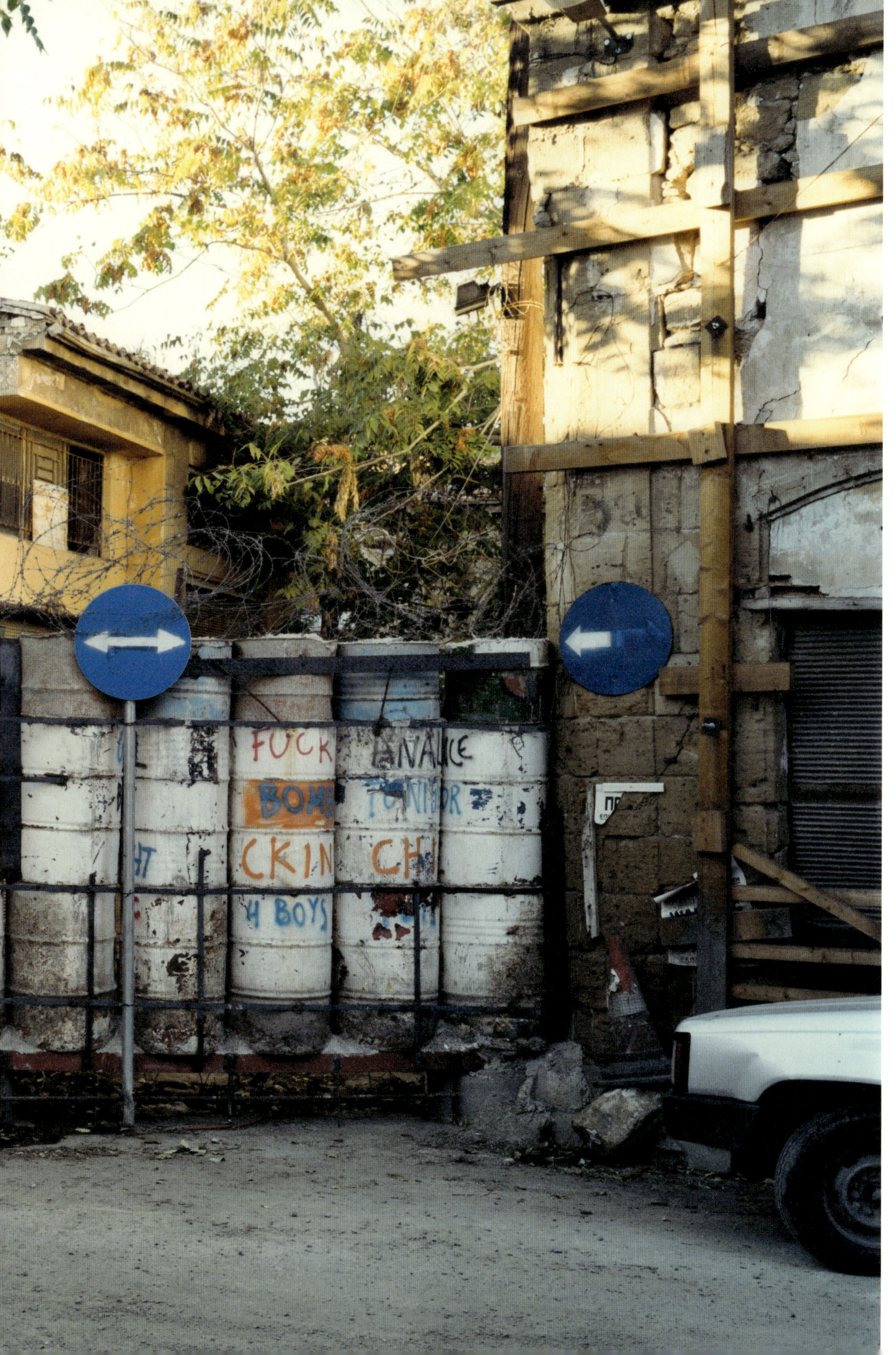

FUCK ANALICE
BOM FONIGR
CKIN CH
4 BOYS

All the countries which flank the Mediterranean have minorities within their borders. In the democracies on the European side of the sea, the rights of these groups are mostly guaranteed. This is an important moral pillar upon which the European Union is built. Consequently, the dubious manner in which Turkey deals with its minorities plays an important role in Turkey's negotiations for accession to the European Union.

At the time of the First World War, the extensive Ottoman Empire lost its right to exist and dwindled to what is now Turkey. Since it was established by Mustafa Kemal Atatürk in 1923, the country has had a tense relationship with the minorities within its borders. In the first year of modern Turkey's existence, an enormous stream of Turkish refugees immediately flowed in from Greece, while Greeks from Turkey travelled in the other direction. In the east of Turkey, a focused campaign had already been in place since 1914 to disarm, expel and kill the Armenians living there. To this day, the Turkish government has denied this Armenian genocide.

With the disappearance of the Armenians and Greeks, the Kurds became the largest minority in Turkey. It was recorded in the country's constitution that every Turkish citizen is a Turk. The Kurds were denied the state they had previously been promised. From that moment, the Turkish government no longer recognized the Kurds as a people but as 'mountain Turks'. Resistance to this notion is an important part of the Kurdish struggle, which has been a constant factor in modern Turkish history ever since, and which has become increasingly radical, particularly since the 80s.

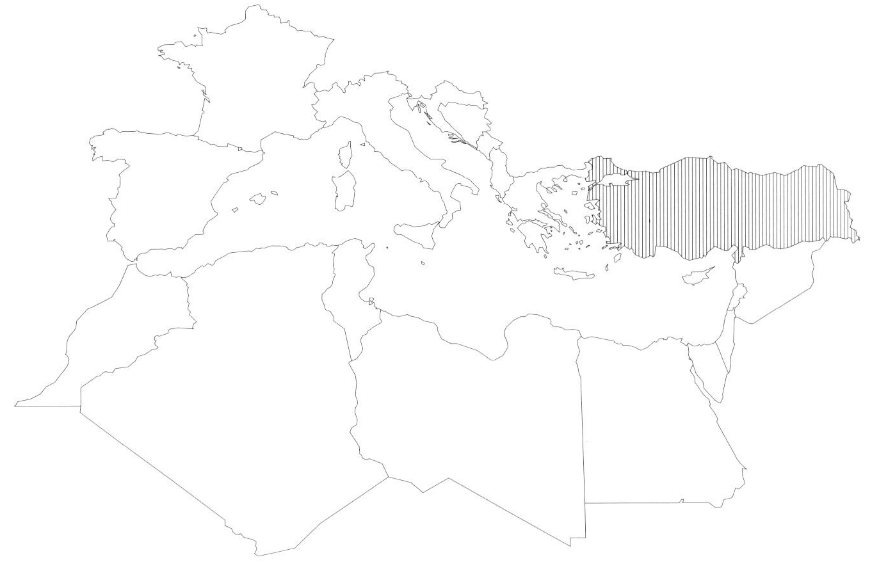

DIFFERENT NATIONALITIES
IN %

GIBRALTAR	1]	
SPAIN	2]	
FRANCE	3]	
ITALY	4]	
CROATIA	5]	
ALBANIA	6]	
GREECE	7]	
CYPRUS	8]	
TURKEY	**9]**	
SYRIA	10]	
LEBANON	11]	
ISRAEL	12]	
W.B.& GAZA		
EGYPT	13]	
LIBYA	14]	
TUNISIA	15]	
ALGERIA	16]	
MOROCCO	17]	

SOURCE : THE CIA WORLD FACTBOOK

1] : GIBRALTARIAN:81.20, UK BRITISH:11.37, OTHER:7.43

2] : SPANIARD:44.9, CATALONIAN:28, GALICIAN:8.2, BASQUE:5.5, ARAGONESE:5, EXTREMADURAN:2.8, ROMA (GITANOS/ GYPSY):2, OTHER:3.6

3] : FRENCH:76.9, ALGERIAN AND MOROCCAN BERBER:2.2, ITALIAN:1.9, PORTUGUESE:1.5, MOROCCAN ARAB:1.5, FLEMING:1.4, ALGERIAN ARAB:1.3, OTHER:13.3

4] : ITALIAN:96, NORTH AFRICAN ARAB:0.9, ITALO-ALBANIAN:0.8, ALBANIAN:0.5, OTHER:1.8

5] : CROAT:89.6, SERB:4.5, OTHER:5.9

6] : ALBANIAN:95, GREEK:3, OTHER:2

7] : GREEK:93, OTHER:7

8] : GREEK:77, TURKISH:18, OTHER:5

9] : TURKISH:80, KURDISH:20

10] : ARAB:90.3, KURDS, ARMENIAN, OTHER:9.7

11] : ARAB:95, ARMENIAN:4, OTHER:1

12] : JEWISH:76.4, NON-JEWISH:23.6

13] : EGYPTIAN:98, BERBER, NUBIAN, BEDUIN, BEJA:1, GREEK, ARMENIAN, OTHER EUROPEANS:1

14] : BERBER, ARAB:97, OTHER:3

15] : ARAB:98, EUROPEAN:1, JEWISH, OTHER:1

16] : ARAB-BERBER:99, EUROPEAN:<1

17] : ARAB-BERBER:99.1, OTHER:0.7, JEWISH:0.2

119. DALYAN
Afternoon in the public park at the Dalyan health resort. Mass tourism has not arrived here yet, although the resort does attract many day-trippers.

121. KEMER
Orange County is a replica of Amsterdam. In front of the entrance stands the Dutch National War Monument. It attracts mainly Dutch and Russian tourists. At 8 o'clock every morning, a cock crows from the loudspeakers and the day's programme begins.

123. LARA
A family from one of the Gulf States in the replica Kremlin. On a small strip of land on the coast, replicas of the Kremlin, Topkapi Palace, Venice and the supersonic jet Concorde have been built.

124. KEMER
The walled resort is shut off from the outside world. And why would you want to go there anyway? Inside the resort, food and drinks are free.

126. DALYAN
Visitors to this mud bath are transported by boat. It is so busy here that it resembles a teeming anthill. Turkey has eclipsed Spain in low-budget tourism.

128. LARA
Conference centre in the replica Kremlin. Outside the tourist season, companies hire the hotels.

131. LARA
Lara's public park stands in shrill contrast to the theme resorts. You see absolutely no foreigners here. The only facility on this expanse of sand is a shower.

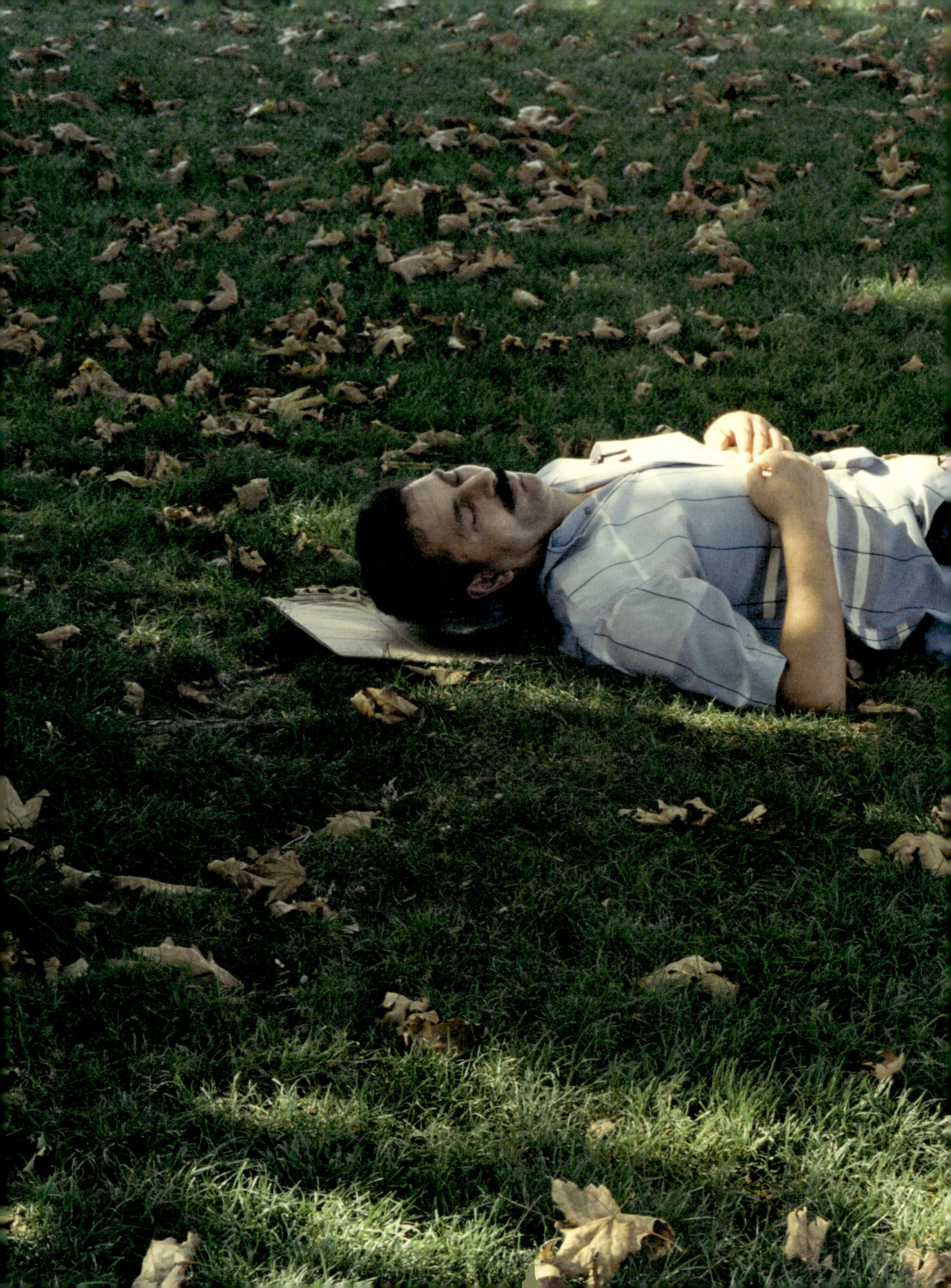

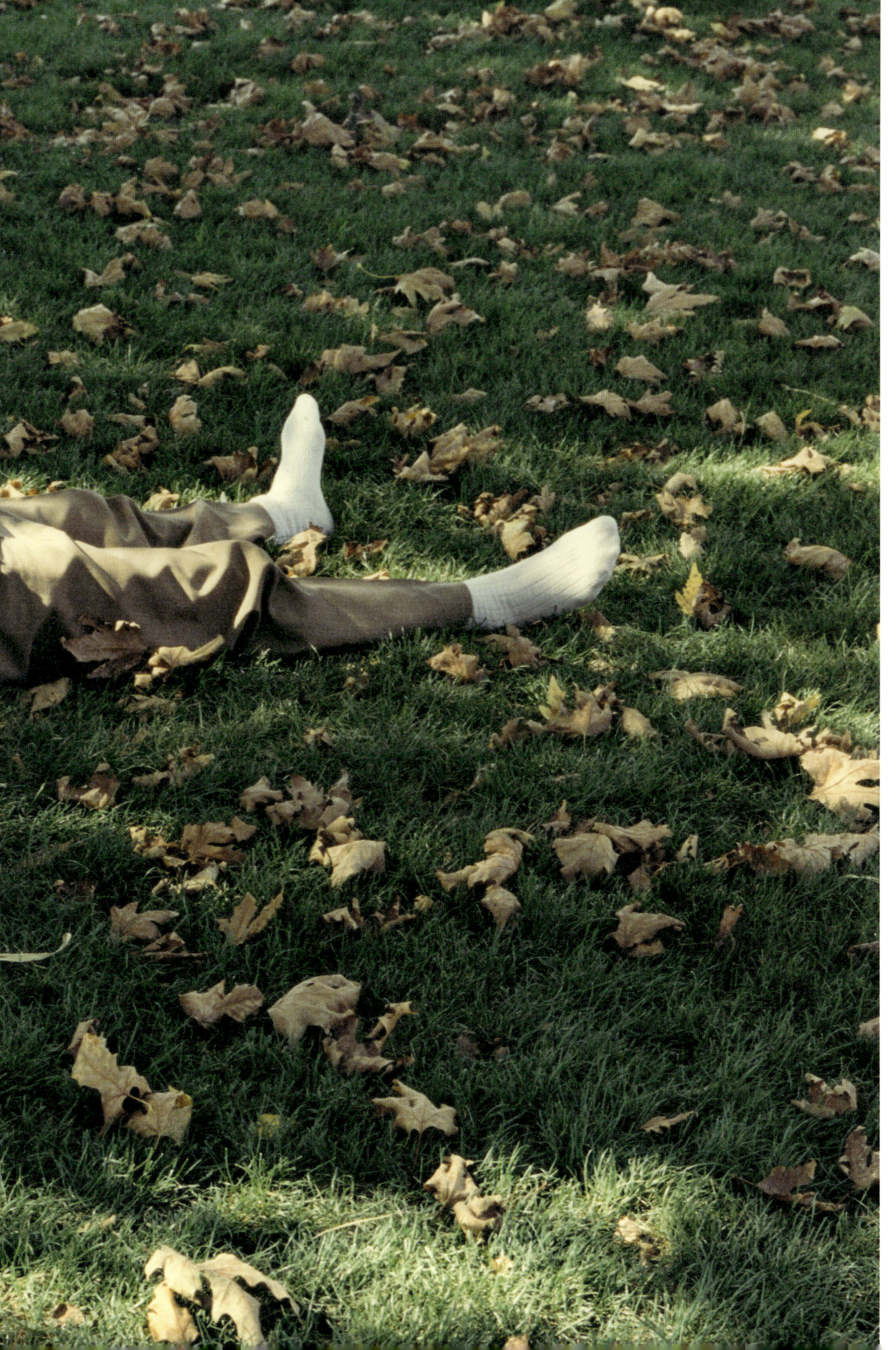

119.

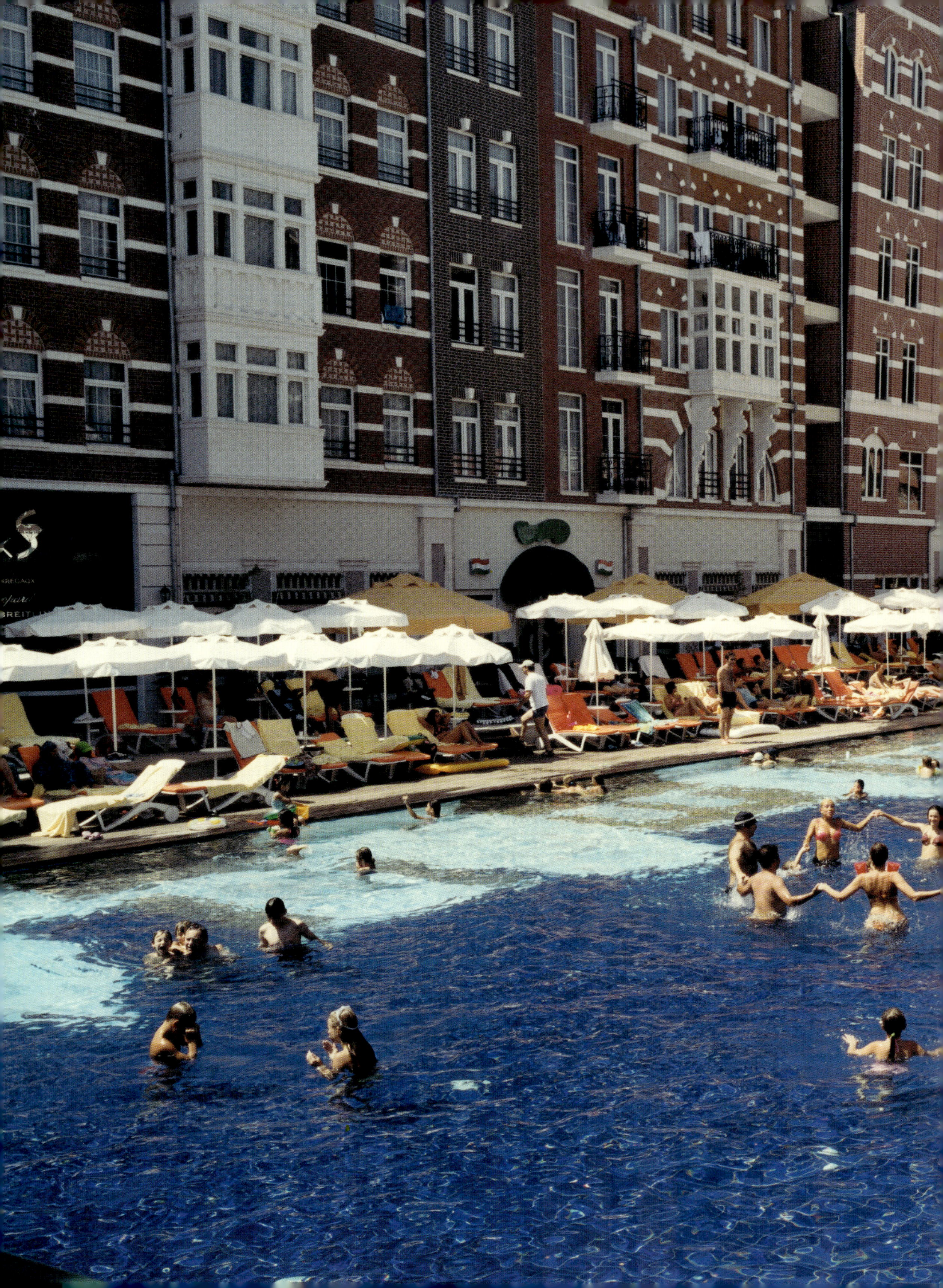

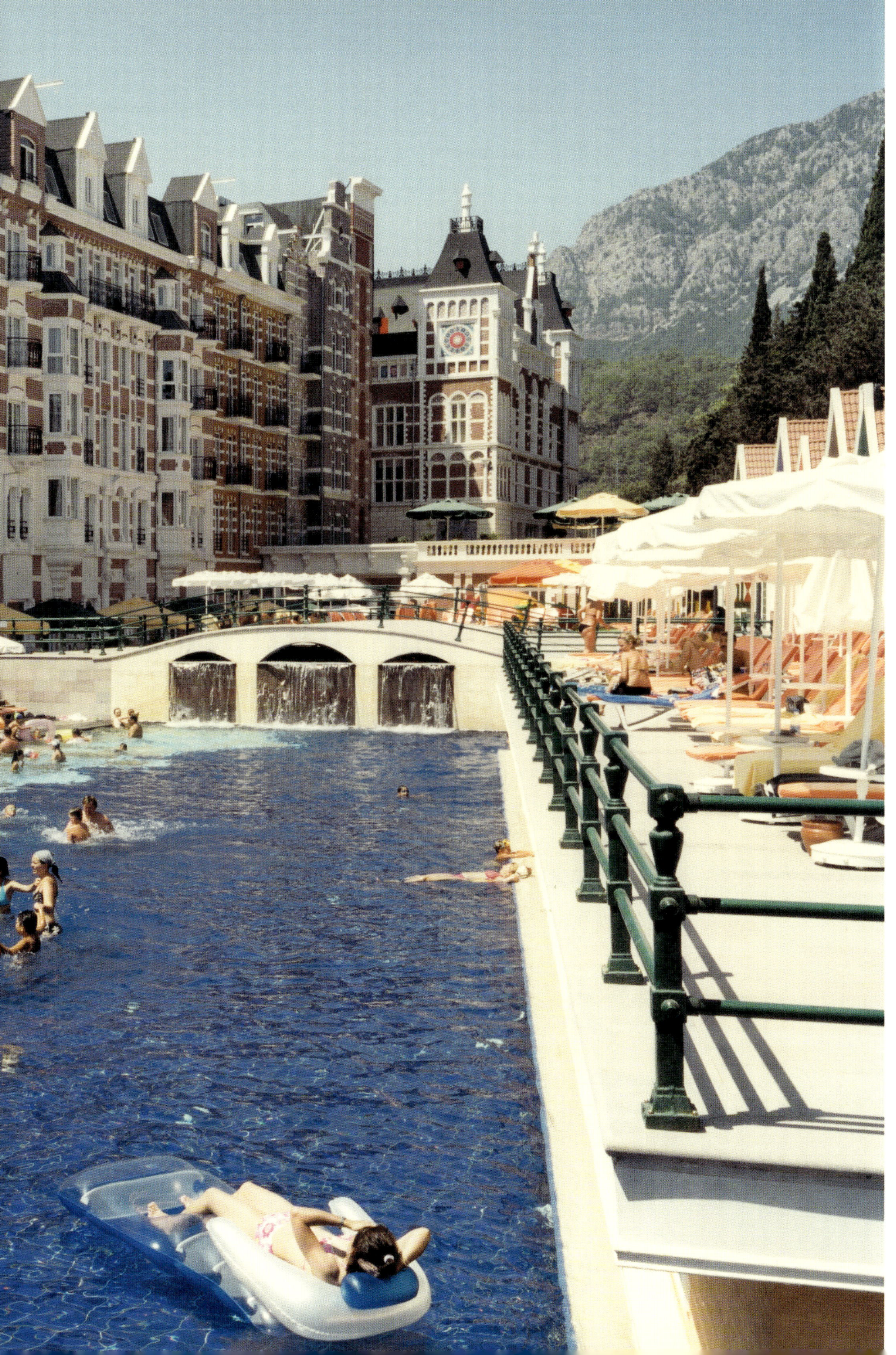

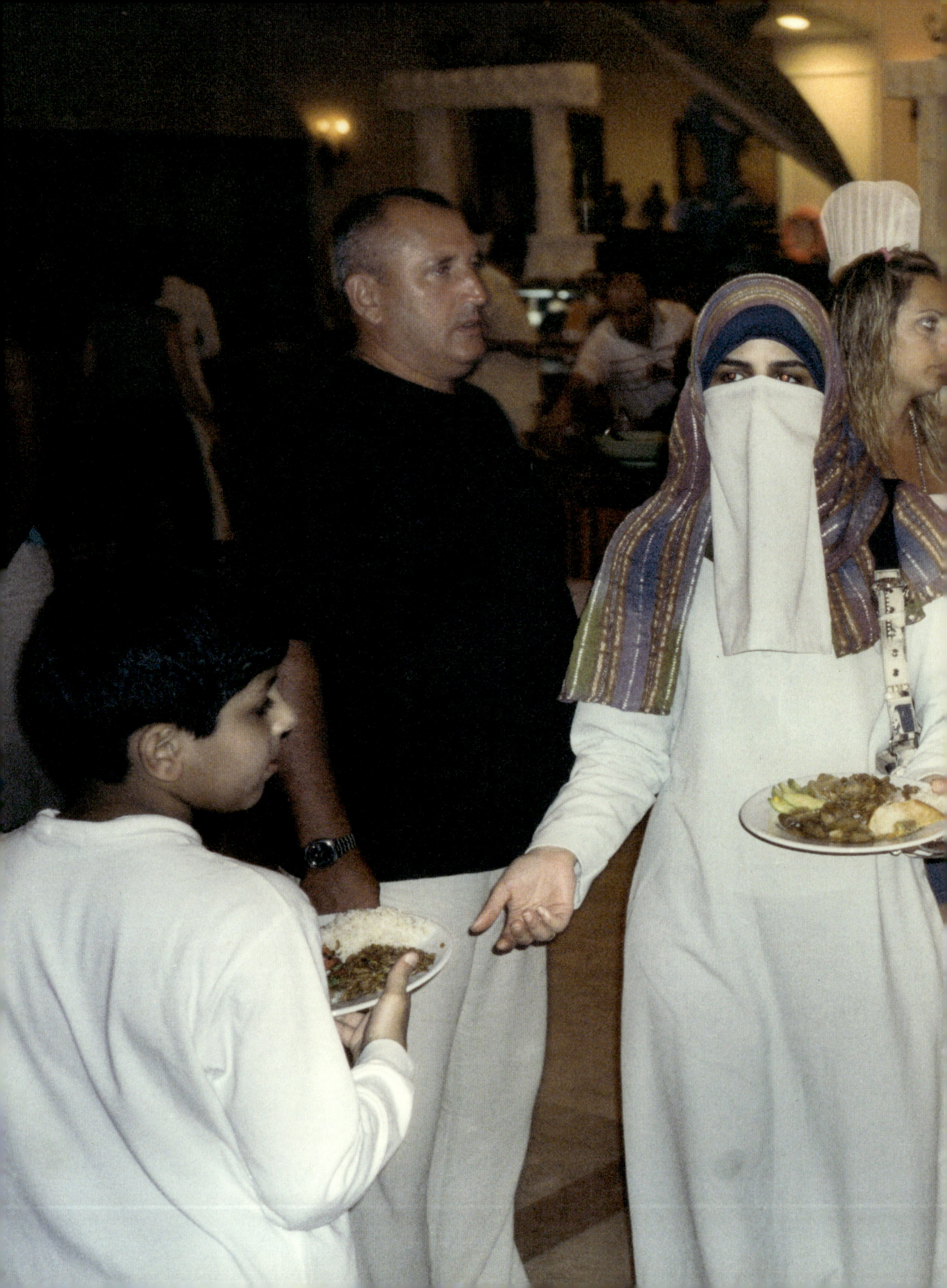

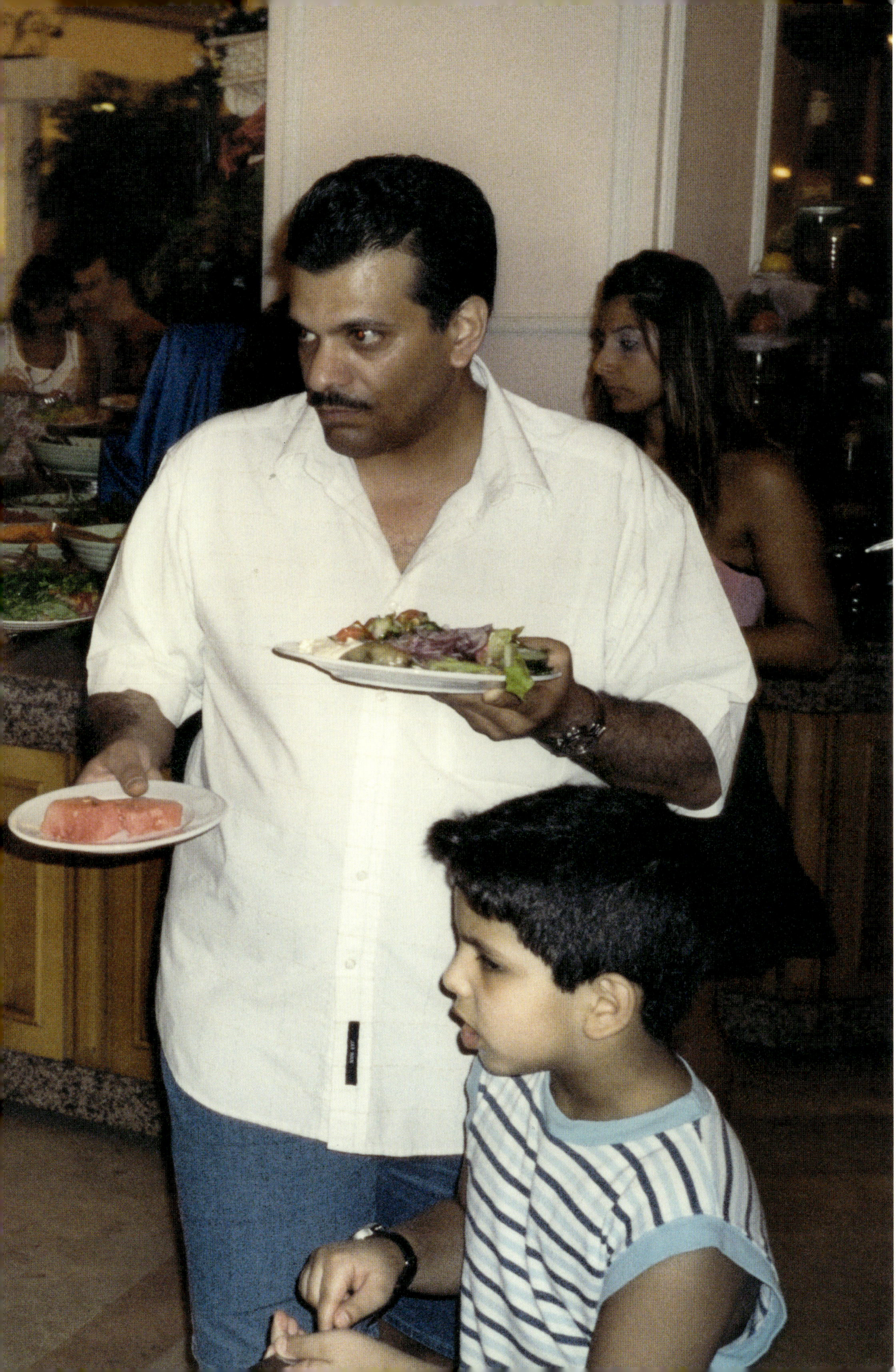

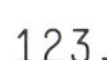

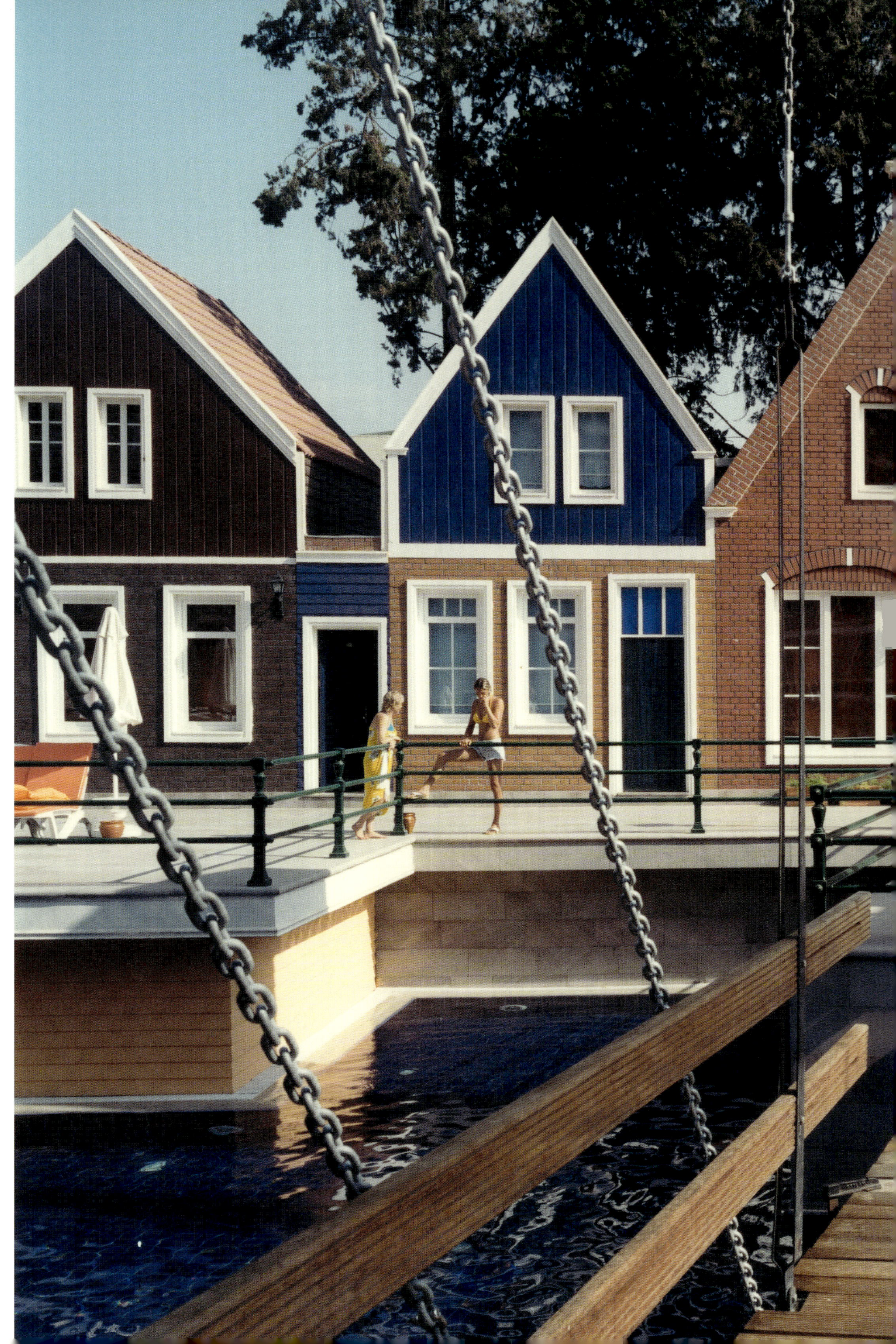

124.

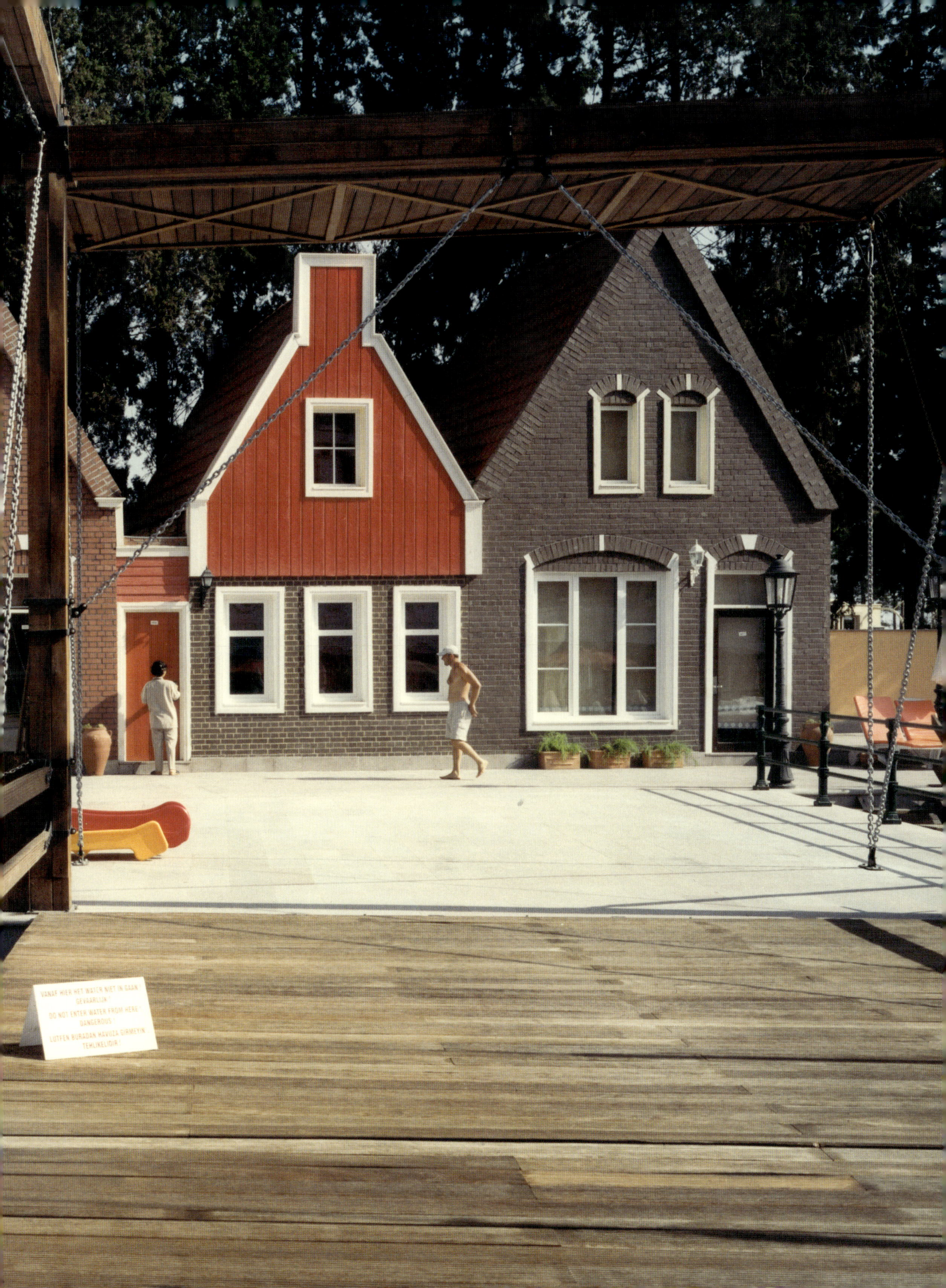
VANAF HIER HET WATER NIET IN GAAN !
GEVAARLIJK !
DO NOT ENTER WATER FROM HERE !
DANGEROUS !
LÜTFEN BURADAN HAVUZA GIRMEYIN
TEHLIKELIDIR !

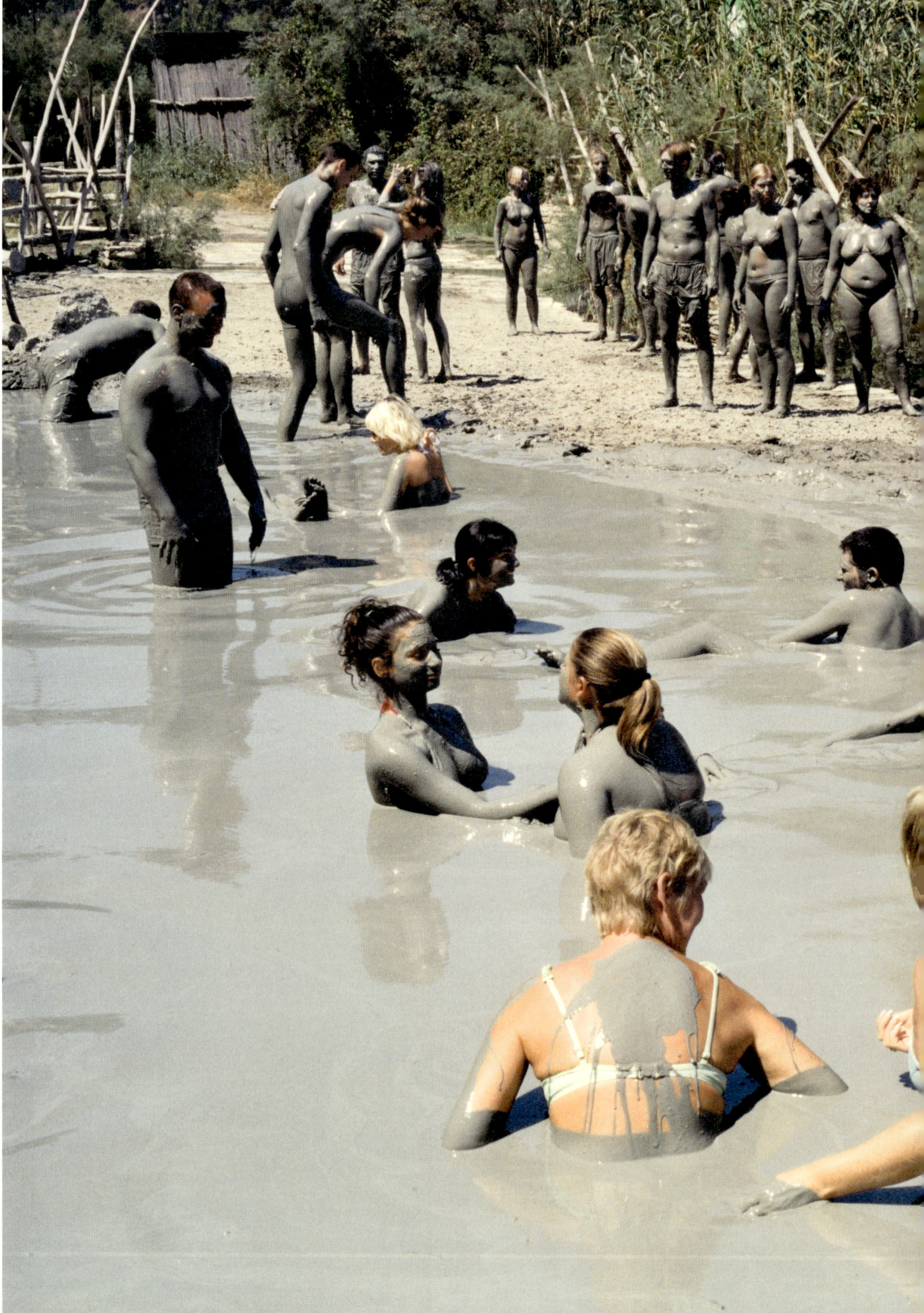

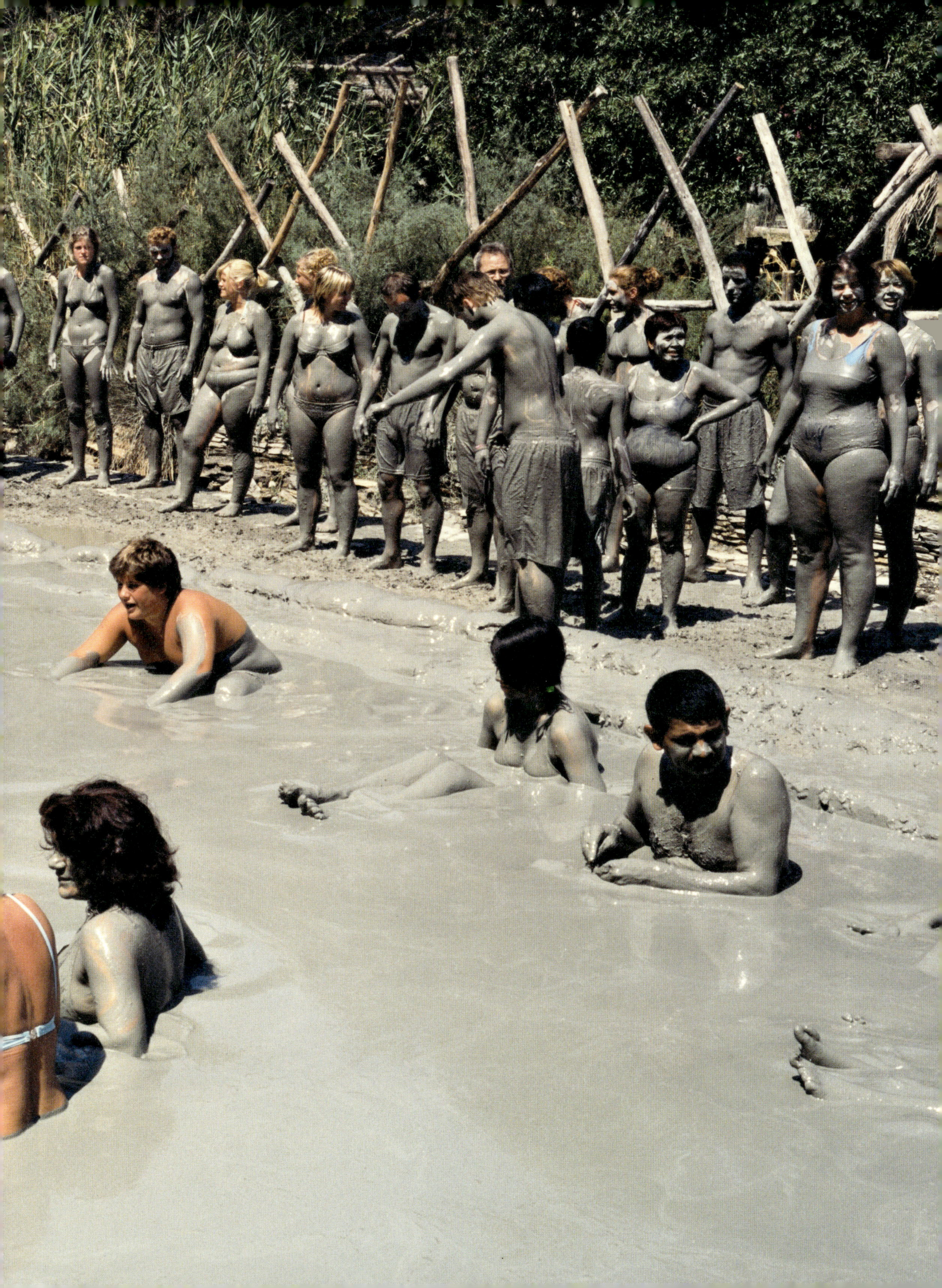

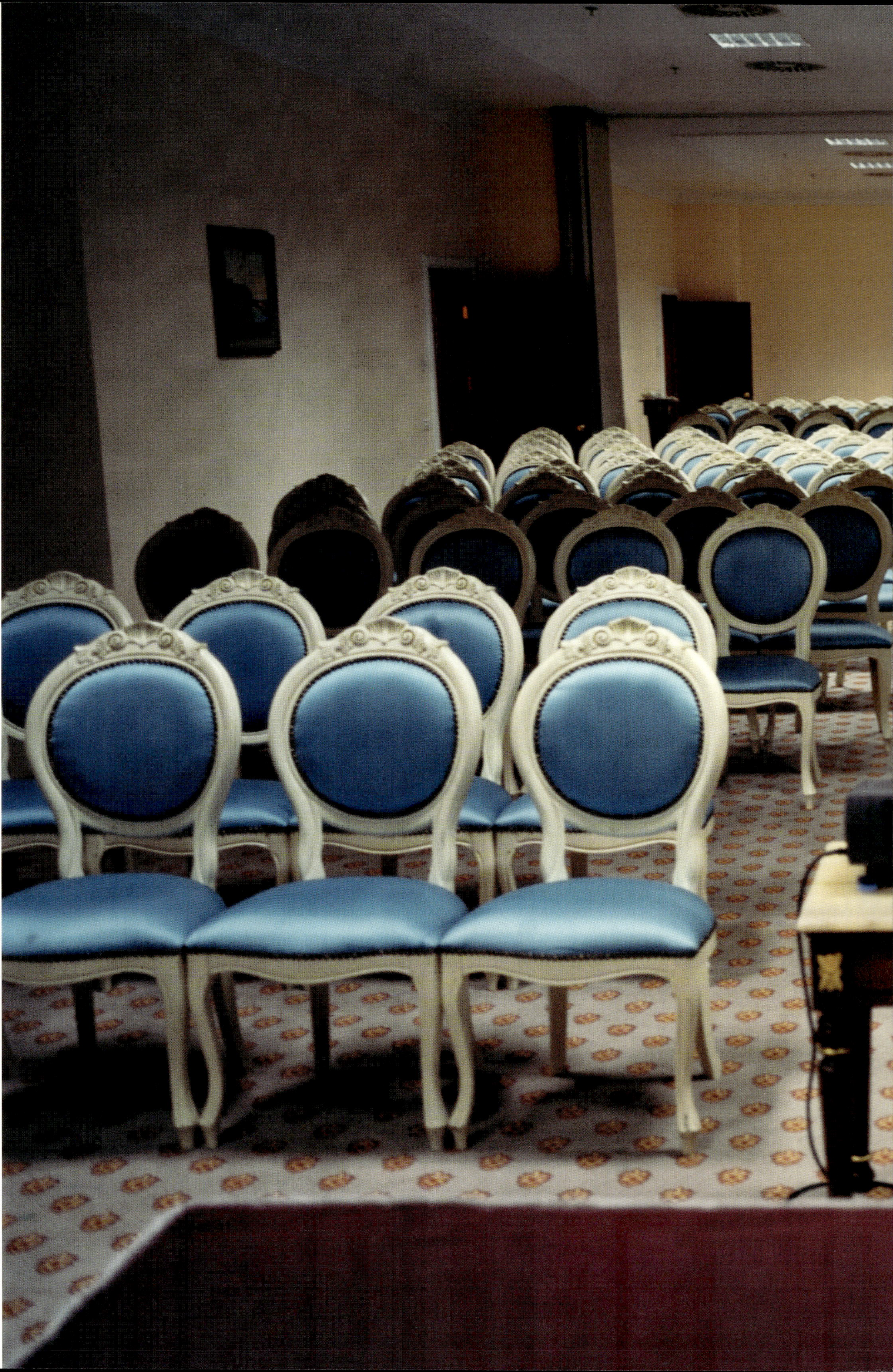

128.

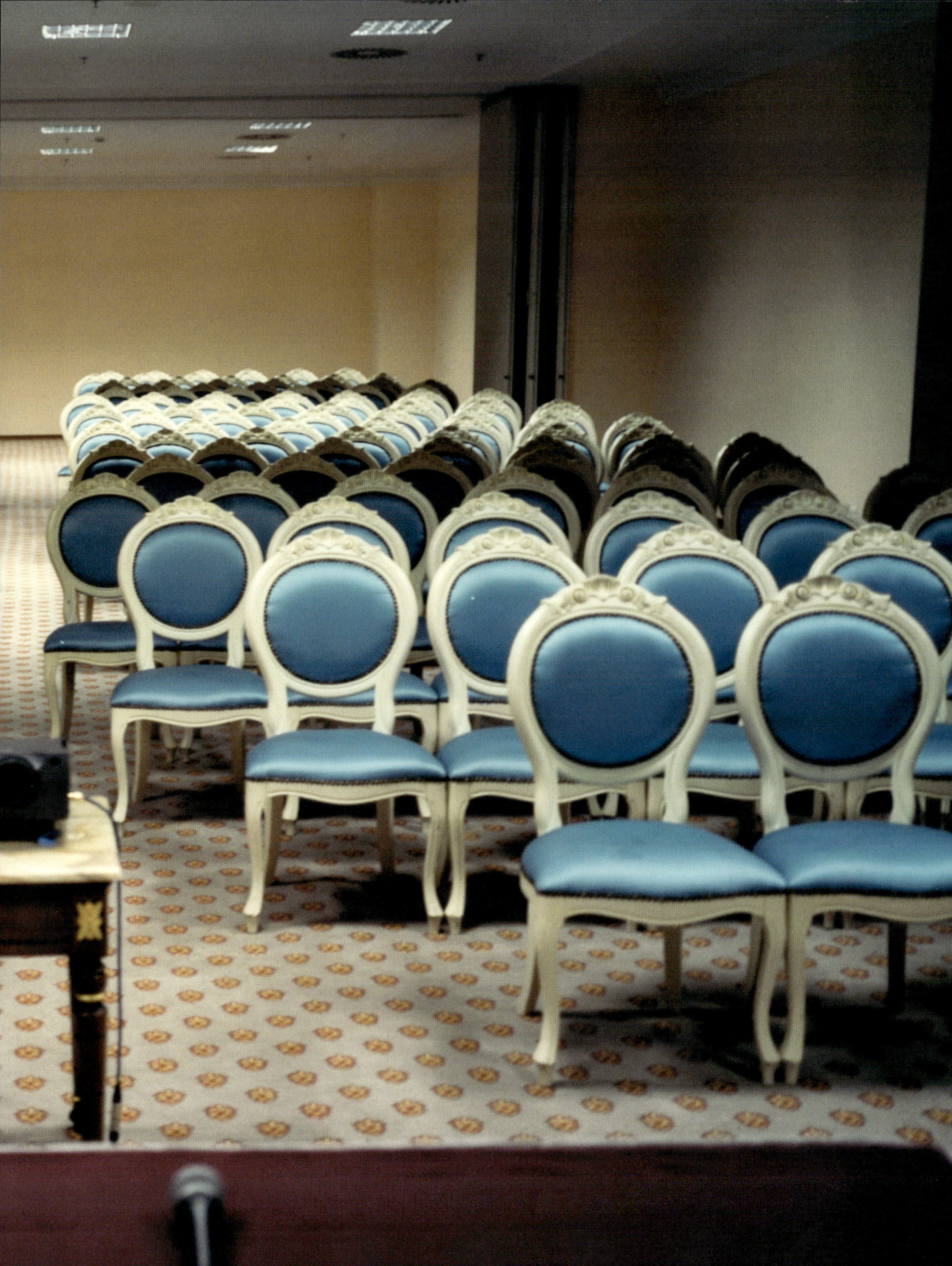

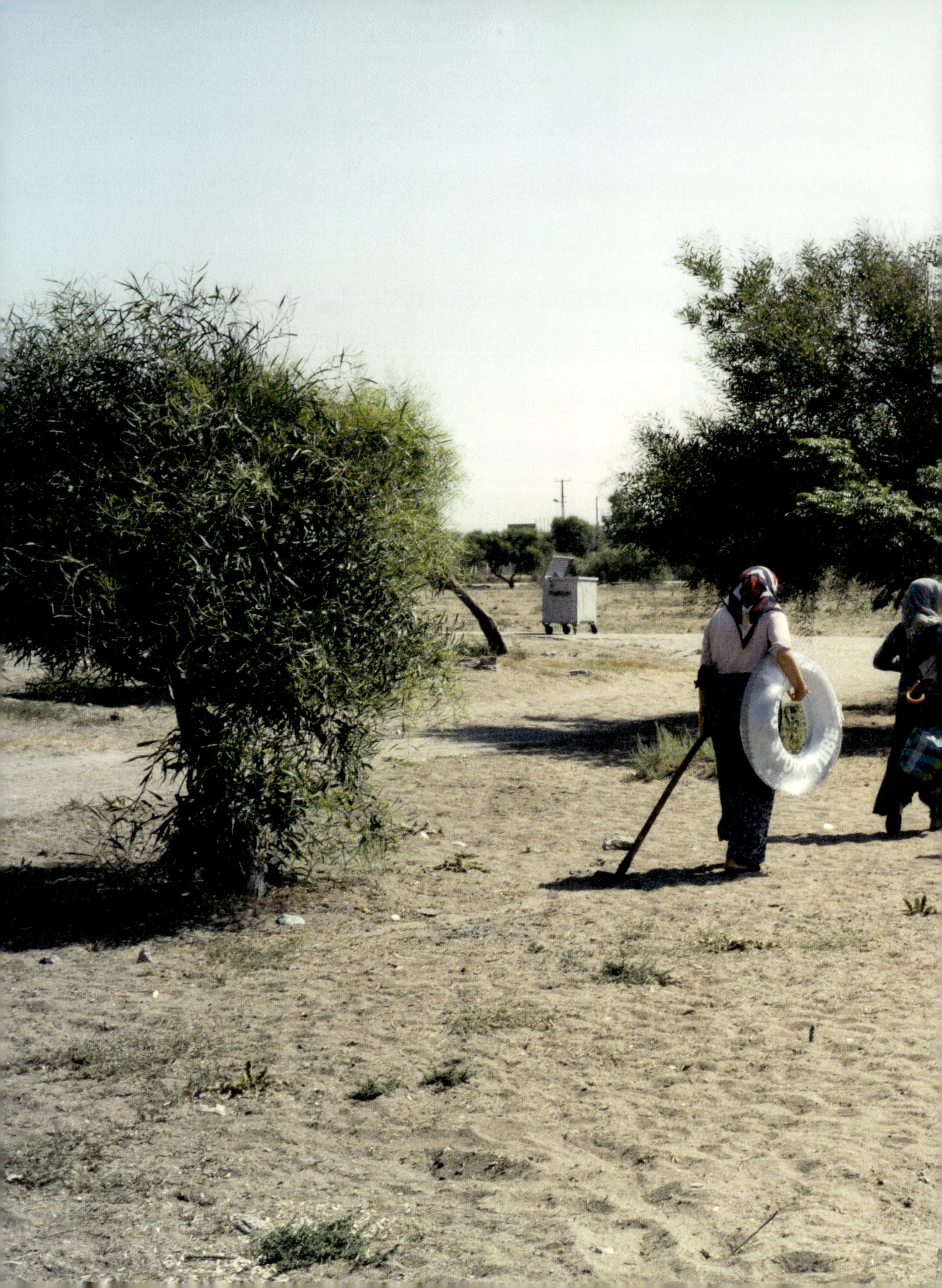

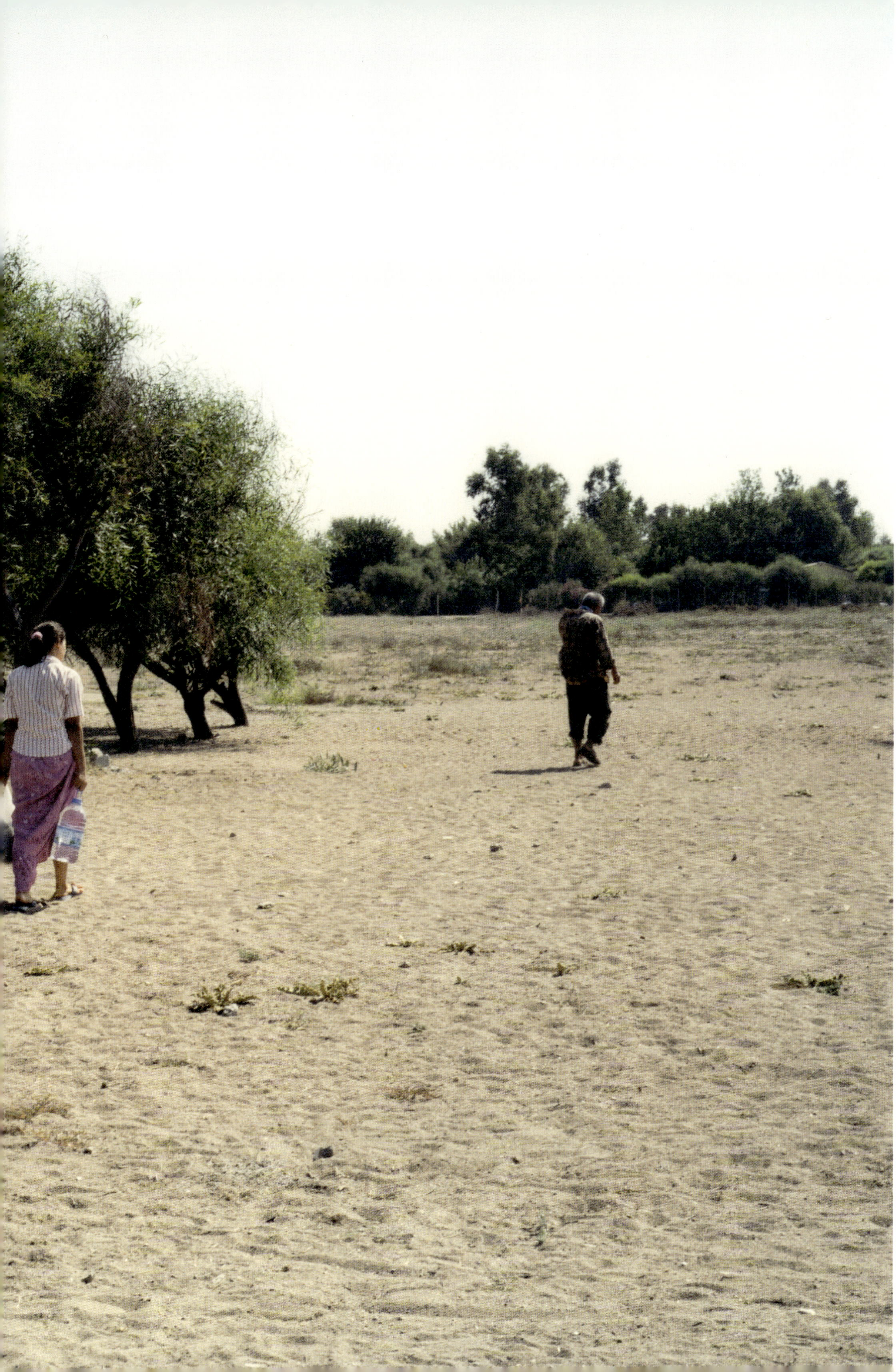

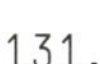

In Algeria they are called 'wall-hangers'. Anyone who has visited a developing country will have seen them: large groups of youngsters who hang around on streets, squares and in parks. Often, they are bored. They don't have much to do, unemployment is high and there is no money to enjoy themselves. The causes of this over-representation of young people are the high birth rate and improved healthcare in developing countries during recent decades. In the Mediterranean, Syria is one of the most extreme examples of this.

More than a third of the Syrian population is younger than 14; almost 60% is younger than 24. The average age is 21. The population grows by 2.5% every year. The effect of this is worrying, because population growth nearly always leads to urbanization, social unrest and heightened tension between youth culture and the country's traditional culture.

Population growth also puts an enormous strain on a country's economy, leading, for instance, to price increases for basic goods such as grain and water. The high percentage of young people also costs the government money in, for example, an increased demand for education. At the same time, young people contribute little to the economy: in Syria's case, 40% of the population is not part of the workforce.

In short, a high birth rate can impoverish a country. As a result, the United Nations sees birth control as one of the most important instruments for halving world poverty by 2015, one of the so-called Millennium Goals the organization established in 2000.

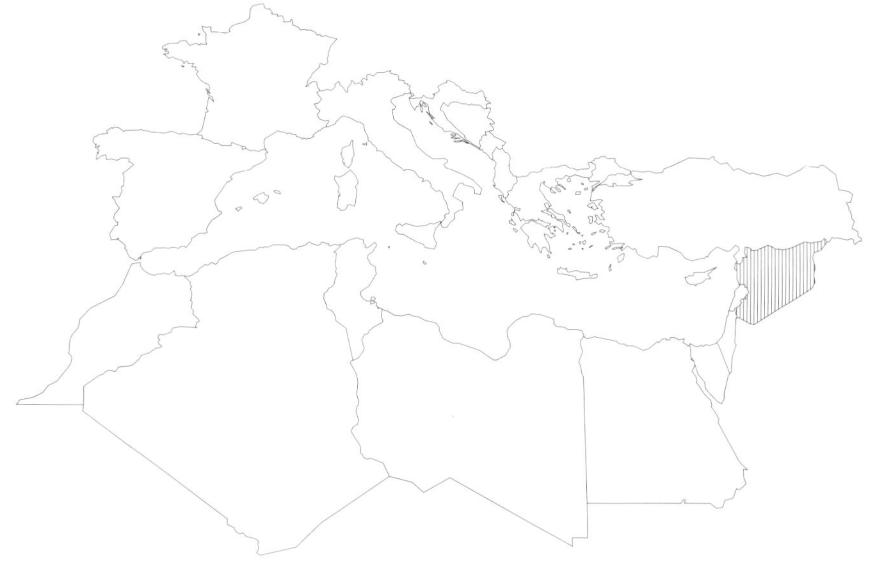

POPULATION UNDER 14

IN %

GIBRALTAR	17.2	
SPAIN	14.4	
FRANCE	18.6	
ITALY	13.8	
CROATIA	16.0	
ALBANIA	24.1	
GREECE	14.3	
CYPRUS	19.9	
TURKEY	24.9	
SYRIA	**36.5**	
LEBANON	26.2	
ISRAEL	26.1	
W.B. & GAZA	45.0	
EGYPT	32.2	
LIBYA	33.4	
TUNISIA	24.0	
ALGERIA	27.2	
MOROCCO	31.0	

SOURCE : THE CIA WORLD FACTBOOK

134. LATTAKIA

On the beach, one kilometre from Lattakia, is a large luxury hotel and villa development, both of which are only occupied during the summer. In the relaxed relationships between men and women you can still see clearly that Syria was once a socialist country.

136. DAMASCUS

Al Ittihad al'Arabi Street is the busiest street in Damascus. When the Four Seasons Hotel was opened by Bashir al-Assad and his Royal Highness Al-Walid bin Talad of Saudi Arabia, the street was completely sealed off.

139. LATTAKIA

Busloads of Iranian religious tourists make the pilgrimage to Zeinab's tomb in Syria. An official guide always accompanies them to ensure moral standards are maintained.

140. TARTUS

Al-Assad is everywhere. Every day, the front pages of the newspapers carry a photo of the president that stretches across three columns with whichever guest he received the day before. Sometimes he also cuts a ribbon or picks up a child.

143. LATTAKIA

After Friday prayers, everyone takes to the streets. Lattakia's boulevard is the central meeting place.

145. DAMASCUS

View from a hotel room. There are streets in Damascus with nothing on them except law firms. This could be because Syria is extremely bureaucratic.

147. BARADA GORGE

No other country has such a strong picnic tradition. Drive through the country on a Friday afternoon, and you will see families sitting everywhere, some of them up to 40 kilometres from their homes.

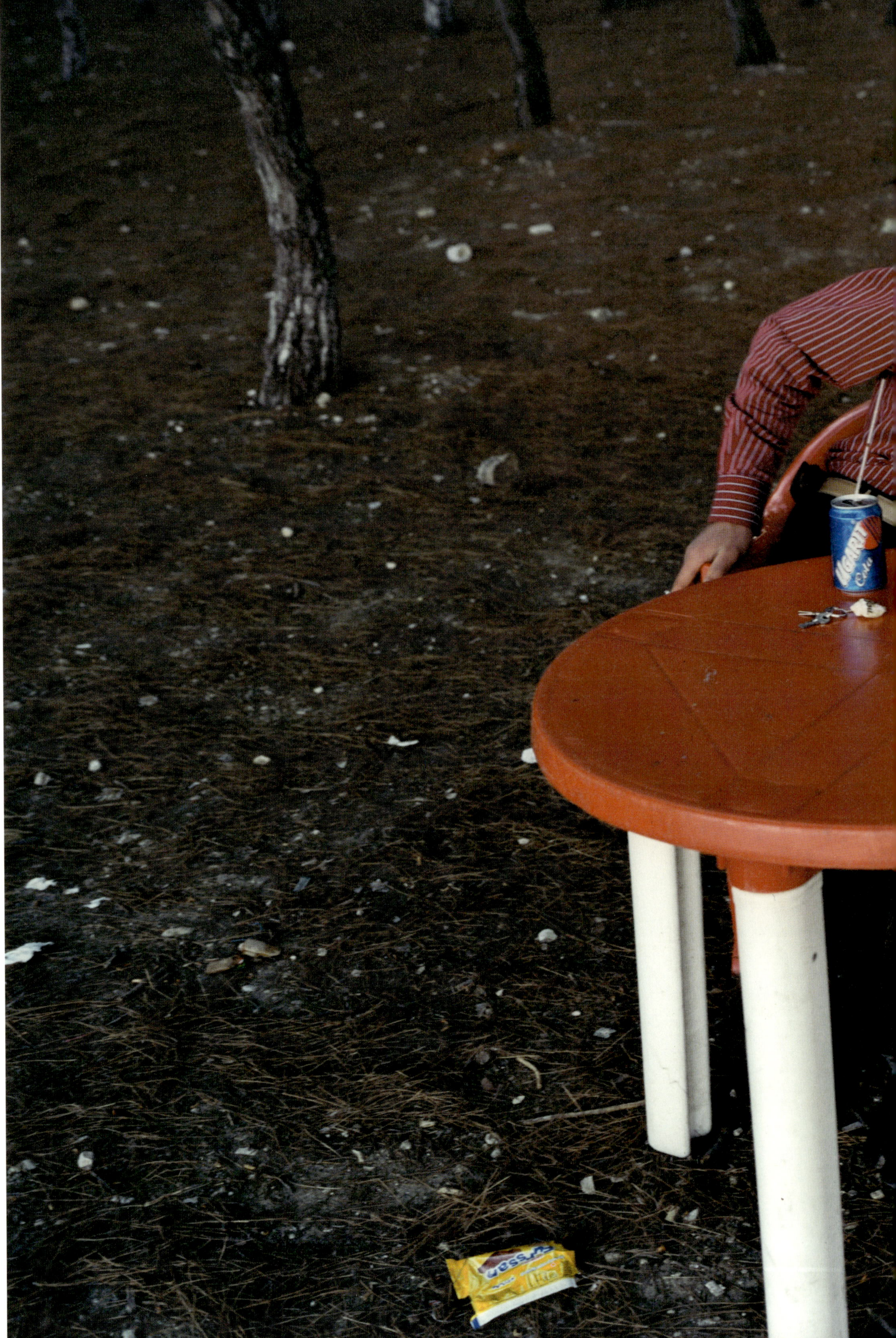

134.

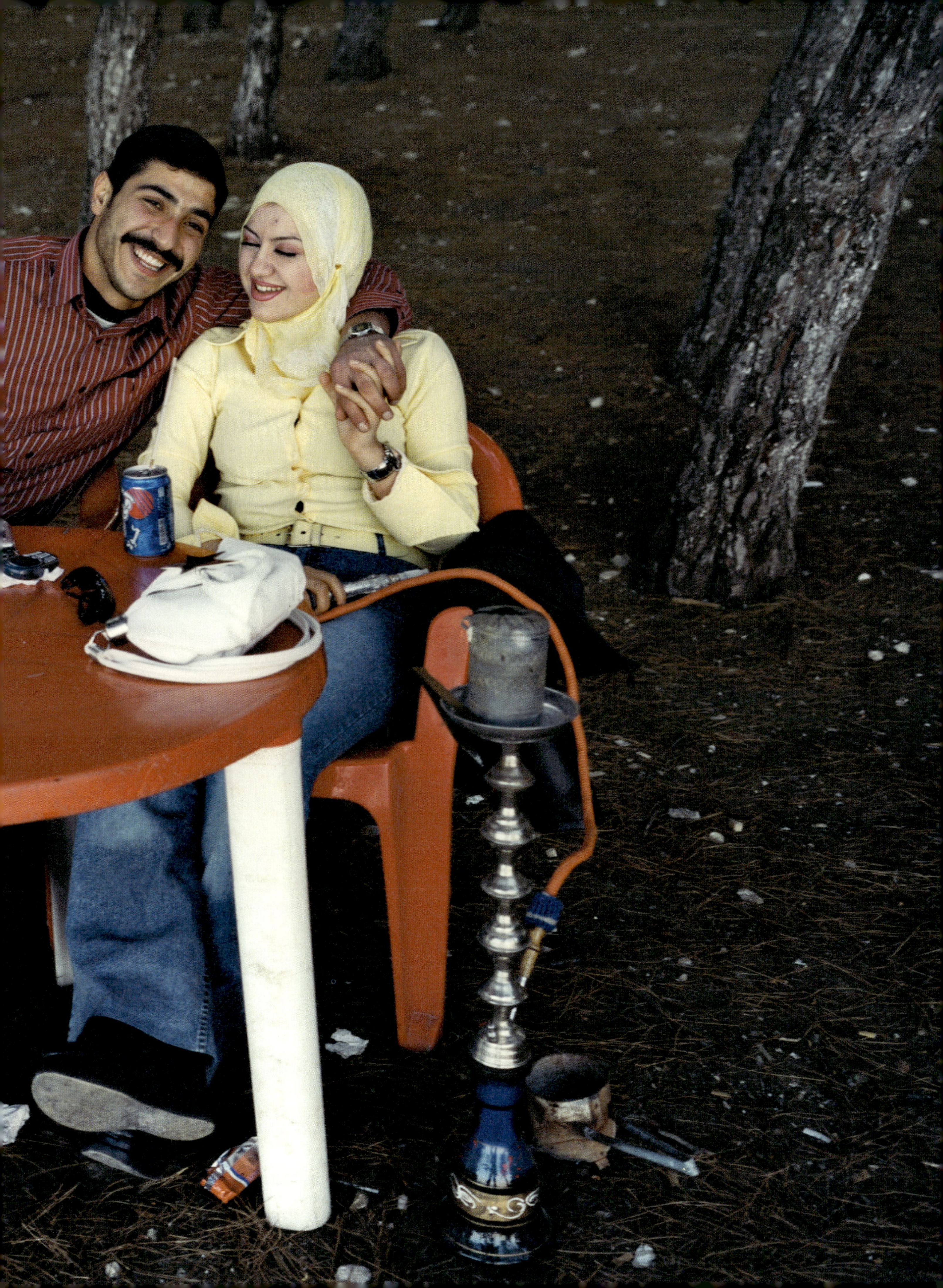

136.

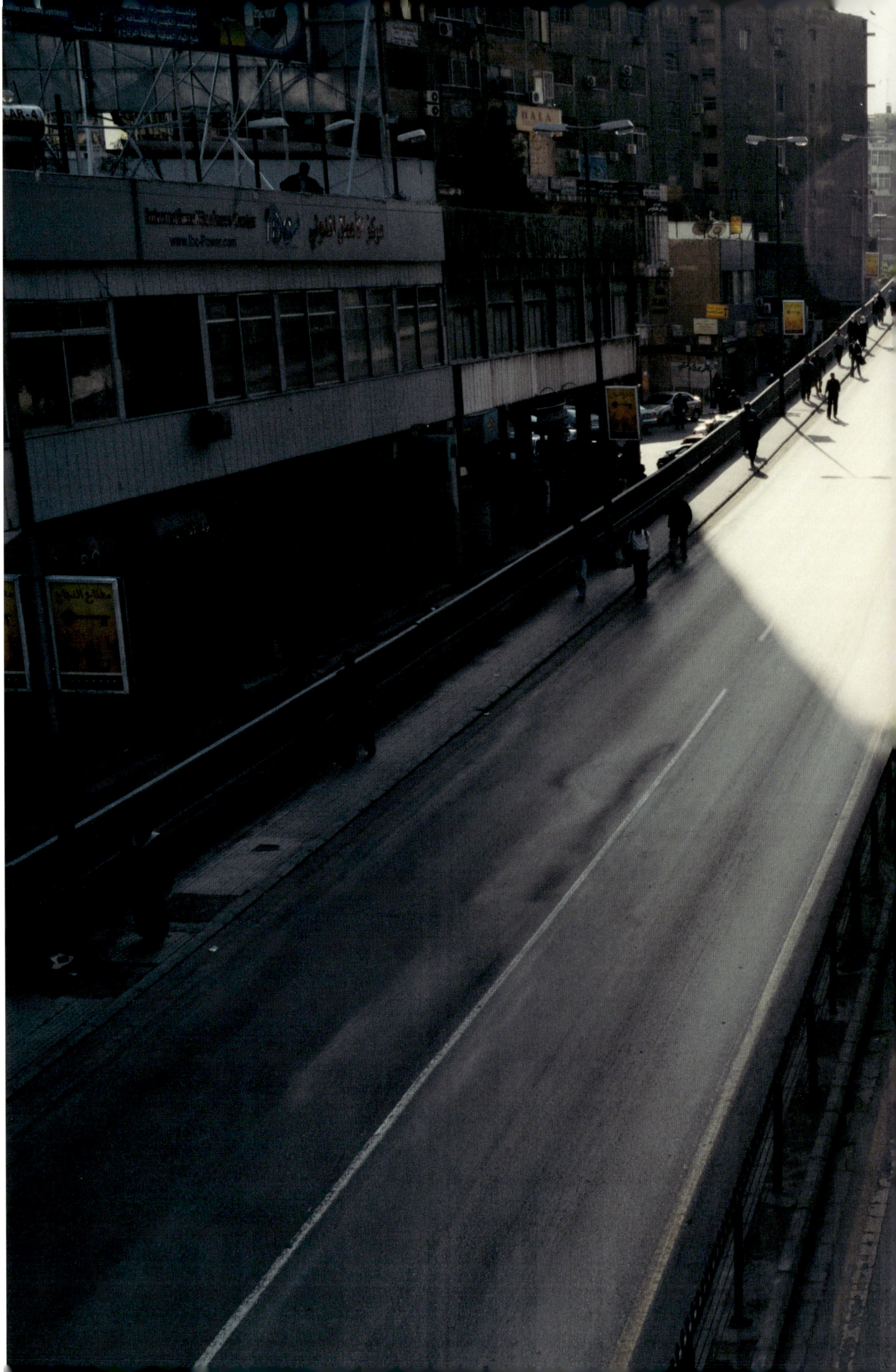

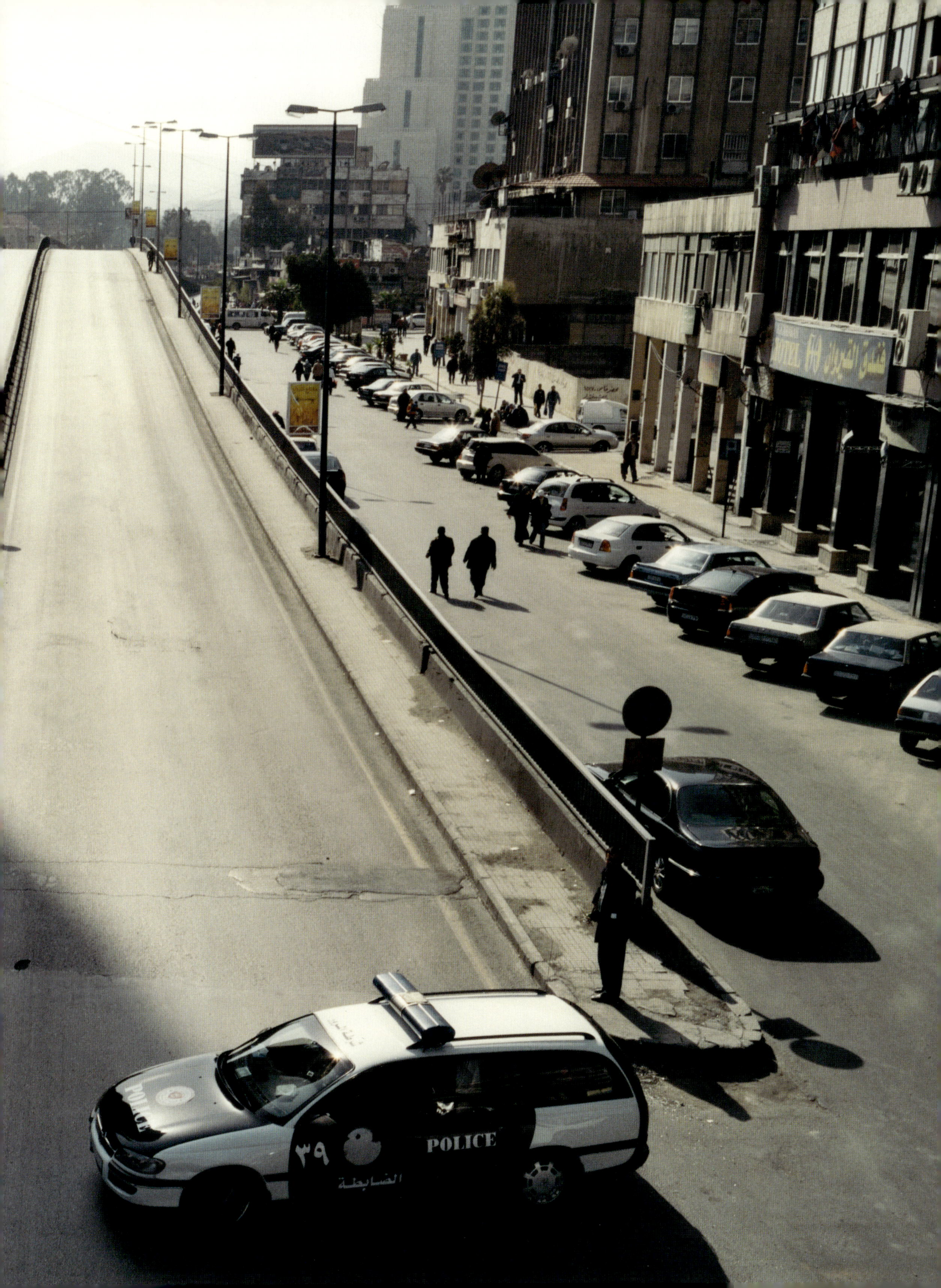
POLICE
٣٩
الضابطة

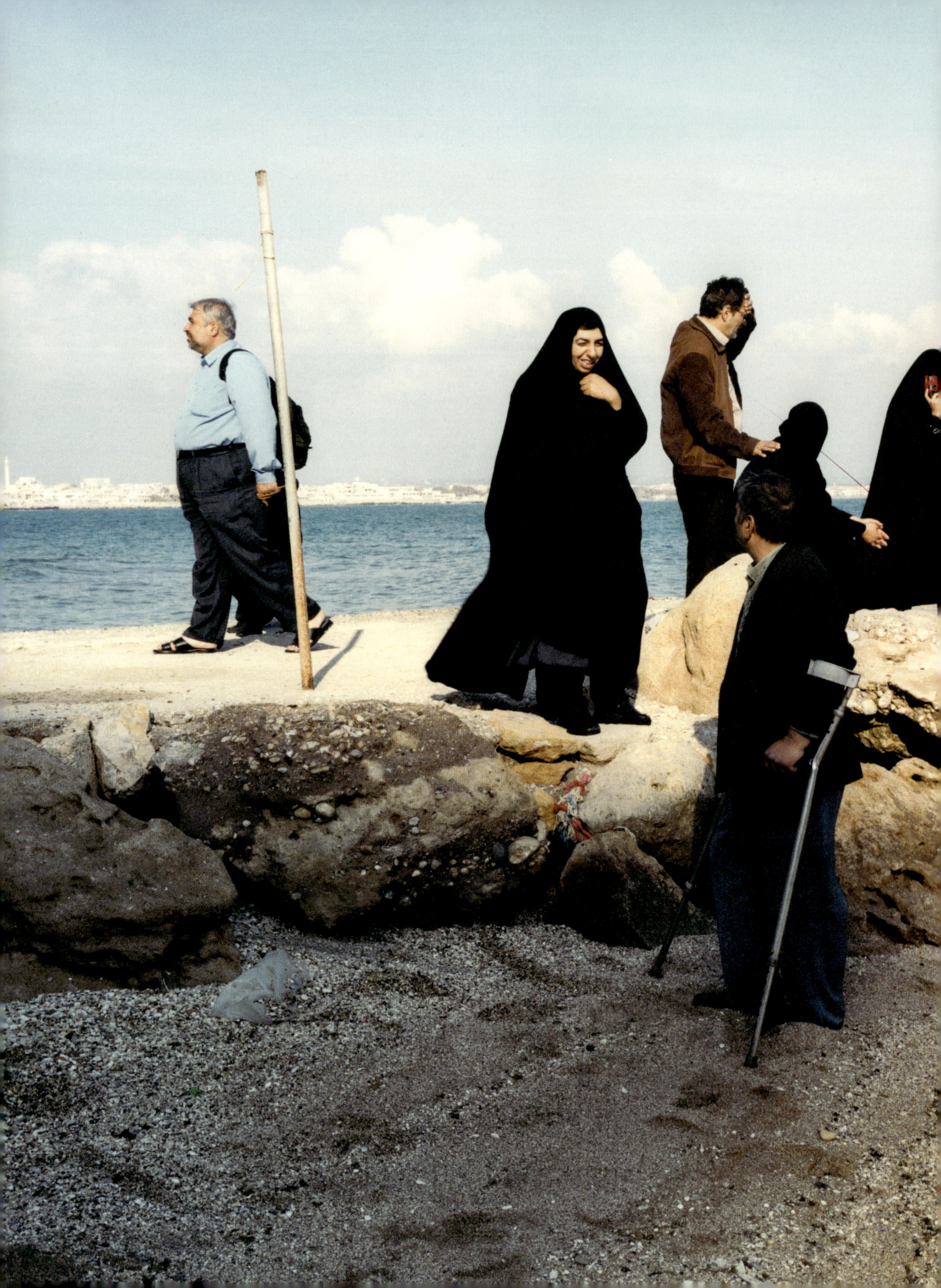

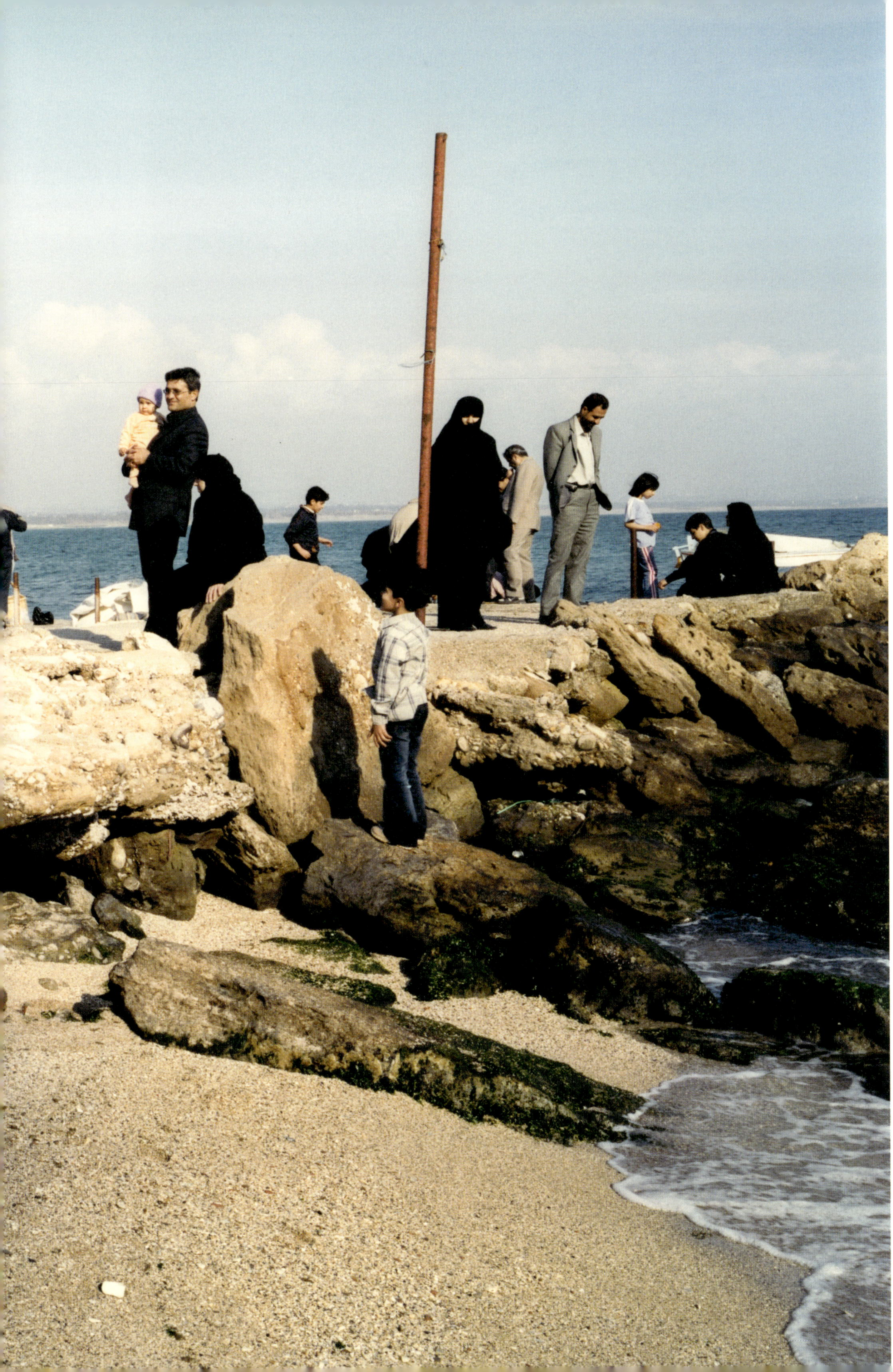

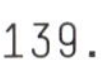

139.

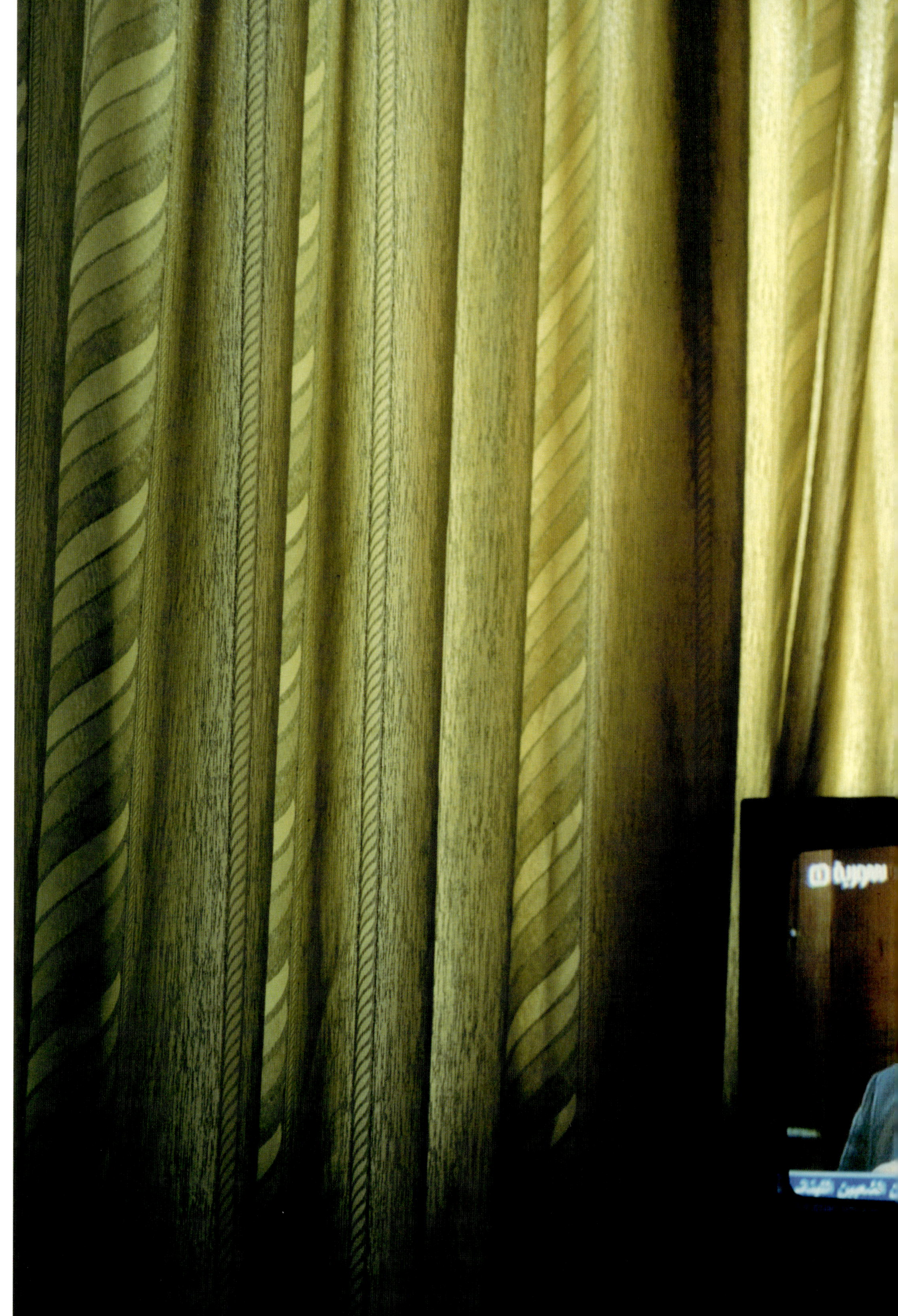

140.

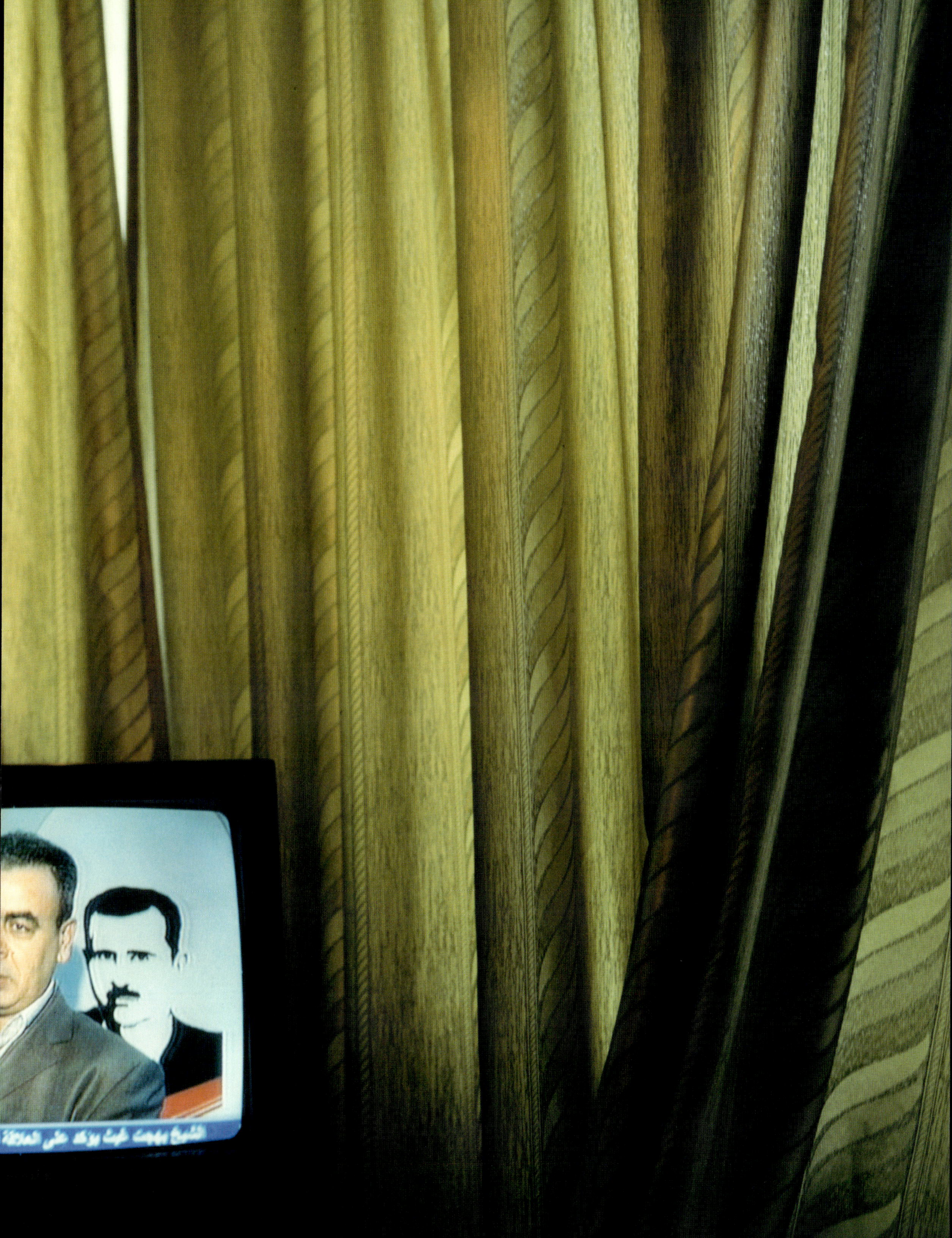

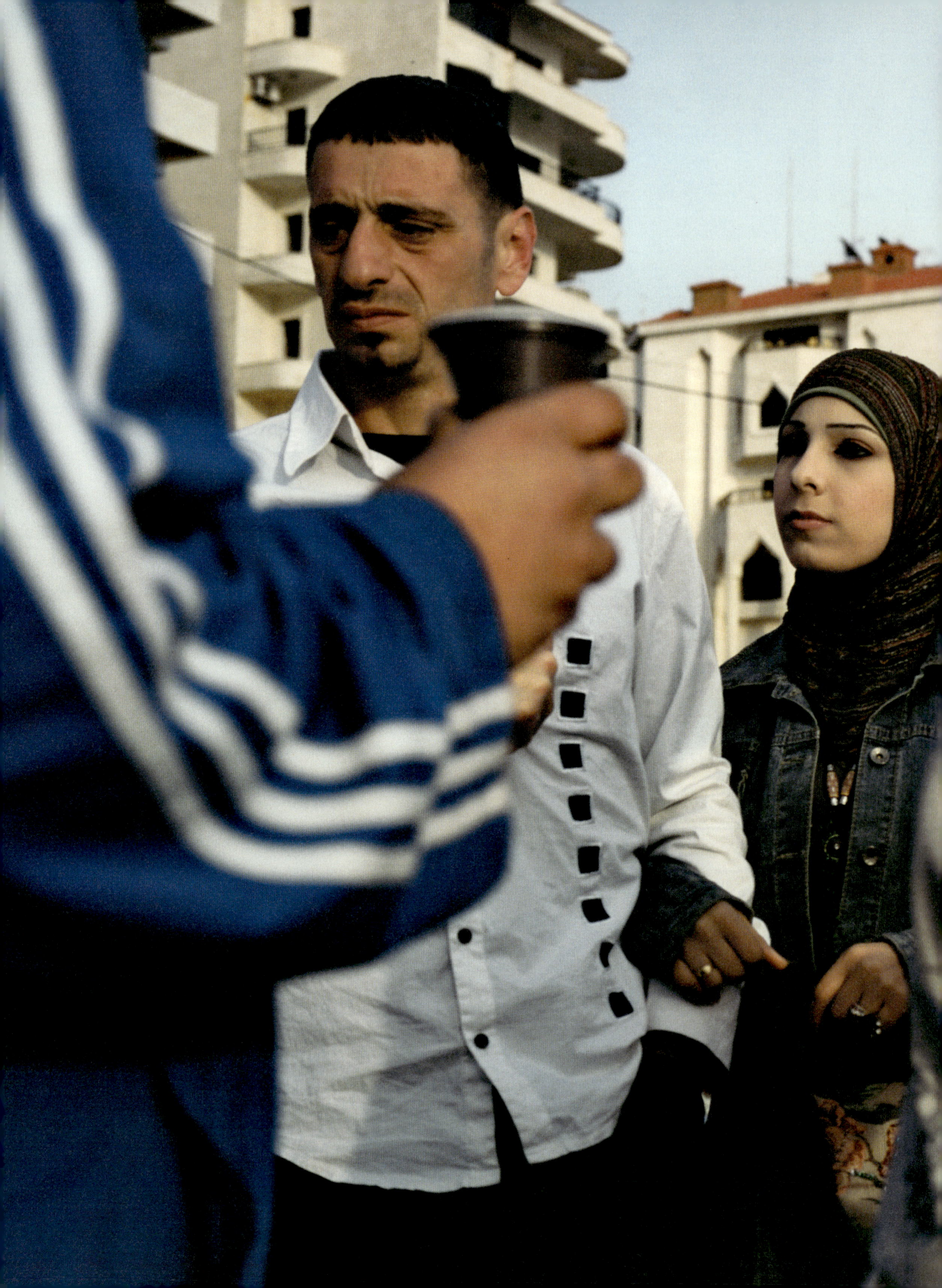

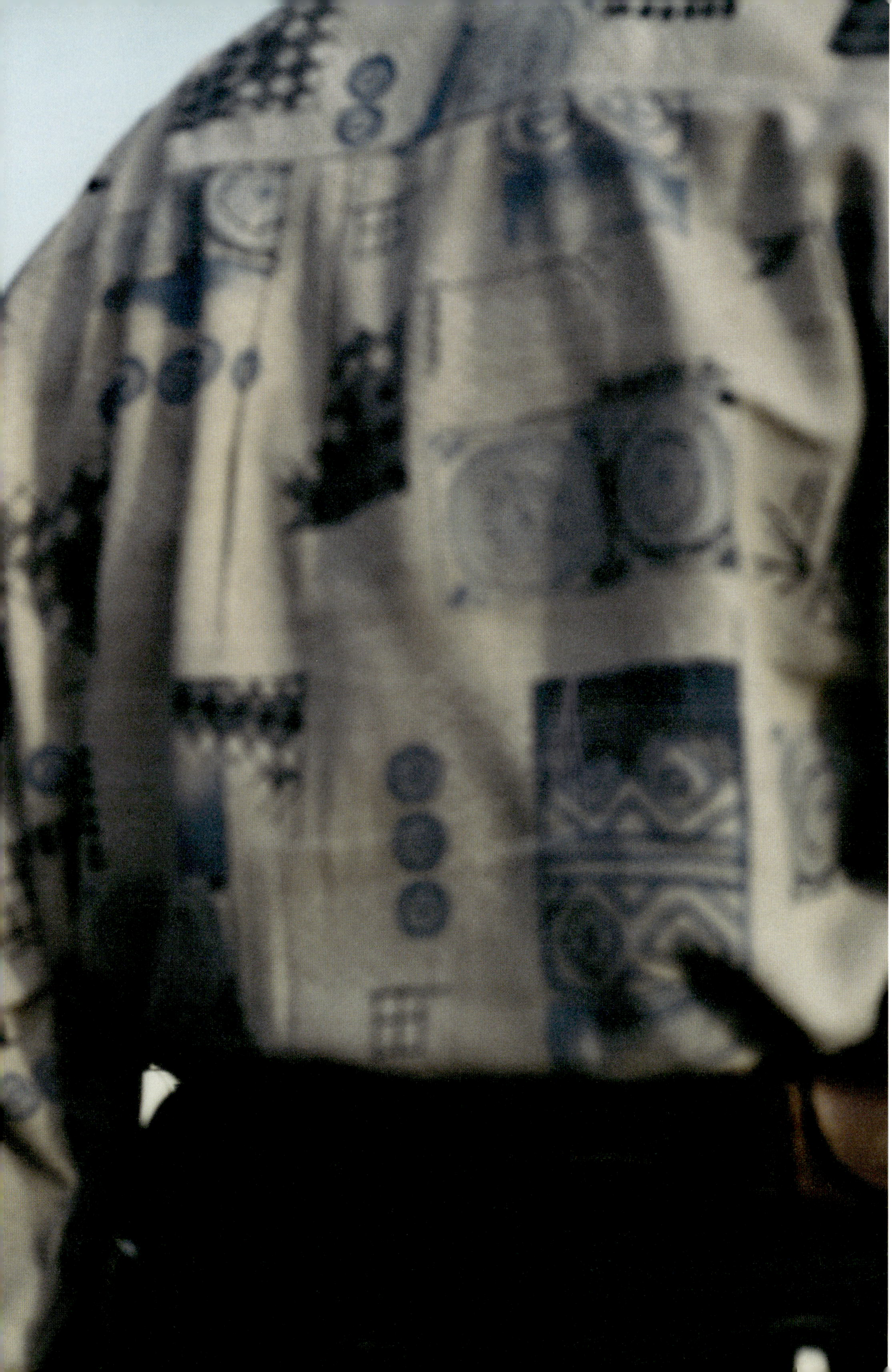

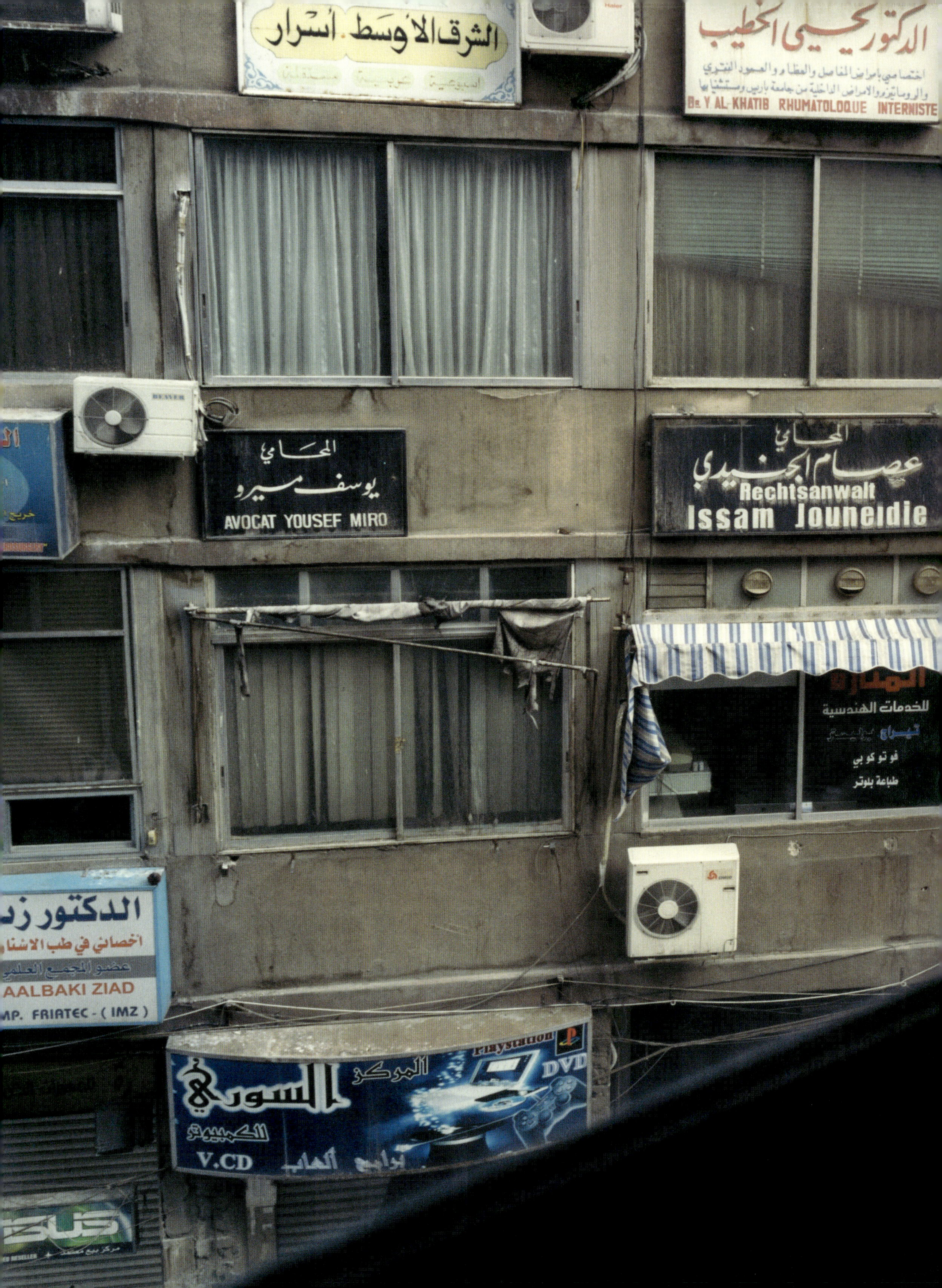
الشرق الأوسط أسرار
الدكتور يحيى الخطيب
Dr. Y AL-KHATIB RHUMATOLOQUE INTERNISTE
المحامي
يوسف ميرو
AVOCAT YOUSEF MIRO
المحامي
عصام الجنيدي
Rechtsanwalt
Issam Jouneidie
الدكتور ز
AALBAKI ZIAD
MP. FRIATEC - (IMZ)
المركز السوري
PlayStation
DVD
V.CD

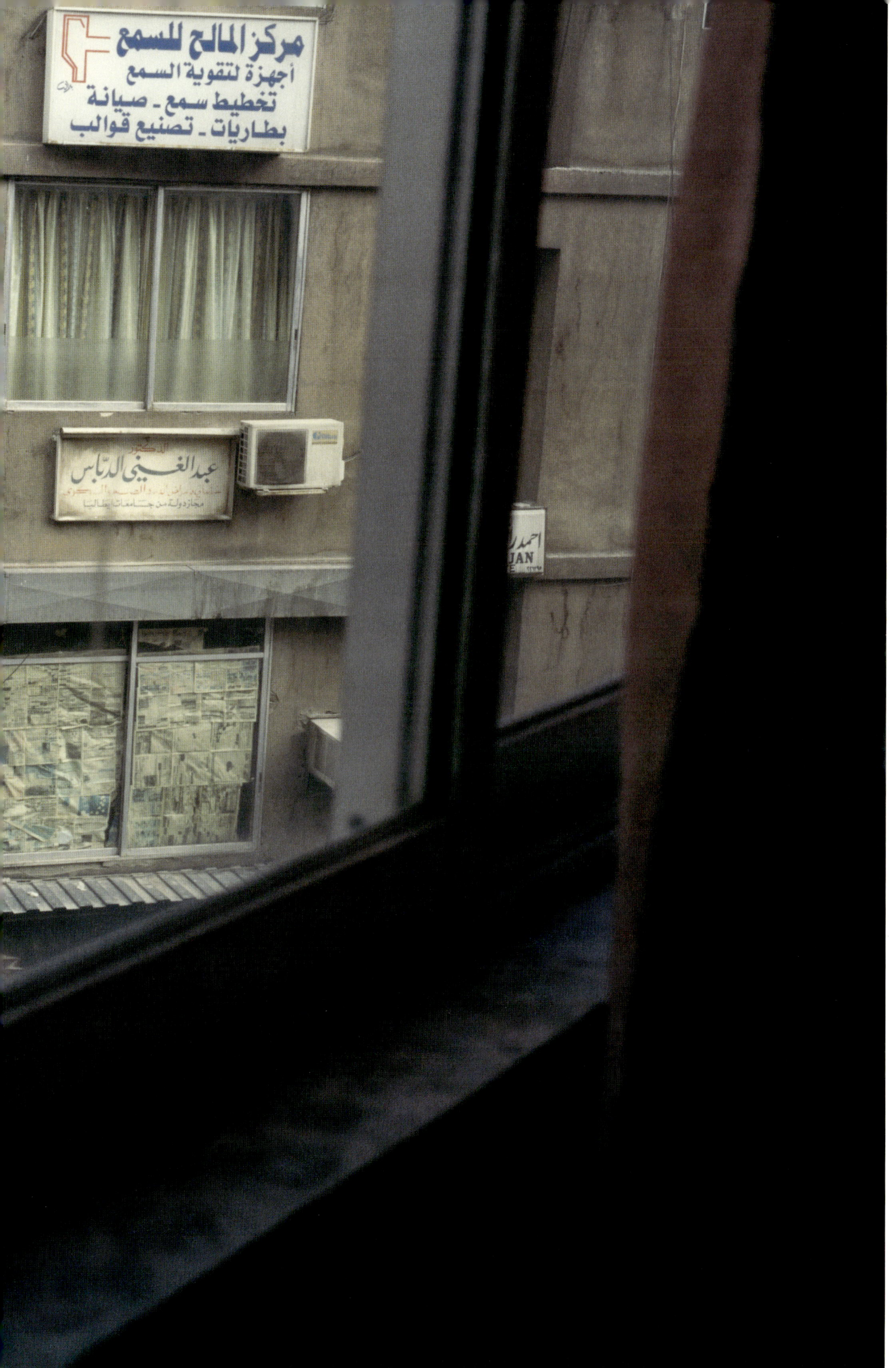

مركز المالح للسمع
أجهزة لتقوية السمع
تخطيط سمع ـ صيانة
بطاريات ـ تصنيع قوالب
الدكتور
عبد الغني الدباس

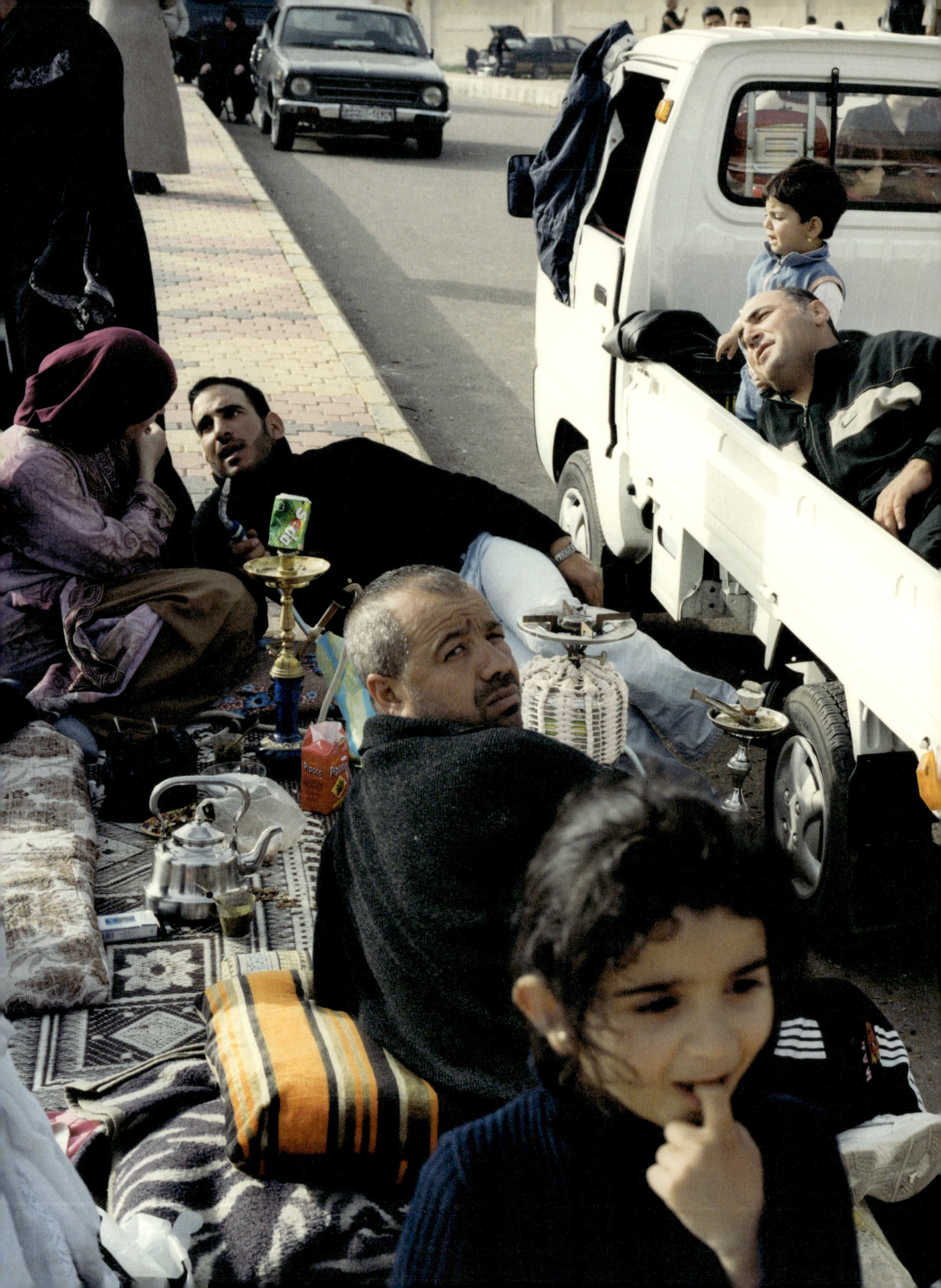

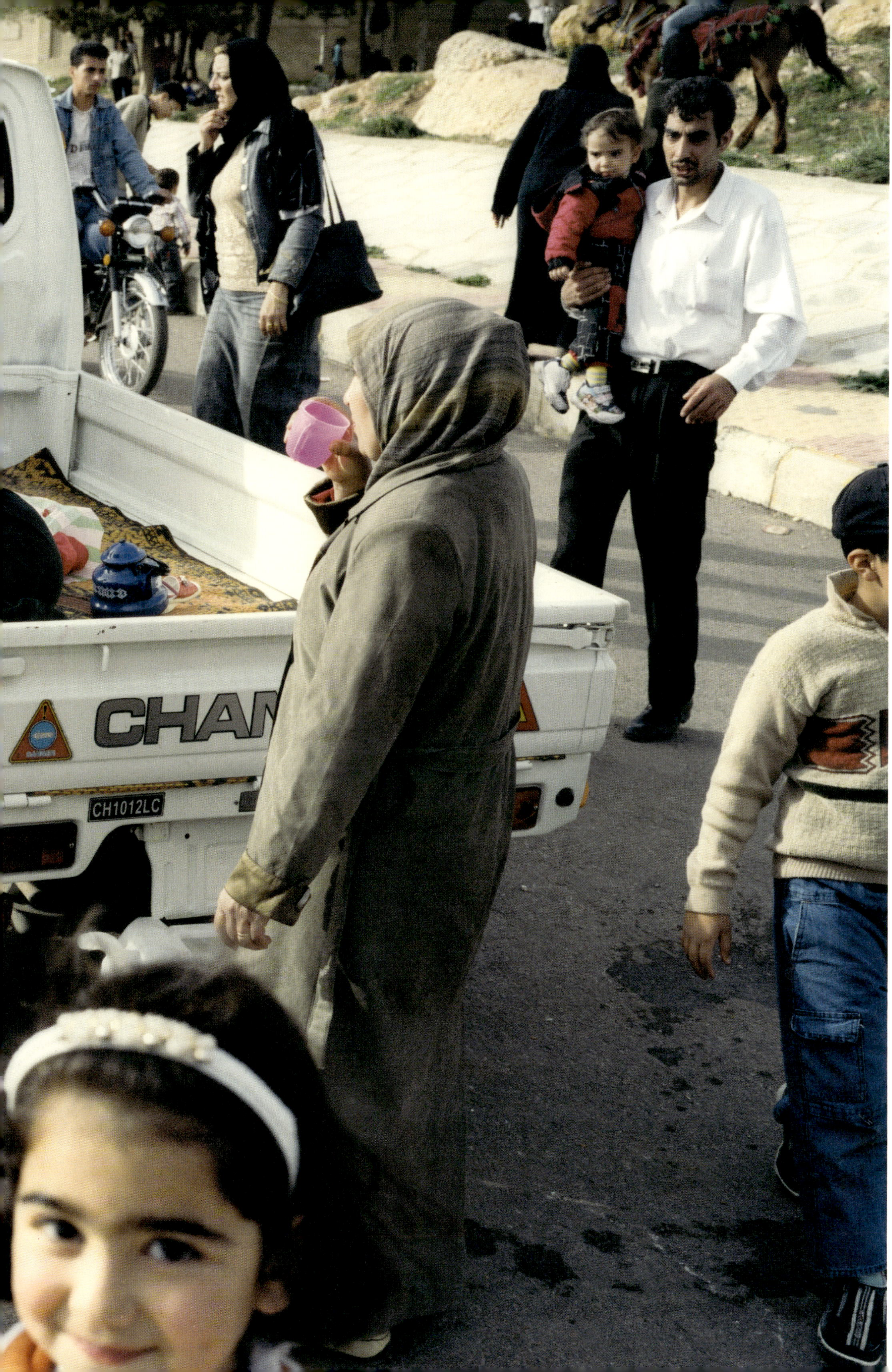

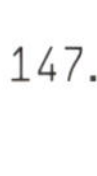

In most of the countries around the Mediterranean Sea, one religion dominates. Lebanon is an exception to this rule. Sixty percent of the population is Muslim, 39% is Christian. But this division is only the start. The country is home to many different religious groups. The Muslims are divided into Sunnis, Shiites, Ishmaelites, Alawites and Druze; the Christians into Maronites, Greek Orthodox and Armenian Orthodox.

In the 50s and 60s, Lebanon was an oasis of calm, prosperity and relatively peaceful cohabitation between the different religious groups. The Lebanese civil war (1975–90) put an abrupt end to this treasured peace when these groups came into direct conflict with each other. The Palestinian struggle for freedom, Israel's foreign politics and Syrian meddling complicated and aggravated the war even further.

At the beginning of the 90s, a battered Lebanon clawed its way back. With his company Solidere, the popular Prime Minister Rafiq Hariri built a new city centre, which was designed to recall the former grandeur of Beirut. The economy recovered and tourists began to return to the 'Paris of the Middle East'. The religious groups rediscovered the will to live alongside each other; however, asking someone about their religious background has become taboo since the civil war.

The murder of Prime Minister Hariri in 2005 signalled the beginning of a new wave of violence and political instability. Syria, which regarded Lebanon as one of its own provinces, was forced to leave Lebanon under pressure from the West. In July 2006, a large part of the country was temporarily occupied by Israel and considerable parts of its rebuilt infrastructure were destroyed. Internal politics reached an impasse and the cautious optimism of the 90s once again gave way among many Lebanese to cynicism and fear of terrorist attacks.

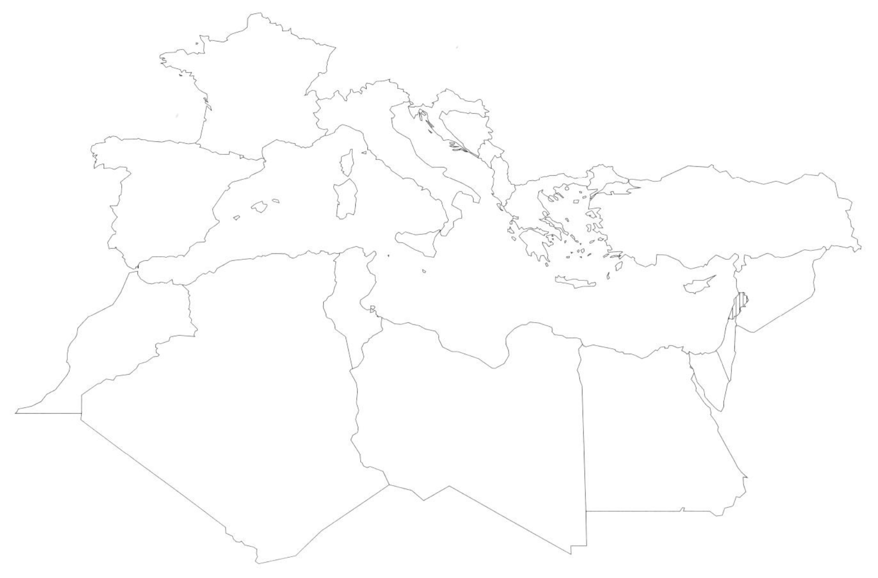

RELIGIONS
% OF POPULATION WHICH IS MUSLIM, CHRISTIAN, JEWISH

	Muslim	Christian	Jewish
GIBRALTAR	4.0	78.1	2.40
SPAIN	1.2	94.0	<0.05
FRANCE	7.5	82.0	0.81
ITALY	1.0	90.0	<0.05
CROATIA	1.3	88.0	<0.05
ALBANIA	70.0	10.0	
GREECE	1.3	98.0*	<0.05
CYPRUS	18.0	78.0*	
TURKEY	99.8		<0.05
SYRIA	85.0	10.0	<0.05
LEBANON	**59.7**	**39.0**	
ISRAEL	16.0	2.1	75.20
W.B.& GAZA	NA	NA	NA
EGYPT	94.0		<0.05
LIBYA	97.0		
TUNISIA	98.0	1.0	0.011
ALGERIA	99.0	<0.5	<0.50
MOROCCO	98.7	1.1	0.20

SOURCE : THE CIA WORLD FACTBOOK

*   : GREEK ORTHODOX

150. EL MINA
The fuse box of block 13, street 93, in El Mina harbour. Whenever they need power, the inhabitants simply plug a cable into the mains. It is like a metaphor for Lebanon itself: explosive and apparently arbitrary.

152. NABATIYE
Ashura, the ritual commemorating the martyr's death of Imam Hussein, the Prophet Mohammed's grandson. Hezbollah dislikes these Shiite traditions, and erects tents where people can donate blood instead.

155. TRIPOLI
A BMW with bullet holes and blacked-out windows. It, at least, has survived the civil war.

157. BEIRUT
Lebanese pay their respects at the grave of murdered former Prime Minister Hariri. During the funeral, I was picked up by the Syrian secret service. Their offices were located under the Lebanese parliamentary building.

159. TRIPOLI
Tripoli is much less Westernized than the capital Beirut. This is the Sunni area of Lebanon. Every religious group has its own territory.

160. BCHARRE
One-and-a-half hour's drive from the sea are snow-covered mountains, one of Lebanon's big attractions. Christians ski down the slopes, while Muslims walk or ride sledges.

163. RAS AD DIN AL BAHR
When I think of grazing cows, I think of lush green meadows. This is not the case in Lebanon. None the less, these well-fed Frisian cows roam freely in the south, where Hezbollah rules the roost.

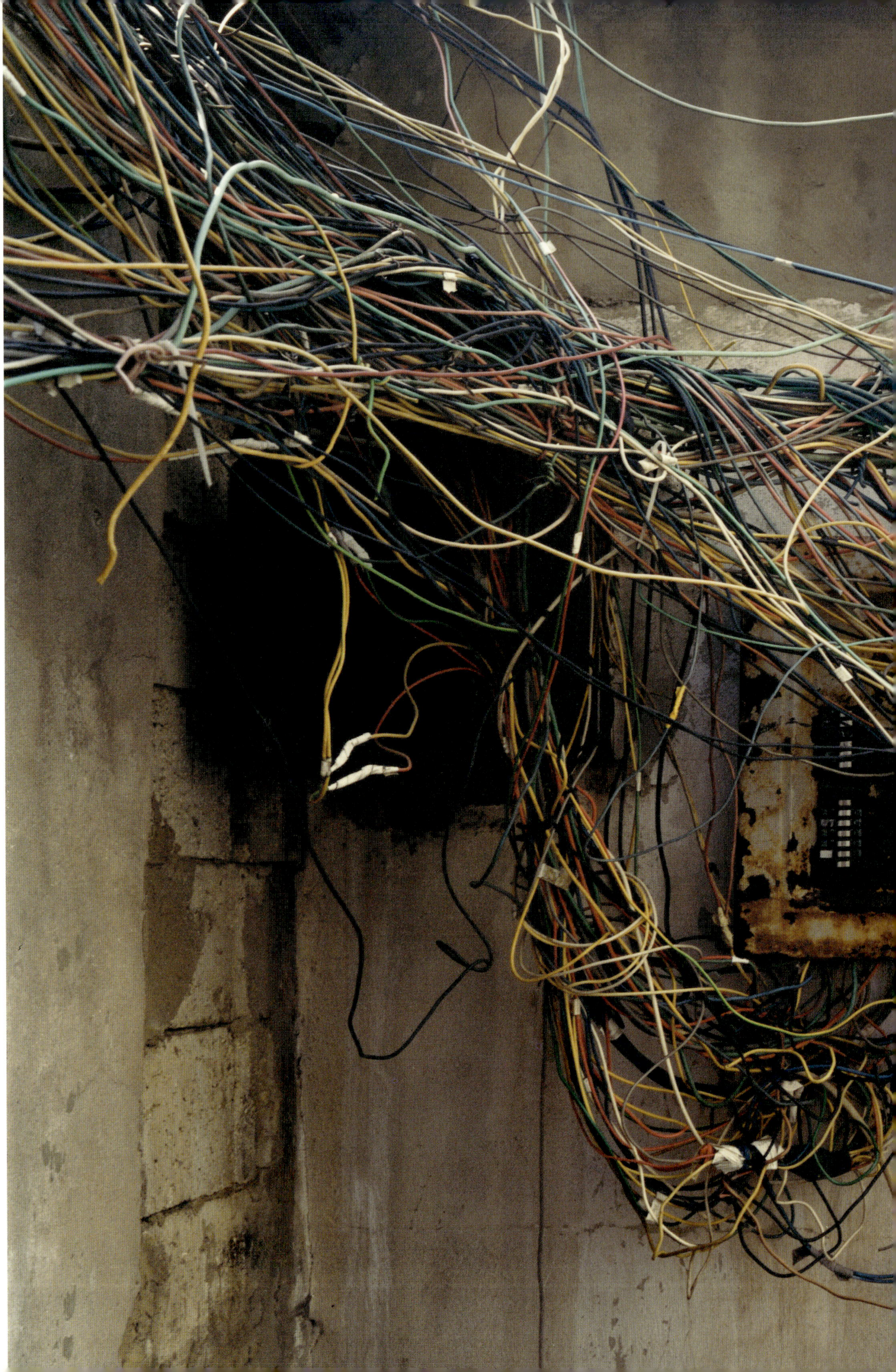

150.

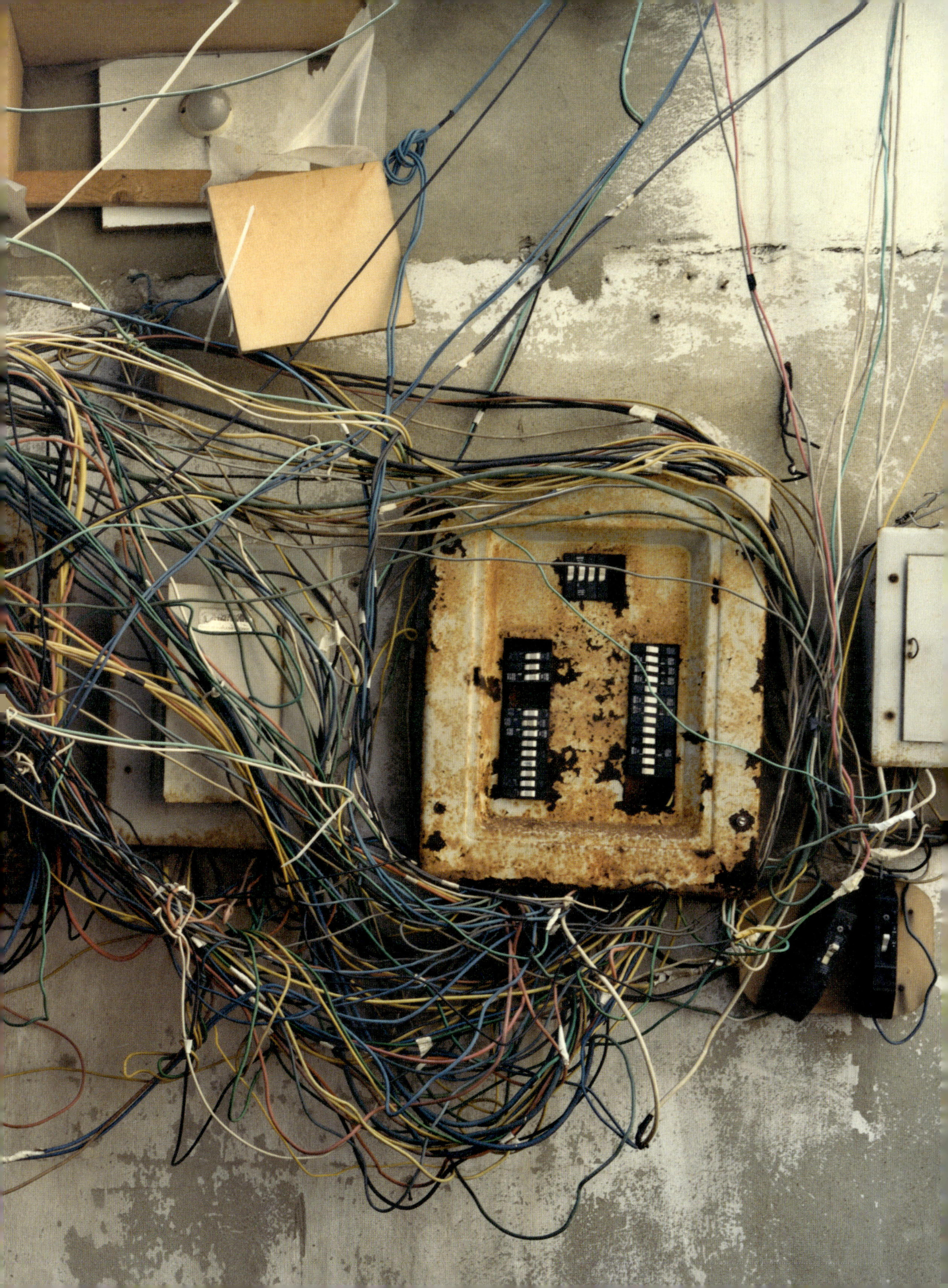

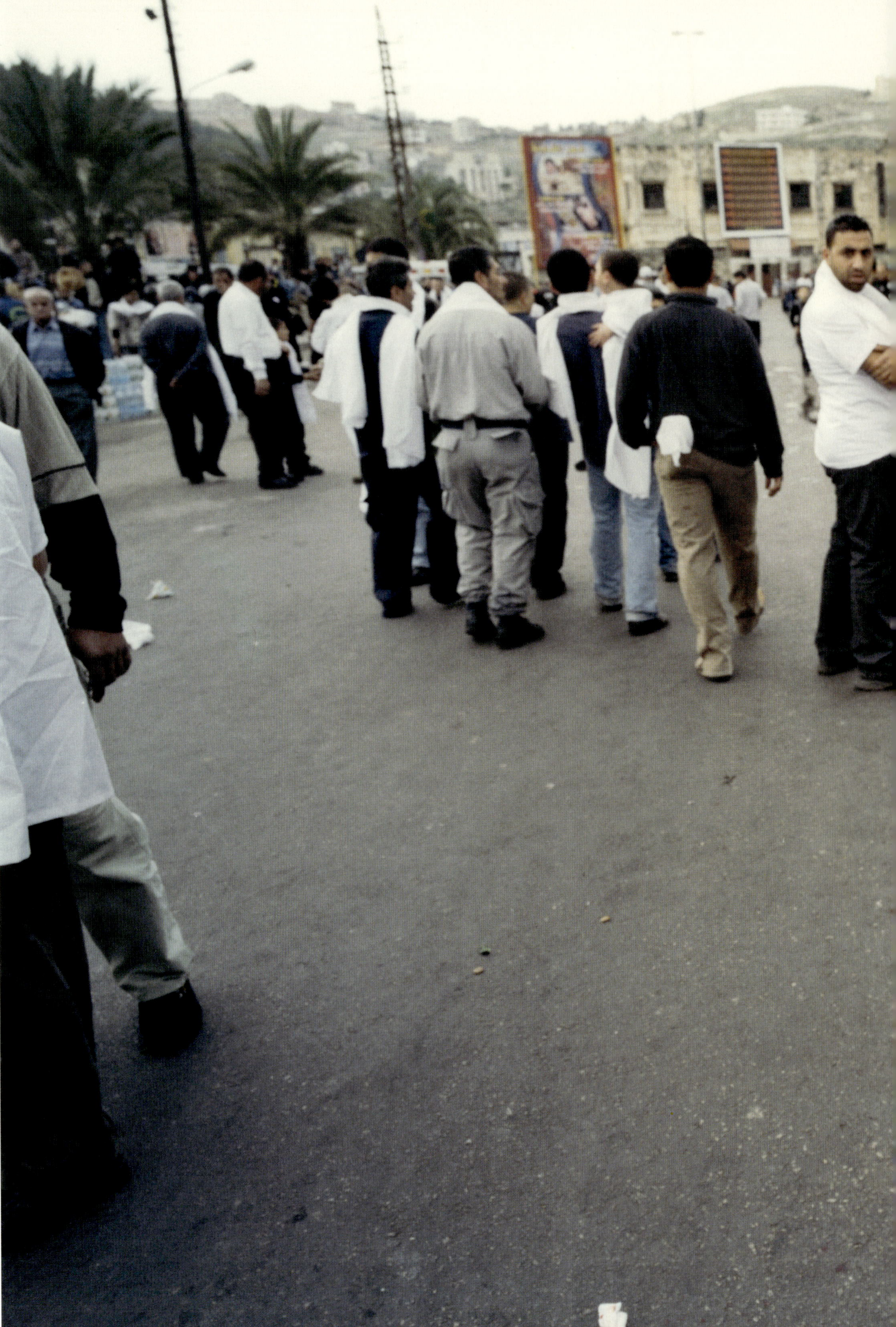

152.

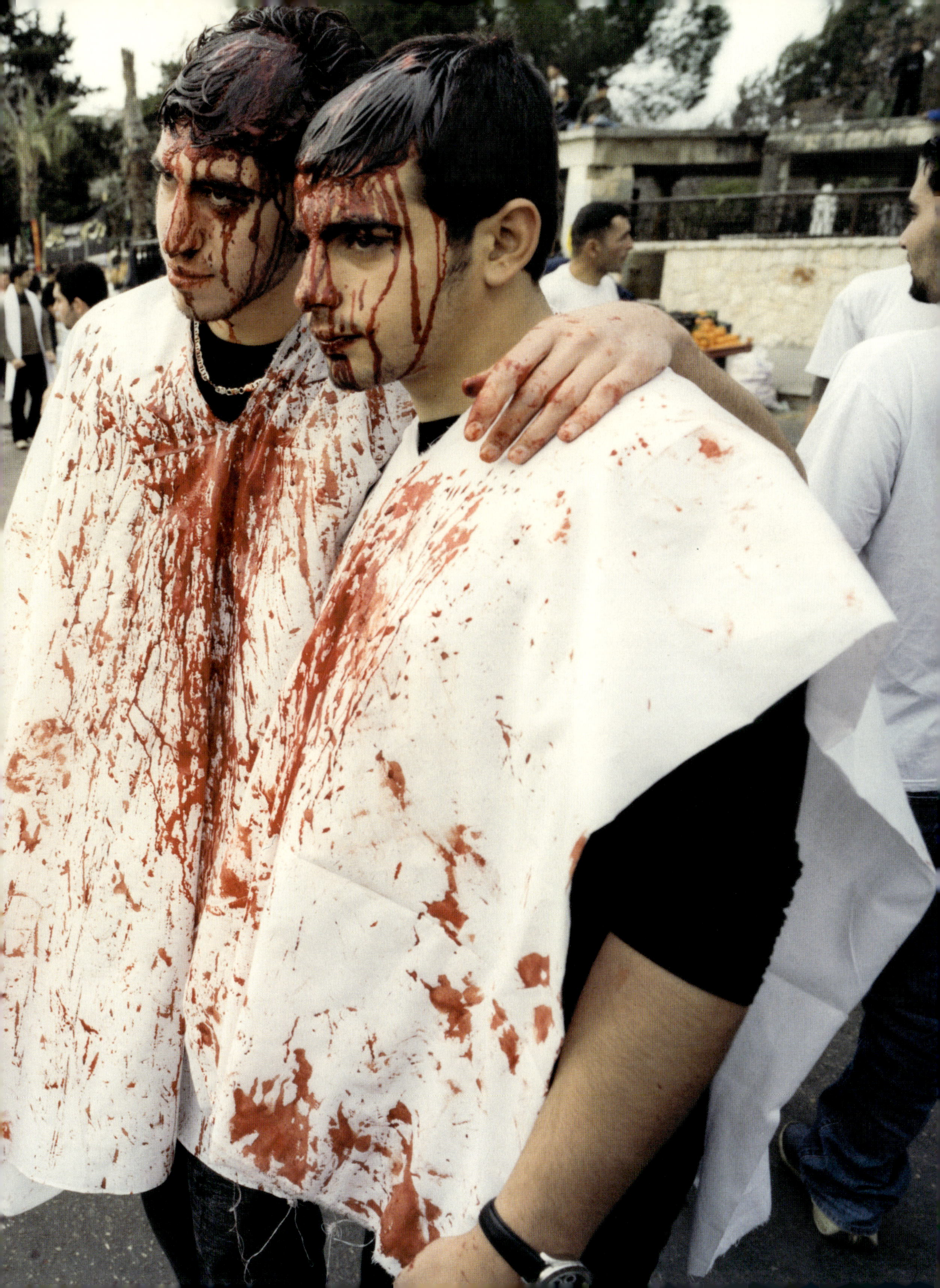

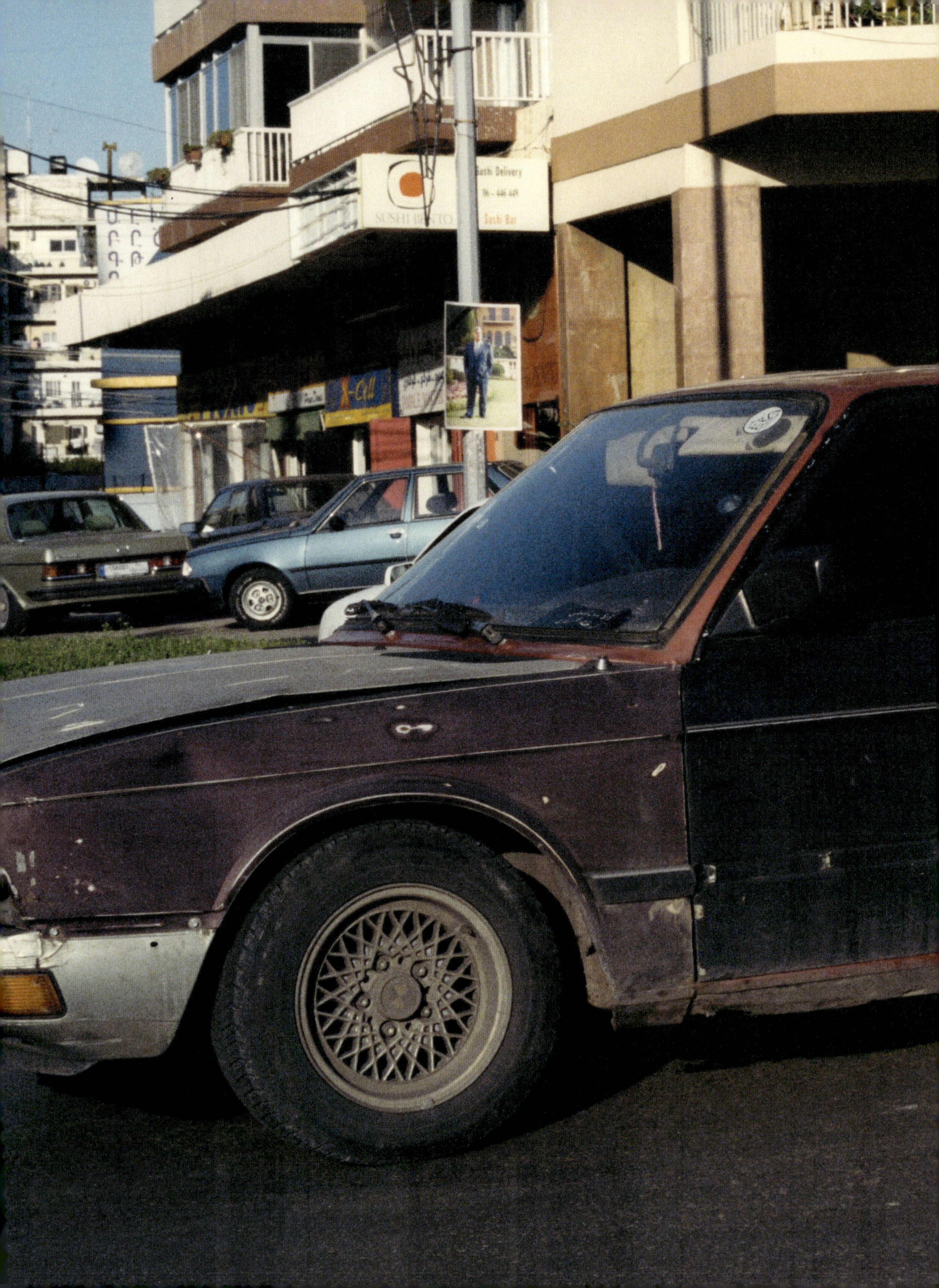

Sushi Delivery
Tel - 446 449
SUSHI RESTO
Sushi Bar
X-Cell

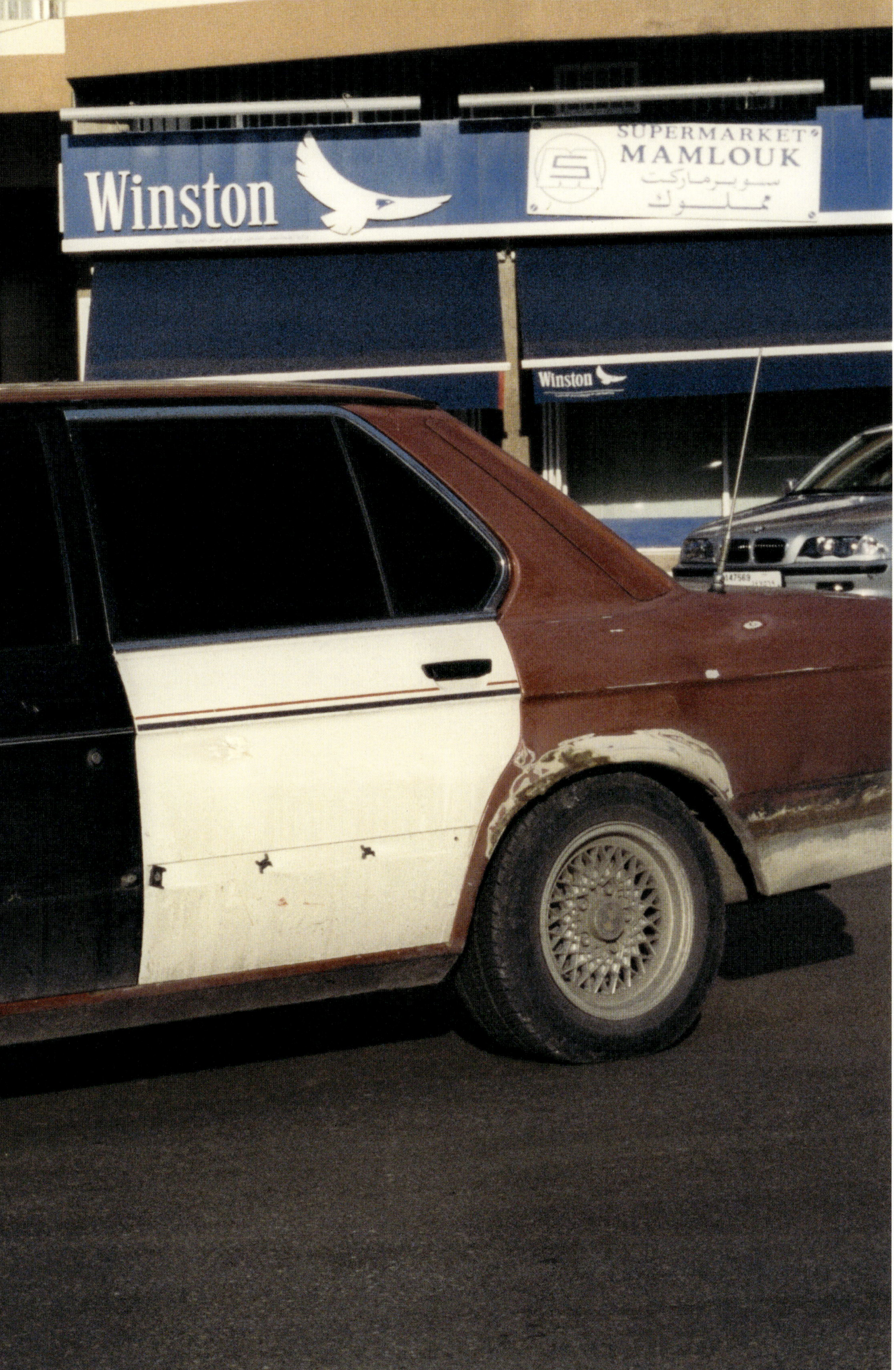
Winston
SUPERMARKET
MAMLOUK
سوبرماركت
مملوك
Winston

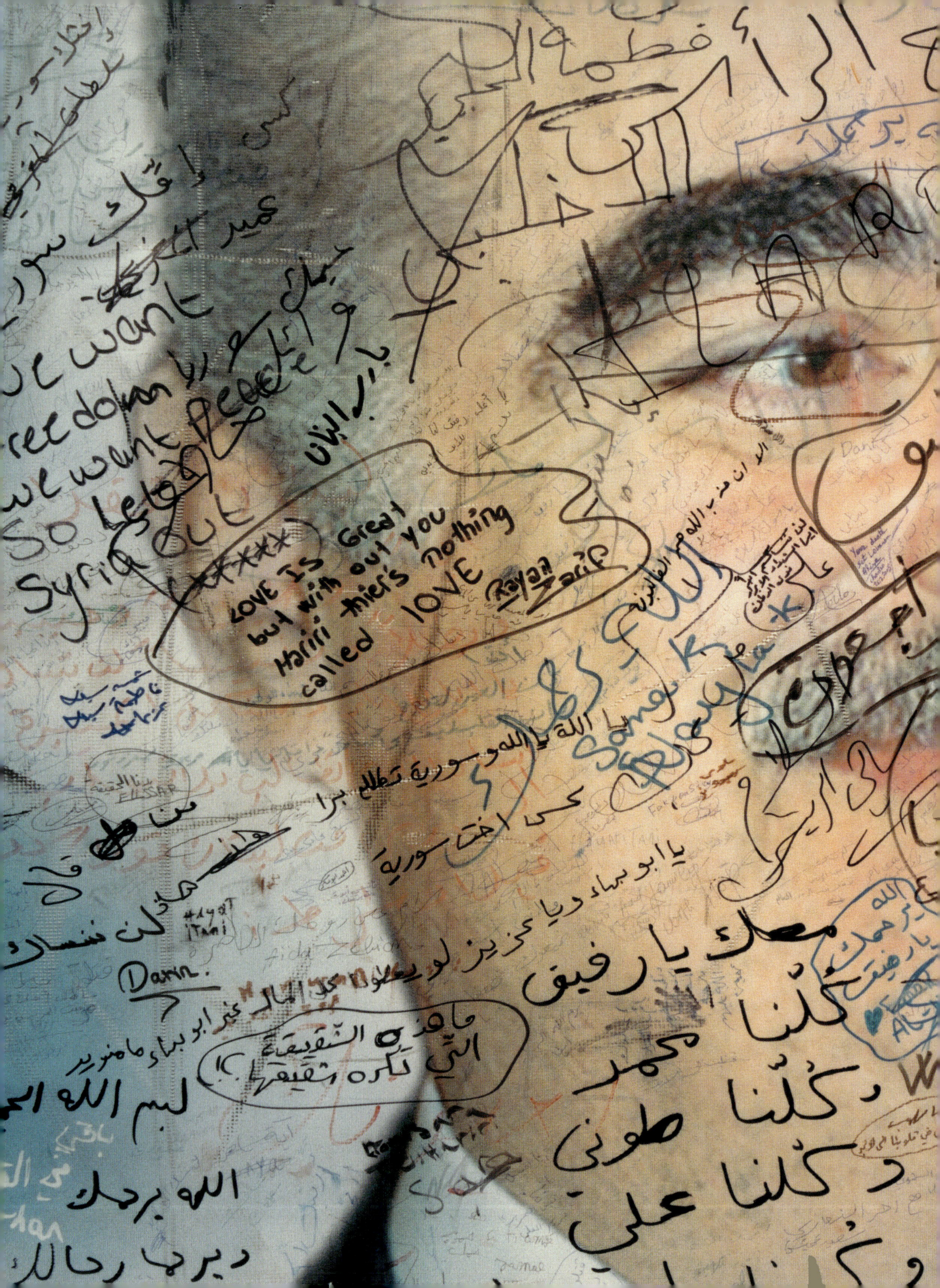
Syria
reedom
we want
so let
we want pece
لبنان
***** Love is great
but with out you
Hariri there's nothing
called LOVE
Rayan

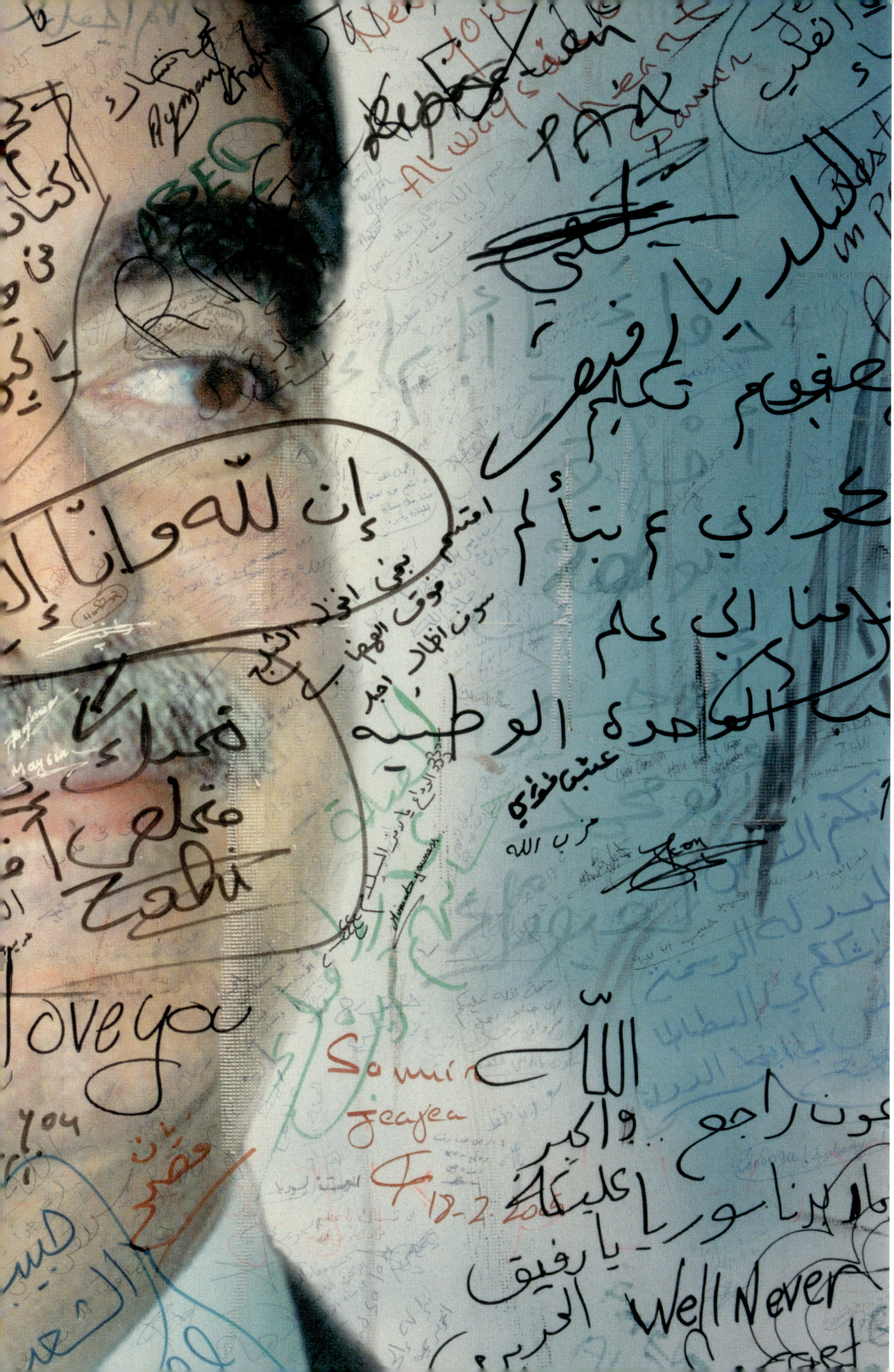

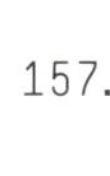

157.

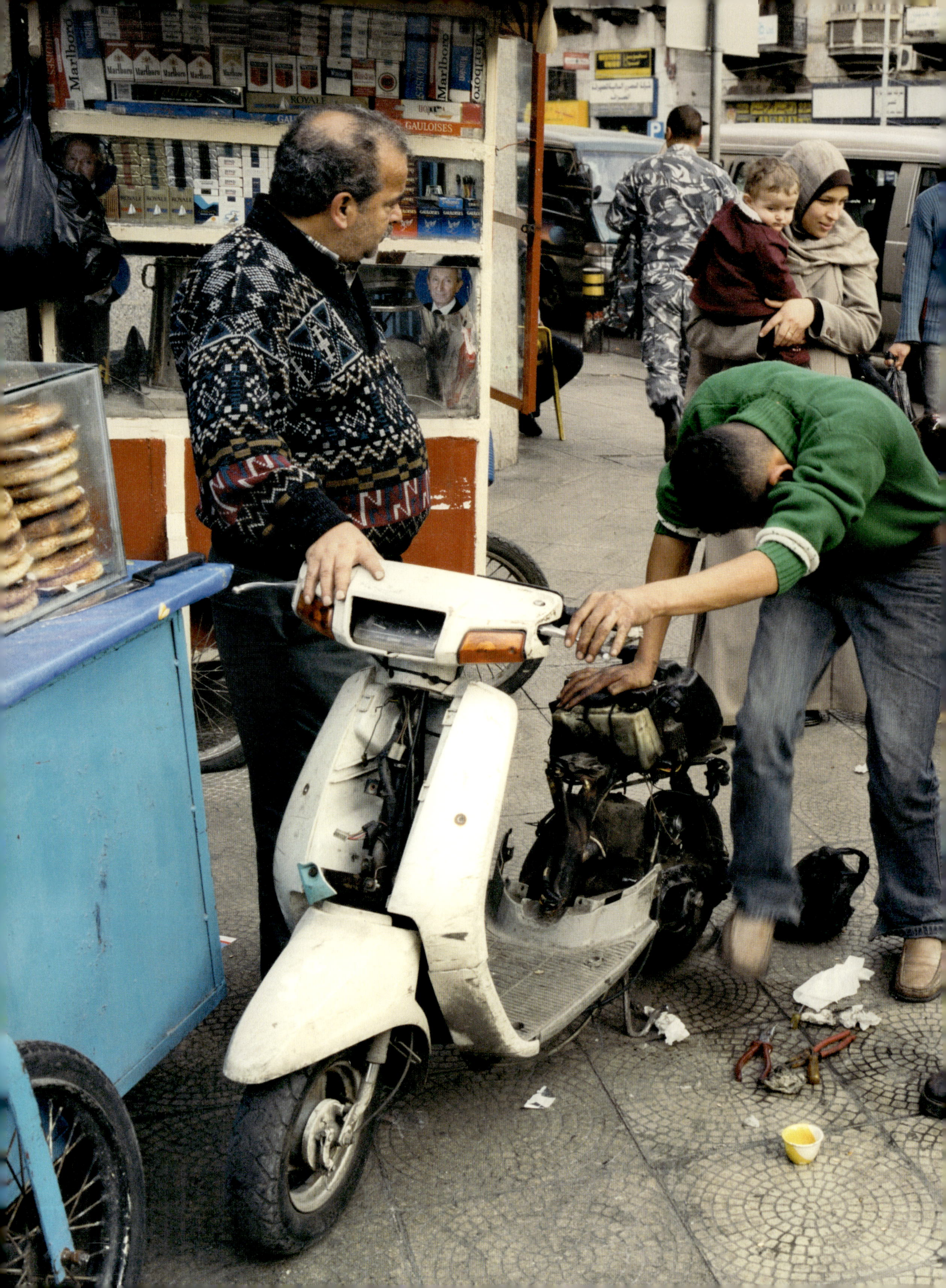

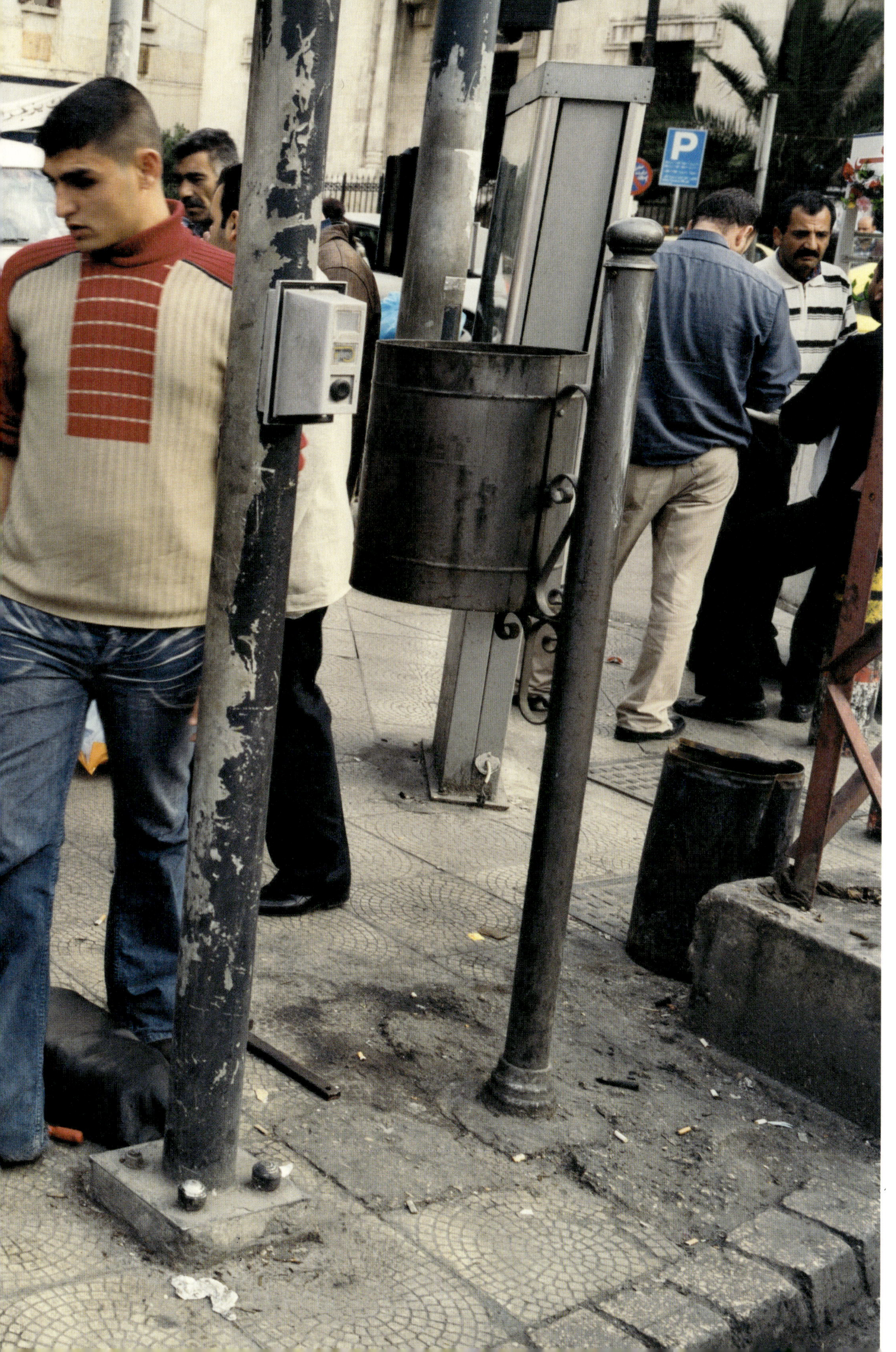

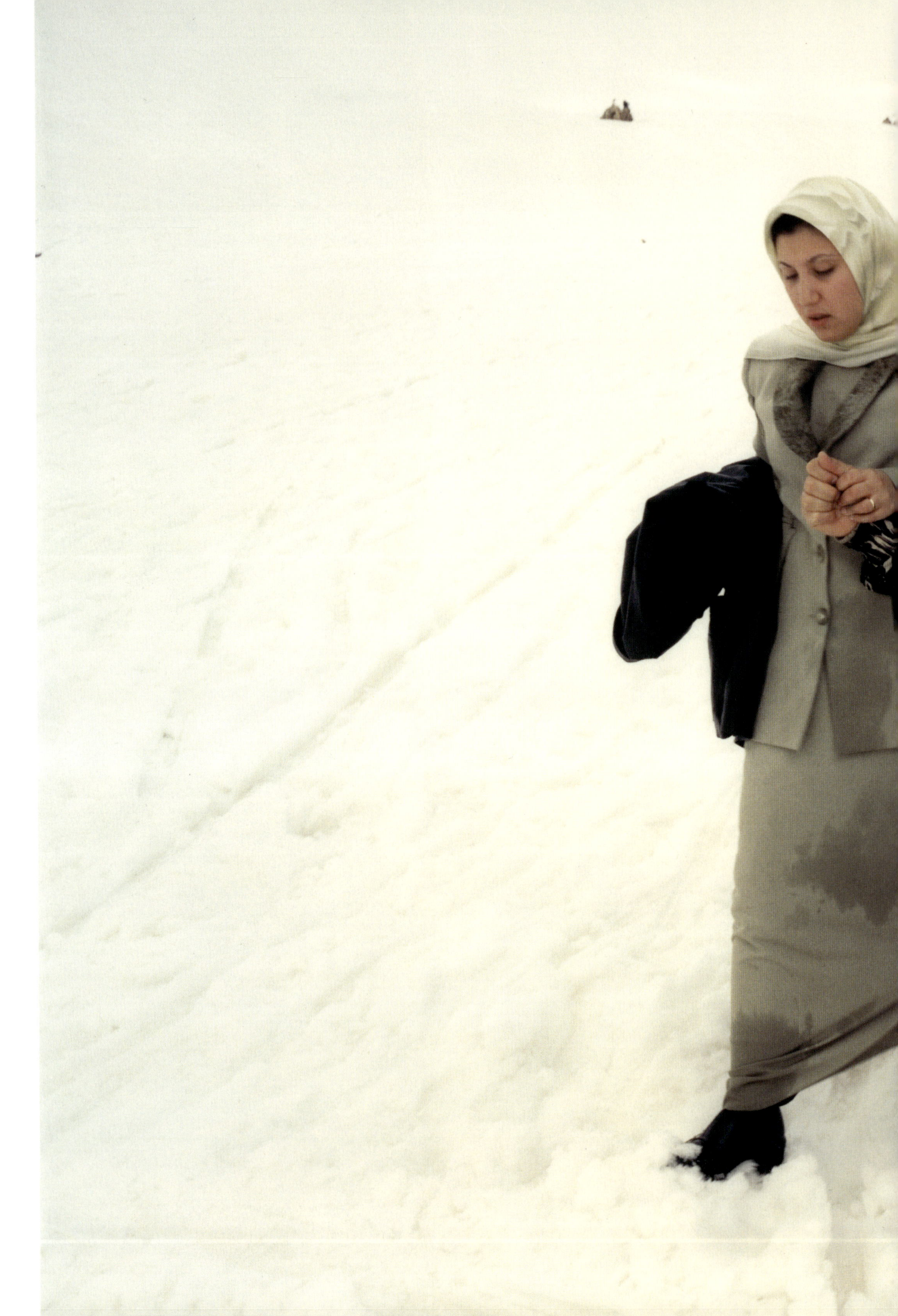

160.

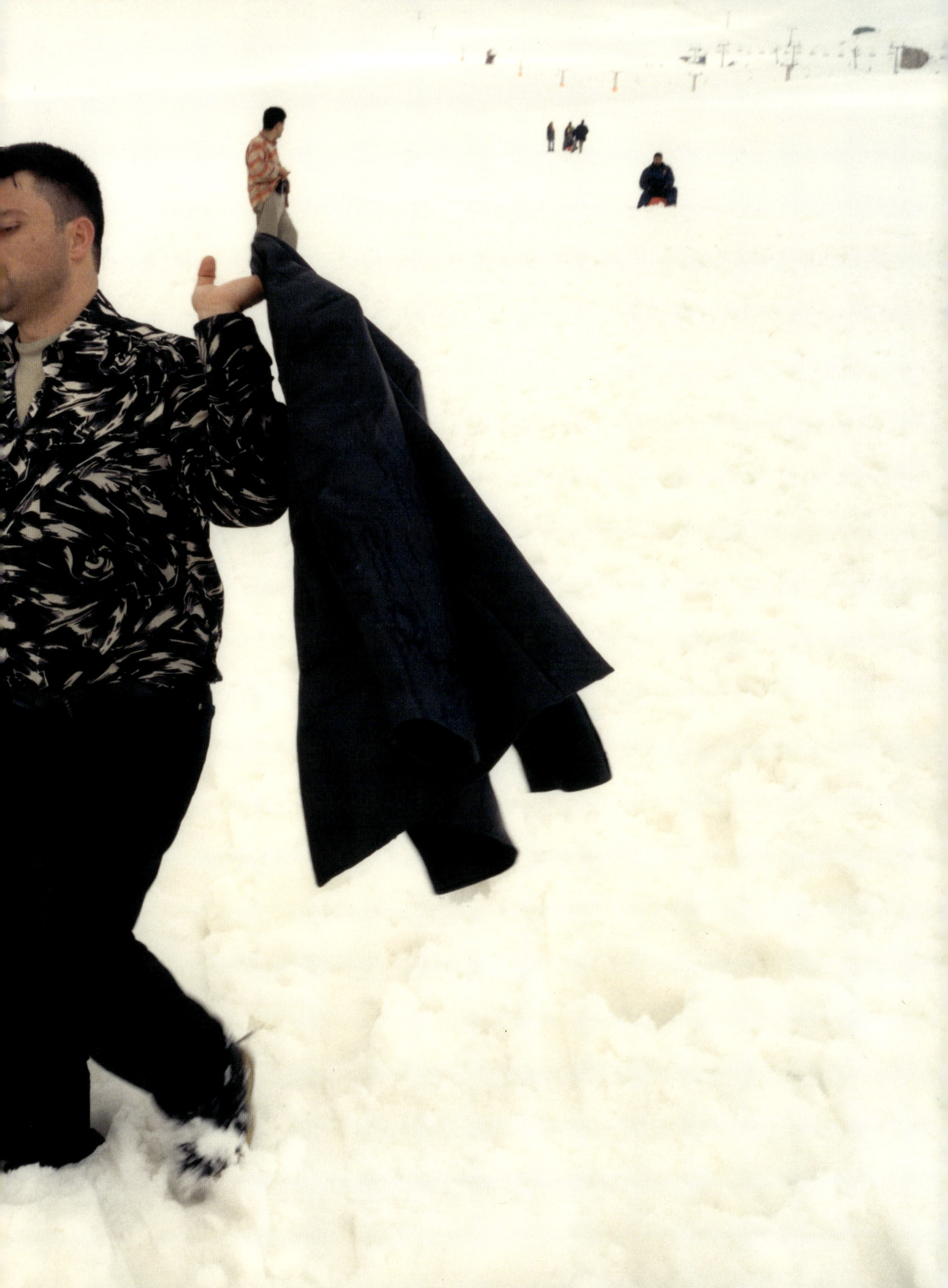

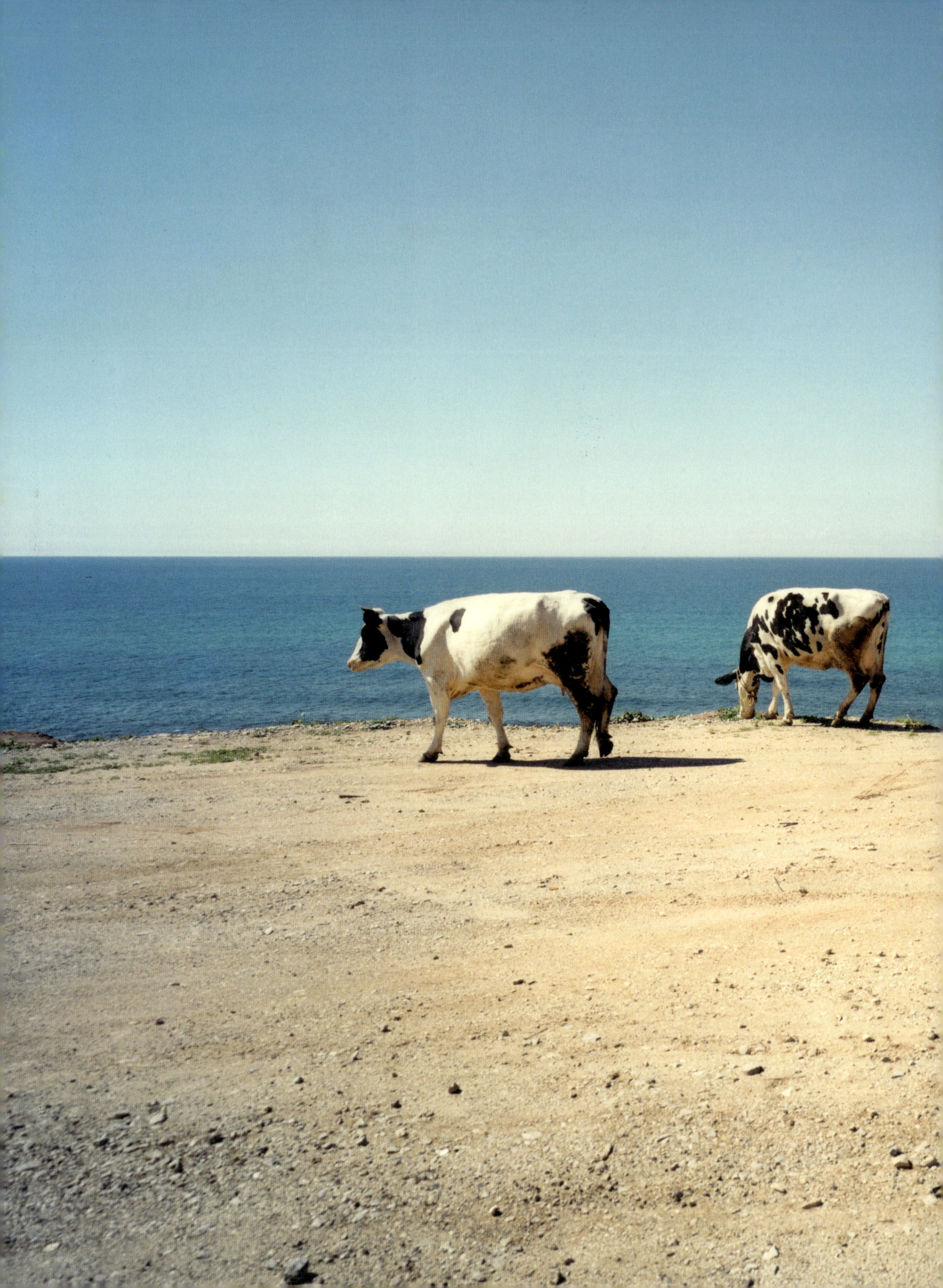

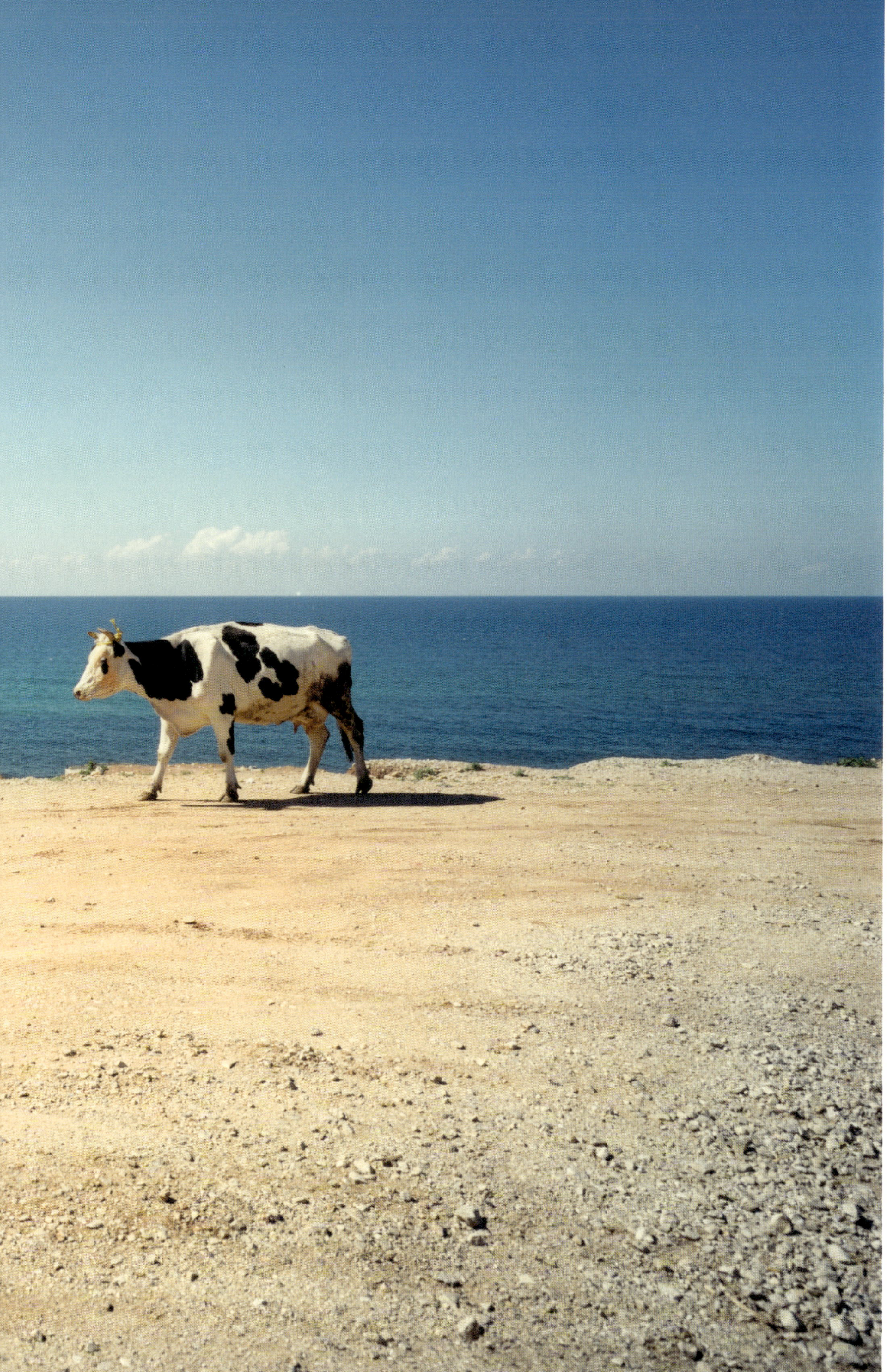

163.

**ISRAEL/
WEST BANK &
GAZA**

Israel is obsessed with new technology. This was where ICQ (read: I seek you), the first functioning online chat service, saw the light of day. Here too, in the Silicon Valley of the Middle East, the first mobile phone was developed in Motorola's laboratory. Israel is now one of the countries with the highest number of telephones per inhabitant. From the beaches and clubs of Tel Aviv, where hip young crowds parade the newest 'bling' mobiles, to the Jewish Orthodox neighbourhoods of Mea Shearim, where kosher telephones – which have been stripped of the temptations of a camera, text-messaging functionality or the possibility of calling a sex line – are making inroads. Mobiles are everywhere: the average Israeli owns 1.3 mobile phones.

For many developing countries, the mobile phone has been a veritable revolution. It enables traders and producers to stay up to date with current prices in the capital and means that villages that were never connected to the old telephone network have suddenly been linked to the world. For Palestinians, mobile telephony is also a godsend at a time when their freedom of movement is increasingly restricted. Since the construction of the Wall and Israeli roadblocks in the West Bank, a journey of just 30 kilometres can sometimes take up to five hours. In these situations, a mobile phone is the ideal way to stay in touch with family and friends. Another use for the mobile phone was demonstrated by the Israeli secret service, Shin Bet, in 1996 when Yahya Ayyash, Hamas's explosives specialist, was blown up by an Israeli-built telephone bomb.

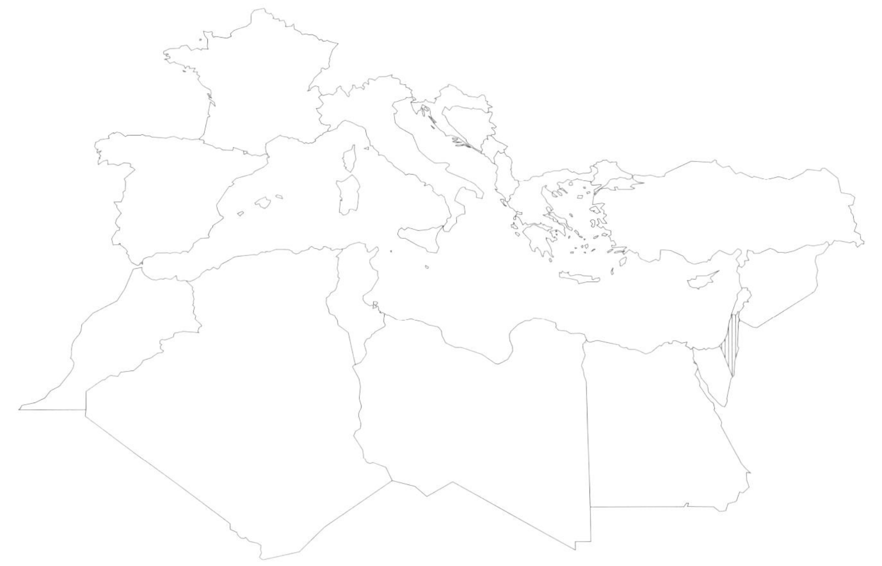

NUMBER OF MOBILE PHONES
PER CAPITA

GIBRALTAR	0.339	
SPAIN	1.023	
FRANCE	0.862	
ITALY	1.217	
CROATIA	1.006	
ALBANIA	0.425	
GREECE	1.037	
CYPRUS	0.986	*
TURKEY	0.740	
SYRIA	0.242	
LEBANON	0.281	
ISRAEL	**1.308**	
W.B. & GAZA	0.273	
EGYPT	0.224	
LIBYA	0.651	
TUNISIA	0.714	
ALGERIA	0.630	
MOROCCO	0.474	

SOURCE : THE CIA WORLD FACTBOOK

*   : IN THE TURKISH REPUBLIC OF NORTHERN CYPRUS THE NUMBER OF
         MOBILE PHONES PER CAPITA IS 0.542

167. KHAN YOUNIS, GAZA
One, two dull booms, a flash; then a silence that lasts minutes, until it is broken by screaming, sirens and flashing lights. The next day, delegations from Hamas, Islamic Jihad and Fatah appear. They shake hands and walk over the rubble of the houses that have been blown to bits.

168. RAMALLAH, WEST BANK
The display of a fashion shop in Ramallah. This is the Palestinian business centre. Ramallah has always been more moderate than the hardliners' strongholds of Jenin, Nablus and Hebron.

170. RISHON LEZION, ISRAEL
The aftermath of a Hamas suicide bomb attack. A gambling-hall technician came to repair the machines. He was carrying a bomb in his toolbox.

172. YENIN REFUGEE CAMP, WEST BANK
A father takes his son for a drive. His car was only six months old when the Israeli army raided Yenin. The centre of the refugee camp was almost completely flattened. But the car still works.

174. EAST JERUSALEM, WEST BANK
Israel continues to build enormous settlements on the West Bank. If this carries on the conflict can never be resolved.

176. KHAN YOUNIS, GAZA
Like hundreds of thousands of Palestinians, Sharif was born in a refugee camp. During the second Intifada, he threw stones and was shot at with rubber bullets. Travelling is only possible at the local photo studio, where he can choose between the French Riviera, the Dutch Keukenhof, a Victorian garden or an idyllic waterfall.

179. TIMARIN, GAZA
Israel vacated this settlement in Gaza in 2005. Timarin was a coastal resort for the Israeli settlers in Gaza. Their agricultural enclaves of just 12,000 inhabitants consumed 60 percent of the water here. The 1.3 million Palestinians who live there had to make do with the remaining 40 percent.

181. WEST BANK
Improvised roadblock on the motorway in the West Bank. Above it runs the road from Jerusalem to Ariel, a large Jewish settlement. Palestinians are not allowed to go there.

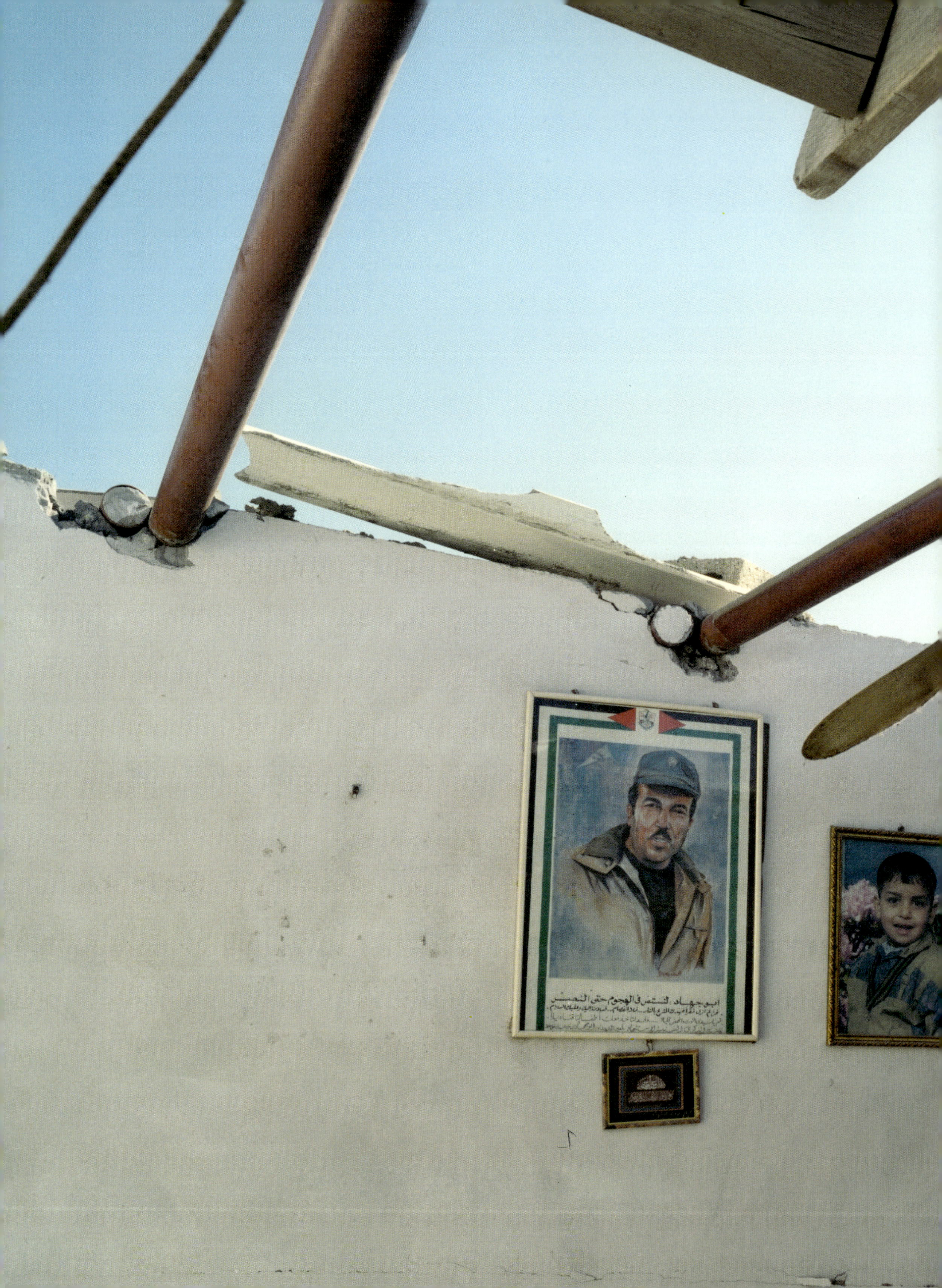

ابو جهاد .. لنتمس في الهجوم حتى النصر

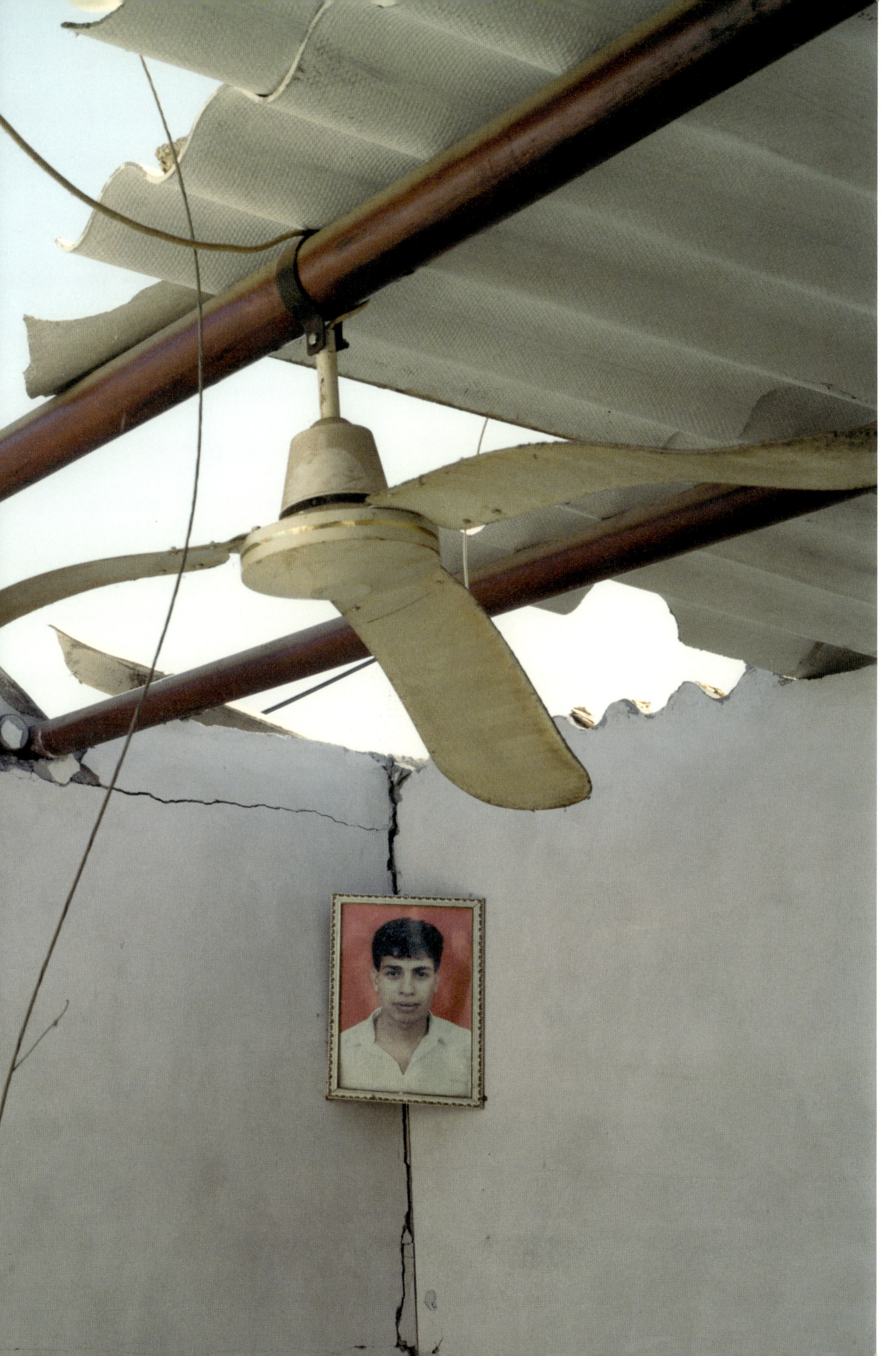

168.

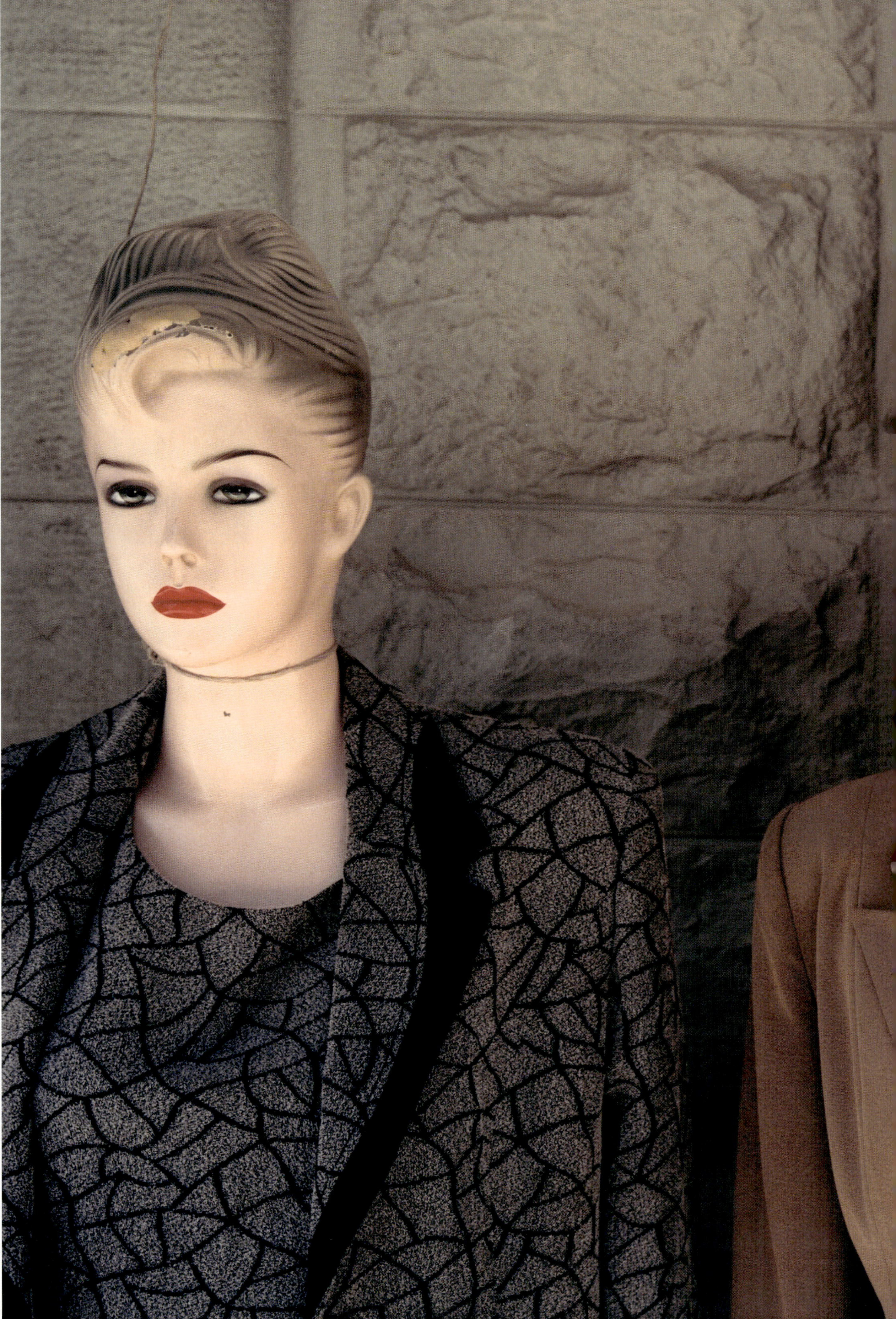

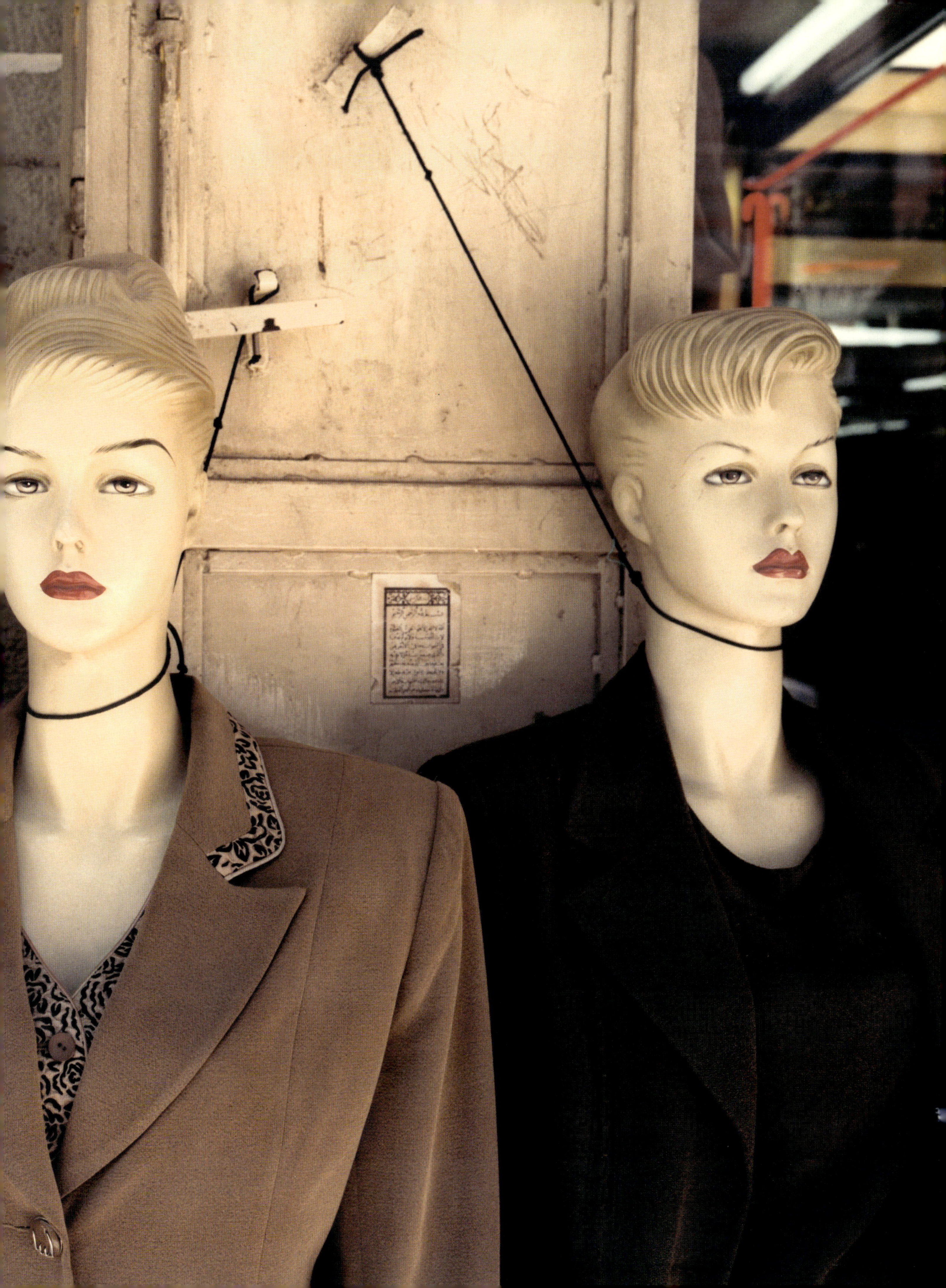

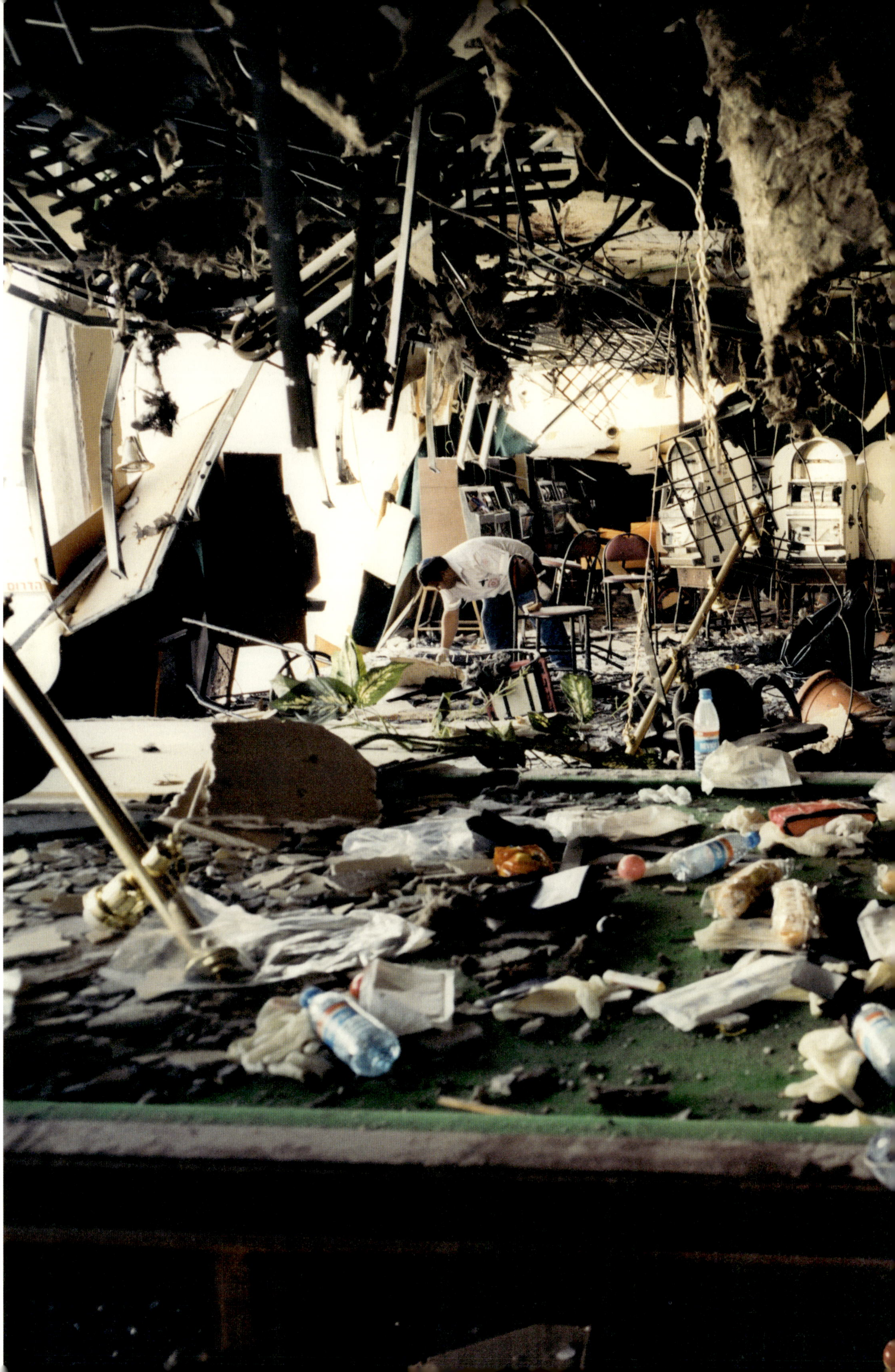

170.

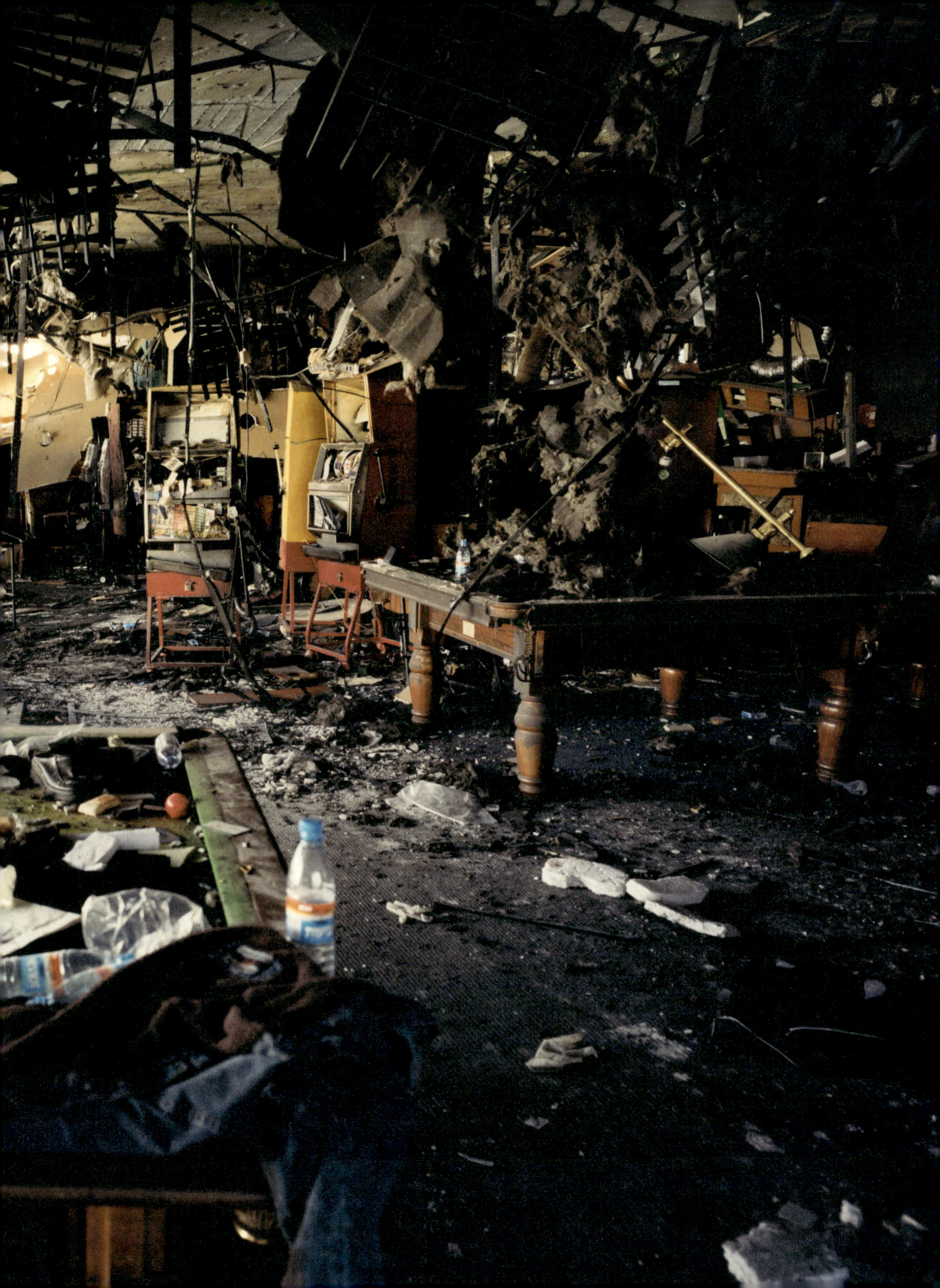

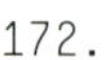

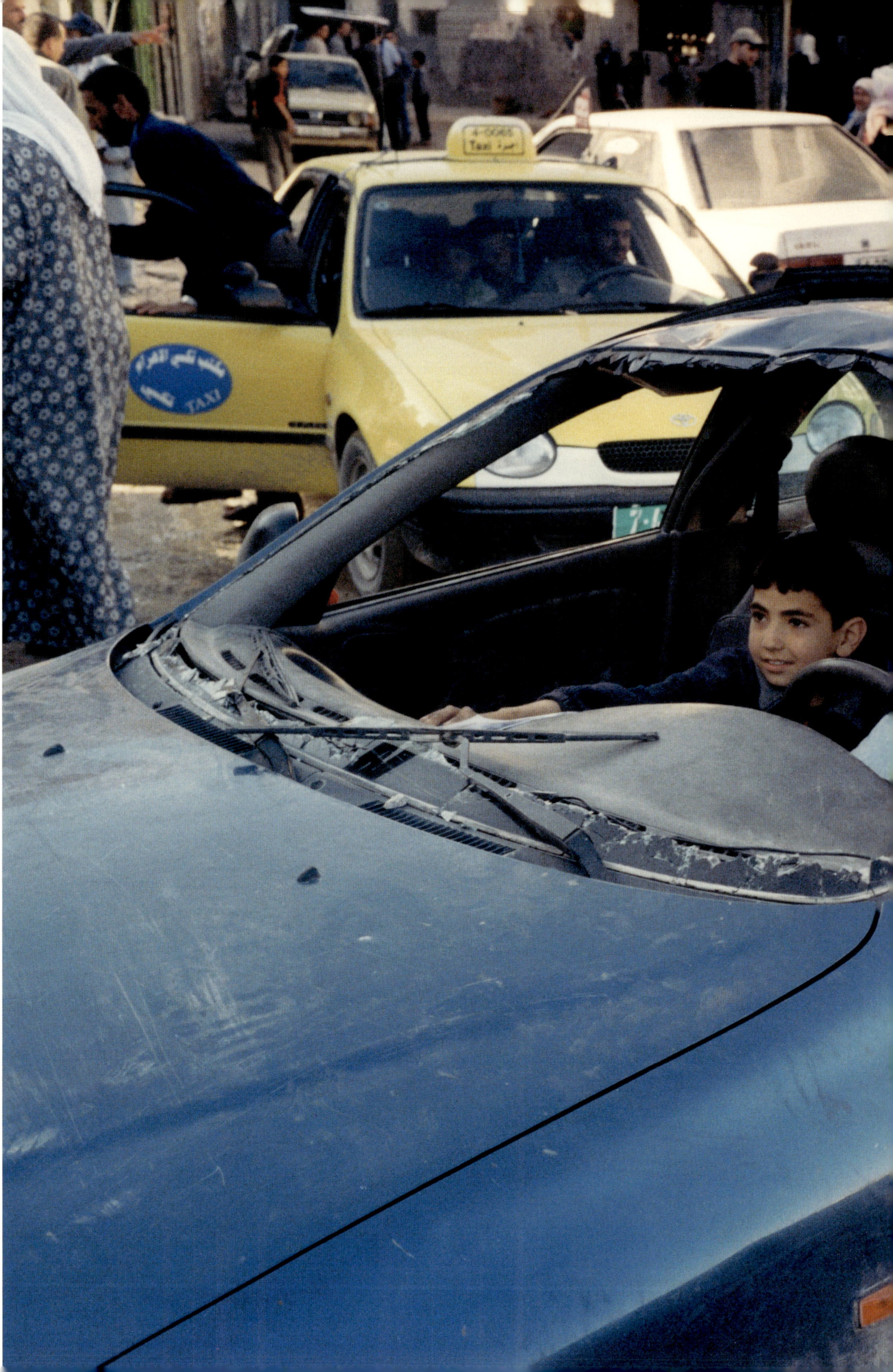

172.

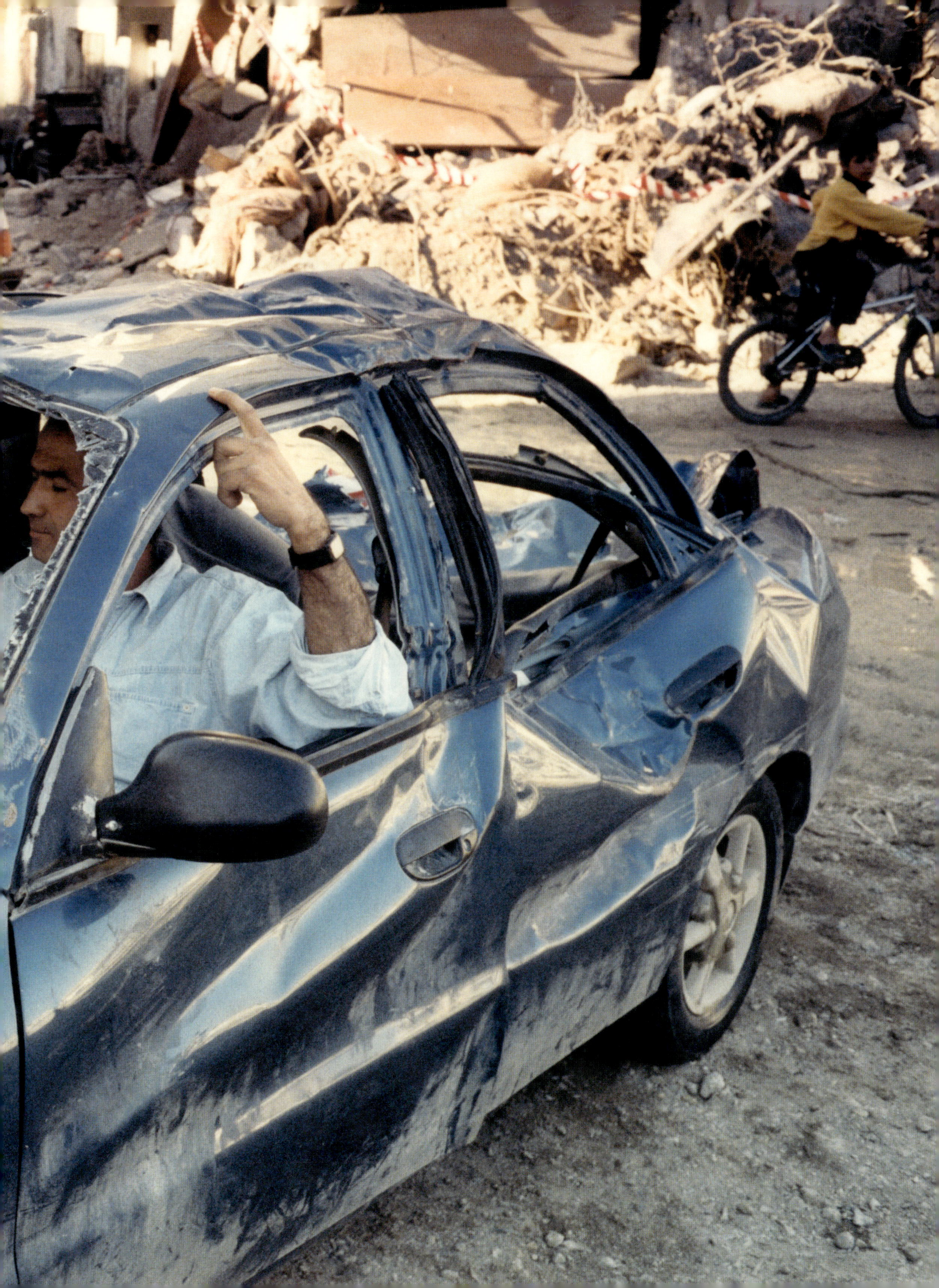

174.

אדם הכפרית
איכלוס מיידי
ס.א.ד
02-5849022 052-4456
לב ב'
5-4 חדרים
נוף
"הבשן"
7(

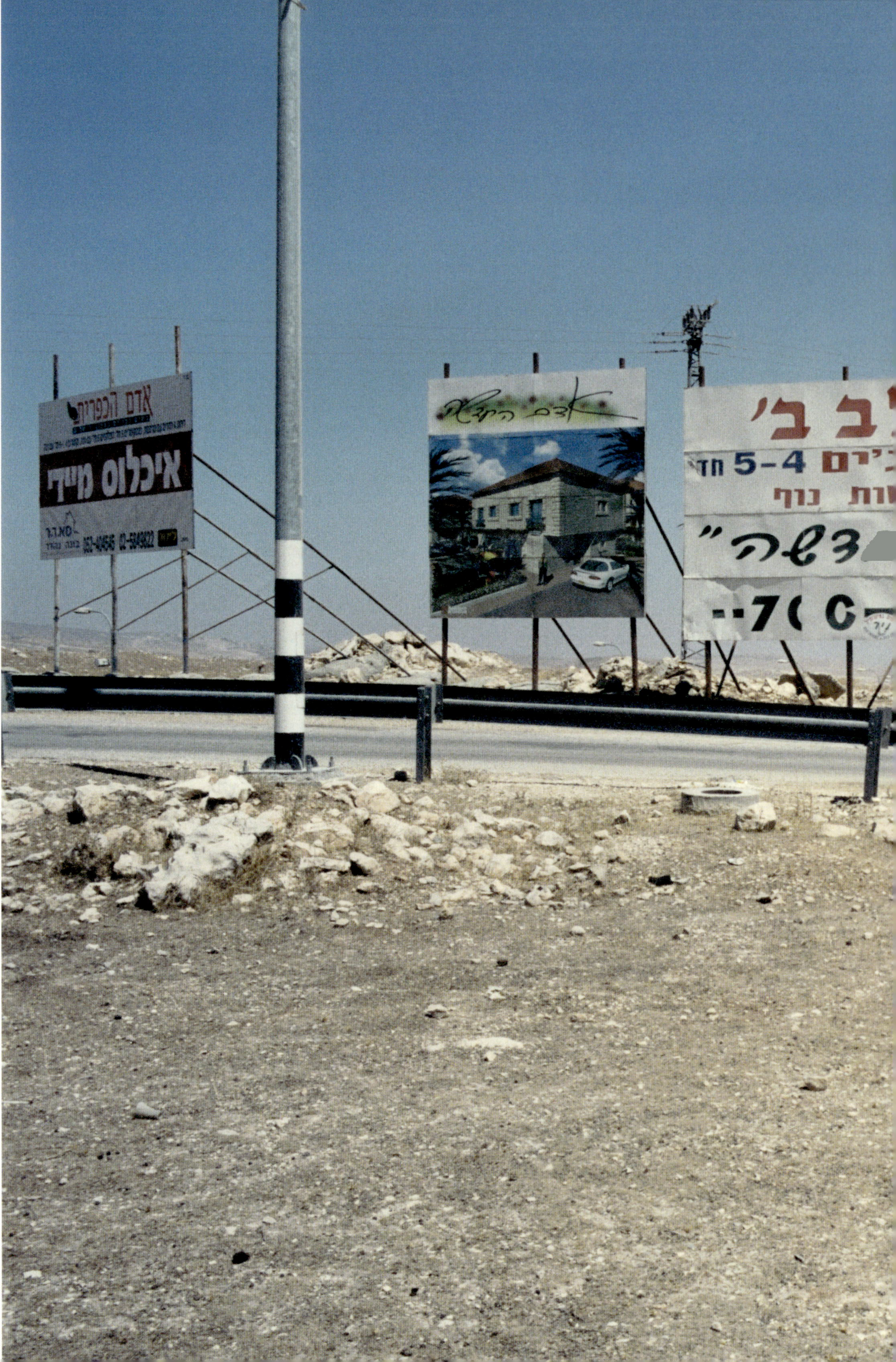

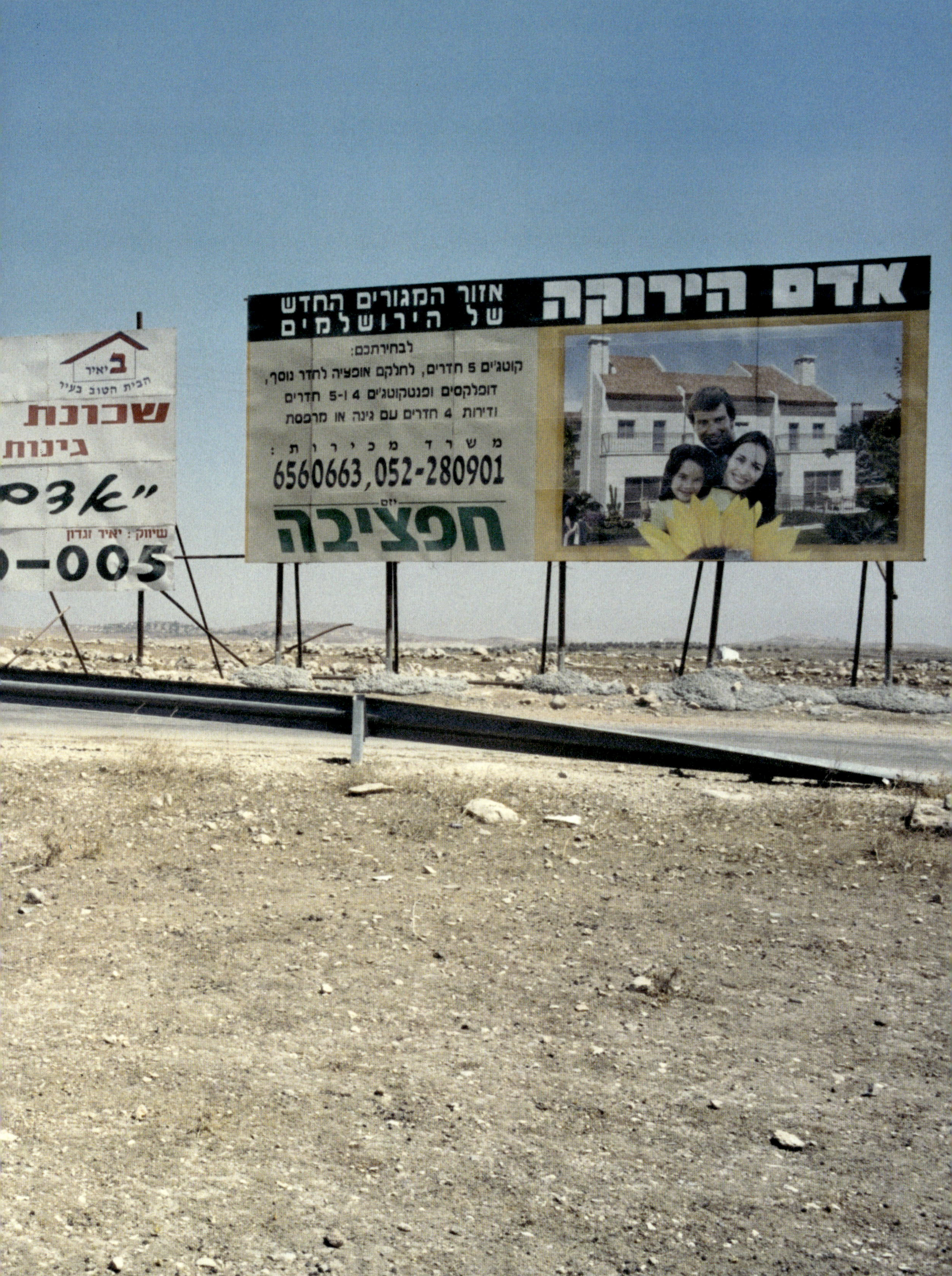
אדם הירוקה
אזור המגורים החדש
של הירושלמים
לבחירתכם:
קוטג'ים 5 חדרים, לחלקם אופציה לחדר נוסף,
דופלקסים ופנטקוטג'ים 4 ו-5 חדרים
ודירות 4 חדרים עם גינה או מרפסת
משרד מכירות:
6560663, 052-280901
יזם חפציבה
ביאיר
הבית הטוב בעיר
שכונת
גינות
"יאיר"
שיווק: יאיר זגדון
005-

176.

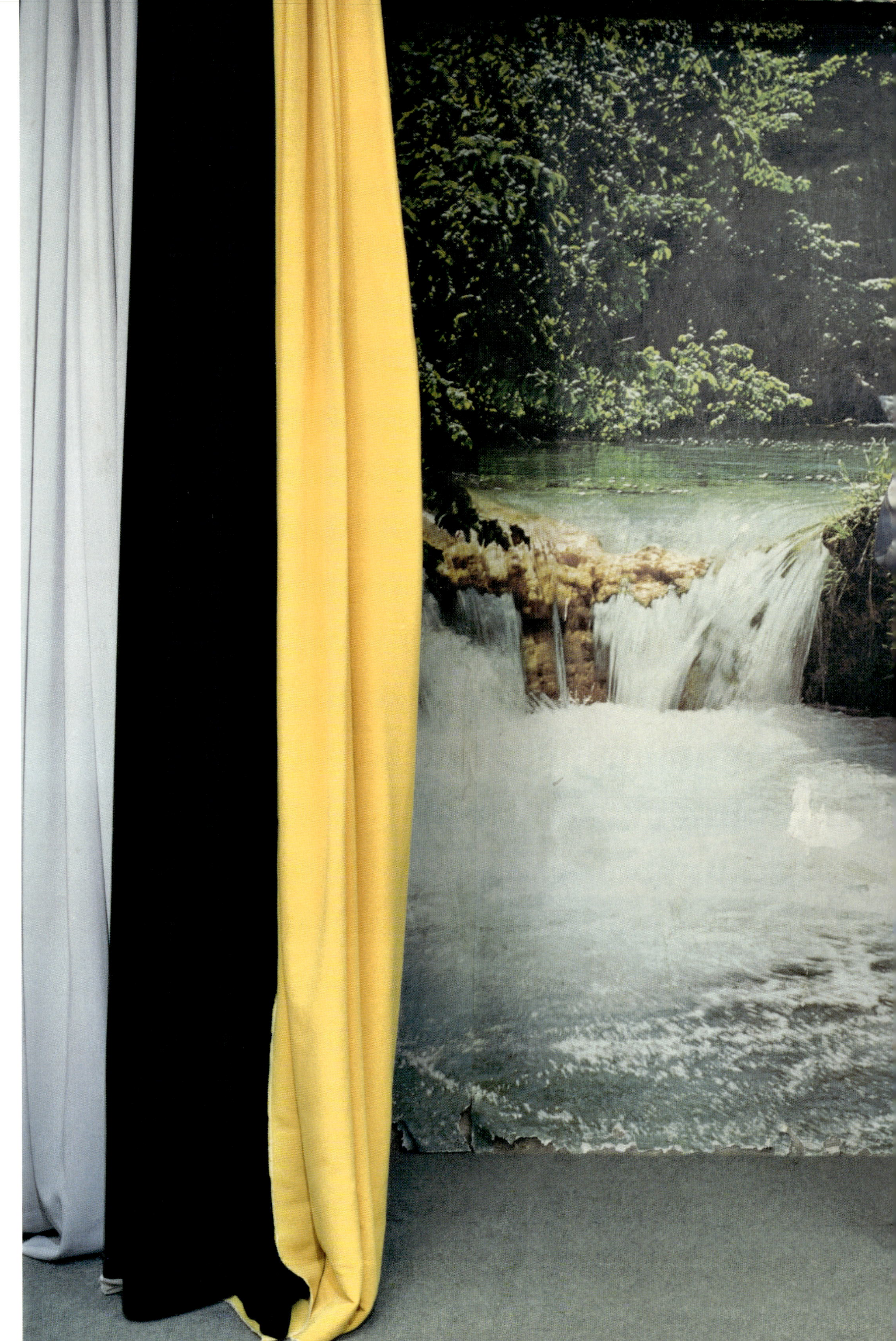

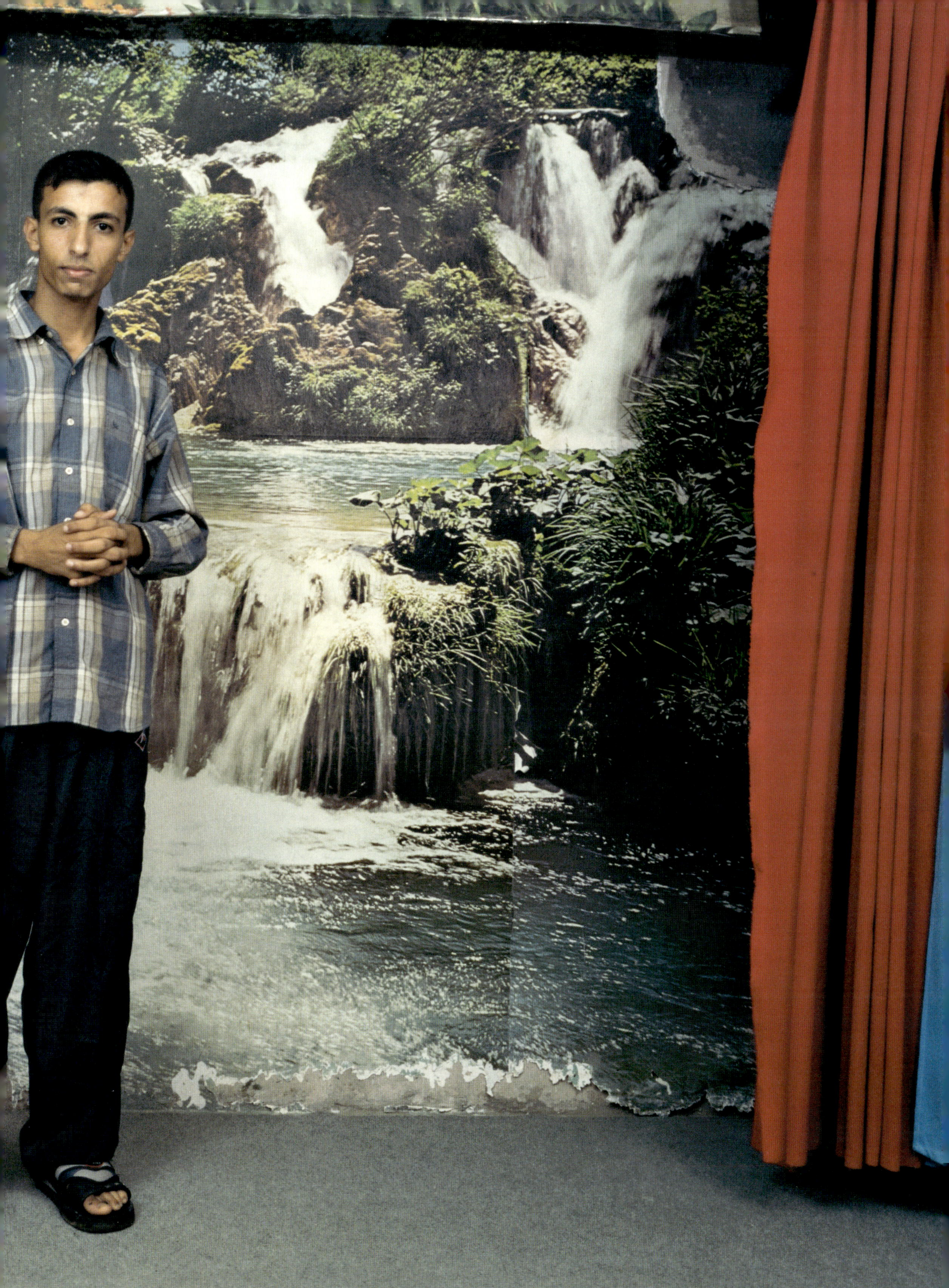

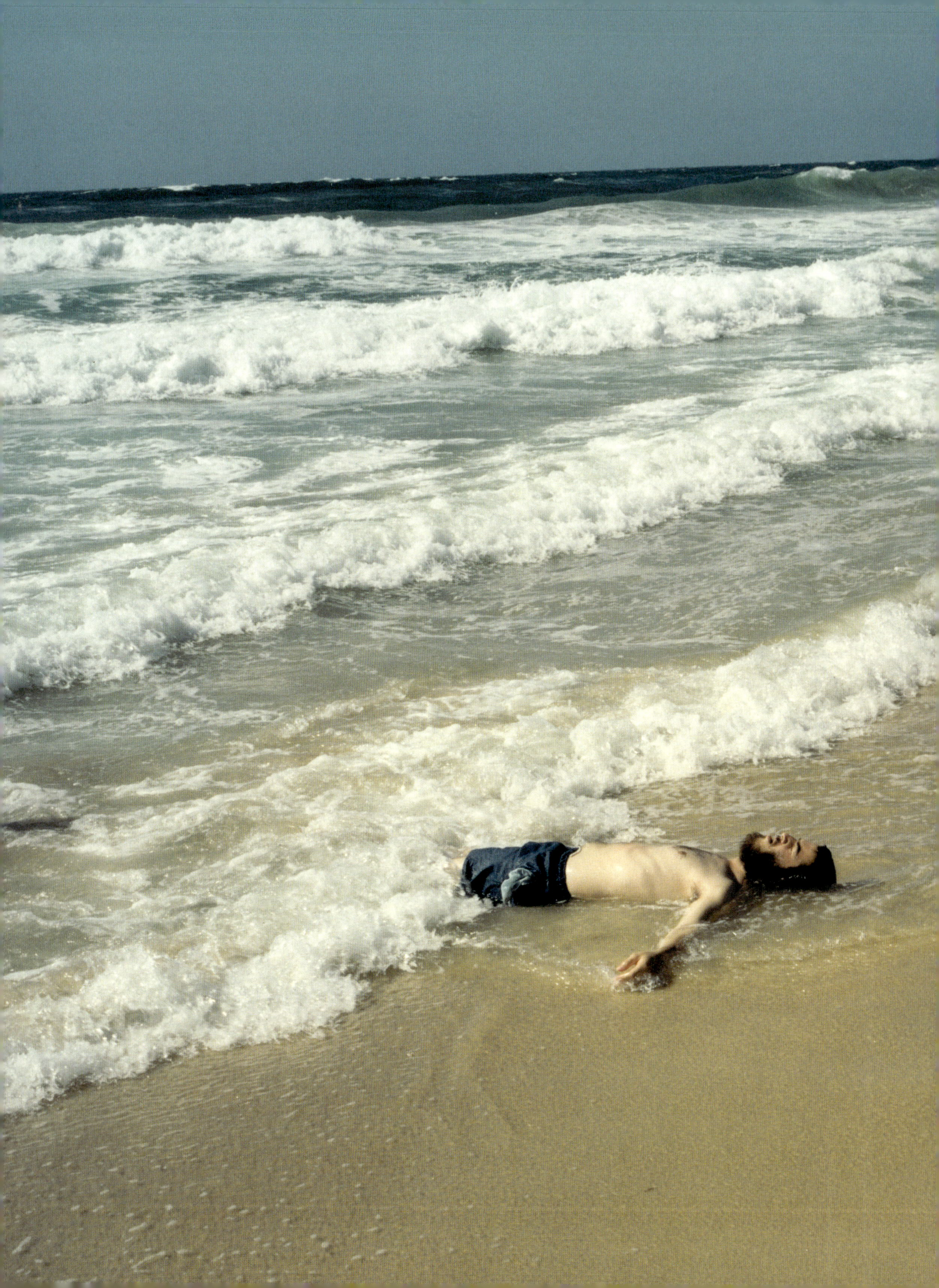

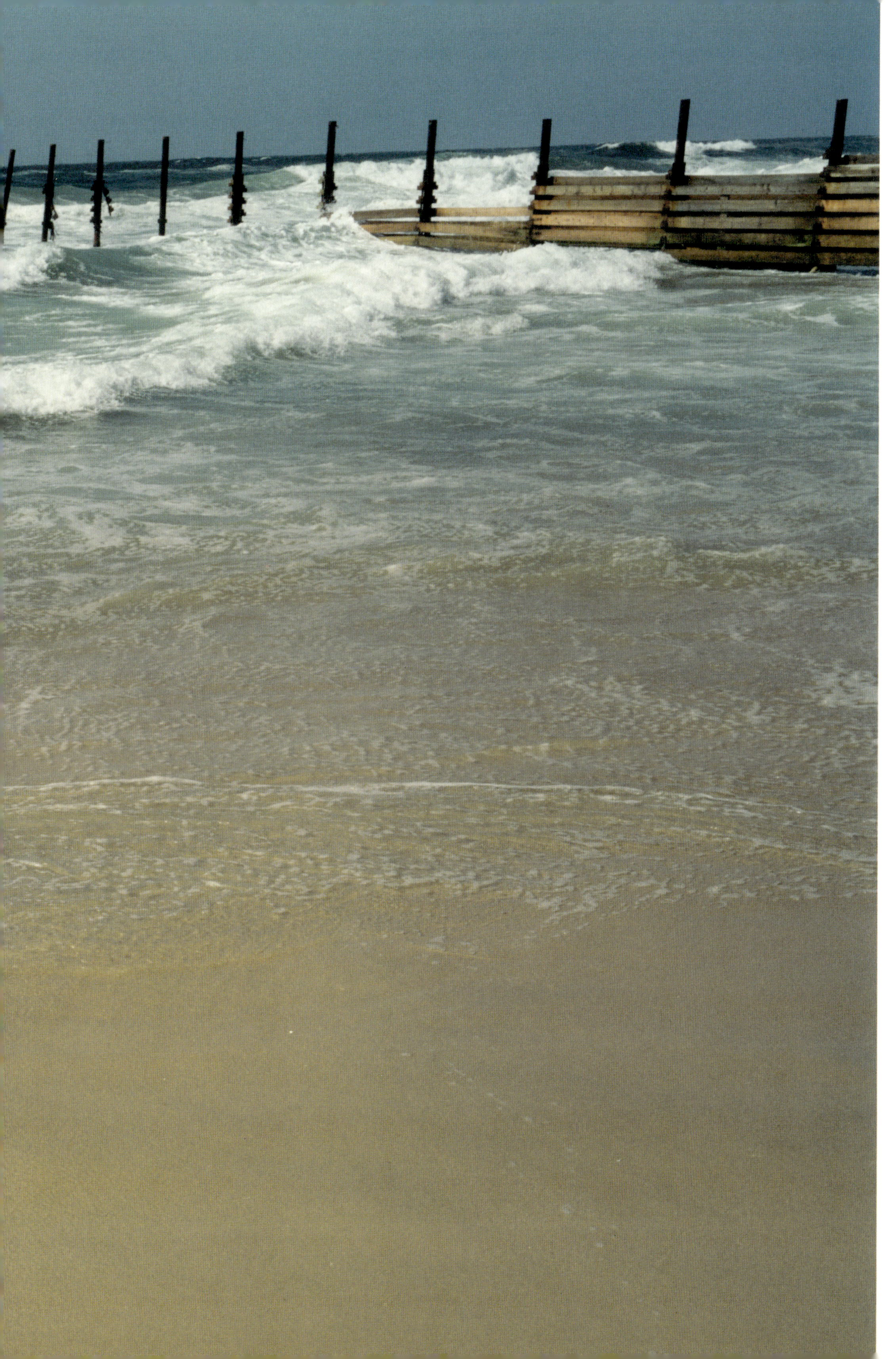

179.

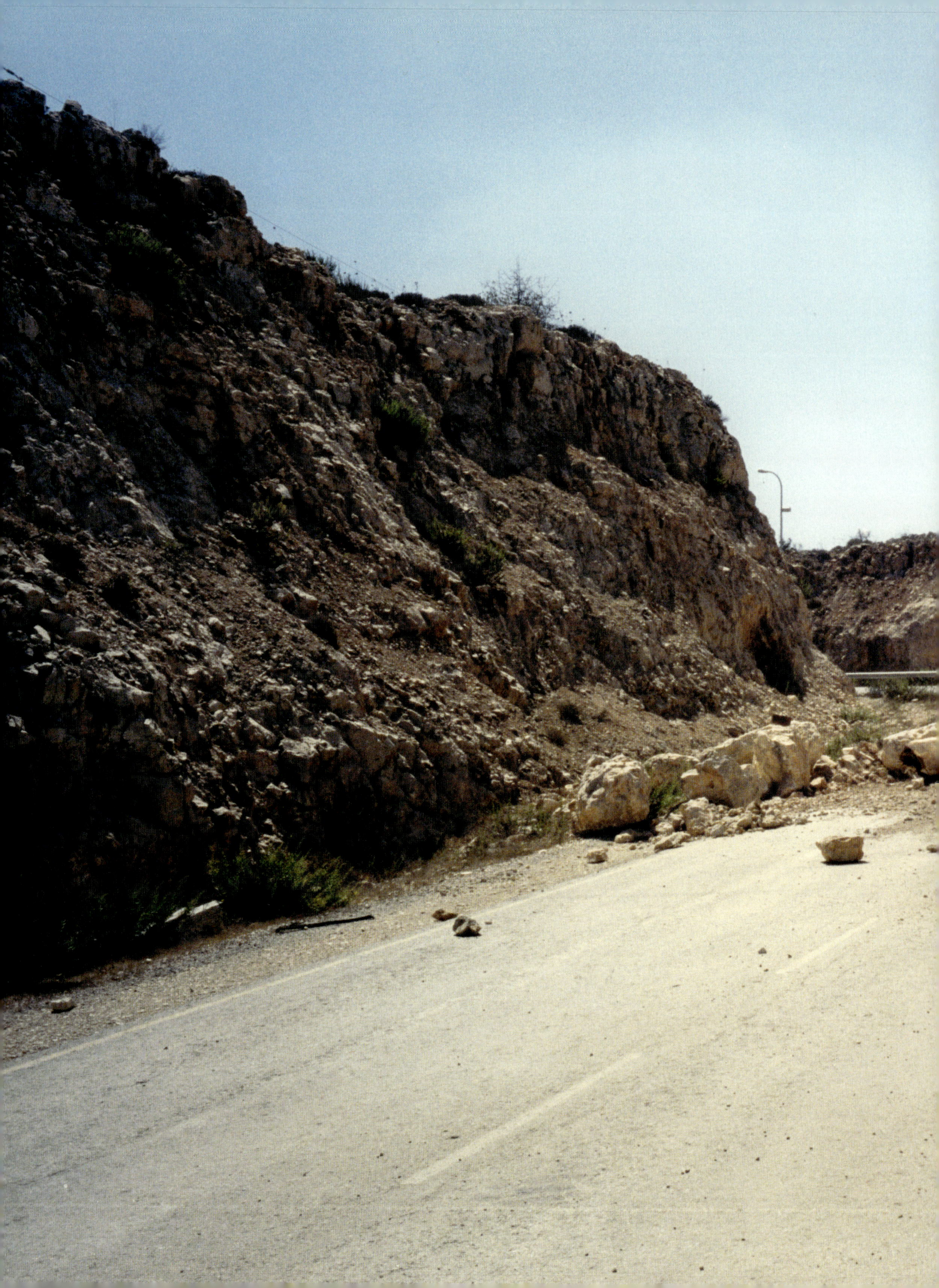

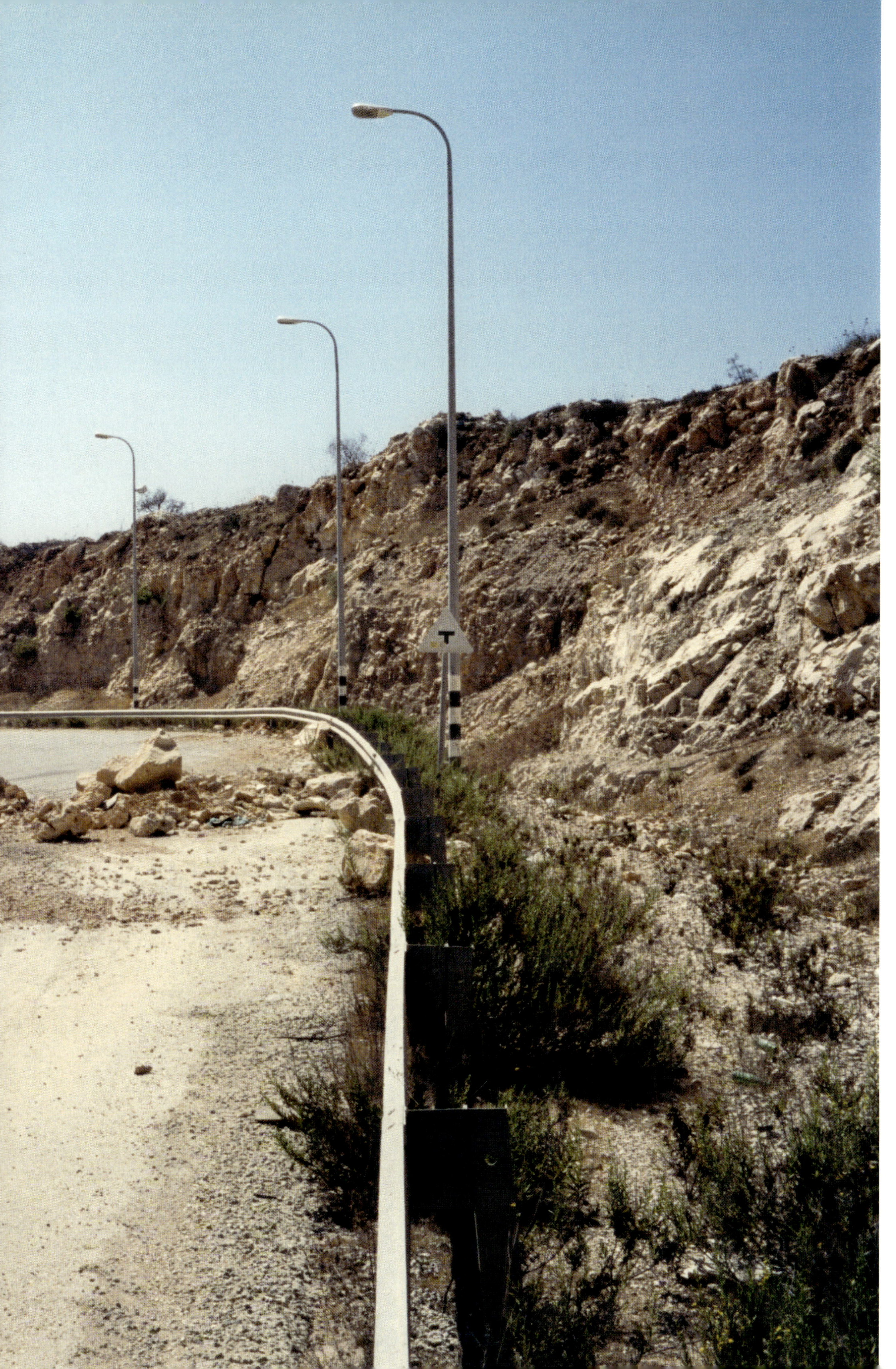

Only in 2007 did the abominable conditions in Egyptian prisons become world news, although organizations such as Human Rights Watch have been criticizing it for a long time. That year, 21-year-old Emad El-Kabir was thrown into prison for three months. He was molested and raped with a wooden stick by several police officers. When the video recorded by the officers found its way into the media twelve months later, it had a domino effect. More videos appeared and the truth about the Egyptian police and prison system, which had been hidden for years, became public.

Imprisonment in many Mediterranean countries is no picnic. Hardly any of the countries has a good record. Stories from Morocco tell of underage prisoners being raped; in Algeria and Libya you run the risk of being dumped in a stifling prison camp in the middle of the Sahara. In Greece and Turkey, regular demonstrations take place against the violent treatment of prisoners by prison wardens; French prisons are overfull; and Spanish prisons are considered the country's biggest breeding ground for Islamic radicals.

In total, around half a million people are in prison around the Mediterranean. One group of prisoners is not included in this statistic. This is the estimated three thousand prisoners suspected of terrorism who have been flown to countries such as Morocco, Egypt and Syria by the American CIA, where they can be harshly interrogated, beyond the reach of lawyers and human rights organizations.

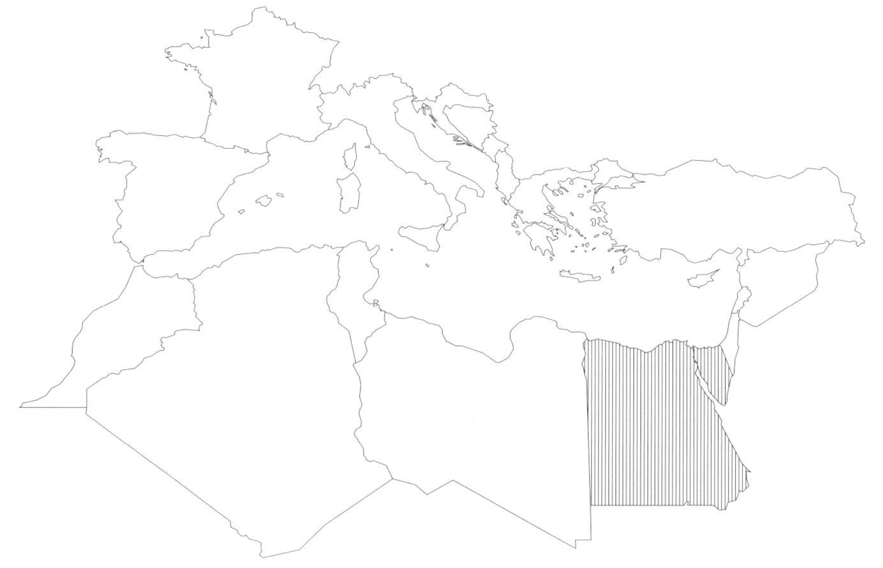

PRISONERS
PER 100,000 POPULATION

GIBRALTAR	136	
SPAIN	145	
FRANCE	85	
ITALY	104	
CROATIA	81	
ALBANIA	111	
GREECE	90	
CYPRUS	76	
TURKEY	91	
SYRIA	58	
LEBANON	168	
ISRAEL	209	
W.B. & GAZA	NA	
EGYPT	**87**	
LIBYA	207	
TUNISIA	263	
ALGERIA	127	
MOROCCO	175	

SOURCE : WORLD PRISON POPULATION LIST

NOTE   : THE NUMBER OF PRISONERS AND THE CRIME RATE [P. 67] SHOW A REMARKABLE DISCREPANCY

185. SINAI DESERT
The Sinai is an enormous sandpit bisected by the Suez Canal. I never saw any work being carried out on this construction site.

187. ALEXANDRIA
Most of the beaches in Alexandria have foreign names. This is Miami Beach. The moral police keep a close watch and ensure everyone behaves themselves.

189. IDKU
President Mubarrak being erected at the Baltim resort. I was ill in bed for two days here; an officer from the security police kept watch in the lobby of the hotel.

191. PORT SAID
Women and cars are men's most expensive possessions. When I took a photo of two women on the beach, one of them ripped off her niqab. 'My brothers say I have to wear it,' she said, 'but you don't think that I'd have my photo taken with this thing over my face, do you?'

192. ALEXANDRIA
Friday afternoon and the man of the house has just come out of the sea. Under President Nasser in 1956, women paraded over the boulevard in the afternoon wearing suits and stilettos.

195. ALEXANDRIA
A family cruises over the Boulevard of the 26th July in a homemade cabriolet.

196. MERSA MATRUH
In the Mövenpick resort, the futile struggle of man against desert goes on.

198. ALEXANDRIA
Trams at the Masr bus and train station. Alexandria is a pleasant and relaxed city. The religious climate is becoming increasingly conservative, however, under the influence of the Muslim Brotherhood.

201. ALEXANDRIA
Arabic versions of soft-porn books are laid out on the pavement. The Arabic models have black strips over their eyes in order to conceal their identity. Women in black niqabs walk along the same pavement. The only thing you can see of them is their eyes.

202. PORT SAID
In the summer families from Cairo flee to walled resorts on the Mediterranean. Women bathe fully clothed and are always accompanied by a family member.

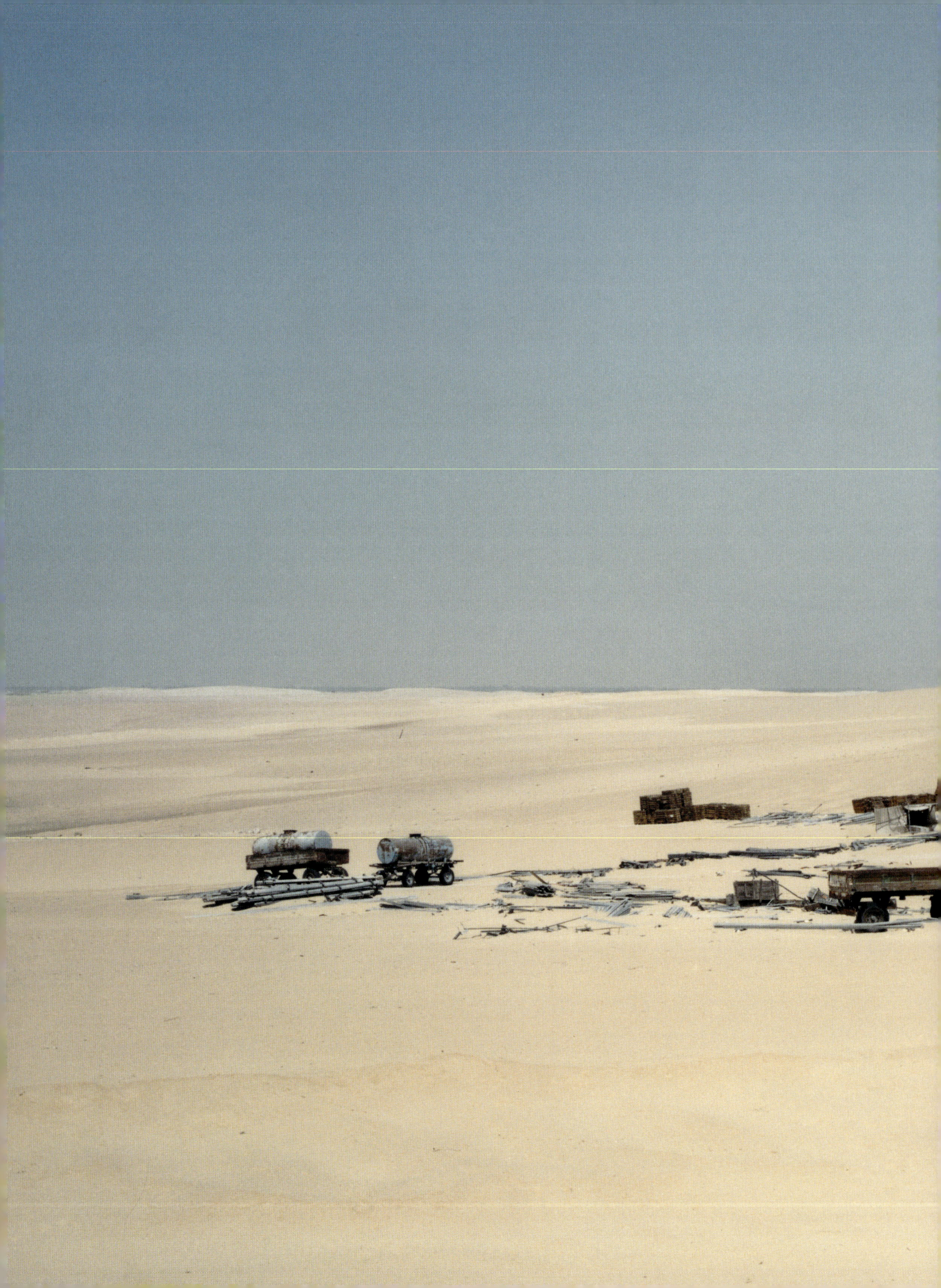

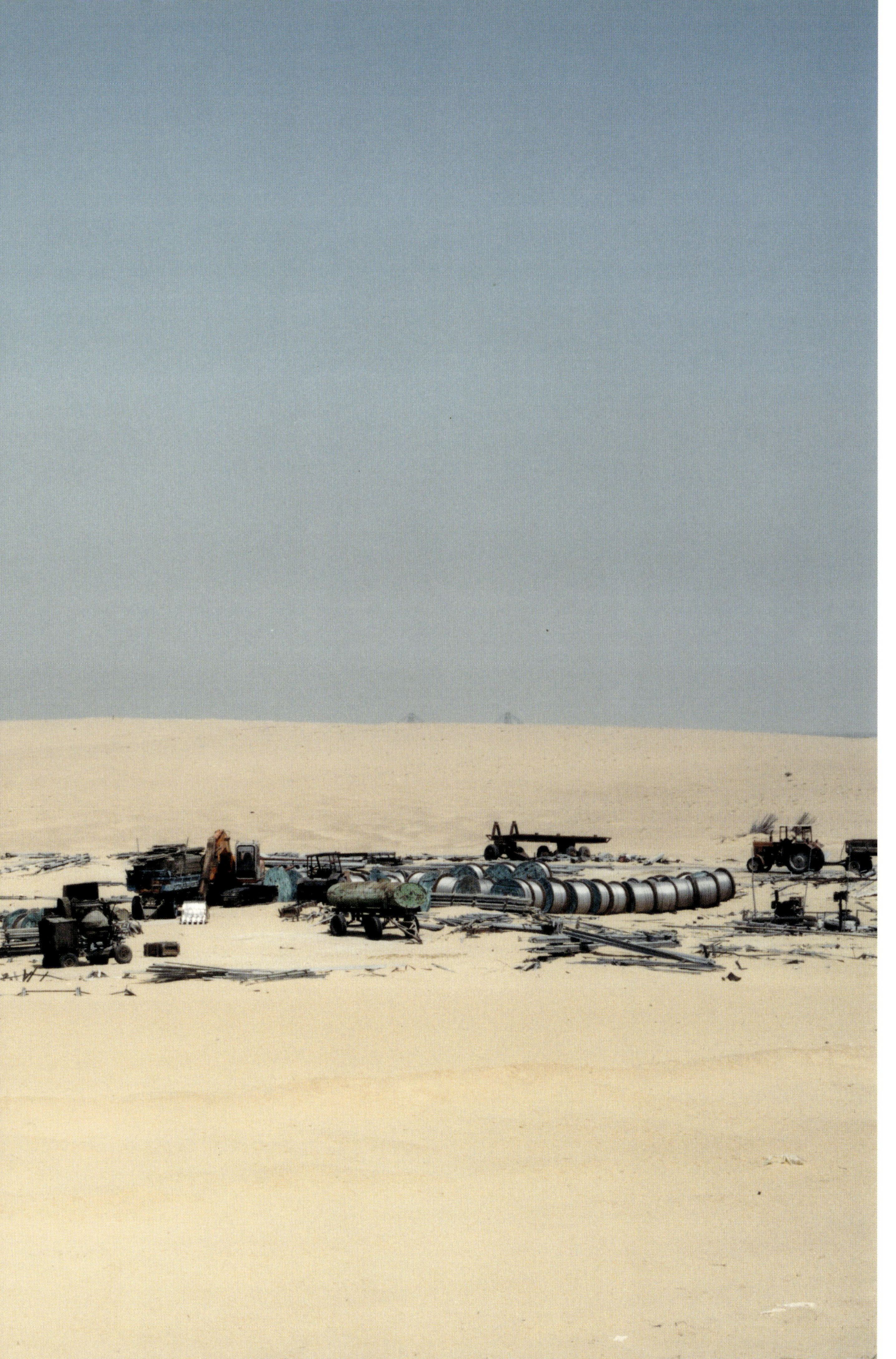

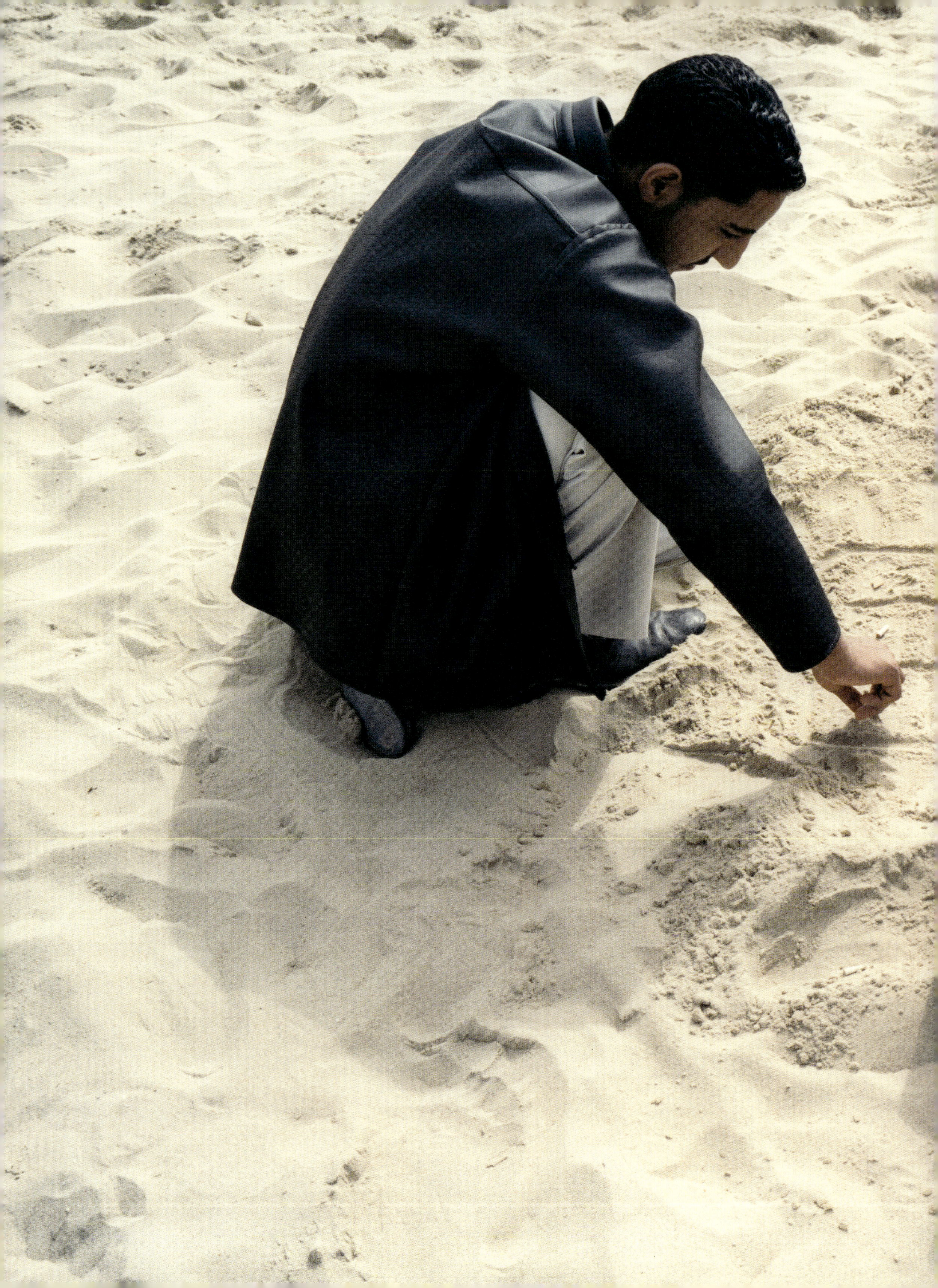

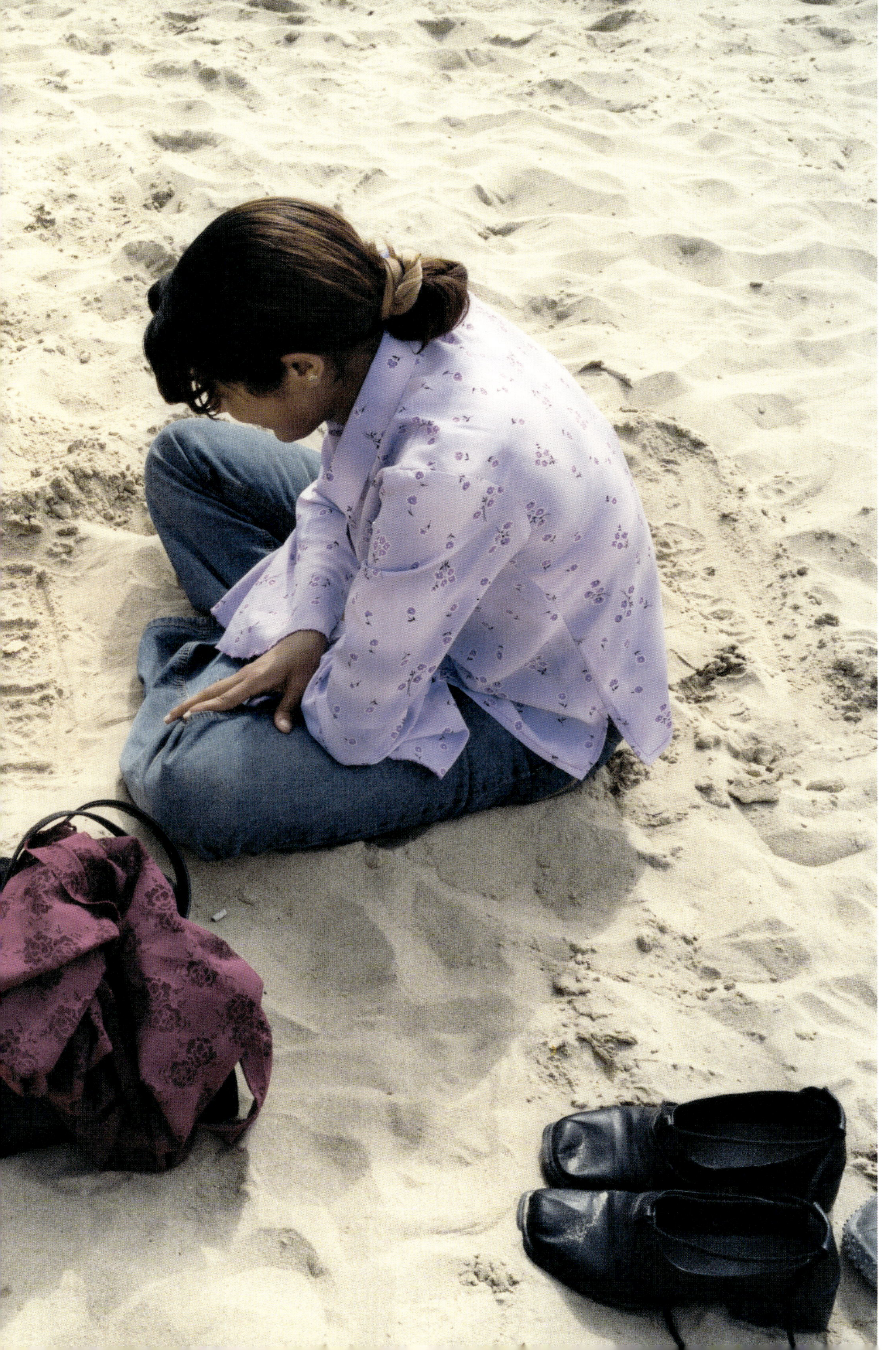

187.

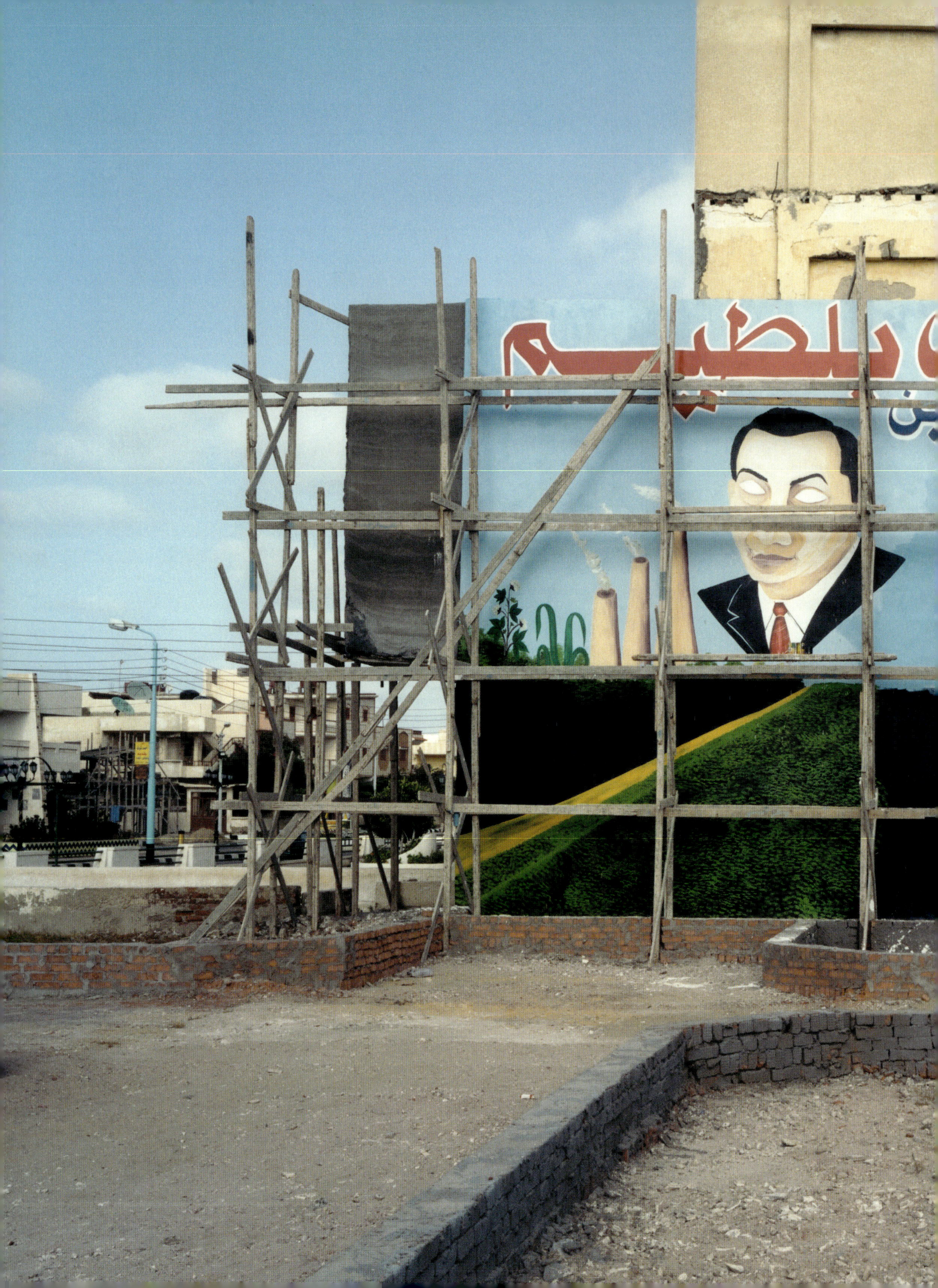

دلضيم
بن

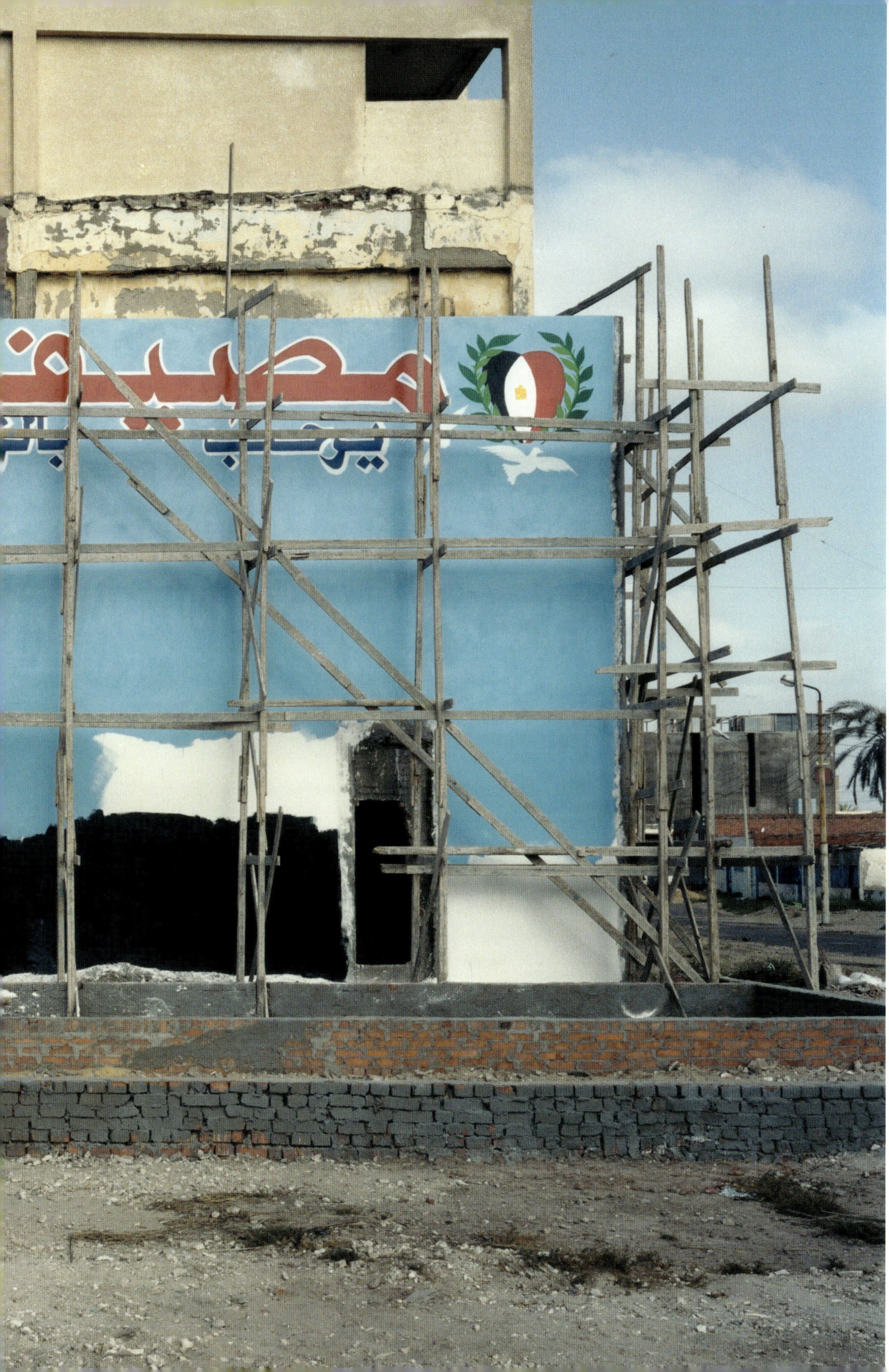

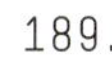

189.

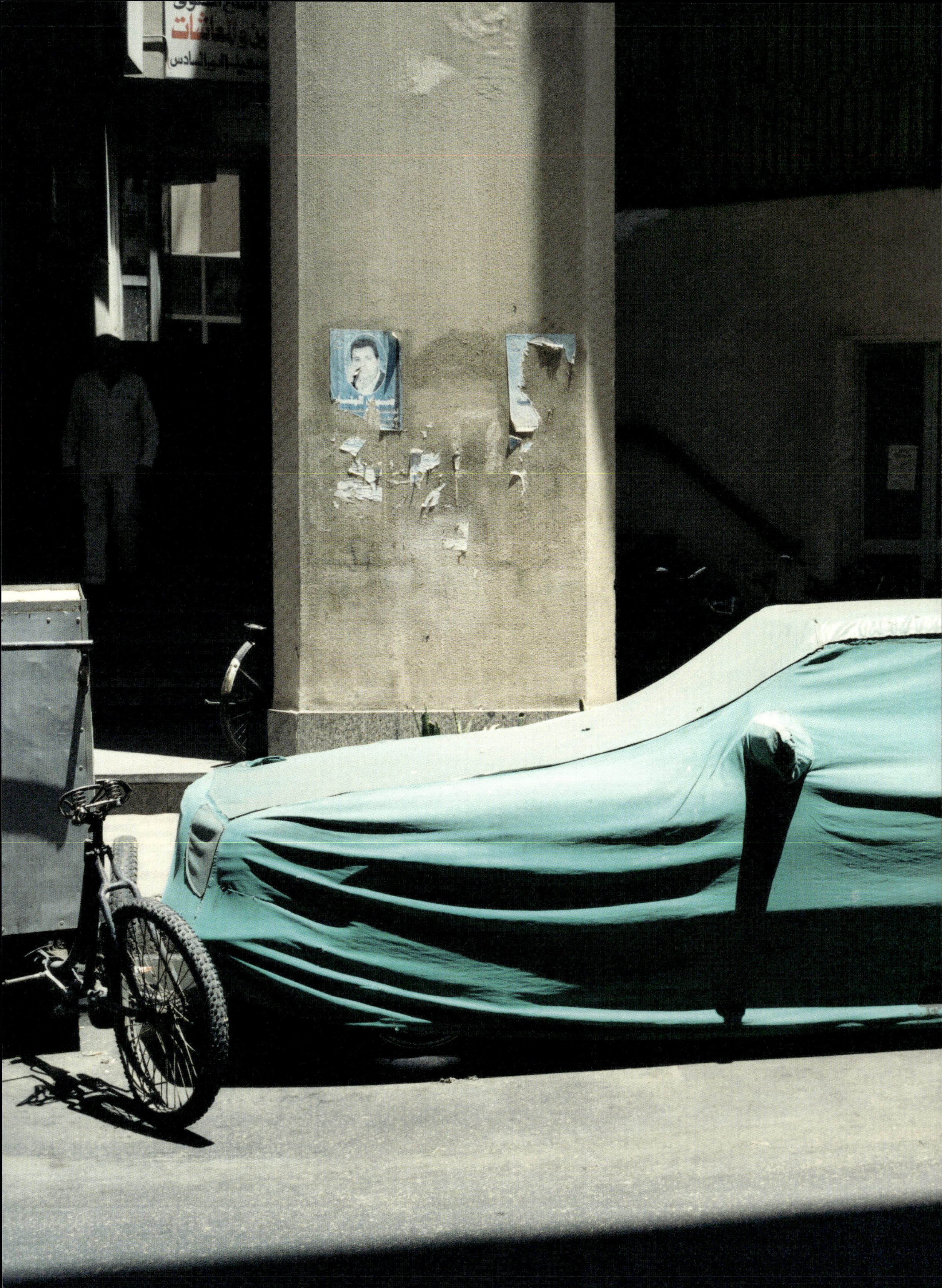
للمعاشات
عبد الحي السادس

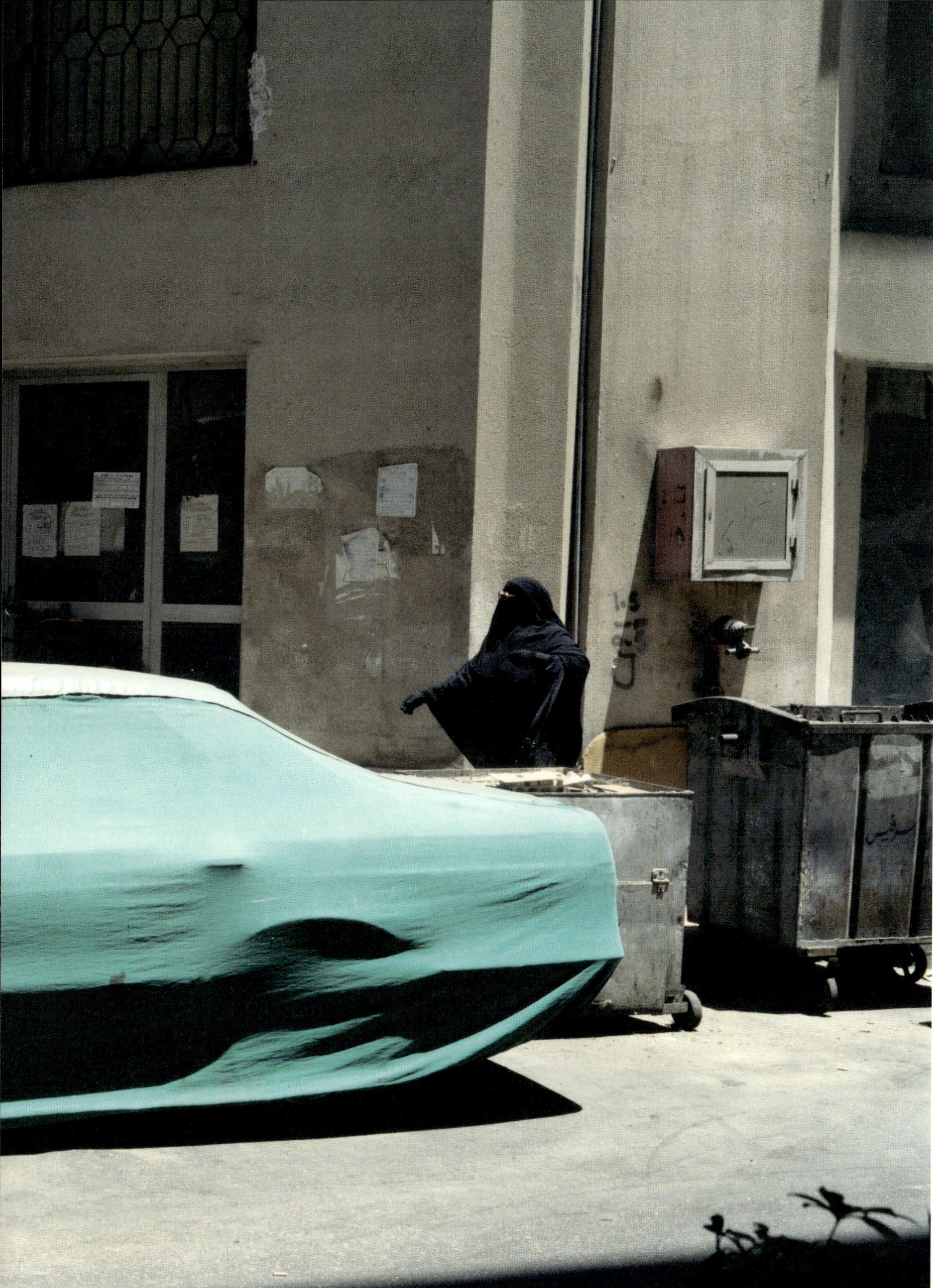

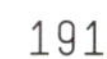

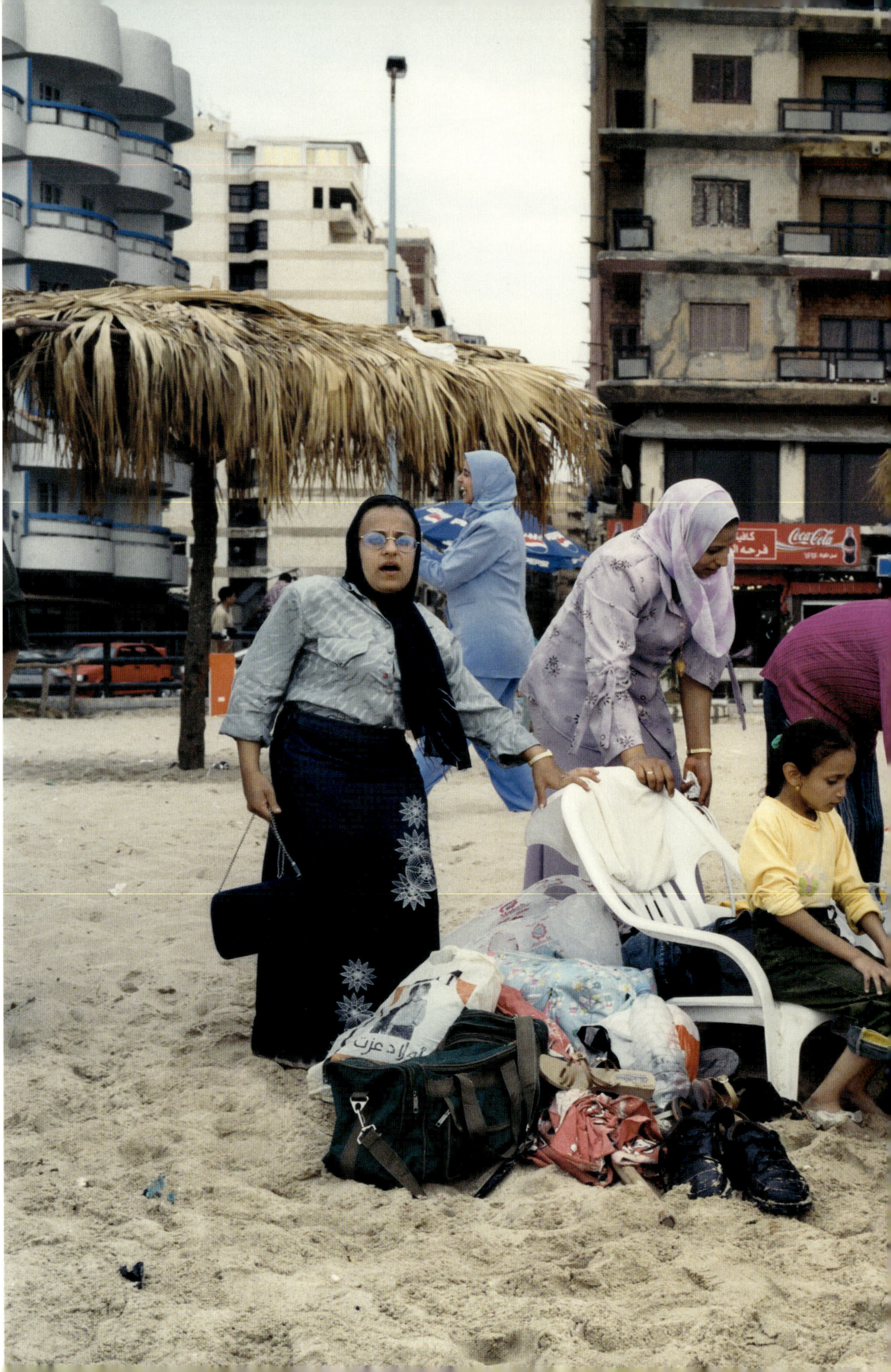

192.

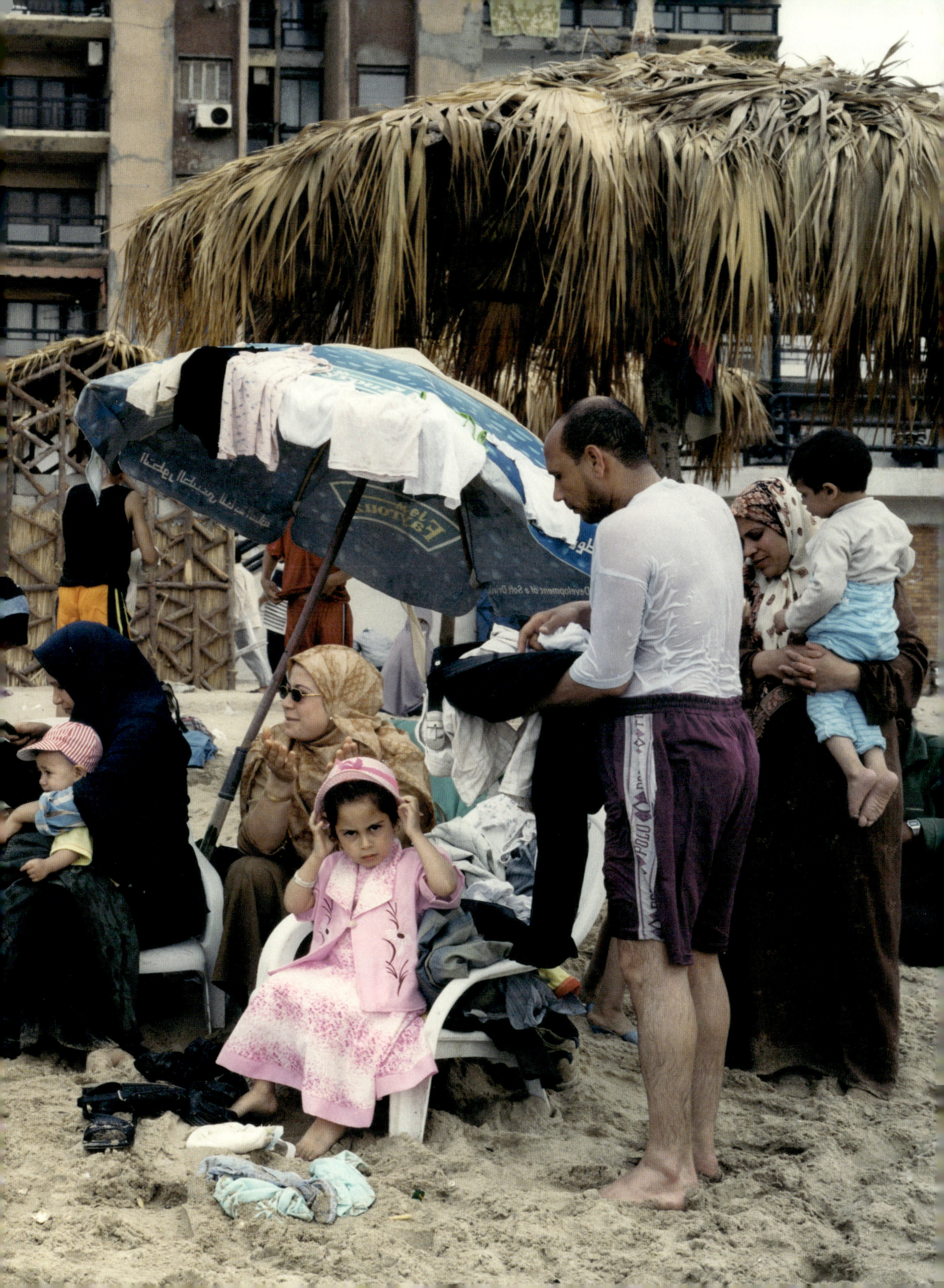

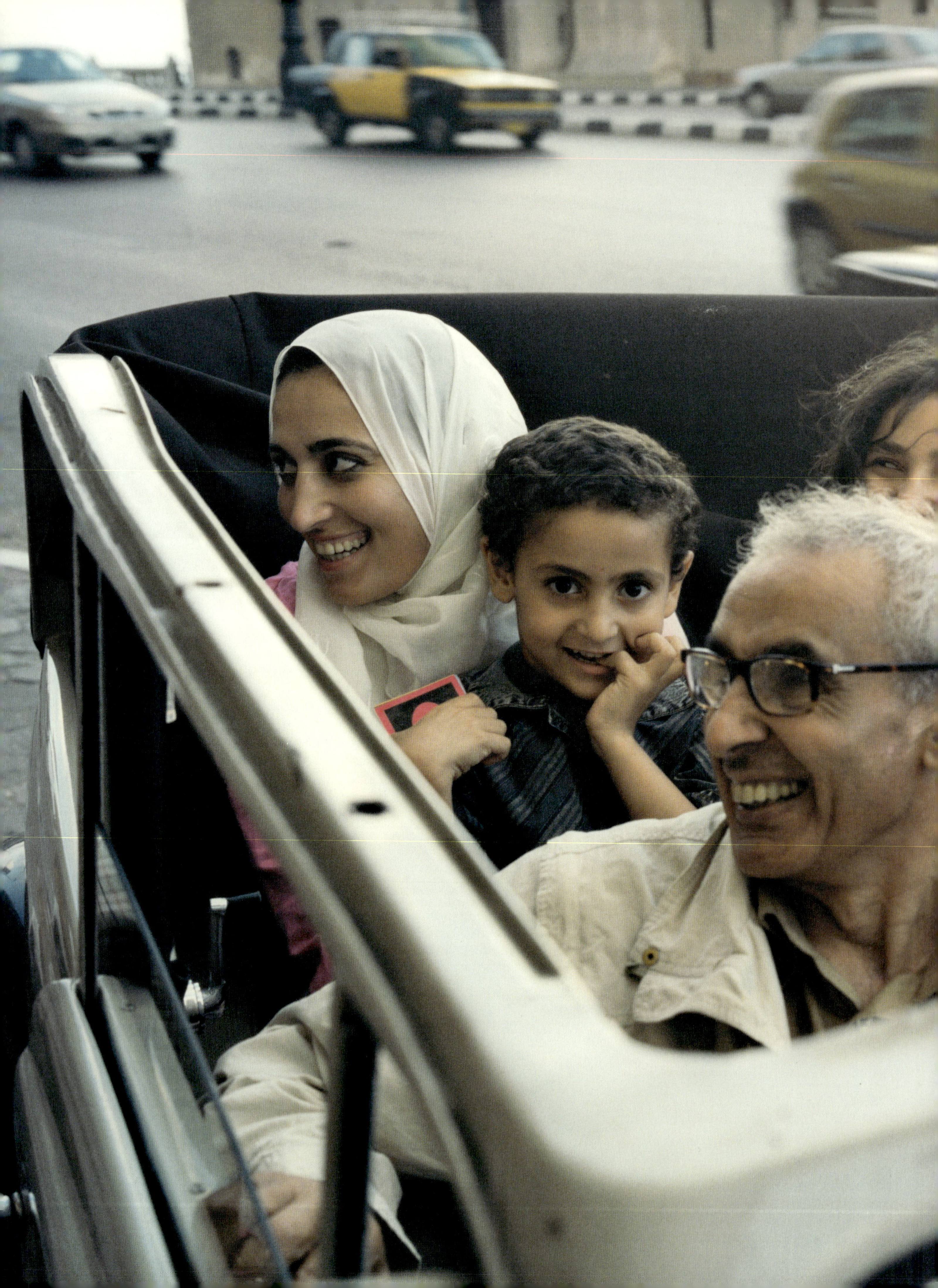

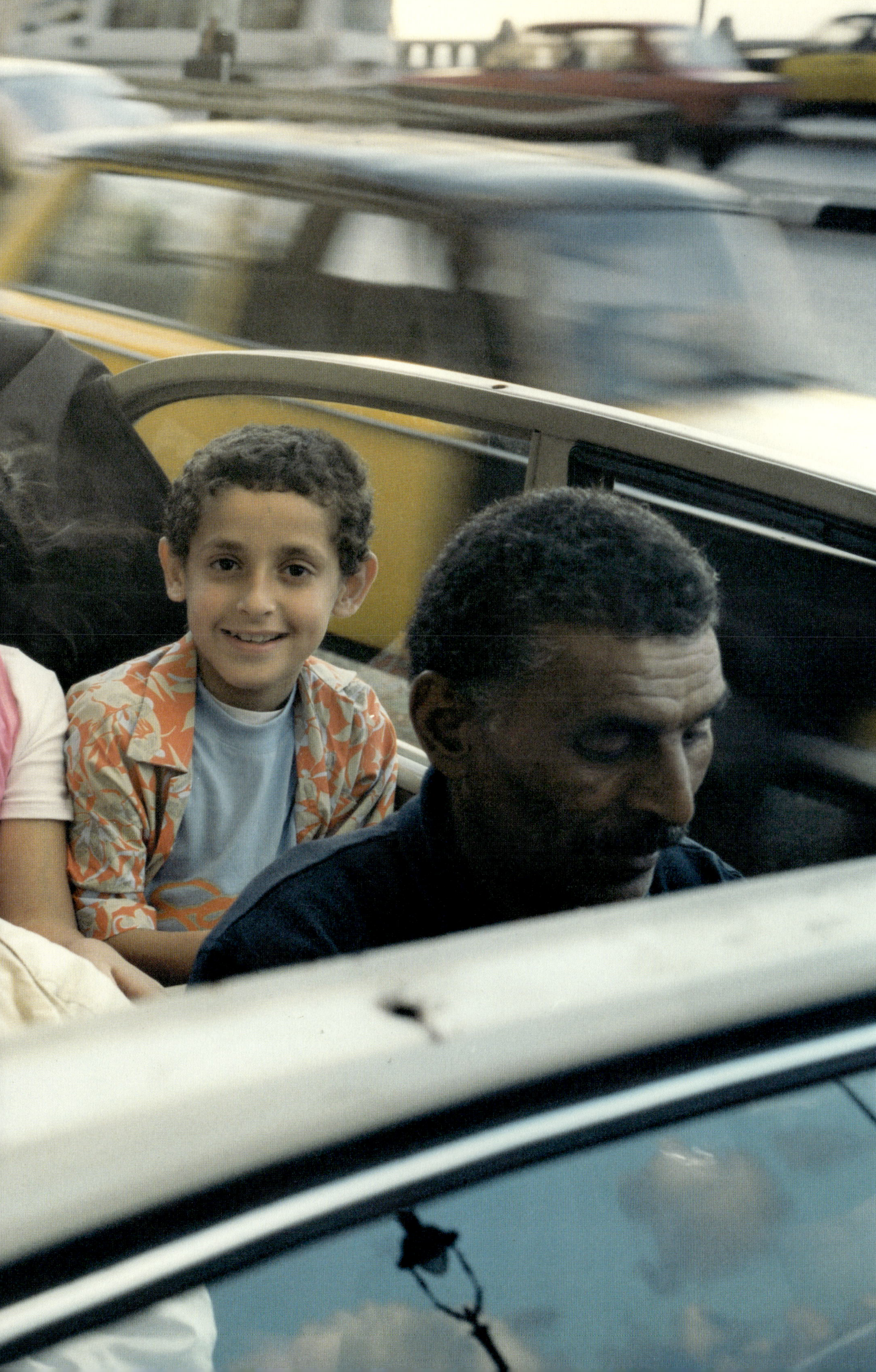

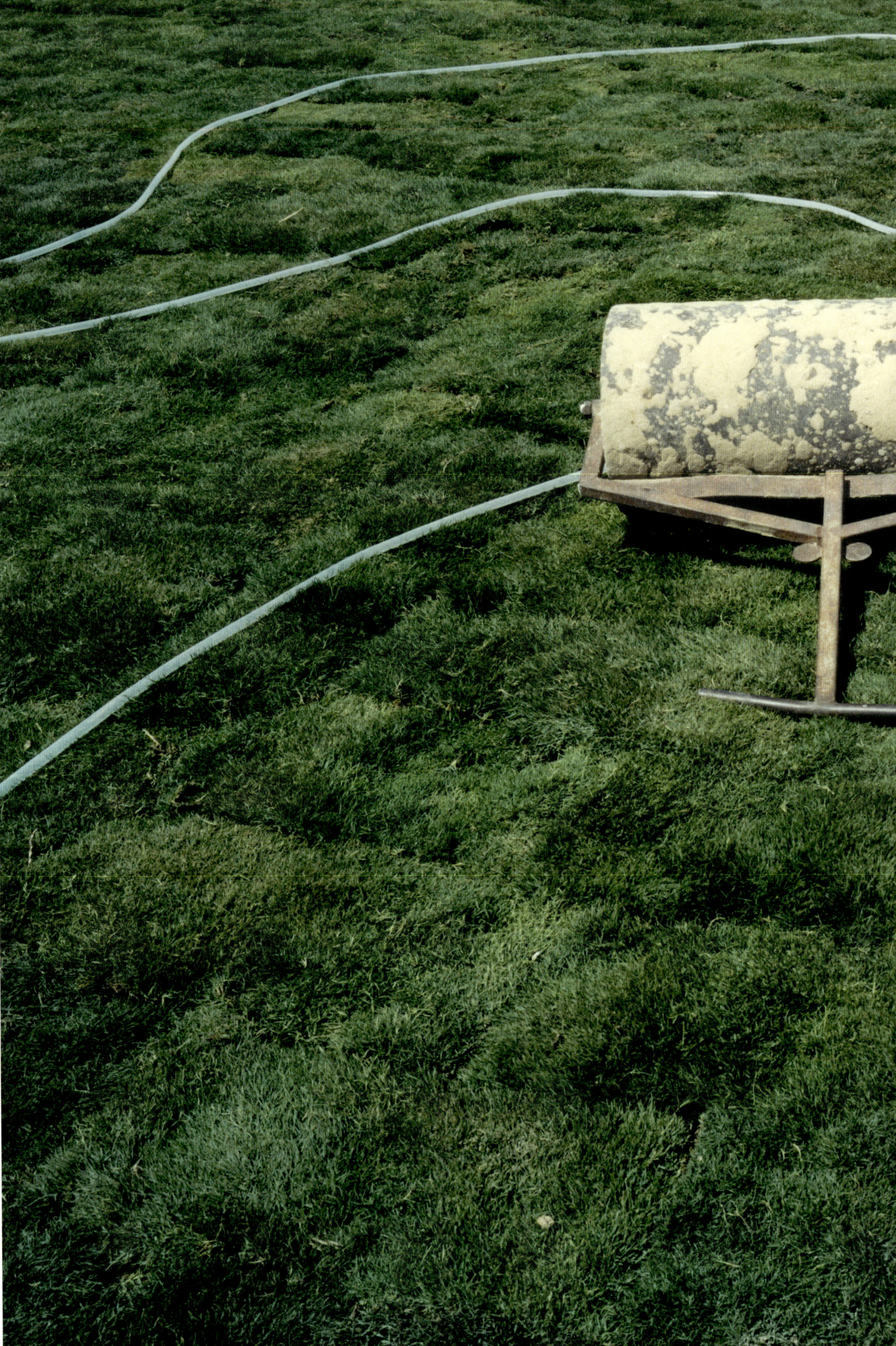

196.

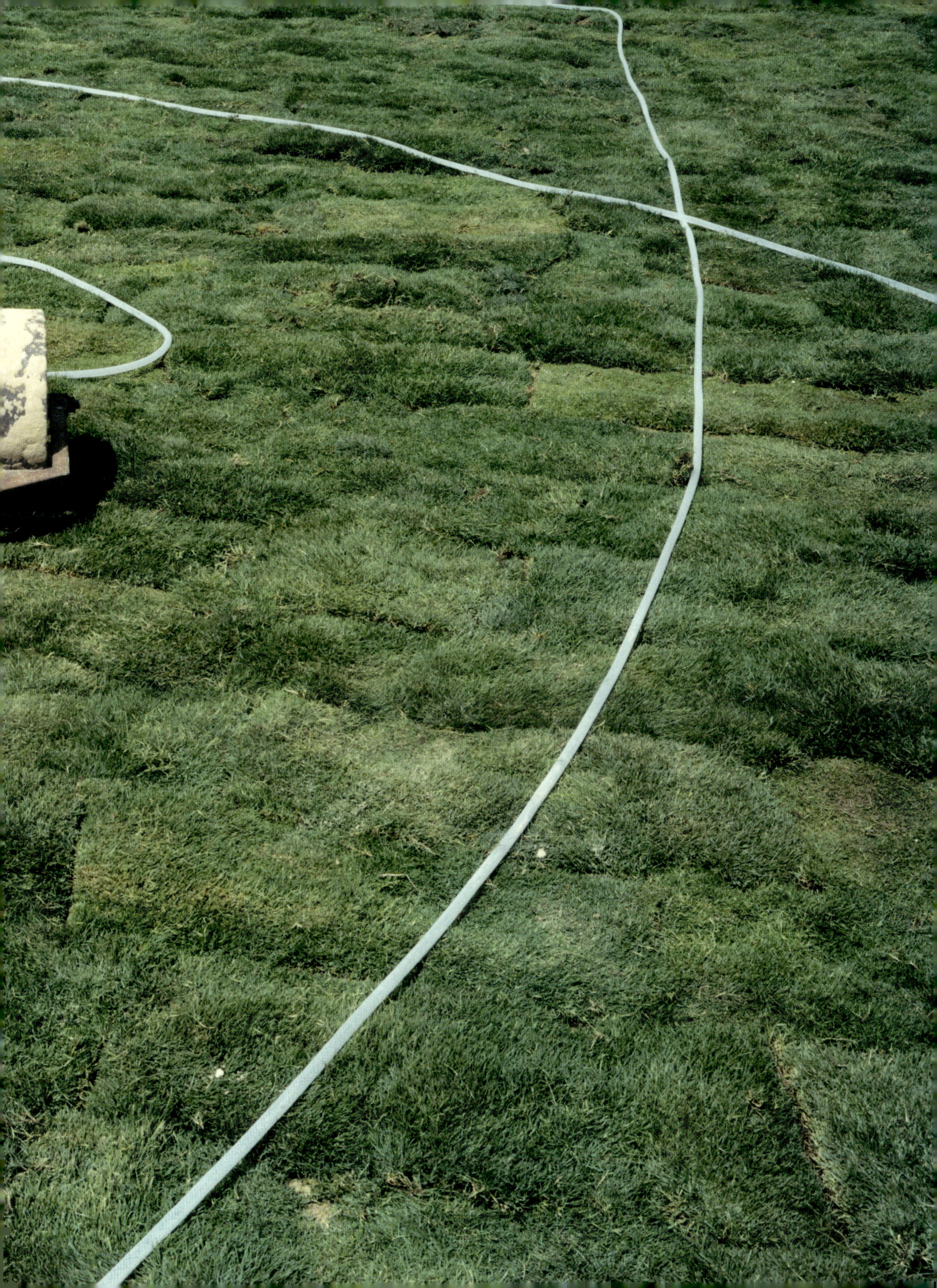

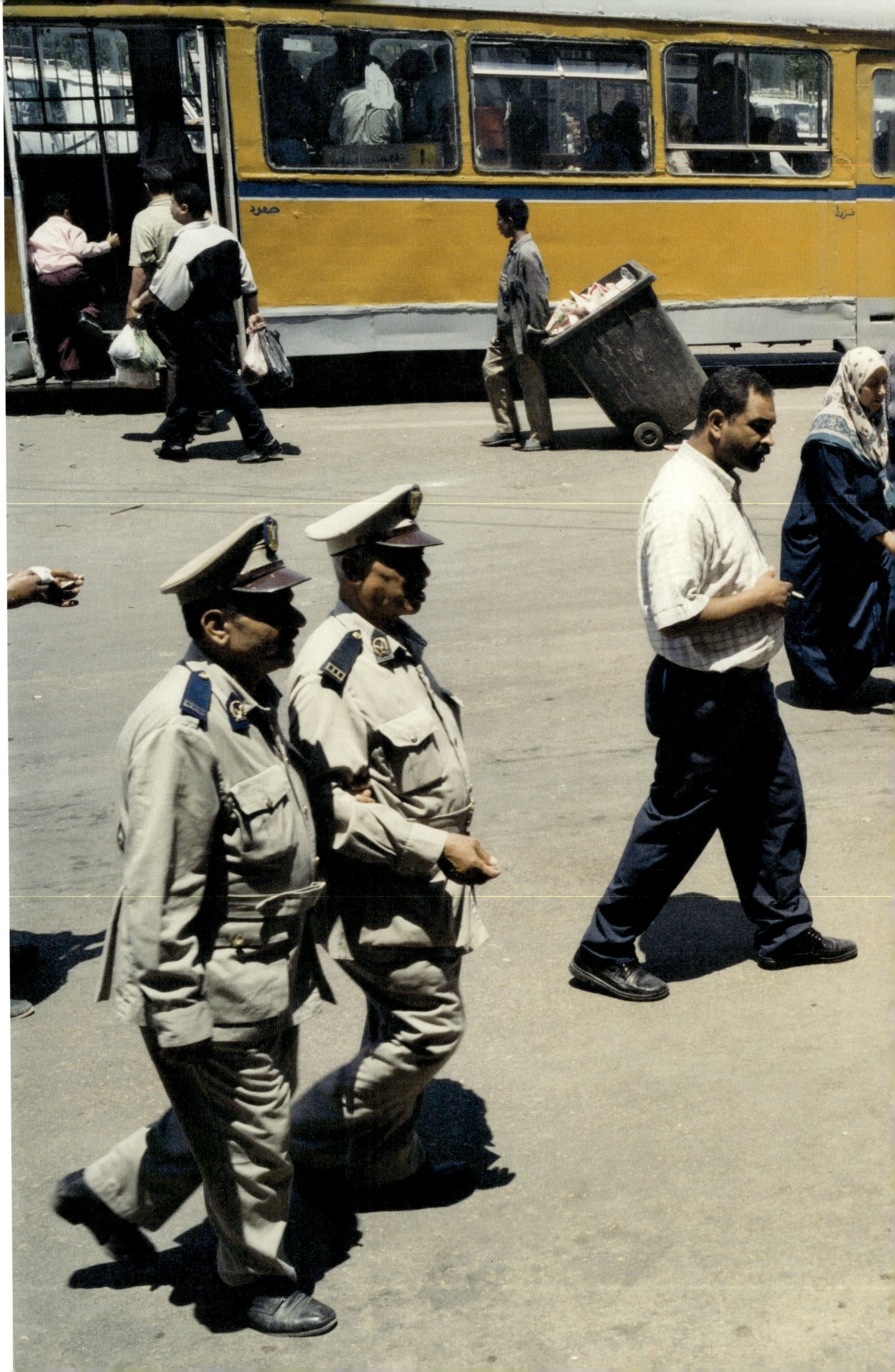

198.

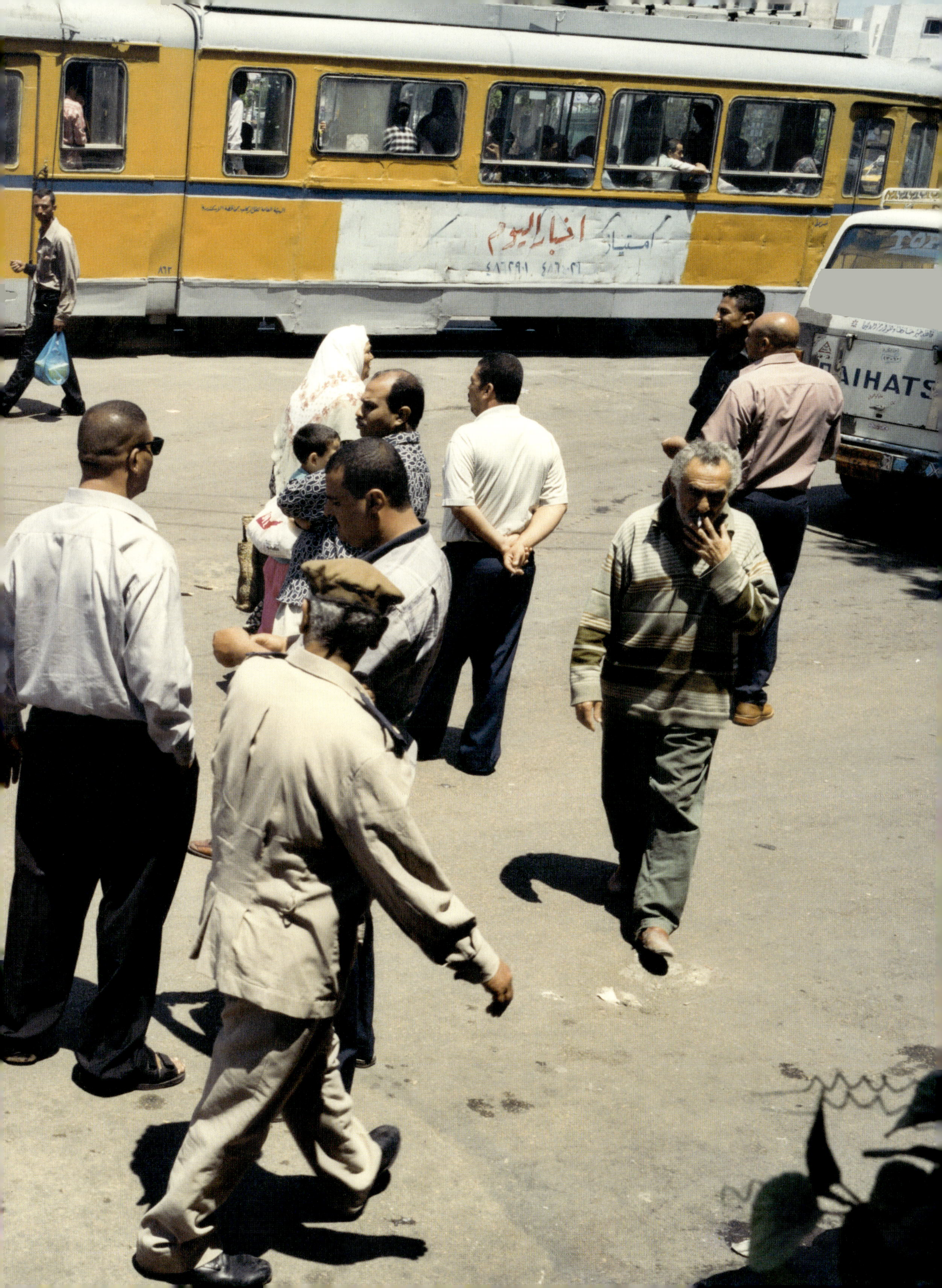

امتياز اخبار اليوم
٥٨٦٢٩١ ٥٨٦٠٦٢
DAIHATS

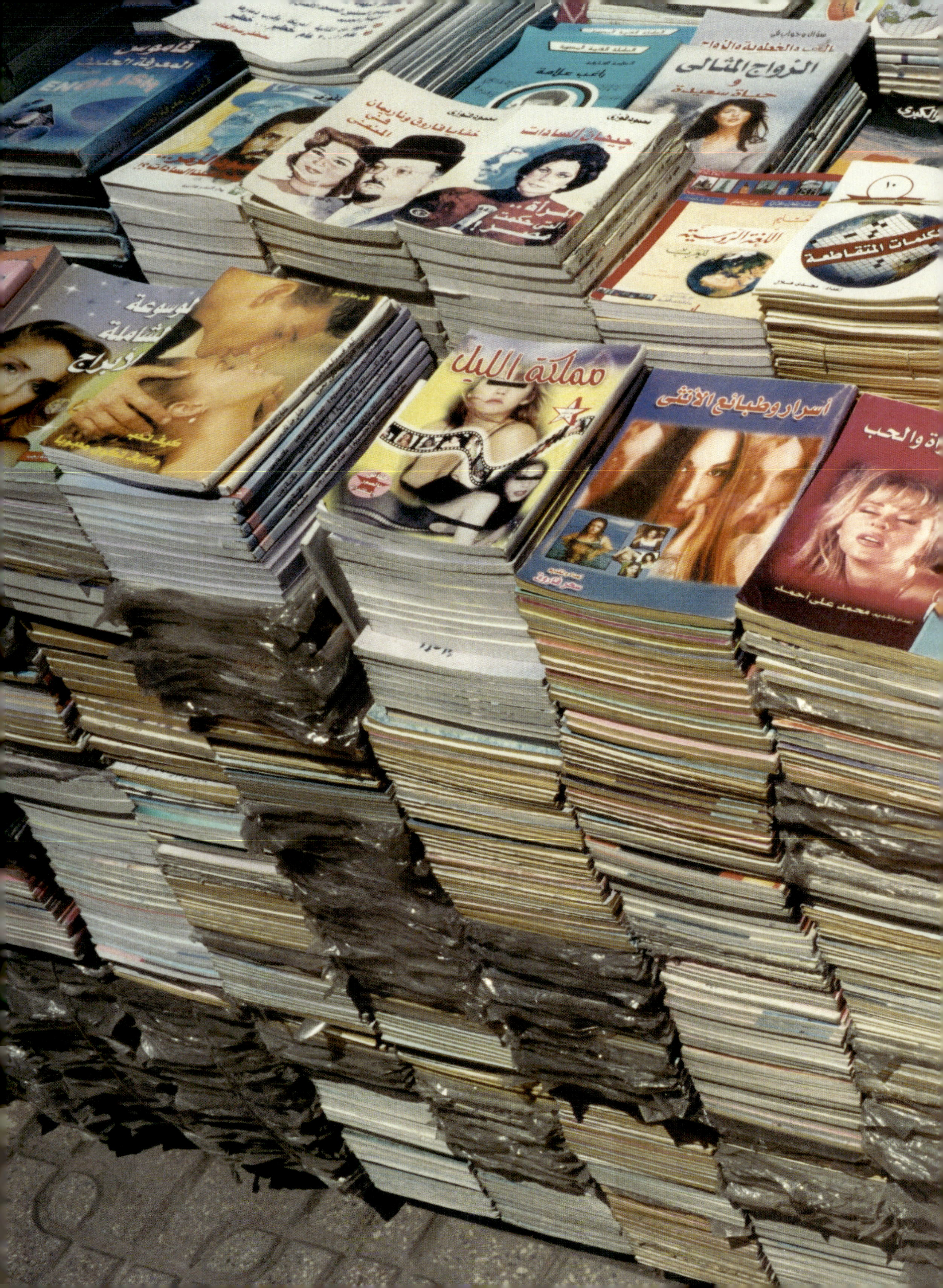

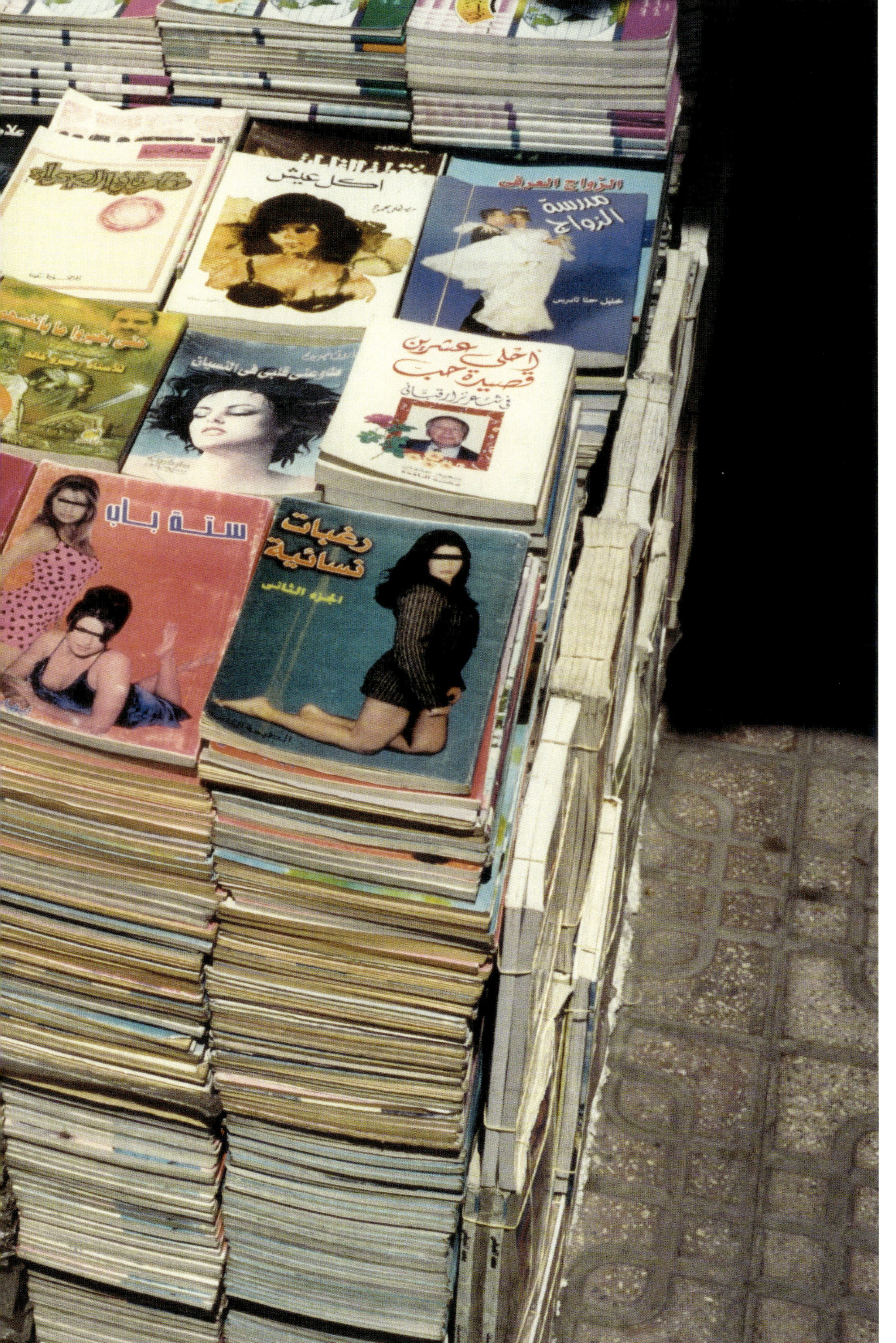

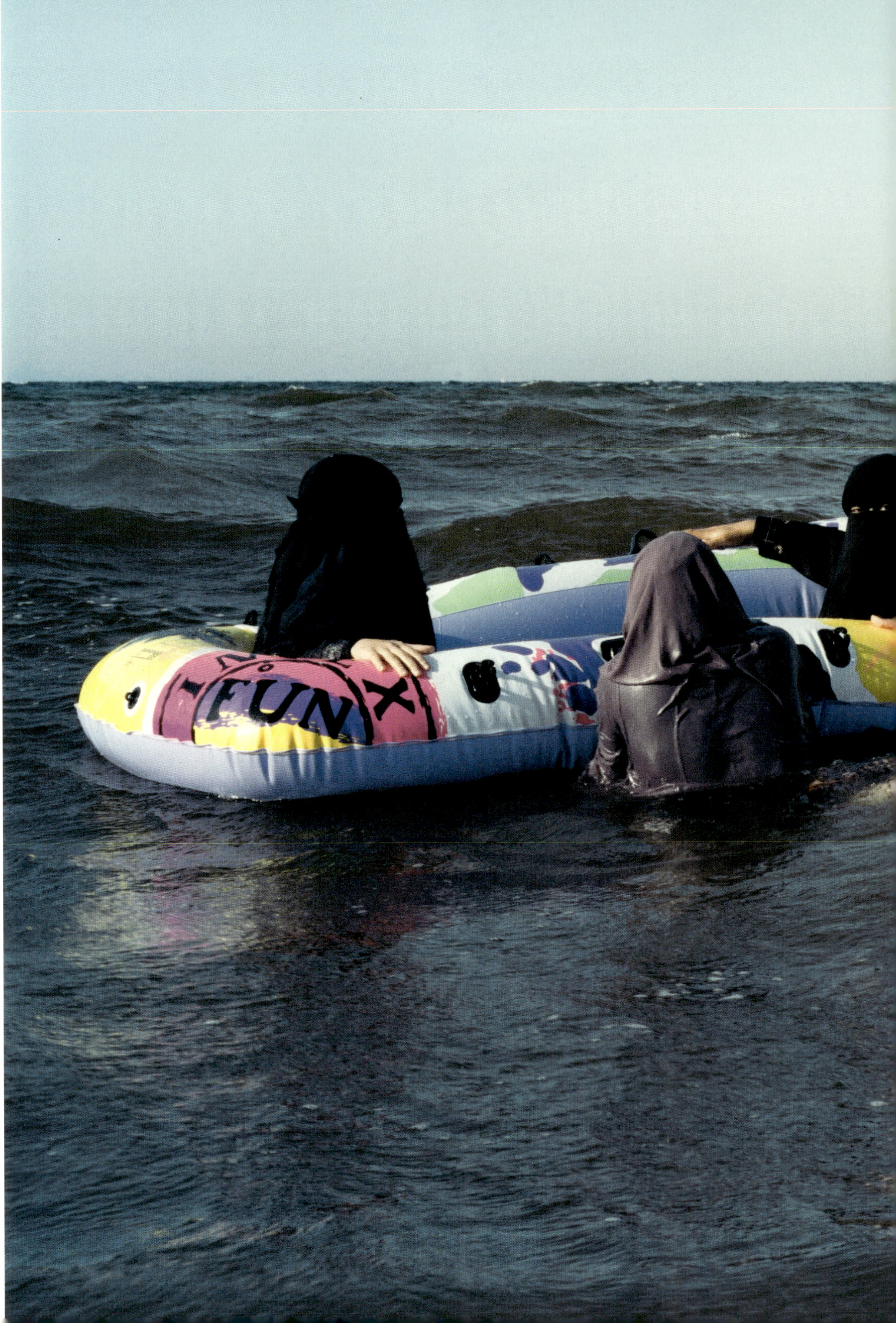
FUN

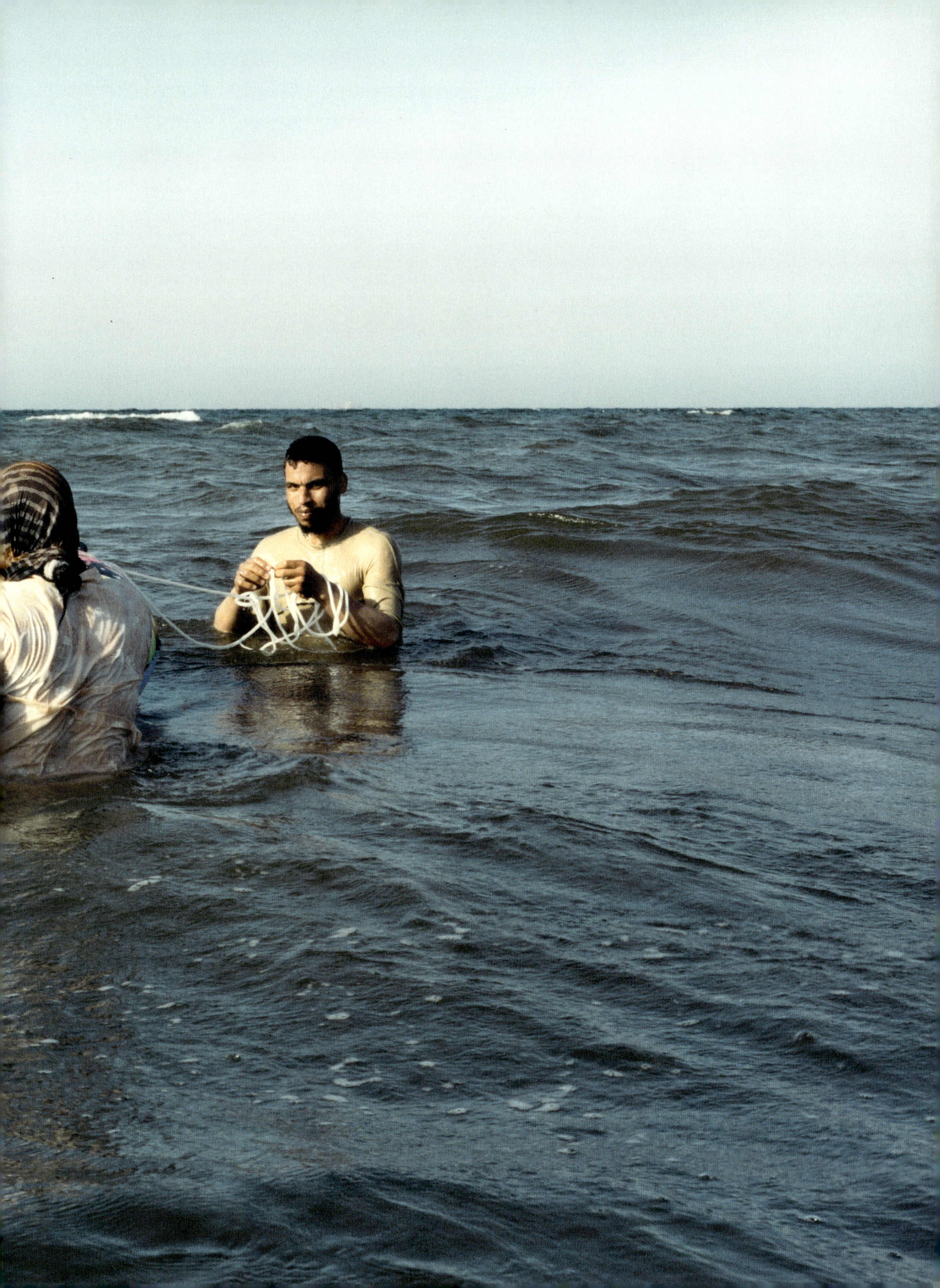

The Libyan economy revolves to a large extent around revenue from its oil industry. Oil contributes about 95% of the country's income from export, and a quarter of its gross national produce (GNP). After Algeria, it is the largest oil exporter in the Mediterranean. While there is oil in abundance, around 28% of the Libyan population does not have access to clean drinking water. Libya is one of the largest countries in Africa, but only 1% of its land is arable.

In order to remain in power, dictator Colonel Gadaffi utilizes Lybia's enormous financial reserves to keep the population happy. Sixty percent of jobs are supplied by the state, education is free, and commodities such as rice, flour and petrol are heavily subsidized. Early 2008, a litre of petrol cost 8 eurocents in Libya. In Italy, on the other side of the Mediterranean, it was around 1 euro 37 cents.

     LIBYA

The oil industry offers many employment opportunities, and Libya is the ideal departure point for the crossing to the Italian island of Lampedusa. As a result, Libya attracts fortune-hunters from all over Africa. It is estimated that nearly two million people stay in the country illegally.

Since December 2003, relations between Libya and the West have improved. Before then, they had been complicated by Libya's involvement in the 1988 bombing of an American plane carrying 259 passengers and crew above Lockerbie, in Scotland. Libya has now asked to join the World Trade Organisation. A condition of membership is that state-owned companies are privatized and state subsidies scaled back. The question is whether the population will be happy with this. Many Libyans already have two jobs just to be able to make ends meet.

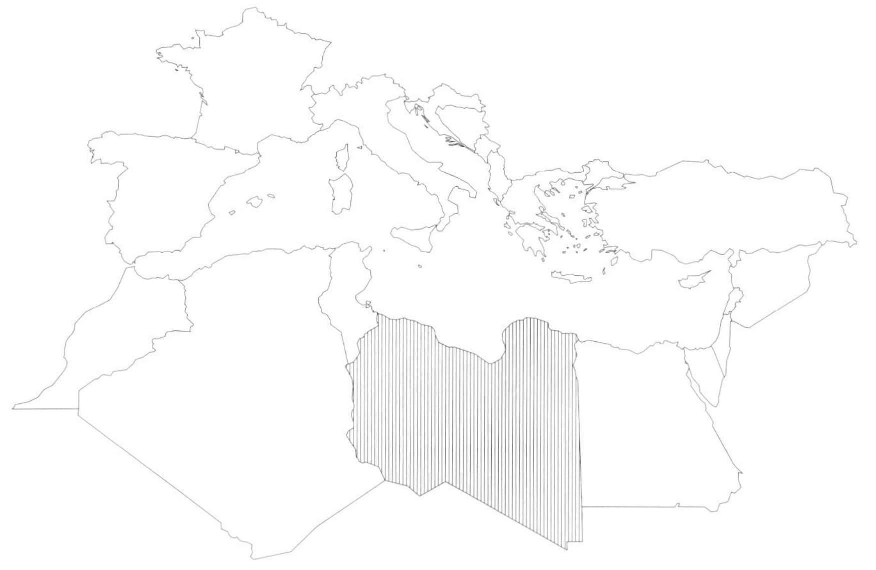

PRICE OF SUPER GASOLINE
EURO/LITRE

GIBRALTAR	0.65
SPAIN	1.10
FRANCE	1.23
ITALY	1.37
CROATIA	0.87
ALBANIA	0.75
GREECE	1.01
CYPRUS	1.13
TURKEY	1.63
SYRIA	0.44
LEBANON	0.58
ISRAEL	1.11
W.B.& GAZA	NA
EGYPT	0.26
LIBYA	**0.08**
TUNESIA	0.64
ALGERIA	0.18
MOROCCO	0.92

SOURCE : SPAIN, FRANCE, ITALY, GREECE: AA ROADWATCH
SOURCE : GIBRALTAR HTTP://WWW.DIGITALSPY.CO.UK/FORUMS/SHOWTHREAD.PHP?P=22033626
SOURCE : CROATIA, MOROCCO, ALGERIA, TUNISIA, LIBYA, EGYPT, SYRIA, ALBANIA, CYPRUS, TURKEY:
        BENZINPREISE.DE
SOURCE : LEBANON, GTZ - GERMAN TECHNICAL COOPERATION

NOTE   : APPROXIMATE PRICING BETWEEN LATE 2007 - EARLY 2008 (DEPENDING ON SOURCE)

206. BIR AYYAD
You can only visit Libya by joining a tour group. You are taken past relics, oases and rock paintings in the constant company of an agent.

209. TOCRA
Before Colonel Gadaffi came to power, the Akka family controlled the Libyan rubbish collection service. Gadaffi feared the power of rich families and devalued the dinar. The rubbish has not been collected since 1973.

210. GERMA
View from a hotel room. Anyone who enters a village to take photos will find themselves in a police station in no time. The Libyans are afraid of no one, they said, except Gadaffi.

213. TRIPOLI
Algerian French footballer Zinedine Zidane's head butt during the World Cup in 2006 has been immortalized in Libya on a matchbox.

215. BENGAZI
A business selling car parts.

216. TRIPOLI
Socializing on Saturdays. The immigrants, mostly from Egypt and Sub-Saharan Africa, live in cramped apartments in the suburbs.

218. BENGAZI
There is a lot of money in Libya, even if it is in the wrong hands. None the less, it is incomprehensible that people do not clean up their own streets.

220. BENGAZI
One of the hundreds of thousands of plastic bags, floating over the street.

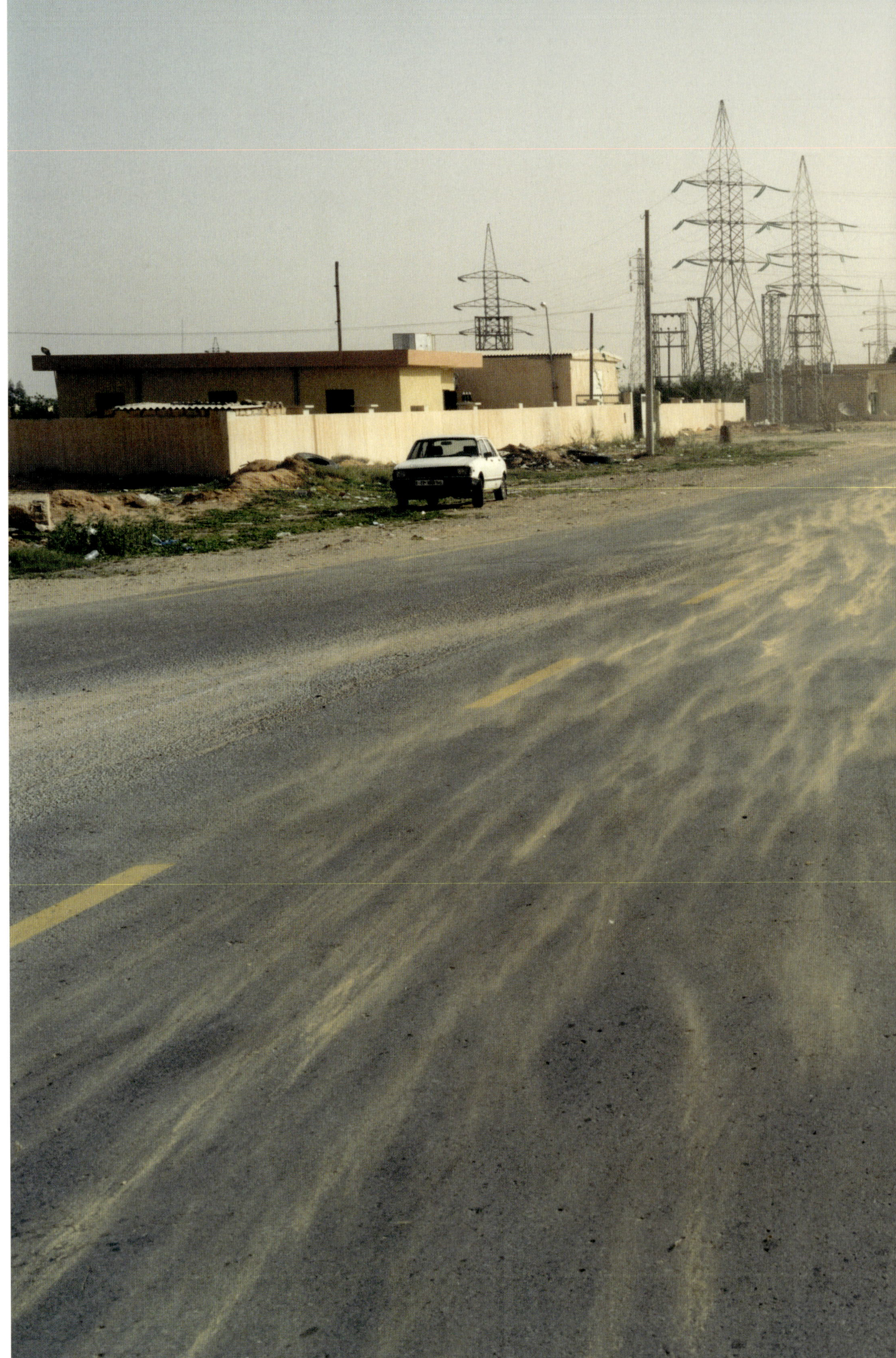

206.

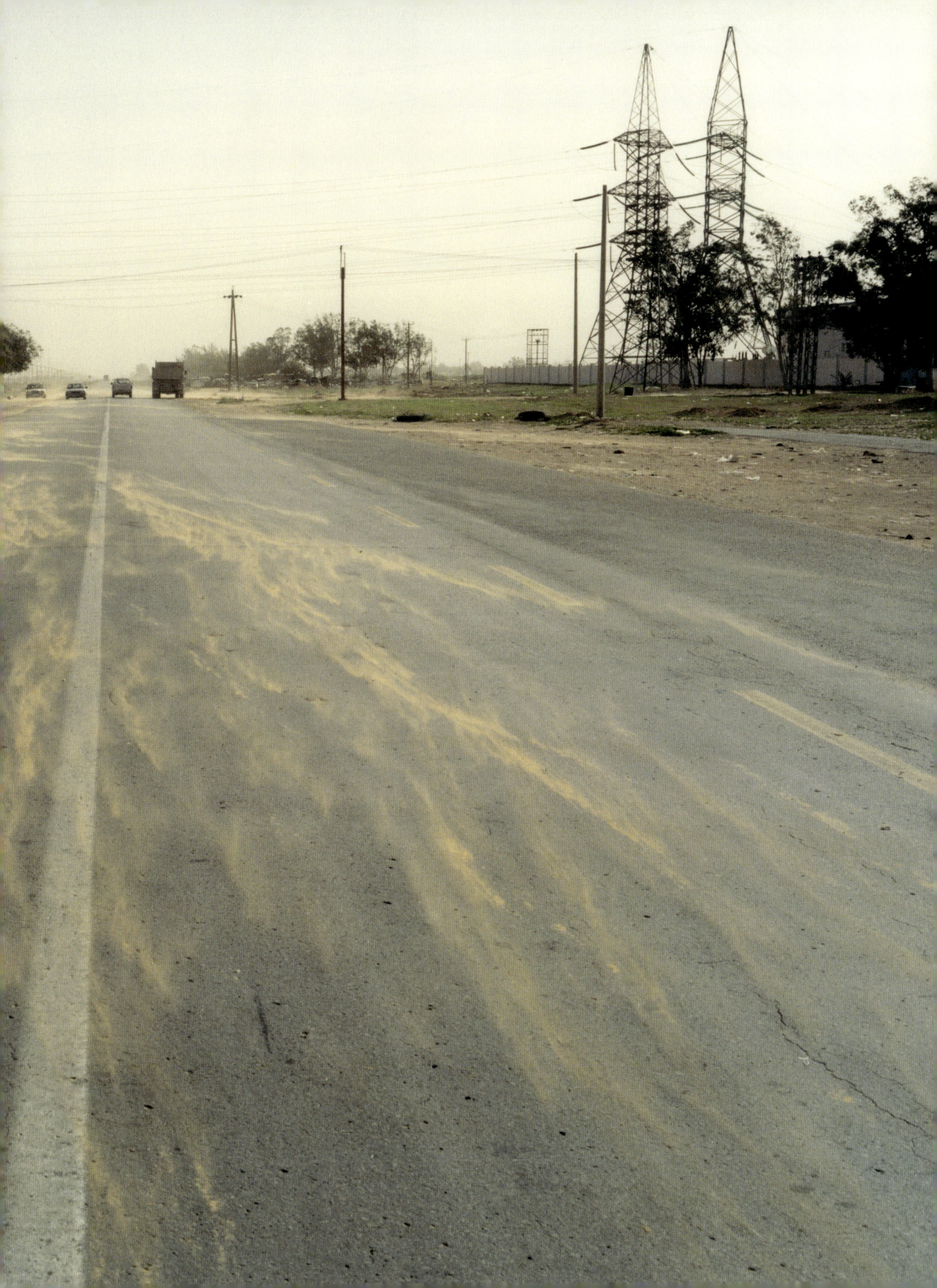

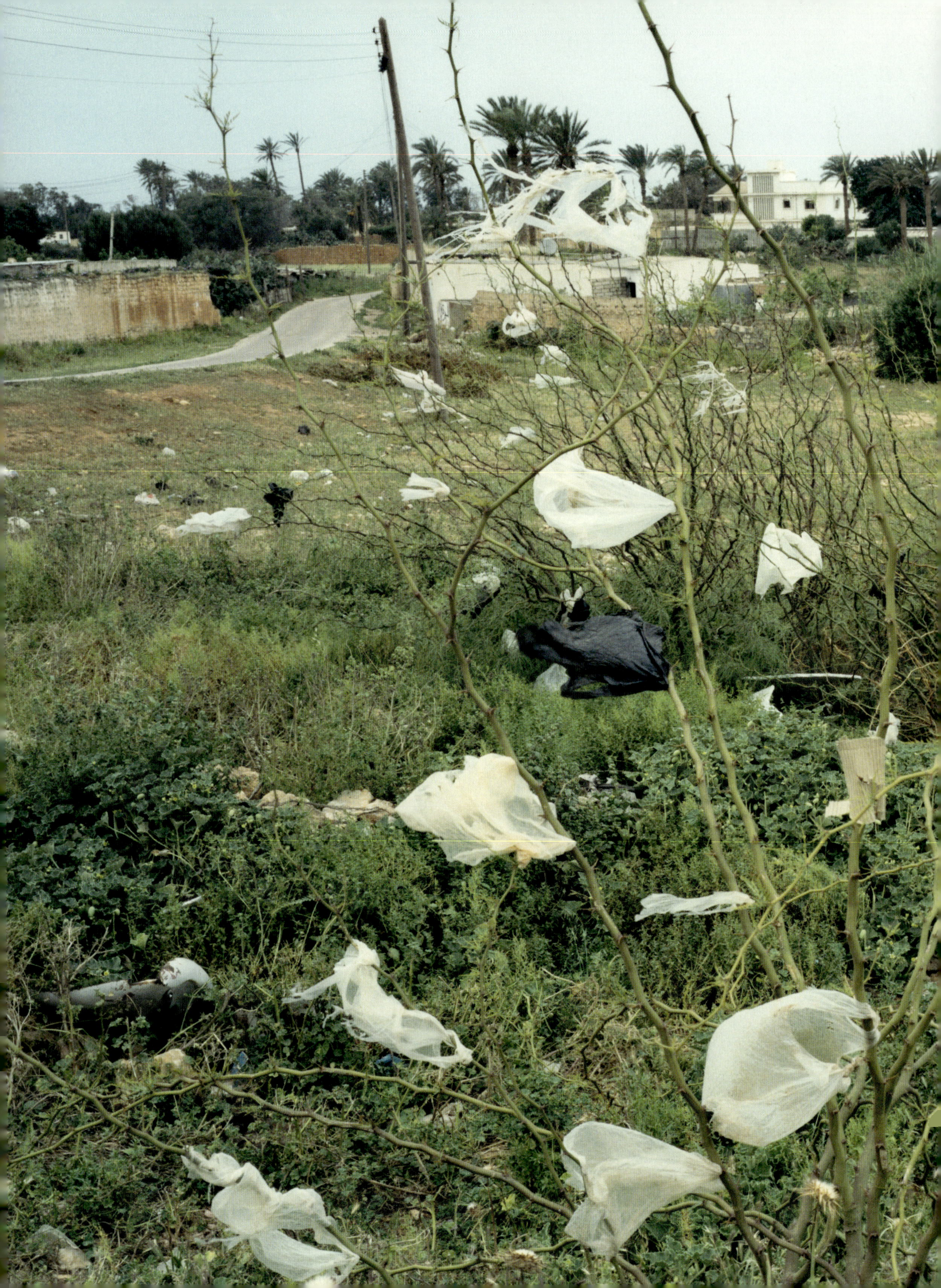

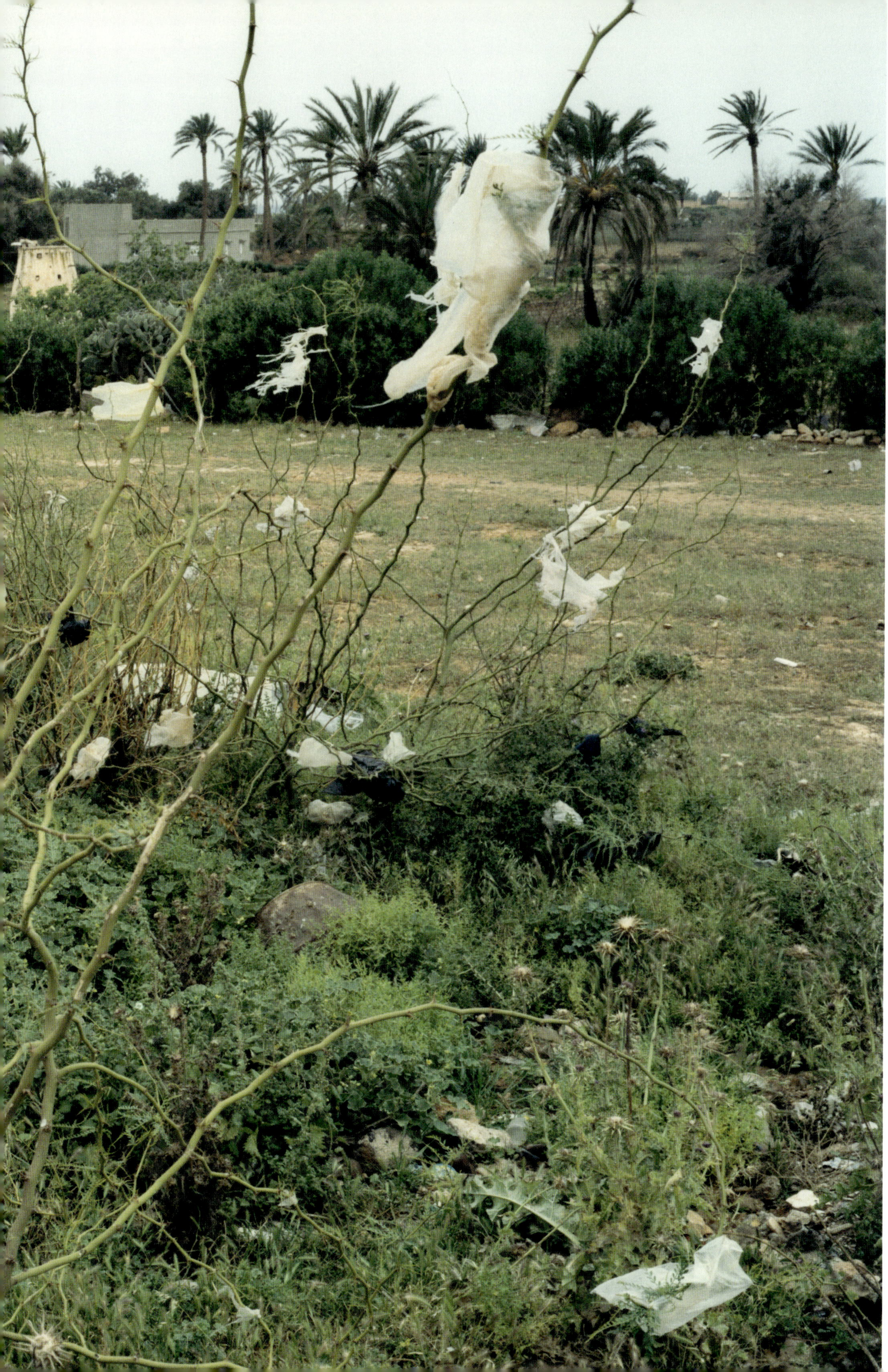

209.

210.

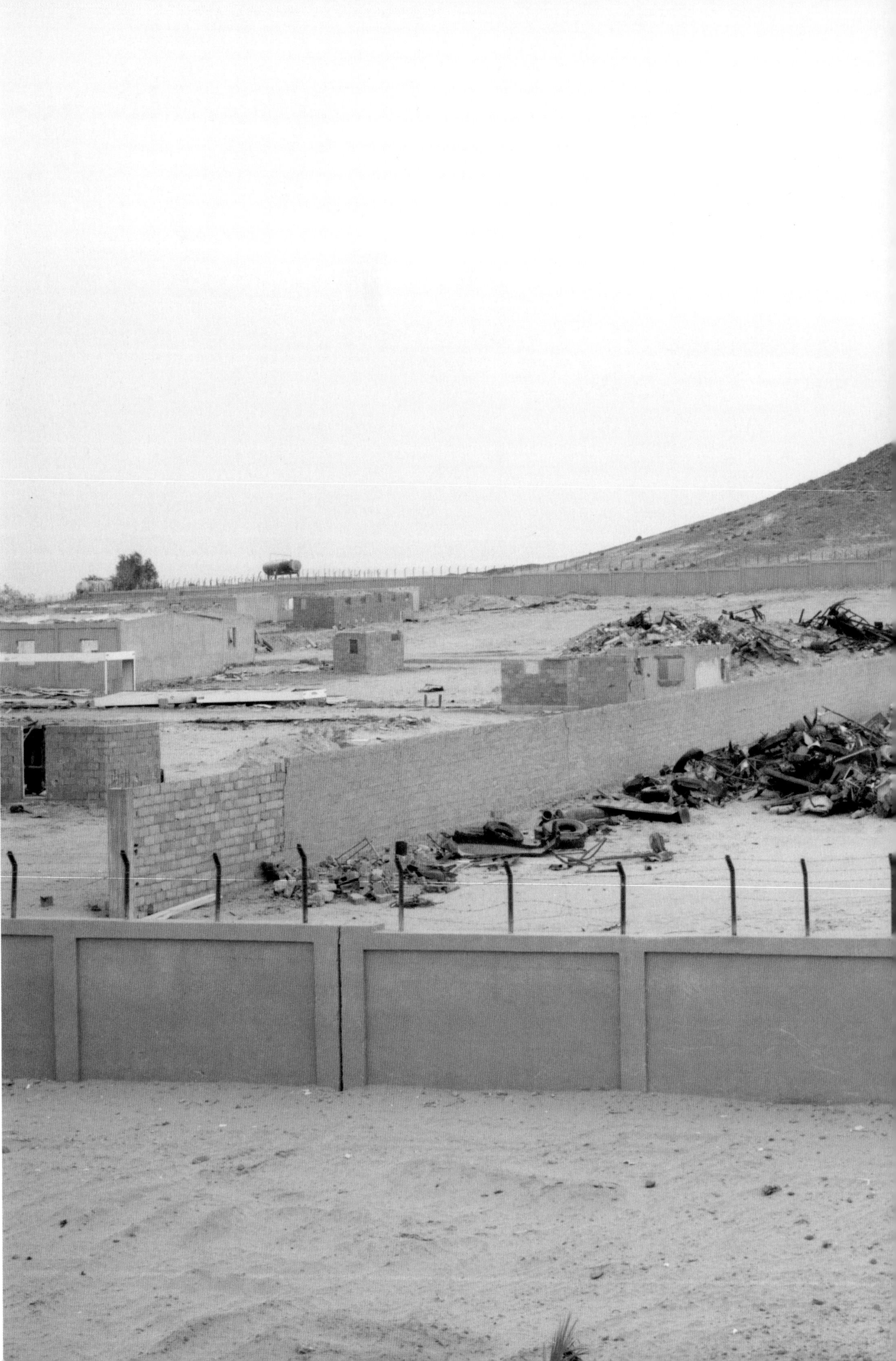

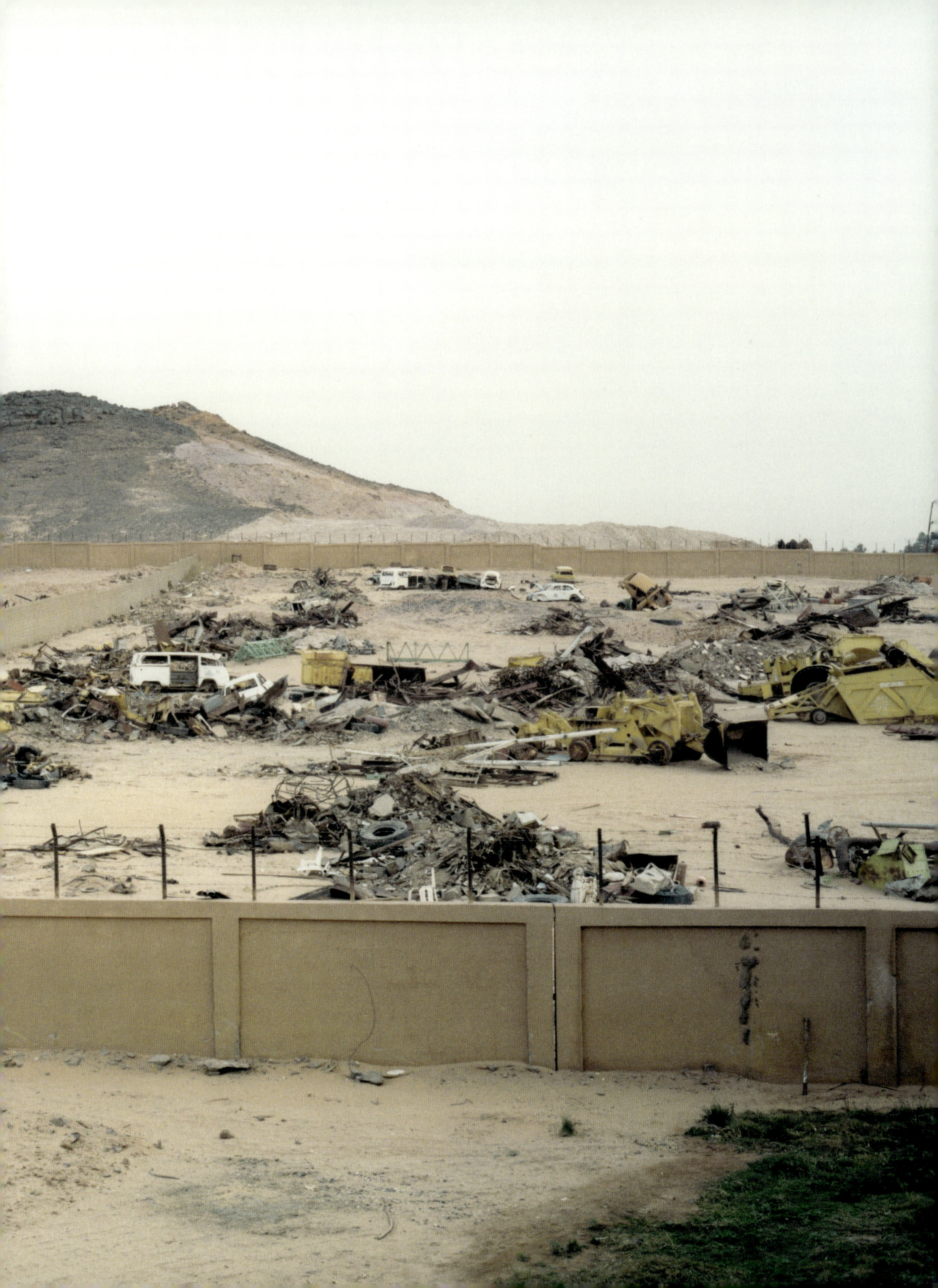

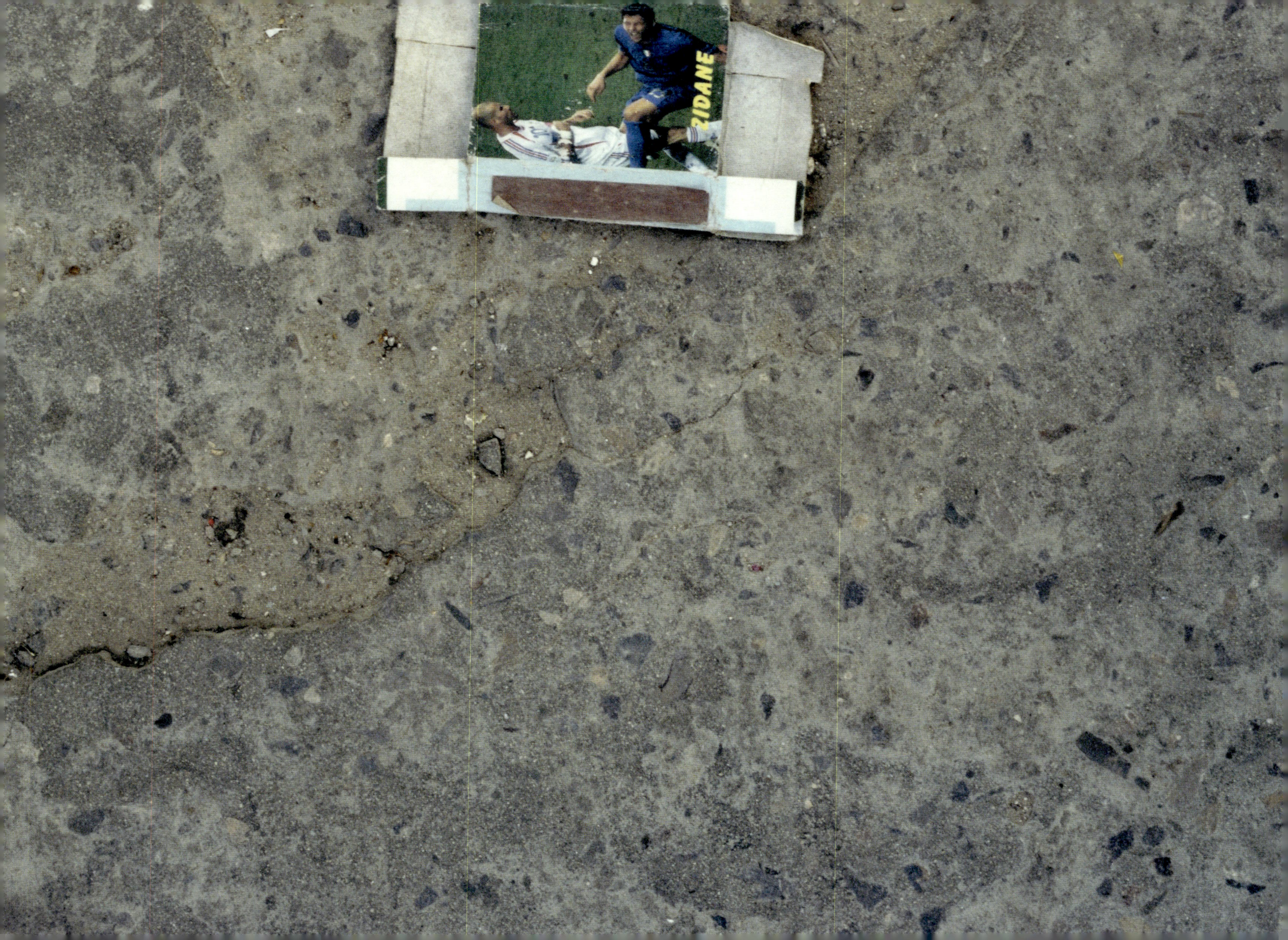
ZIDANE

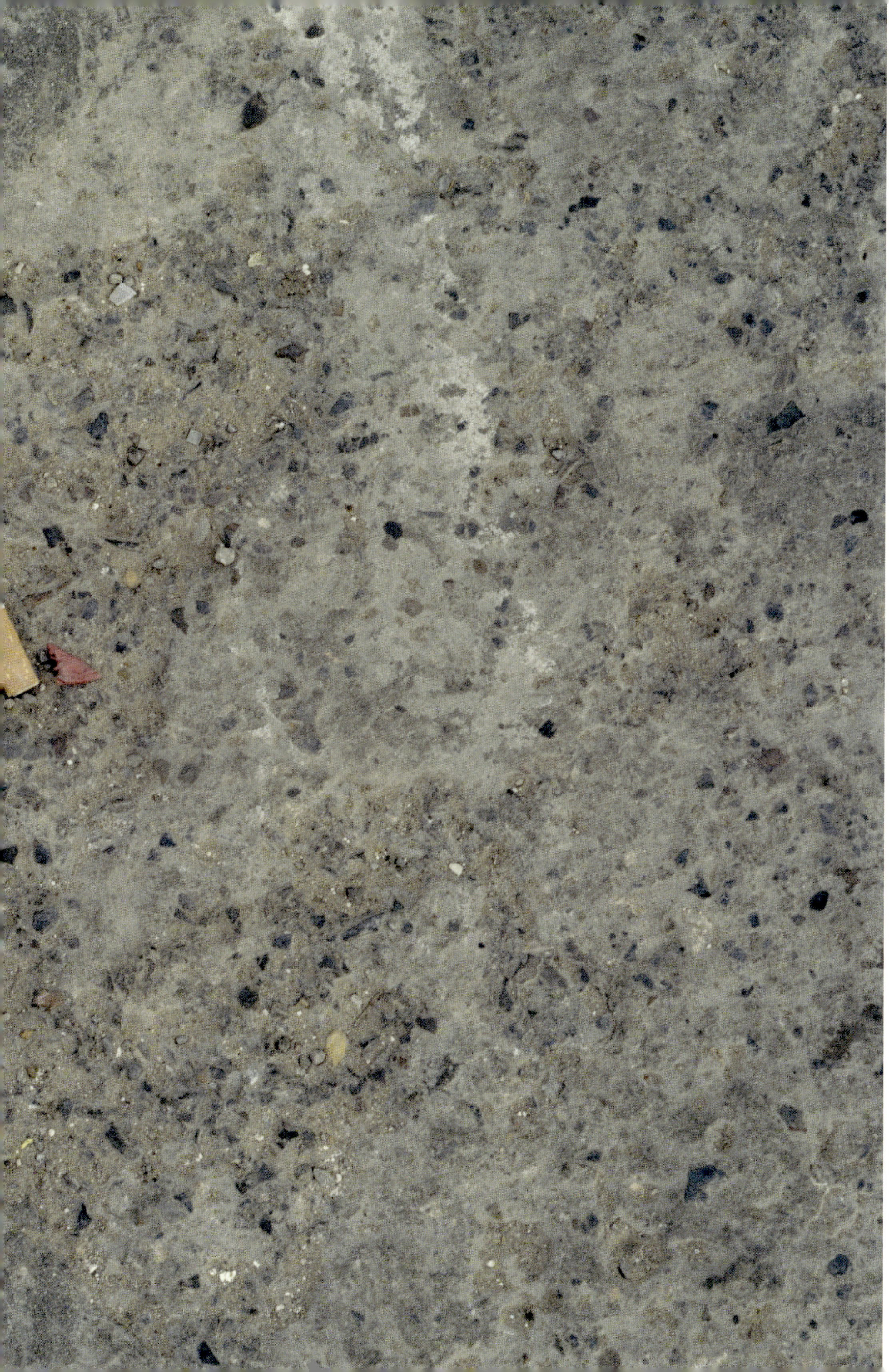

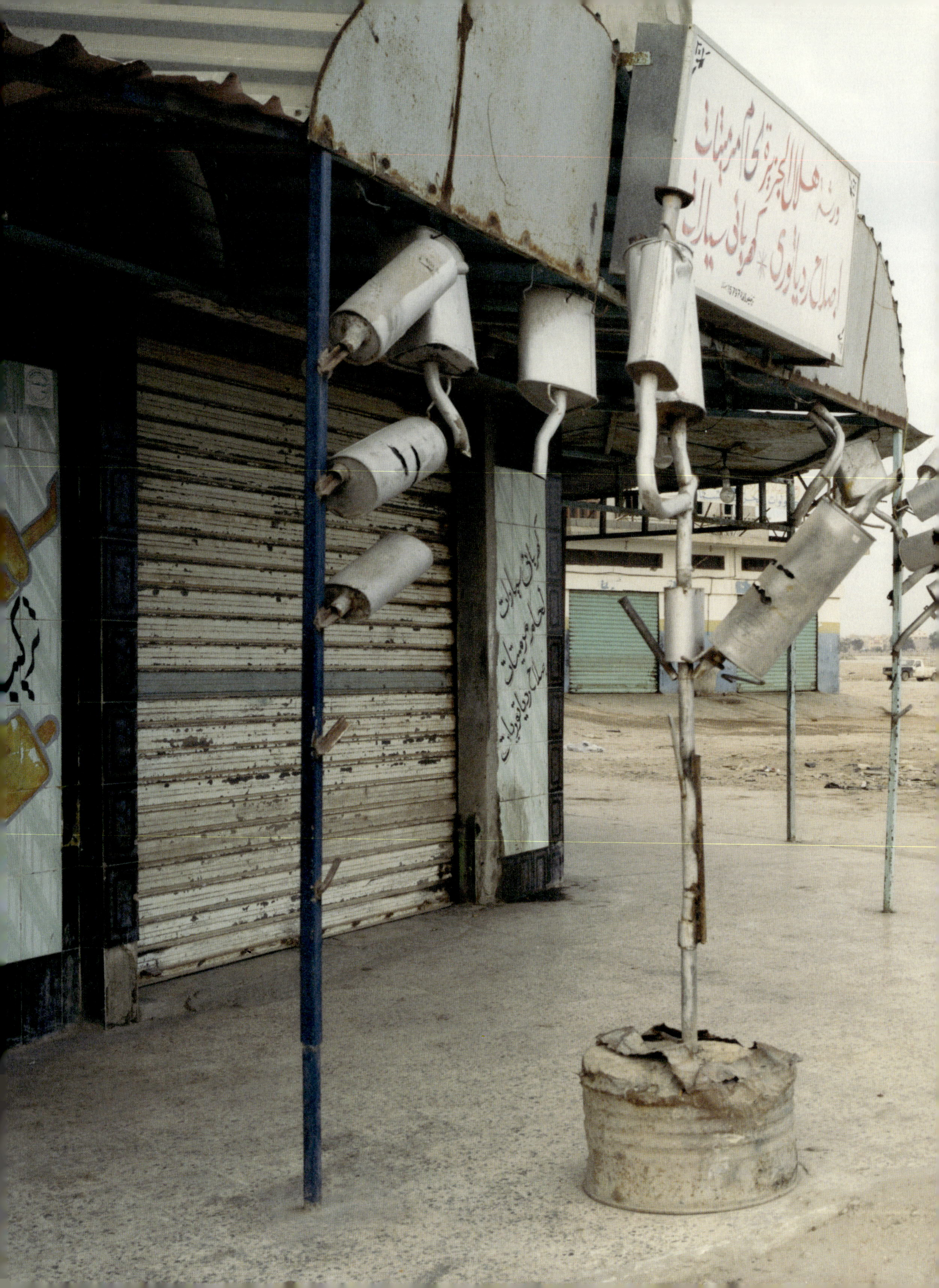
ورثہ ہلال الجبیرہ تلحام آمر میھاٹ
اصلاح ریاوری * کھوپائی سیارات

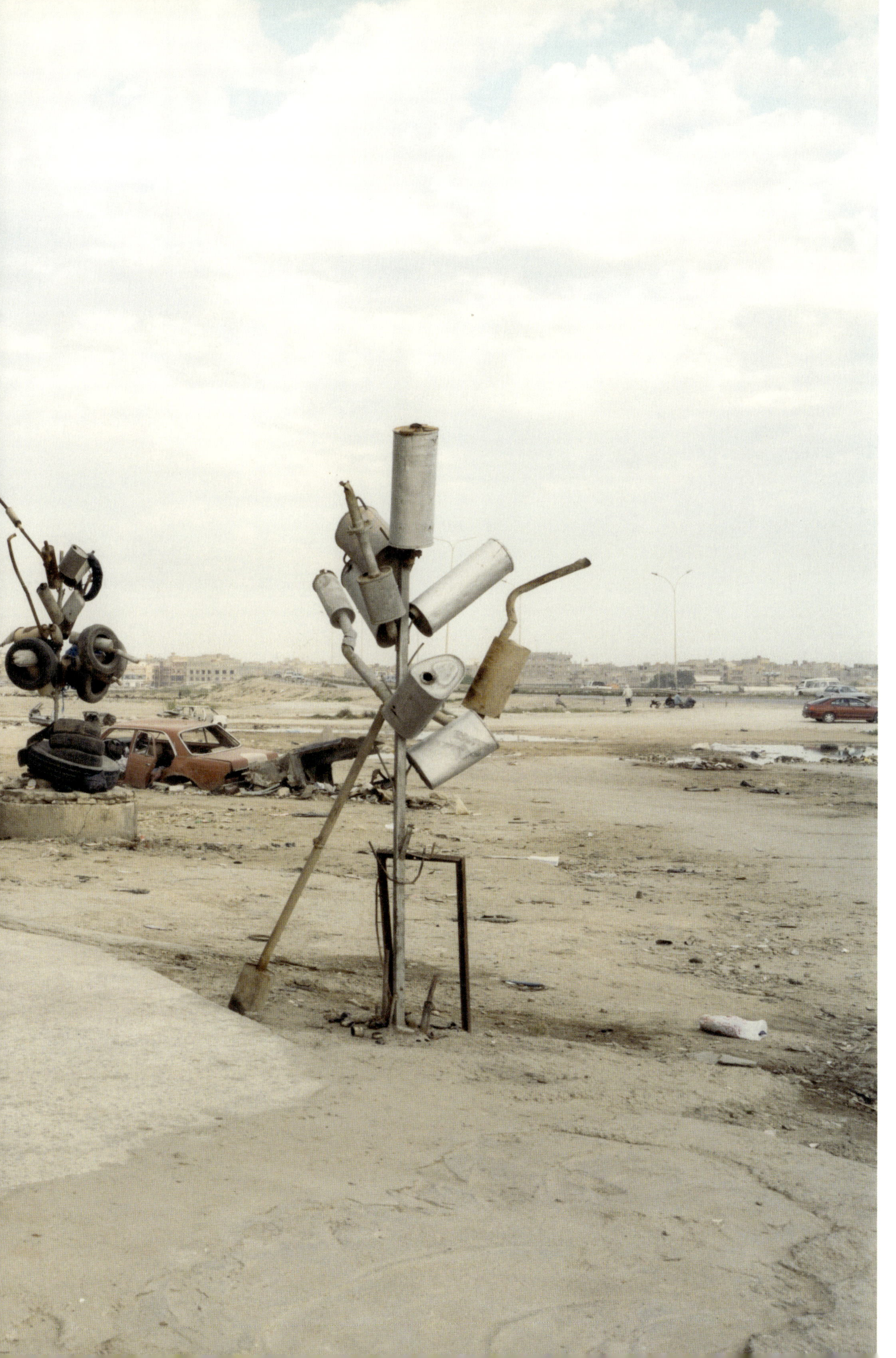

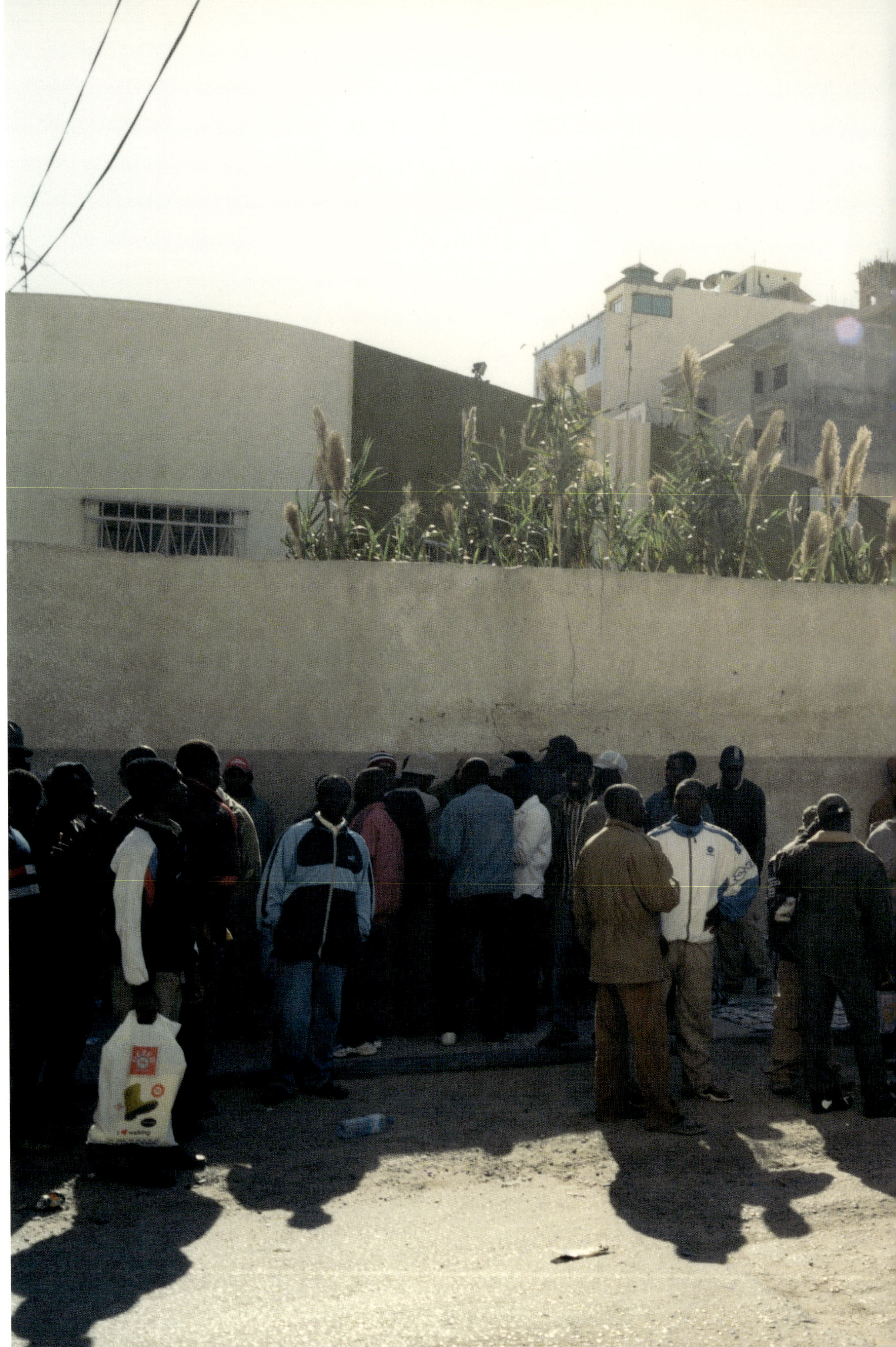

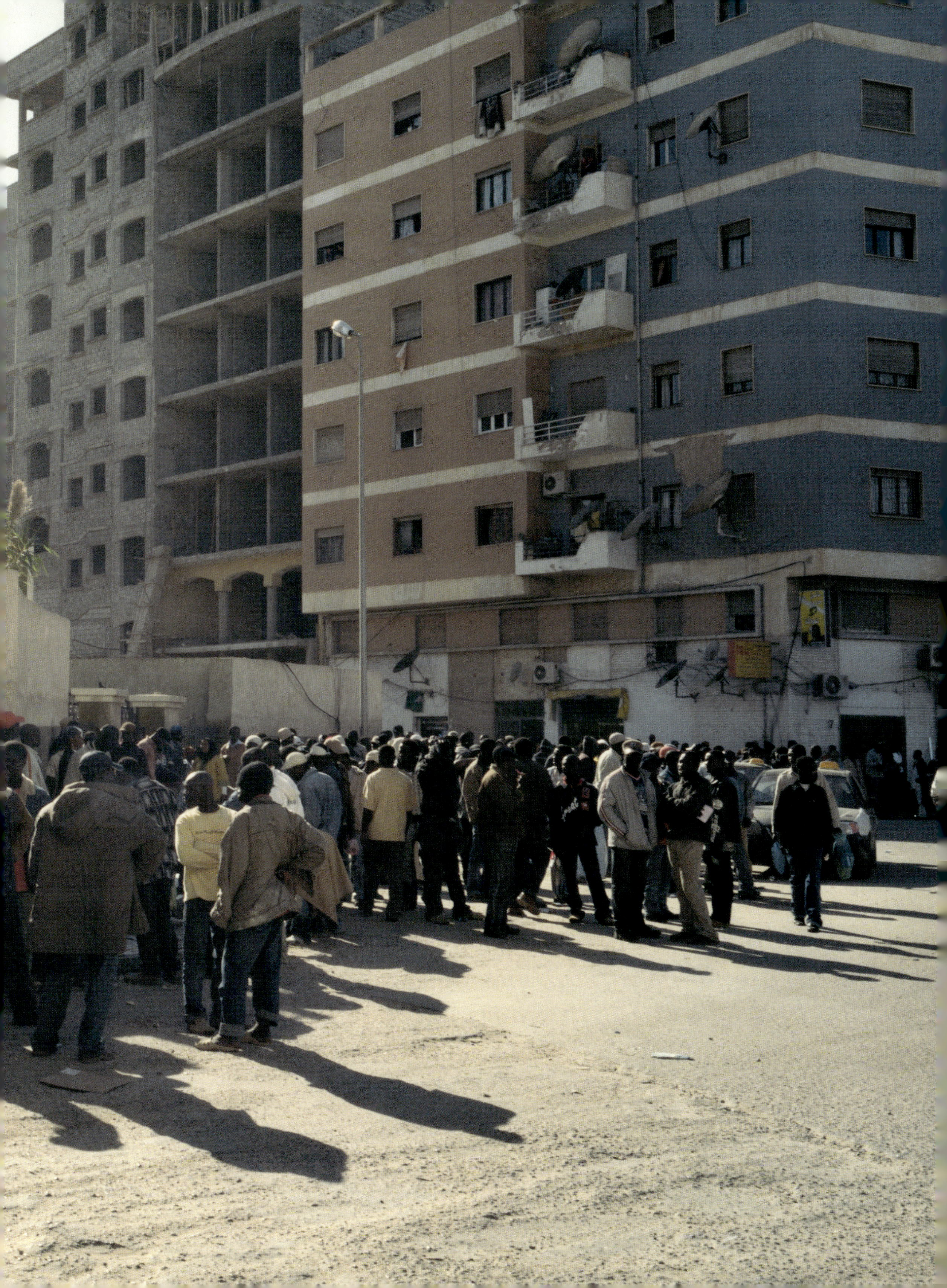

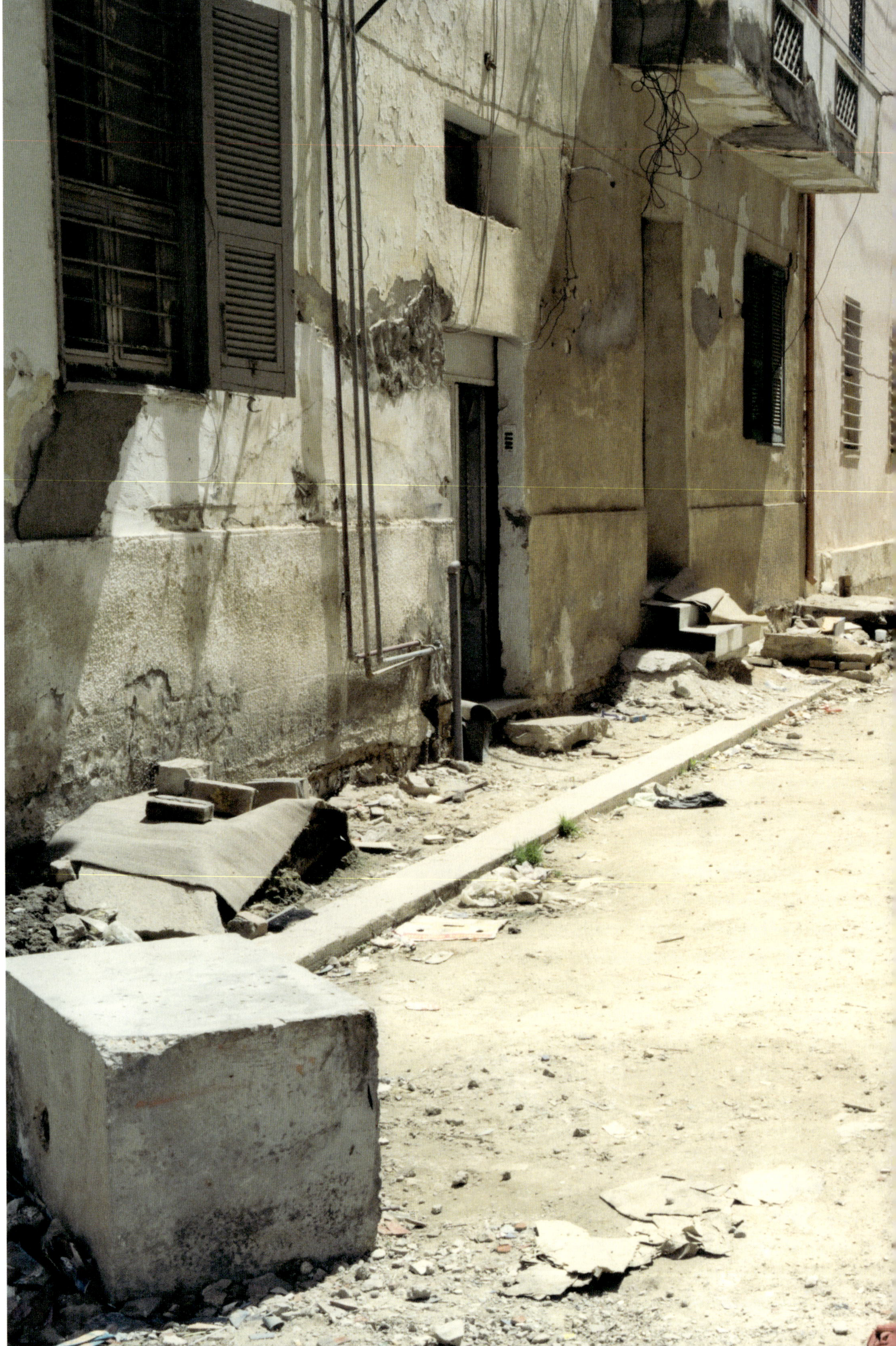

218.

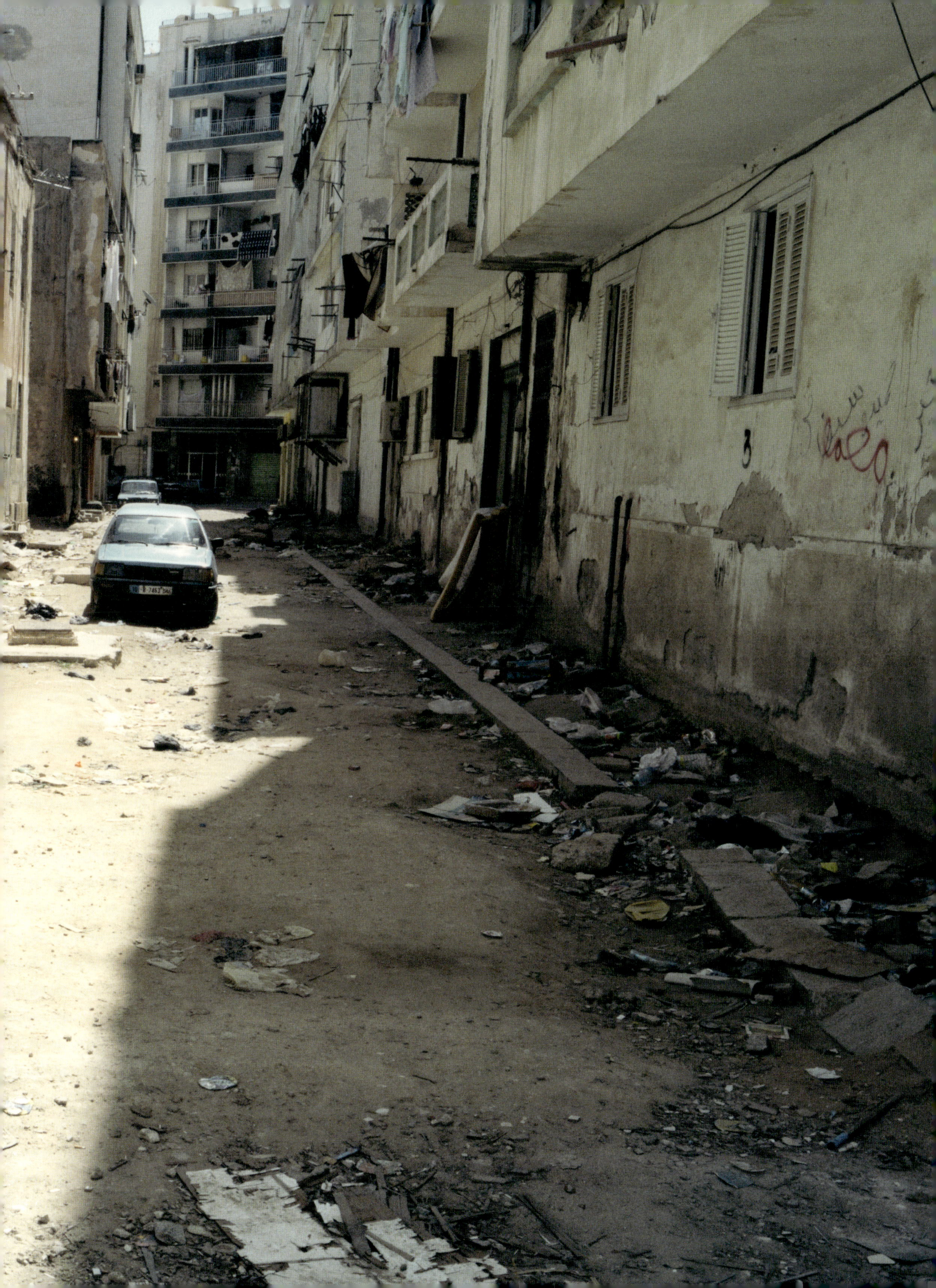

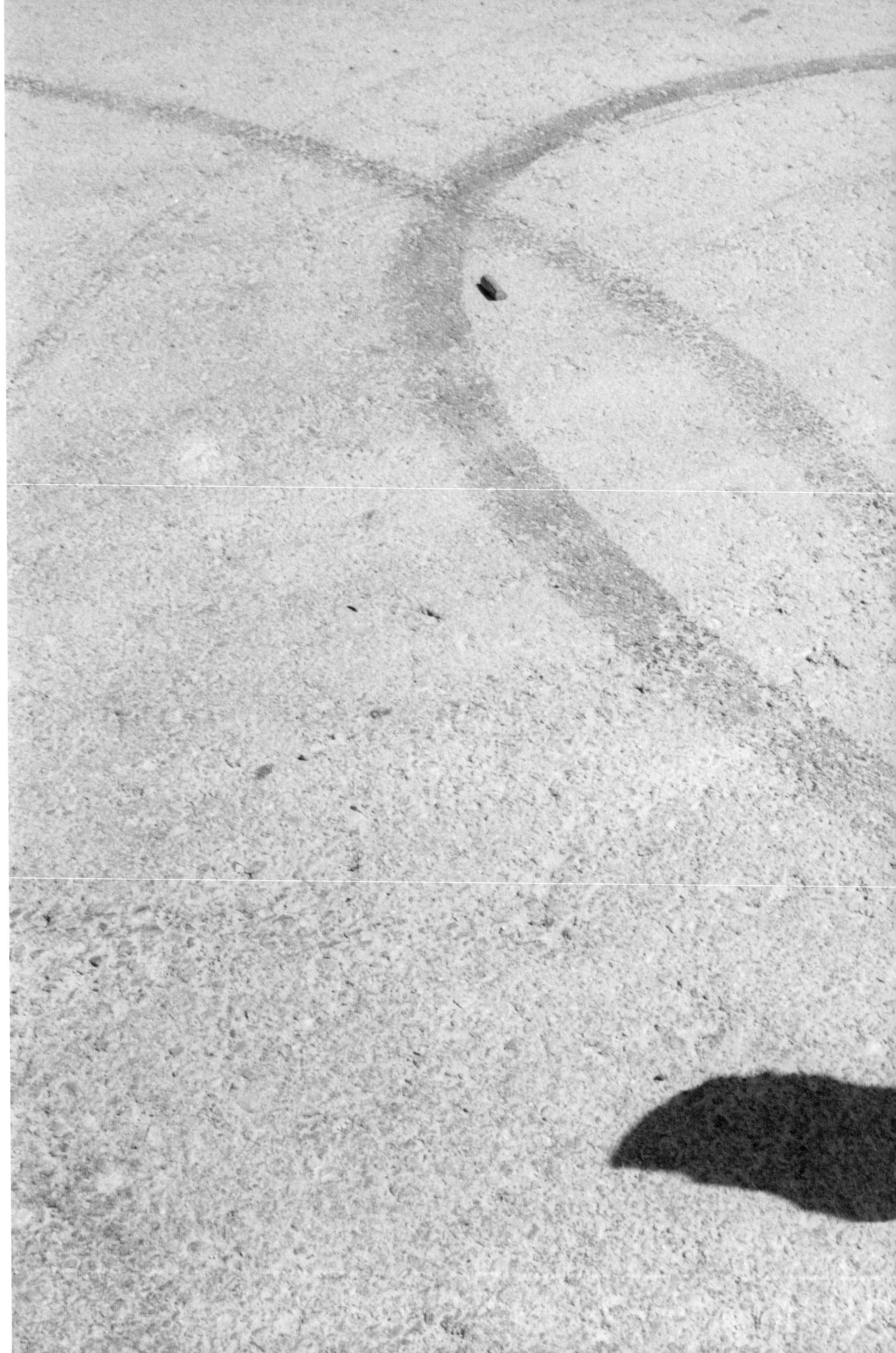

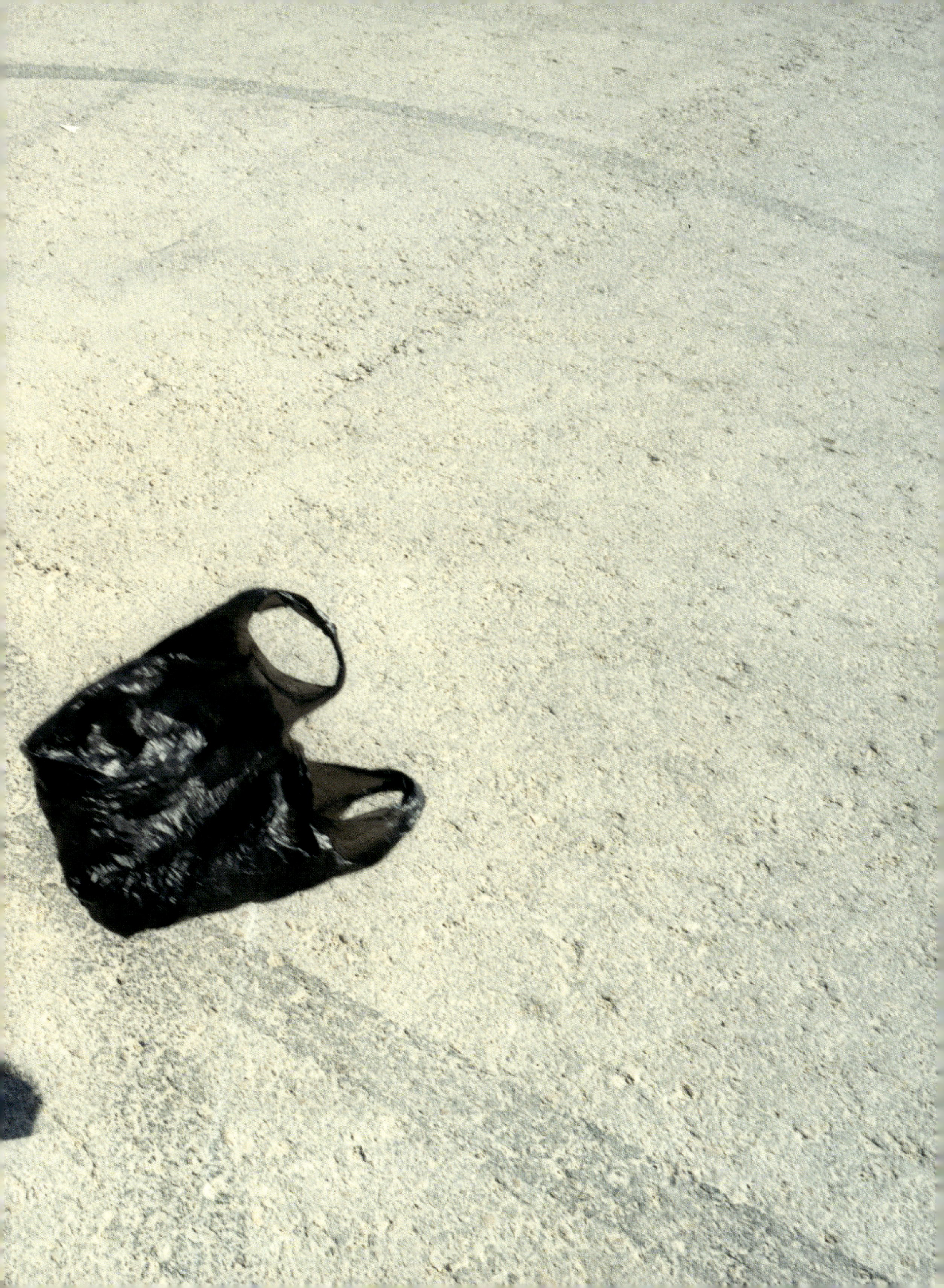

Of all the figures that can be gathered from the Mediterranean countries, illiteracy is one of the most troubling. In the North African countries, at least a third of the population is illiterate. This is an enormous number of people who are unable to absorb written information and are dependent on others to handle their affairs with official bodies. New media – extraordinarily significant in an educational and democratic sense – mostly pass this group by.

In addition to the number of people who are illiterate, there is also something called 'functional illiteracy', the so-called low-literates: those who can just about read the signs at the baker, but who get lost in longer texts. In Spain, 10 million people, or around 20% of the population, are considered low-literates. In some countries, not being able to understand a computer or modern communication tools is also regarded as functional illiteracy.

As far as the fight against illiteracy is concerned, Tunisia has taken significant steps. On various occasions, the country has even been hailed by UN organizations as a glowing example for developing countries, due to the way in which it has tackled its social problems. Compared to its neighbours, Tunisia is also relatively enlightened in the area of women's rights. Even so, at 42%, illiteracy among women is considerably higher than the 16% among Tunisian men.

TUNISIA

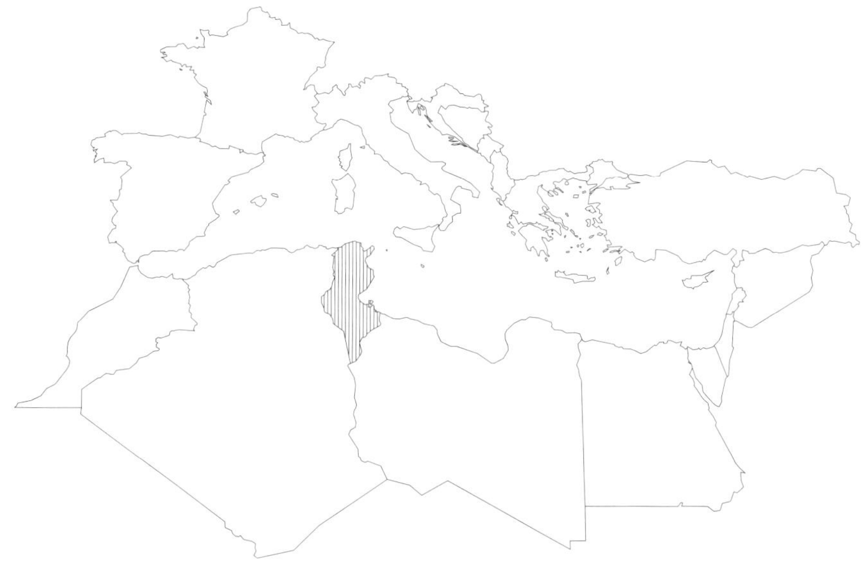

ILLITERACY
% OF POPULATION

GIBRALTAR	NA	
SPAIN	2.1	
FRANCE	1.0	
ITALY	1.4	
CROATIA	1.5	
ALBANIA	13.5	
GREECE	2.5	
CYPRUS	2.4	
TURKEY	13.5	
SYRIA	23.1	
LEBANON	12.6	
ISRAEL	4.4	
W.B.& GAZA	7.6	
EGYPT	42.3	
LIBYA	17.5	
TUNISIA	**25.8**	
ALGERIA	30.1	
MOROCCO	48.3	

SOURCE : THE CIA WORLD FACTBOOK

225. SOUSSE
A bull waits on the street for the butcher. Tunisia is one of the most popular tourist destinations in the region. The insanity has also set in here. Replicas of entire Arabic souks are being built.

226. ISLE OF DJERBA
The Saudi-funded Hotel Hasdrubal under construction. A suite will cost 800 euros a night. The land here is so saline that agriculture is no longer possible. The whole island is now dedicated to tourism.

229. SKANES
The swimming pool at the Houdi resort. After dinner, the visitors relax for a while. At the same time, the sprinklers on the adjacent golf course come on, sending a cloud of mosquitoes into the air. The visitors run quickly inside.

230. KERKER
Tunisia is not very religious. The author-itarian President Zine El Abidine Ben Ali banned women at public functions from wearing the veil.

232. SKANES
The Reception at the Houdi resort. Travel-ling used to be an adventure, and so expensive that it was unaffordable for most people. These days, it can be as easy as hopping on and off a plane, then lying en masse by the pool.

235. GABES
People leaving the mosque on a Friday afternoon.

236. SOUSSE
On Sousse's public beach. She is French. I don't know if he was successful. This was right at the very beginning, and a lot still had to happen.

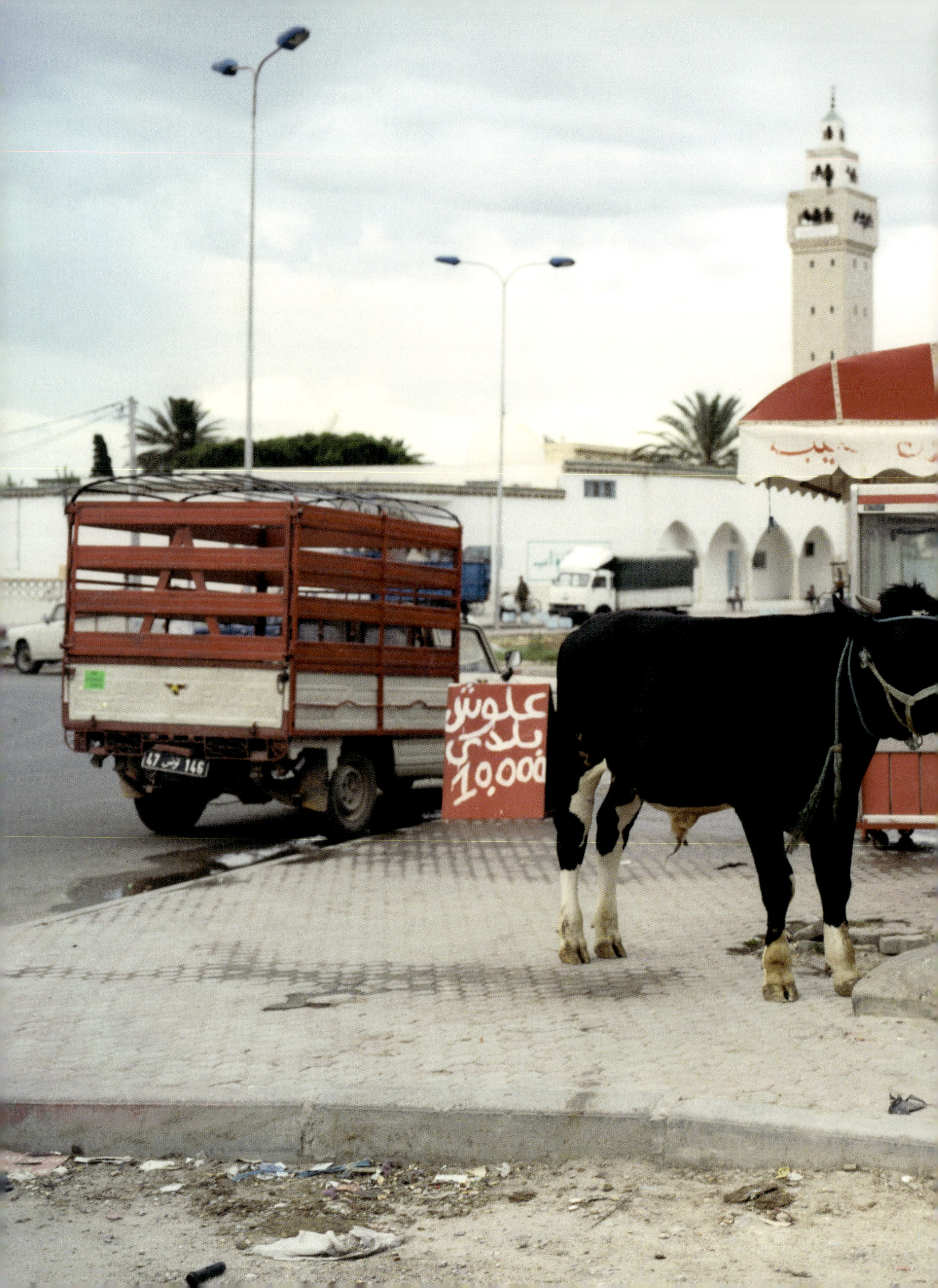
علوش
بلدي
10,000

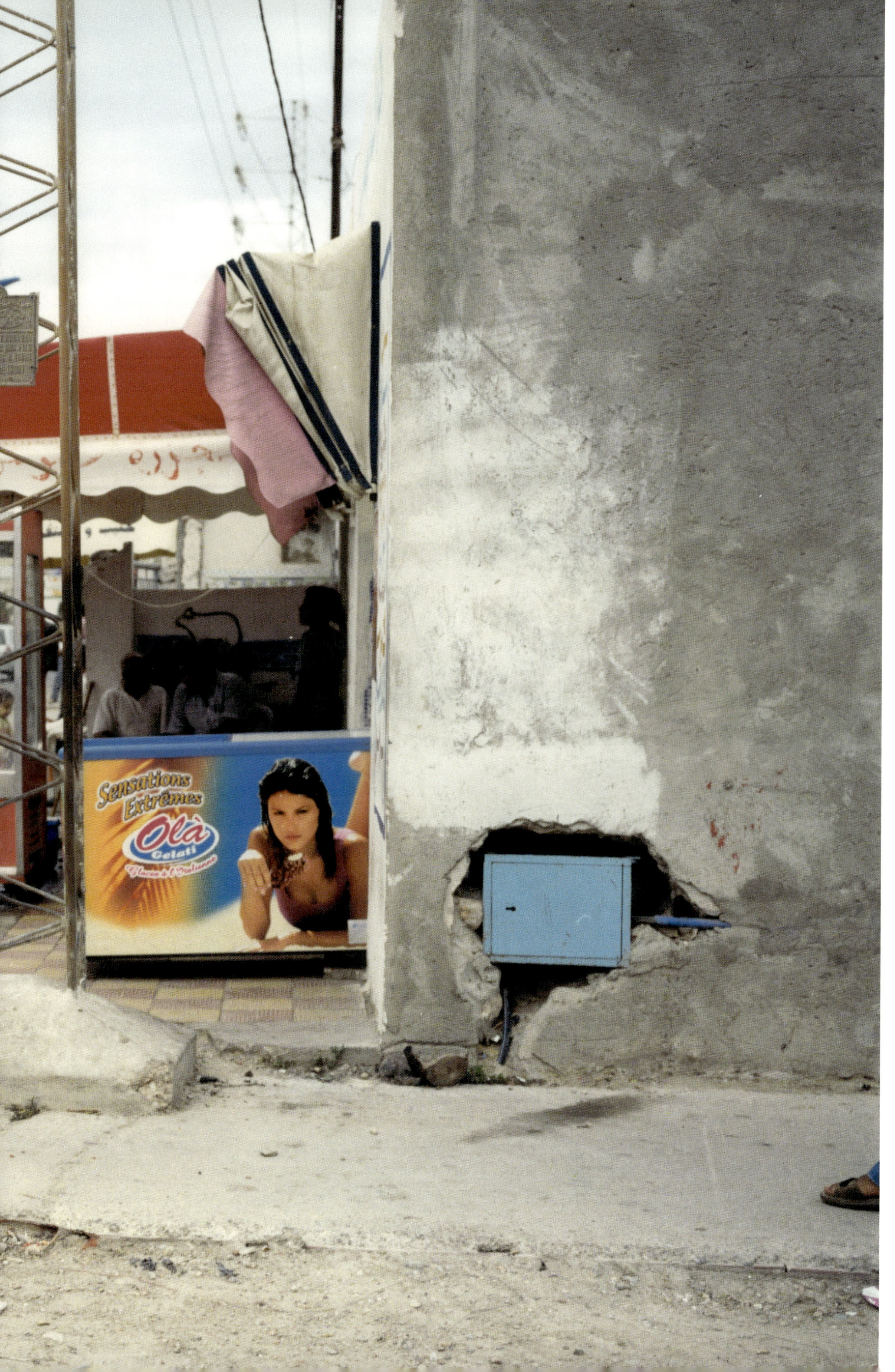

Sensations
Extrêmes
Olà
Gelati
Glaces à l'italienne

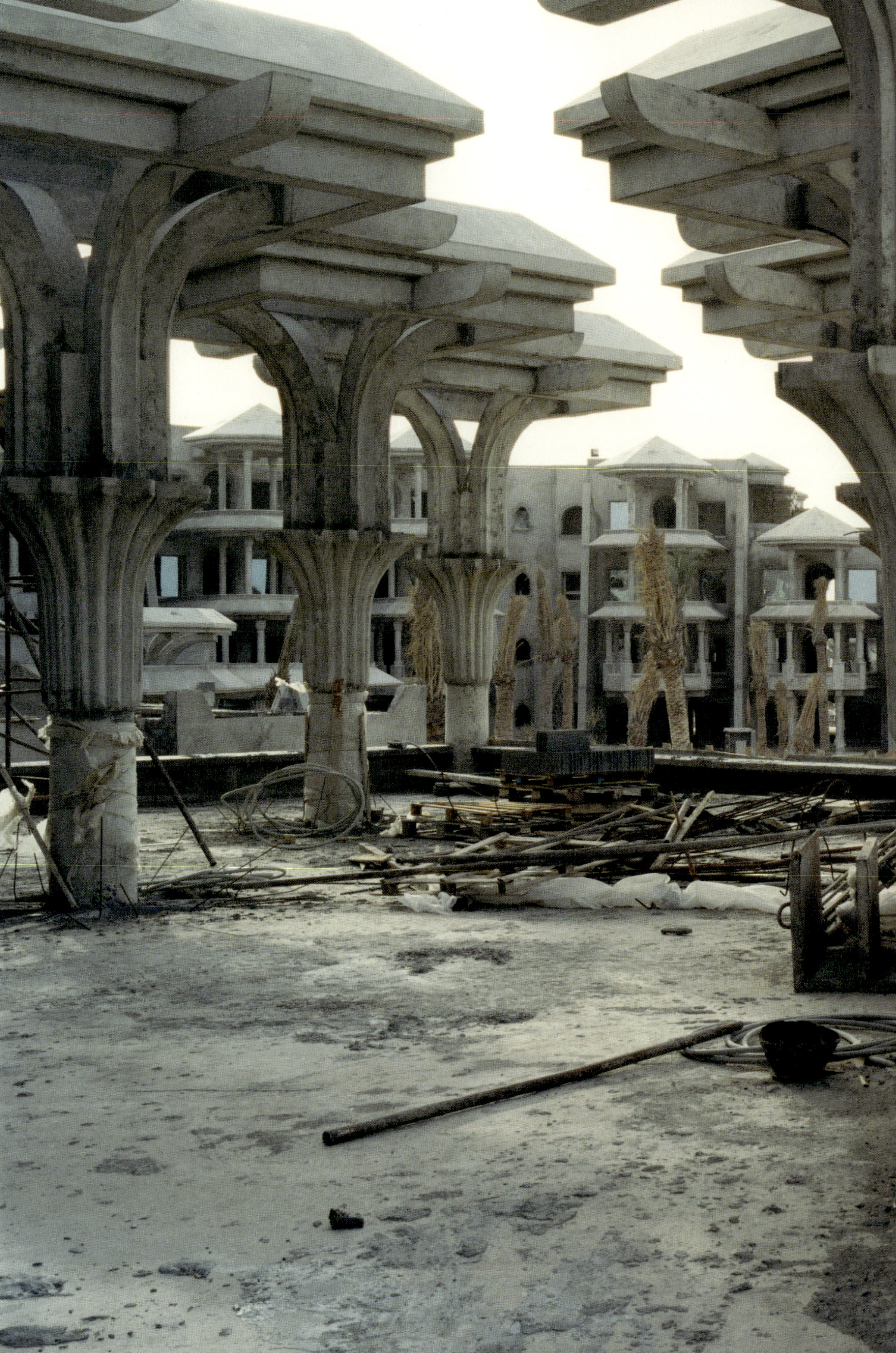

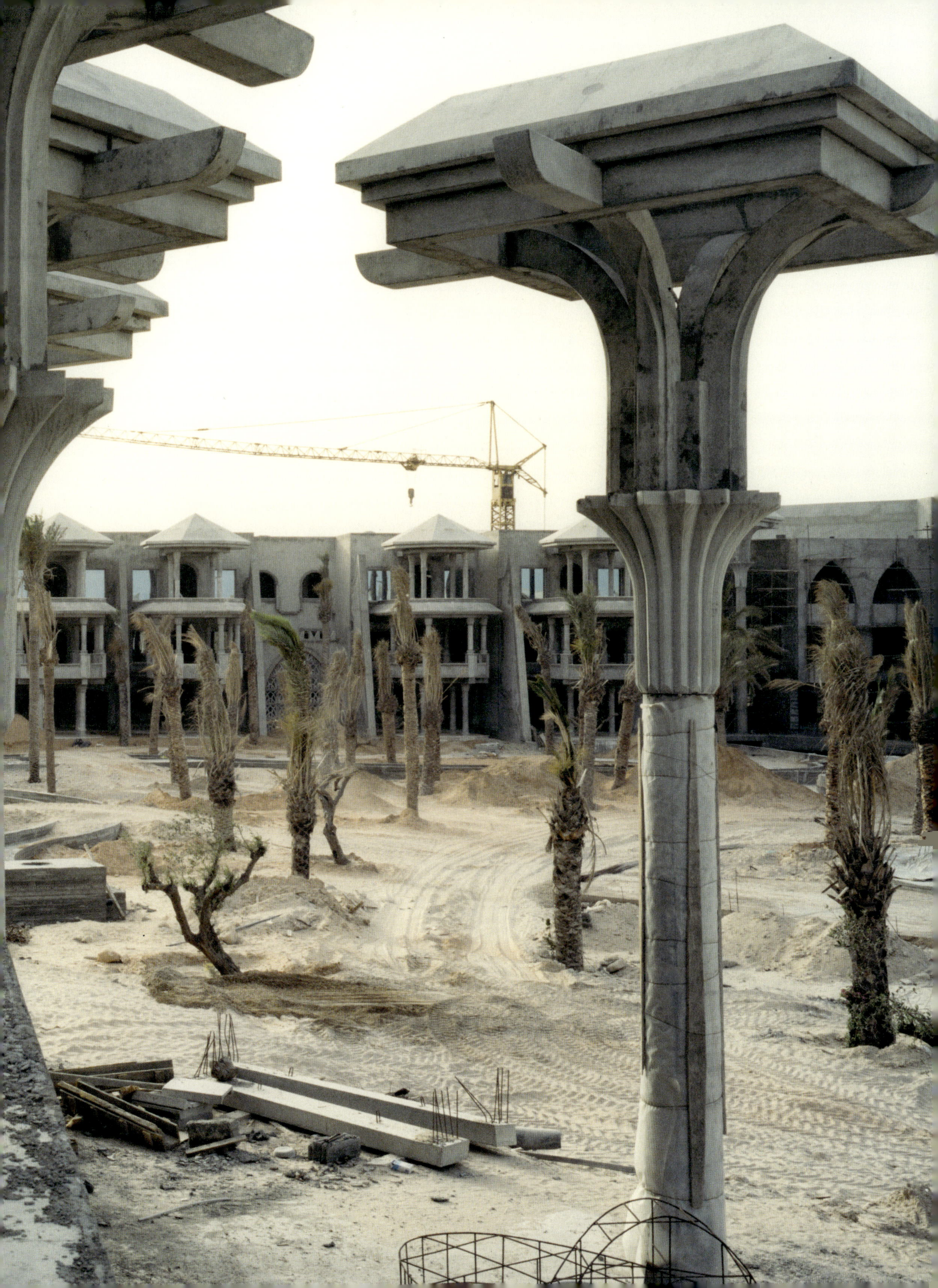

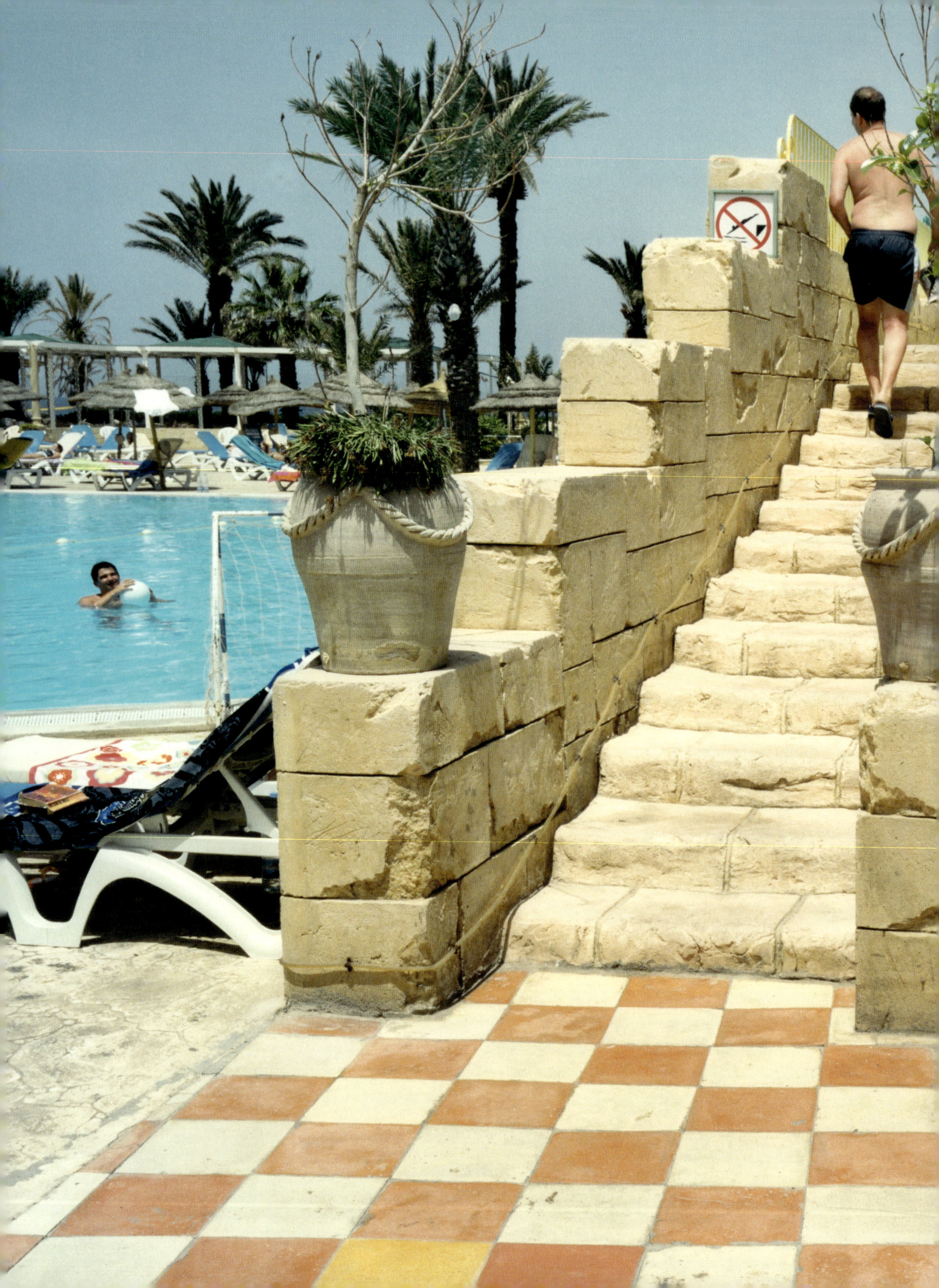

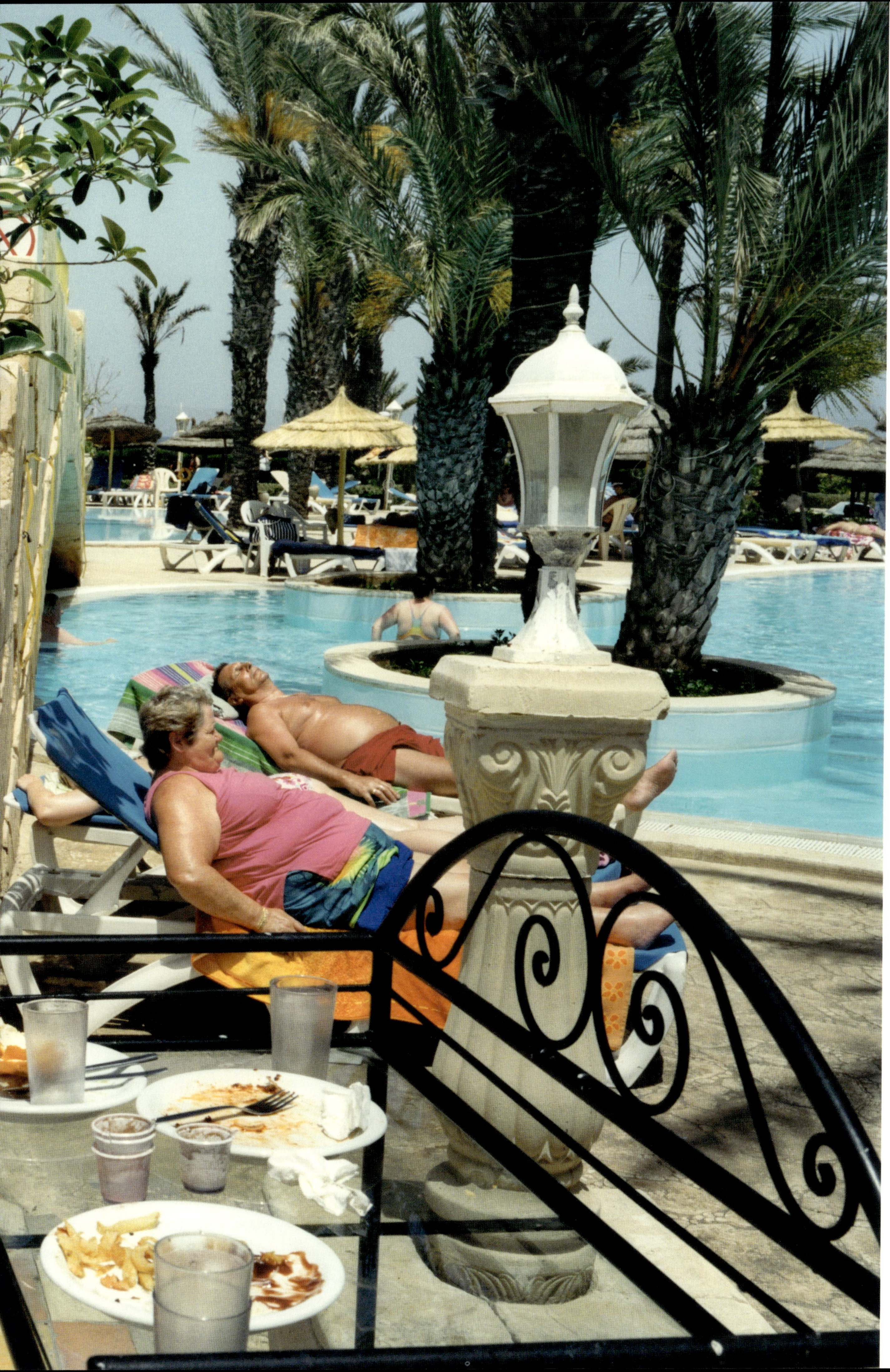

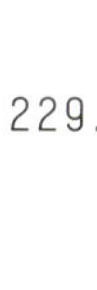

230.

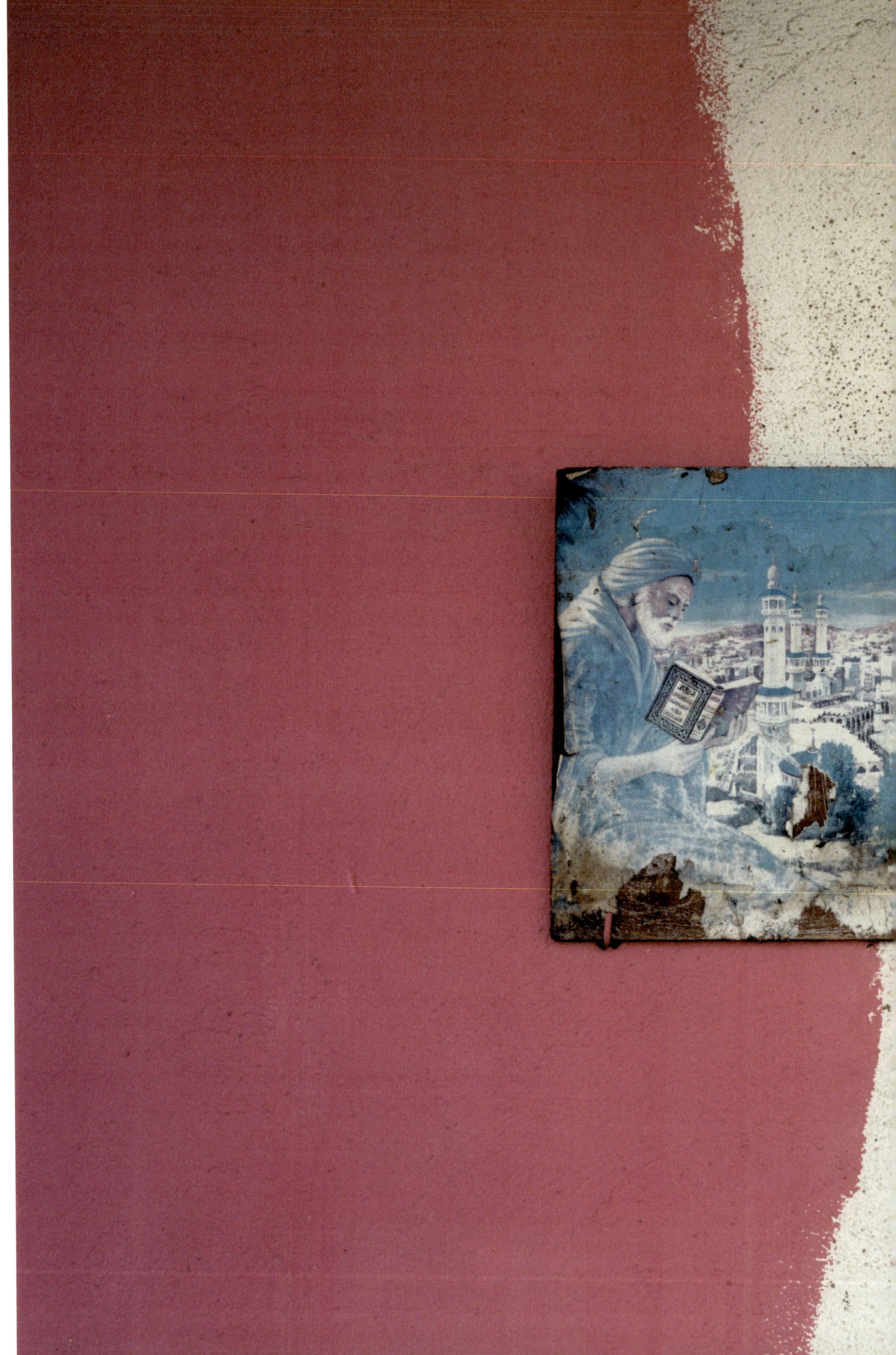

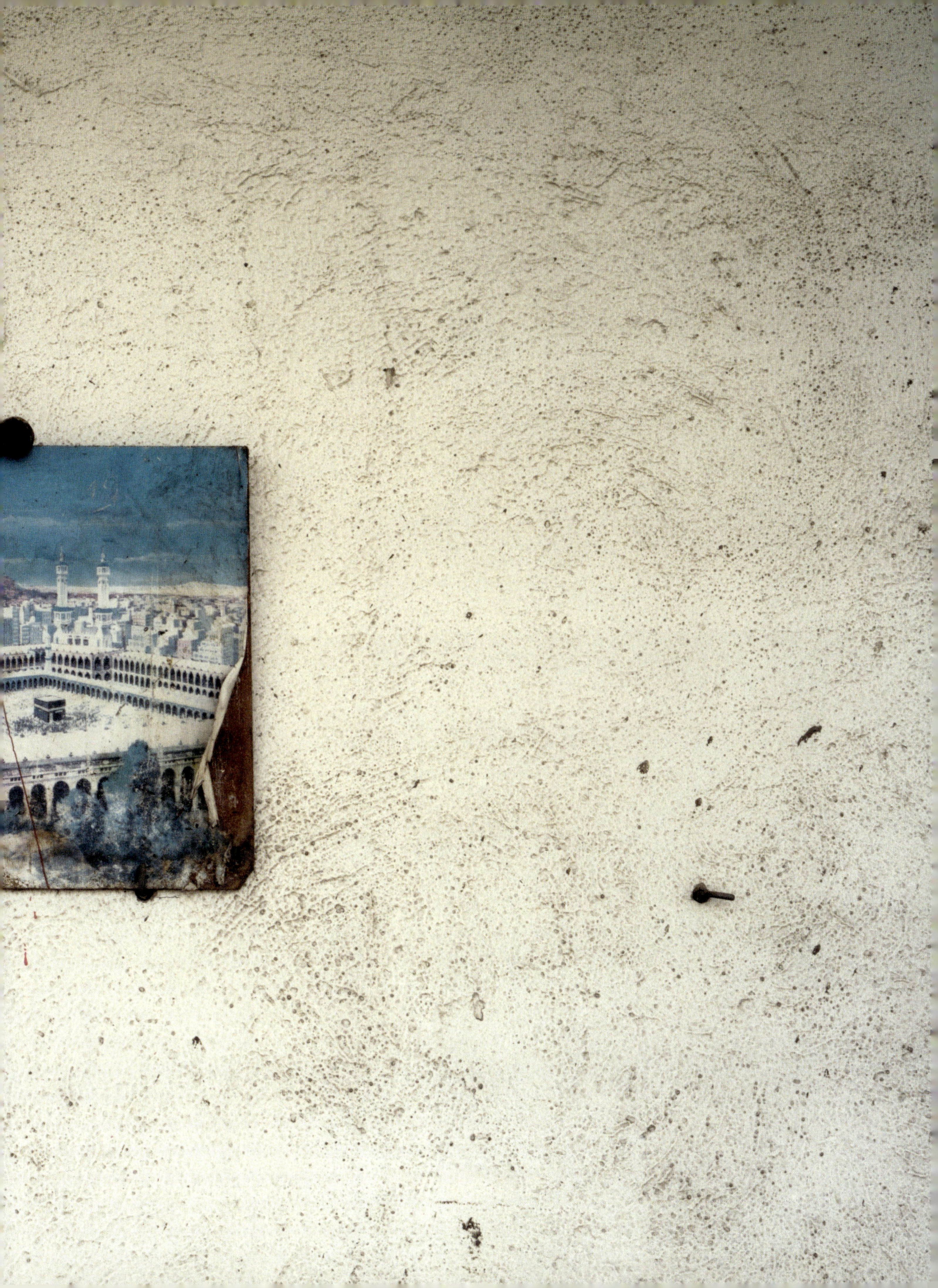

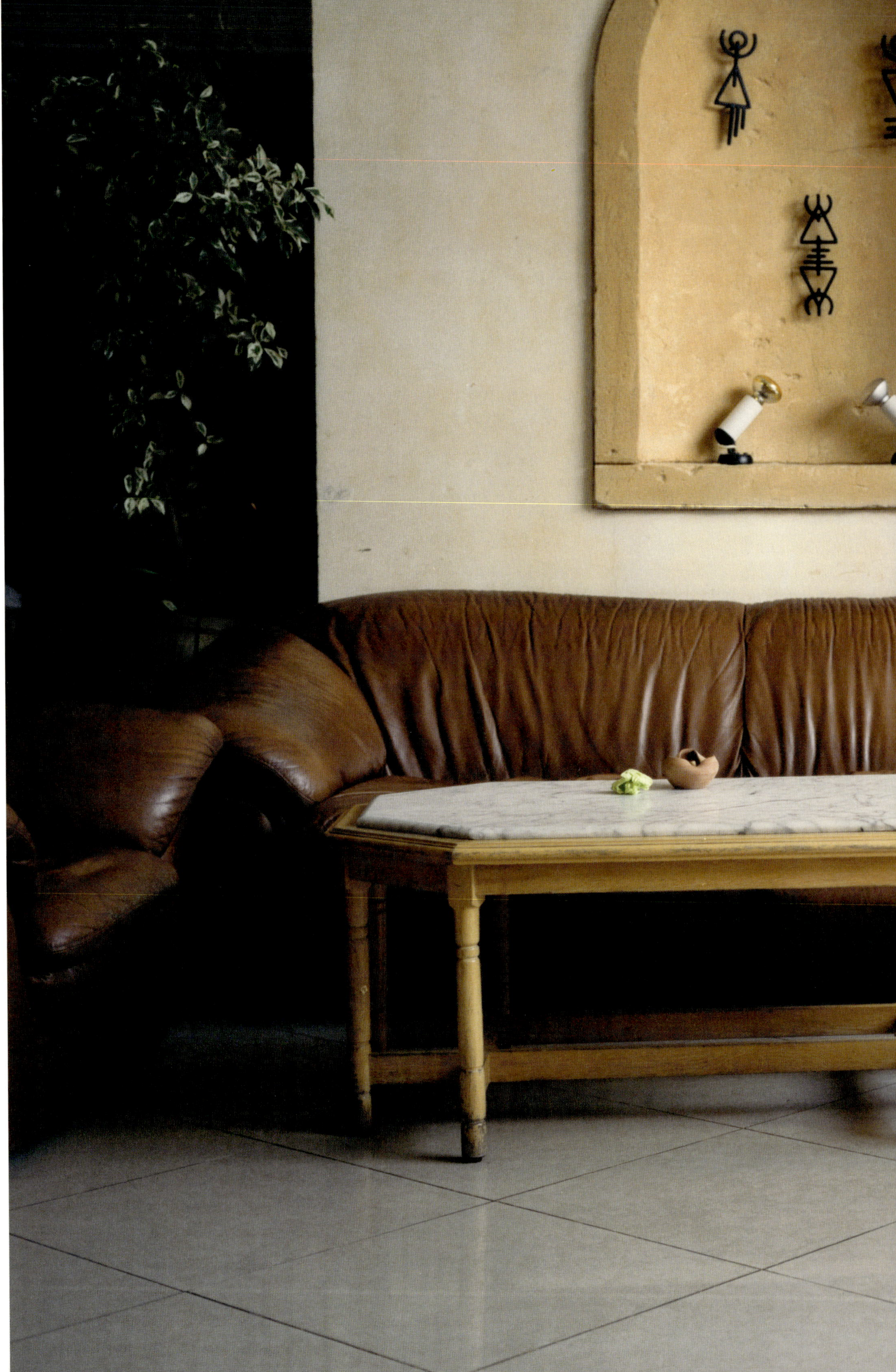

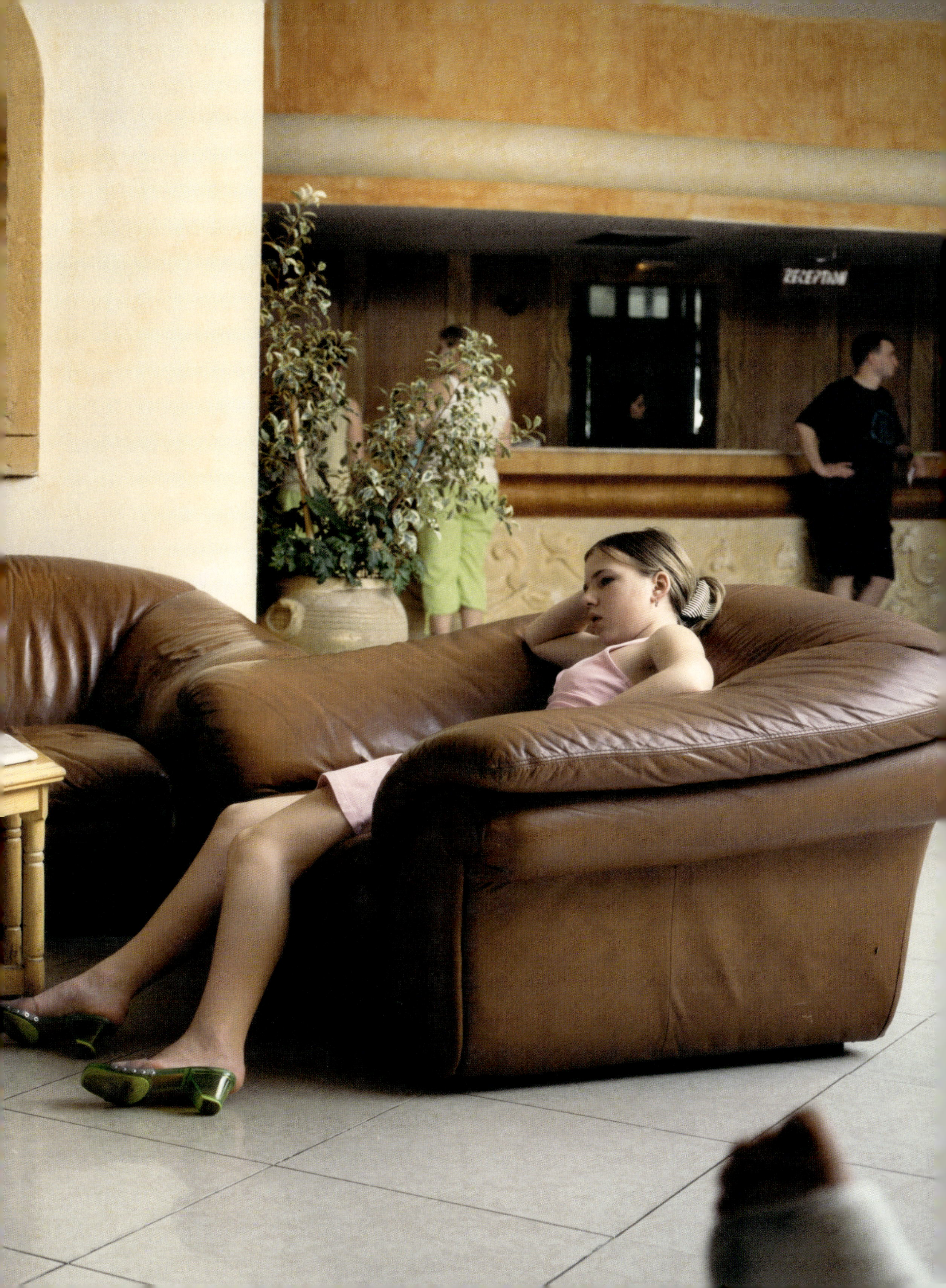

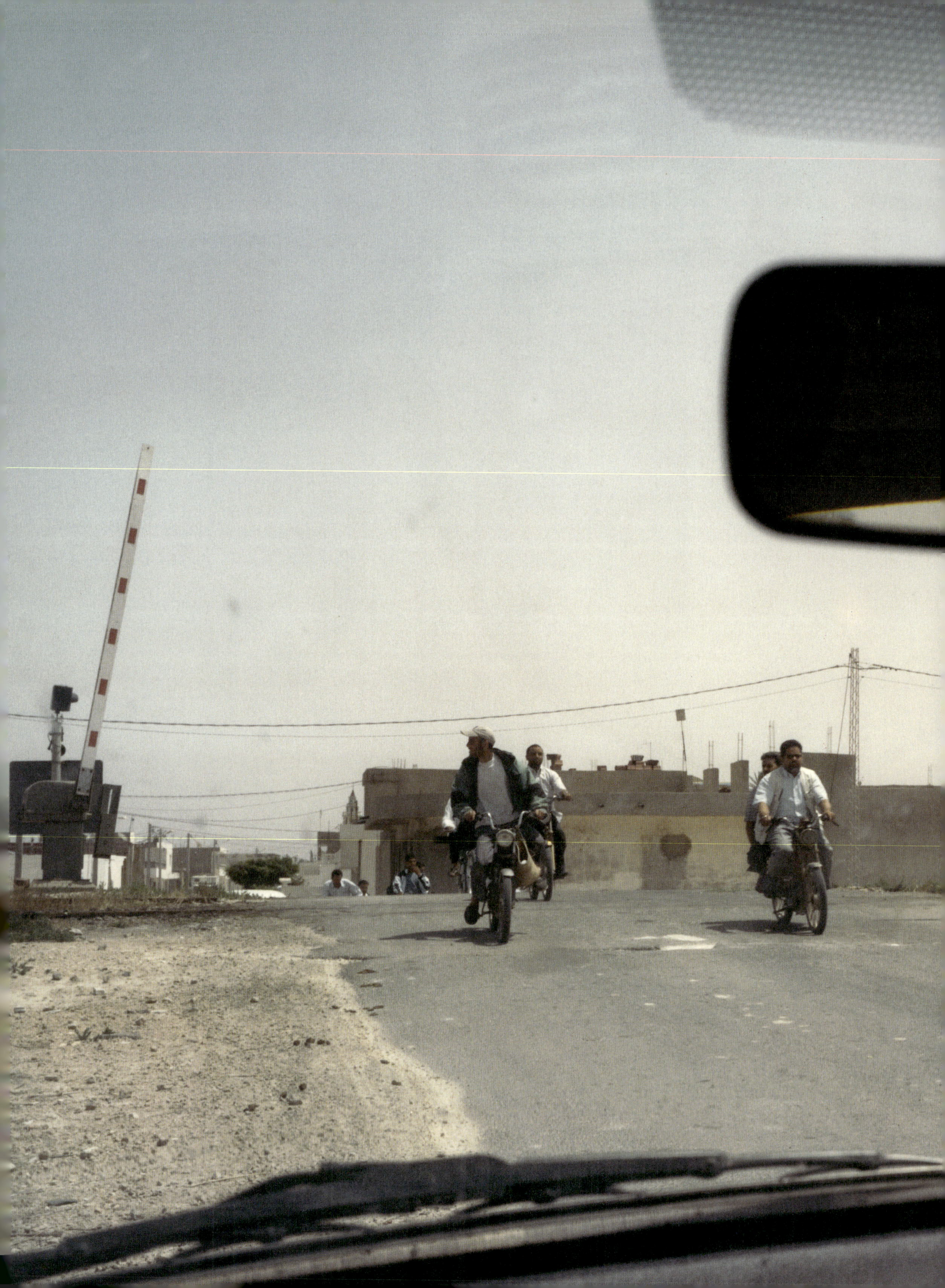

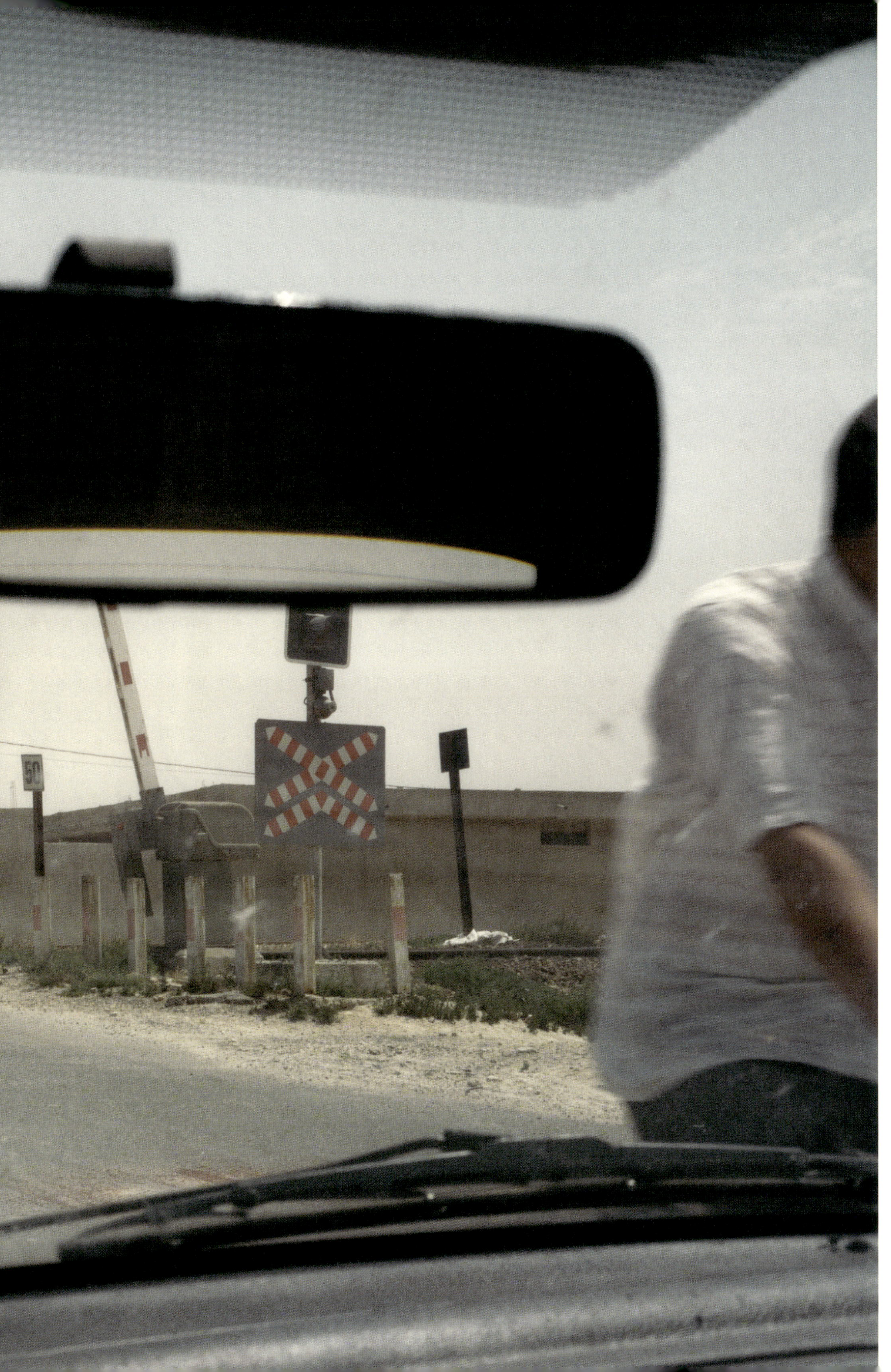

235.

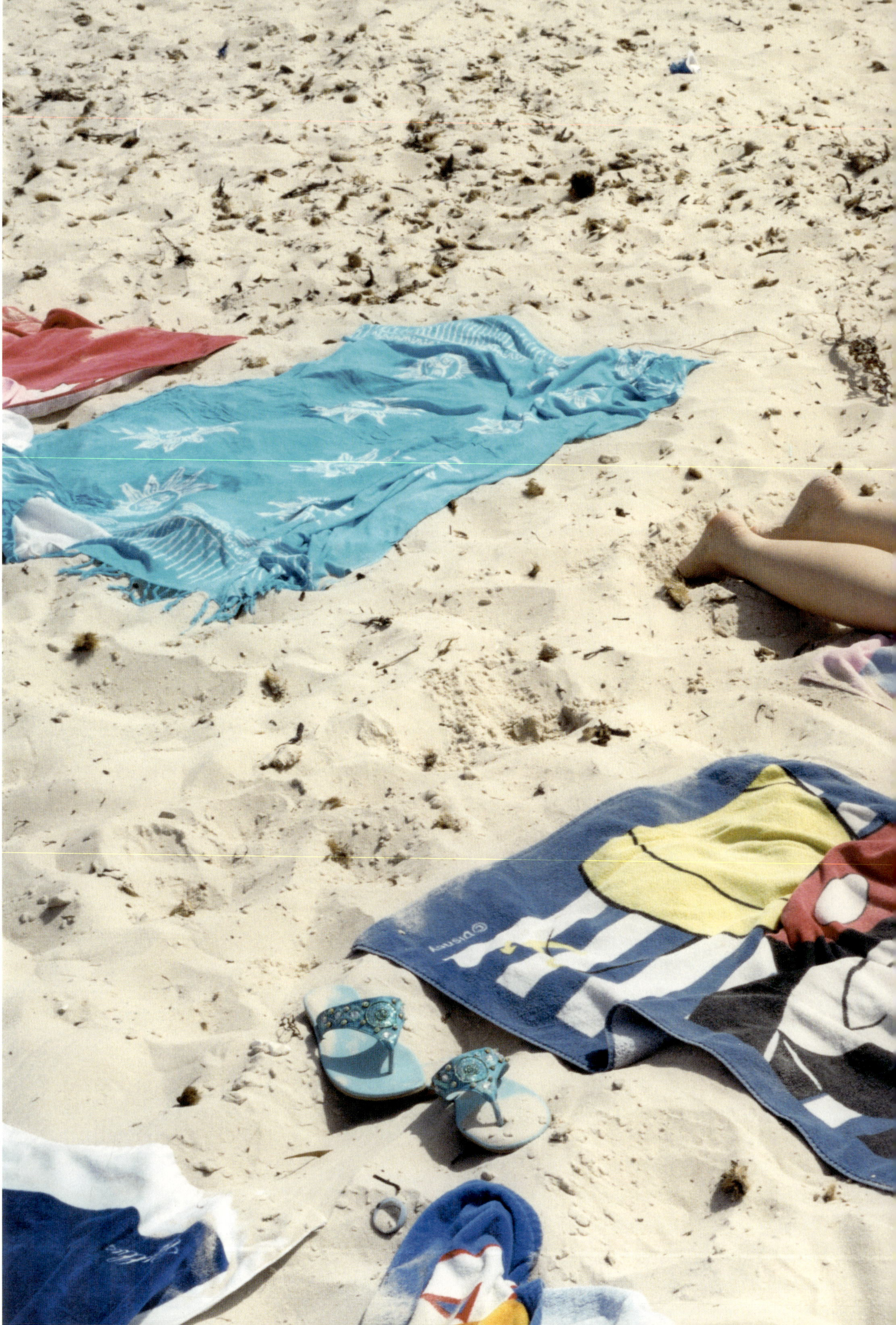

236.

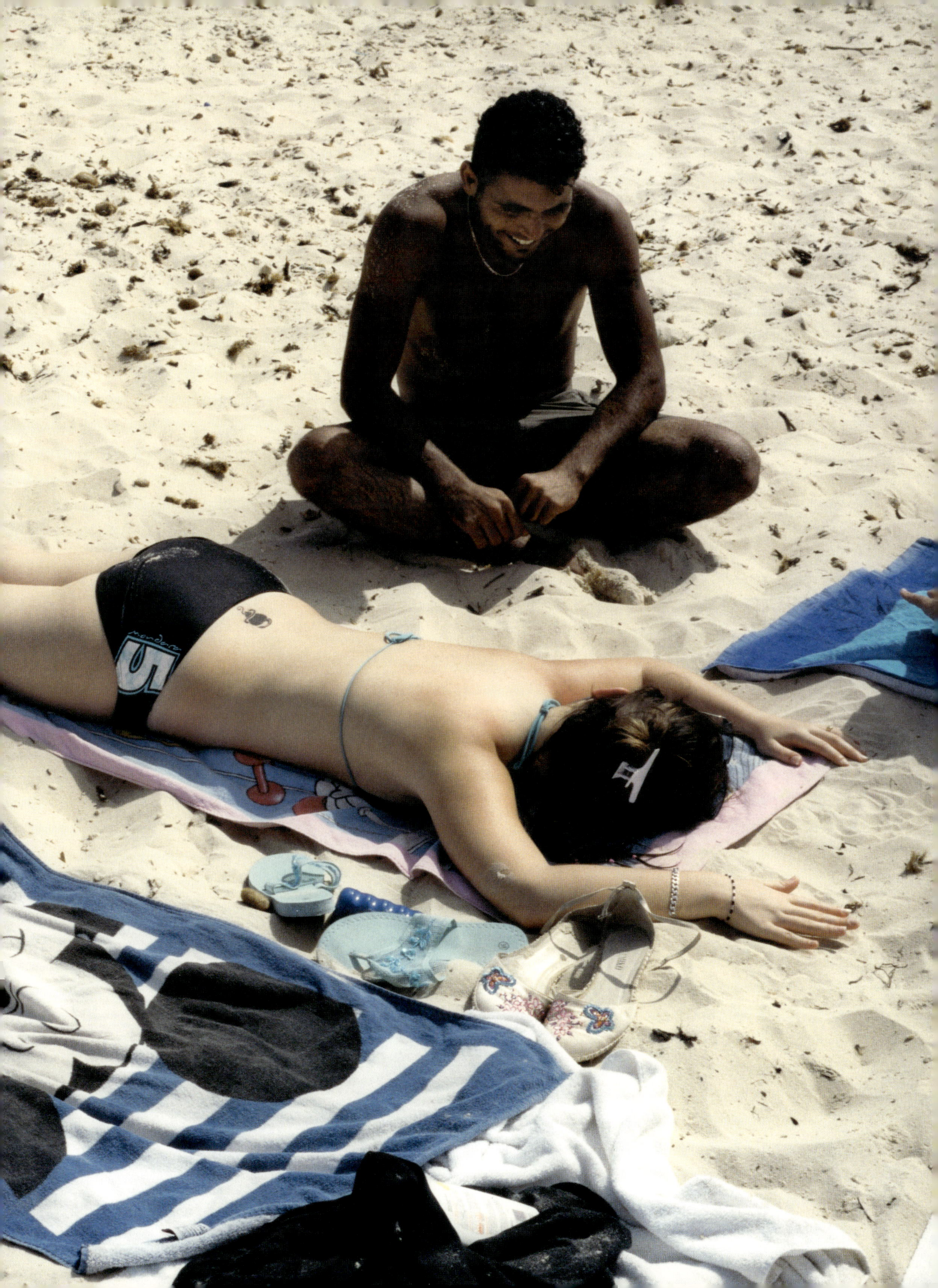

Many statistics about the countries around the Mediterranean divide the region sharply in two. The number of cars to the north of the sea is several times higher than on the southern and eastern coasts, Albania being the major exception. There is, of course, only one logical explanation for this, and that is poverty. Cars are expensive. Secondhand cars from Europe are very popular as a result. Even these are steeply priced, however, and for many still unaffordable. You often see patched-up bangers – third, fourth, fifth hand even – that are kept running with difficulty. In Cairo, for example, 76% of the taxis are more than 12 years old, of which 41% are more than 20 years old.

But the end could be drawing nigh for this arsenal of old and often polluting cars. Large producers such as Tata in India and Chery in China have discovered a lucrative market in developing countries. They are capturing the market with low-priced models that undercut the European, American and Korean brands. In Morocco and Egypt, production plants are being established so that the dream of prosperity many Europeans had after the Second World War – a car for every family – can also become a reality in Algeria and other countries on the southern side of the Mediterranean.

   ALGERIA

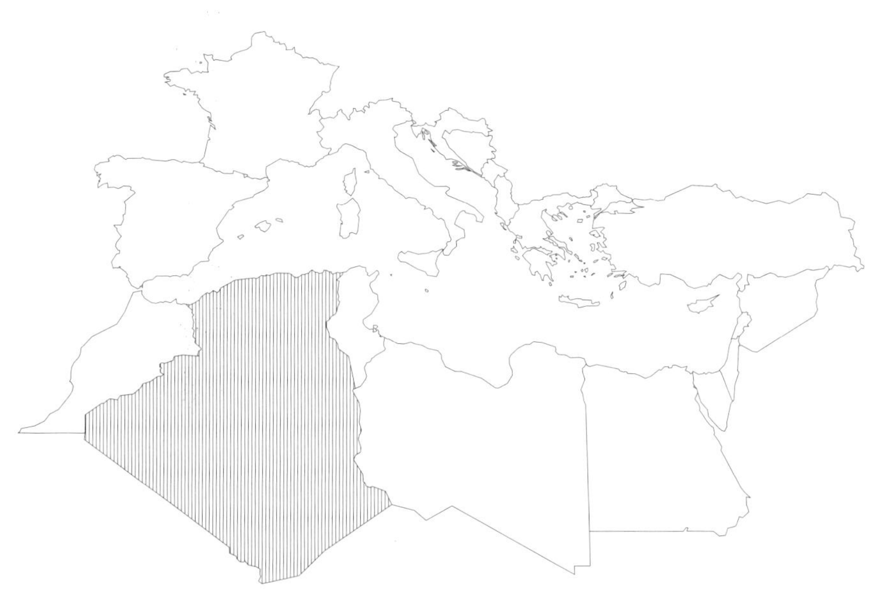

NUMBER OF CARS
PER 100,000 POPULATION

GIBRALTAR	8.36	
SPAIN	515.92	
FRANCE	499.54	
ITALY	605.00	
CROATIA	352.85	
ALBANIA	56.68	
GREECE	440.68	
CYPRUS	383.78	
TURKEY	71.91	
SYRIA	9.00	
LEBANON	418.16	
ISRAEL	290.92	
W.B.& GAZA	NA	
EGYPT	21.93	
LIBYA	172.86	
TUNISIA	62.60	
ALGERIA	**72.58**	
MOROCCO	47.29	

SOURCE : WELTINZAHLEN.DE

241. ORAN
Lunchrooms are places where young lovers go to meet each other. Girls can smoke cigarettes here and boys and girls can touch each other – small things that are forbidden outside.

242. SIDI-FERRUCH
Near a metropolitan bathing place schoolchildren sit on the beach. After this photograph was taken, they all went into the sea in small groups.

245. ORAN
Of all the Mediterranean countries, Algeria is most visibly an ex-colony. In Algerian coastal cities you often feel as if you are in Marseilles. There are still cafés here where both men and women can enjoy a drink together.

247. SIDI-FERRUCH
Fear of terrorism deters most tourists from visiting Algeria, even though it is a beautiful and pleasant country. At the entrance to the fashionable, walled bathing area Sidi Ferruch, all bags are checked for explosives. The civil war might officially be over, but the tension is not.

249. KHADIA
The coast road between Algiers and Oran. Members of the AIS (Armée Islamique du Salut) used to hide in the trees and lie in wait for their victims, who were shot or had their throats slit on the spot. The Algerian Army rendered the hiding place useless by cutting the tops off the trees.

250. AIN BENIAN
A funeral, attended by the whole village. Muslims must be buried within 24 hours.

252. ZERALDA
A car bomb exploded on this spot 10 years ago. All the façades have since been repaired. The terraces and restaurants are once again full and families cruise through the streets in their cars.

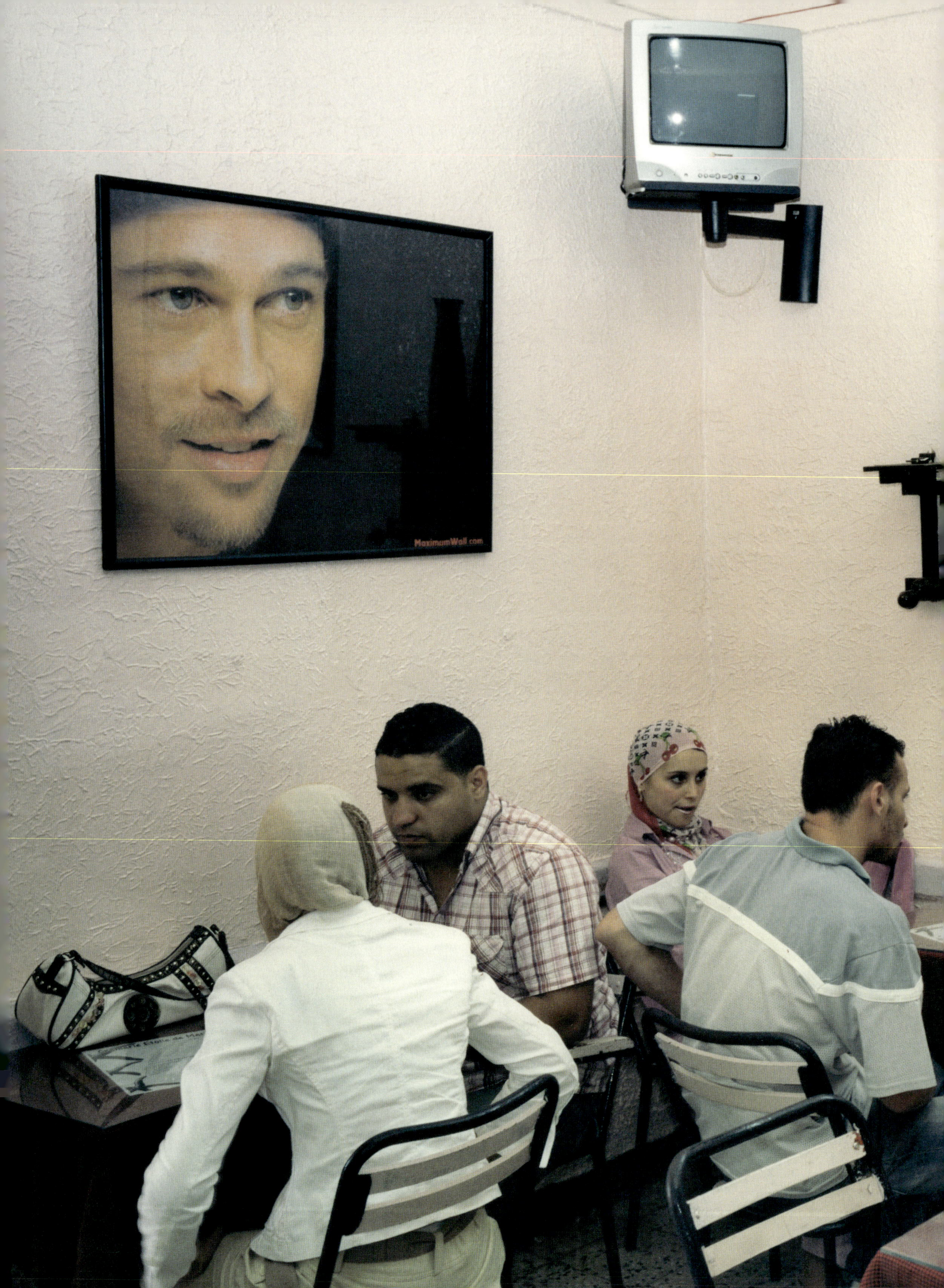
MaximumWall.com

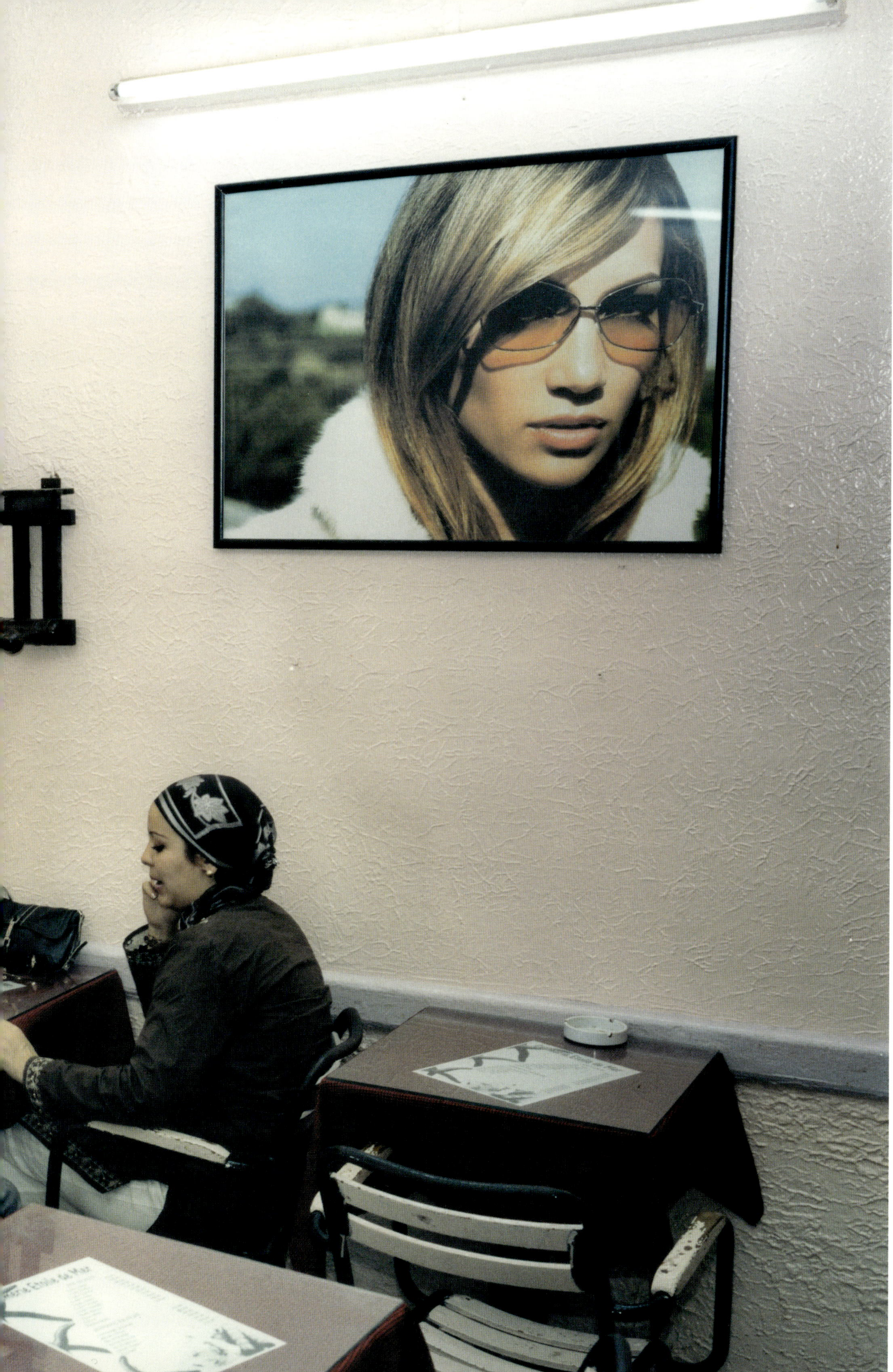

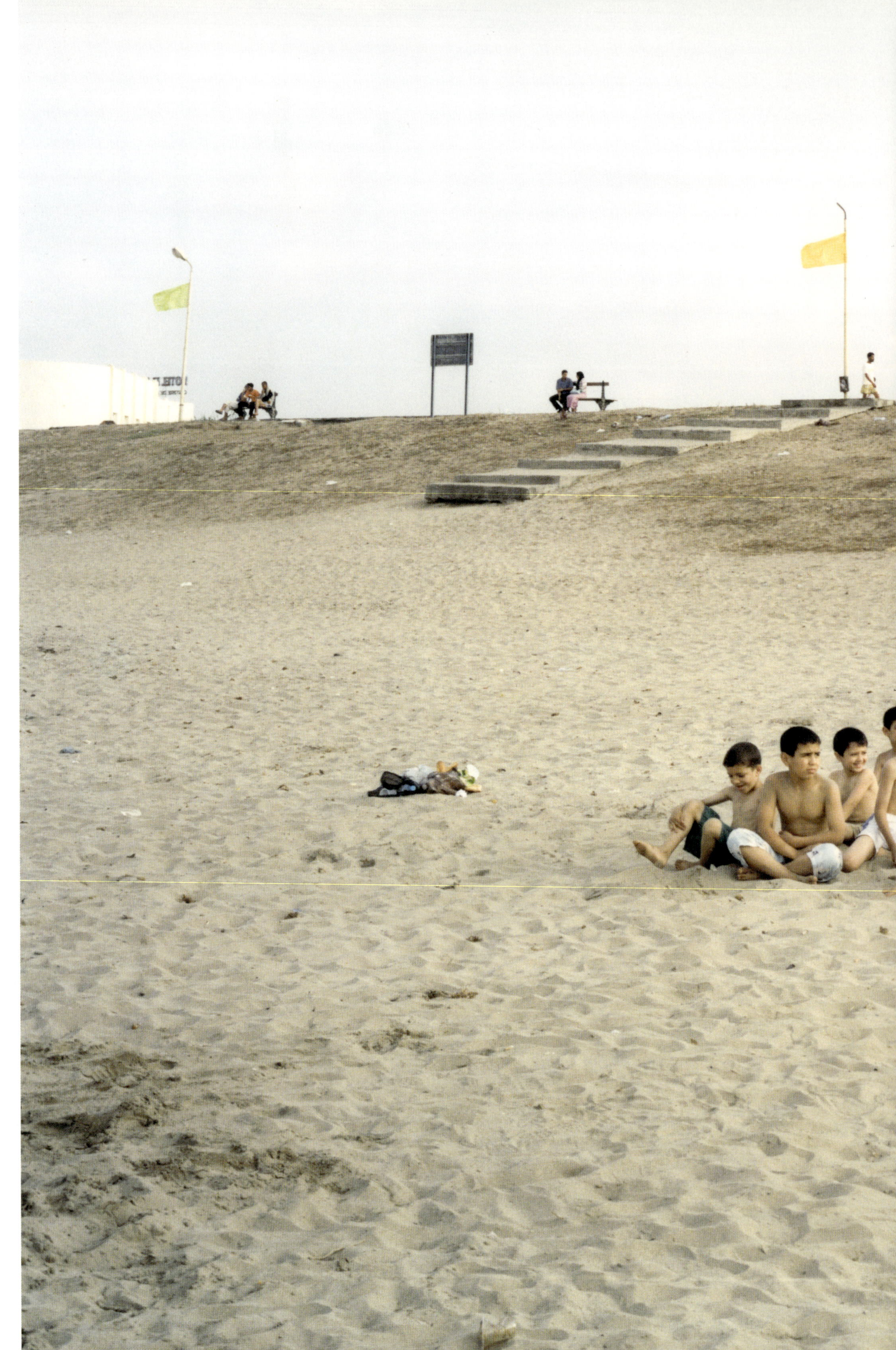

242.

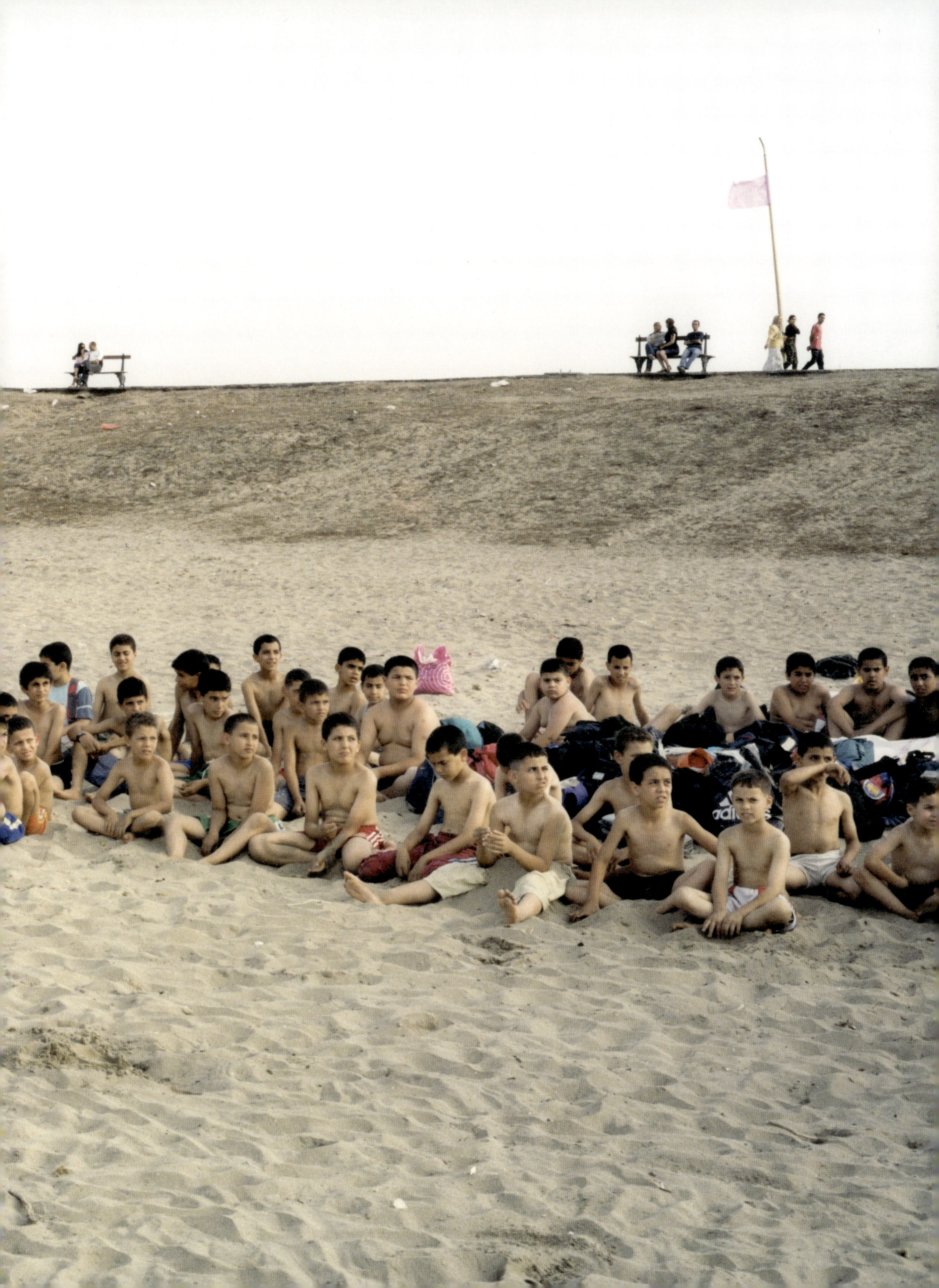

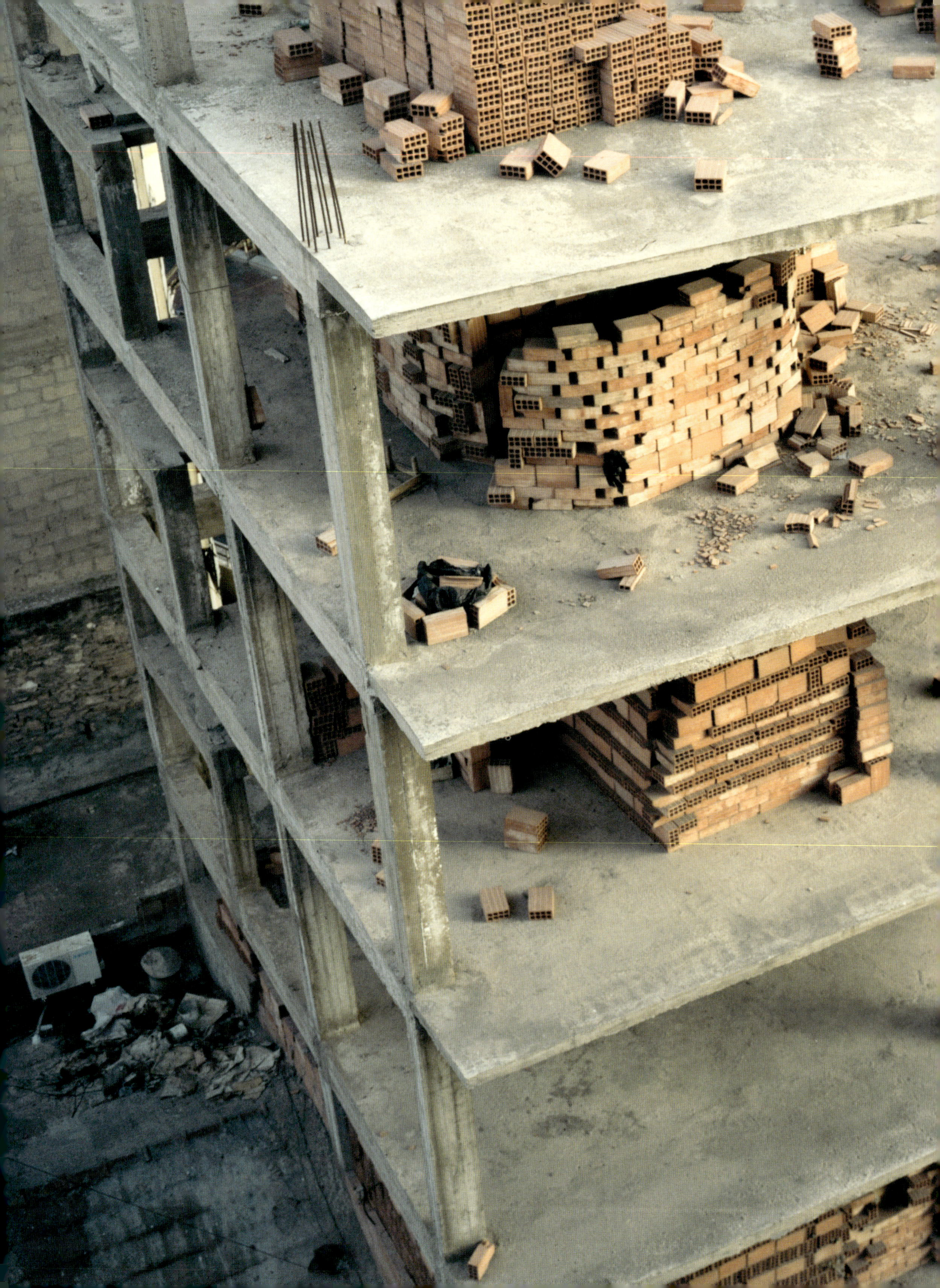

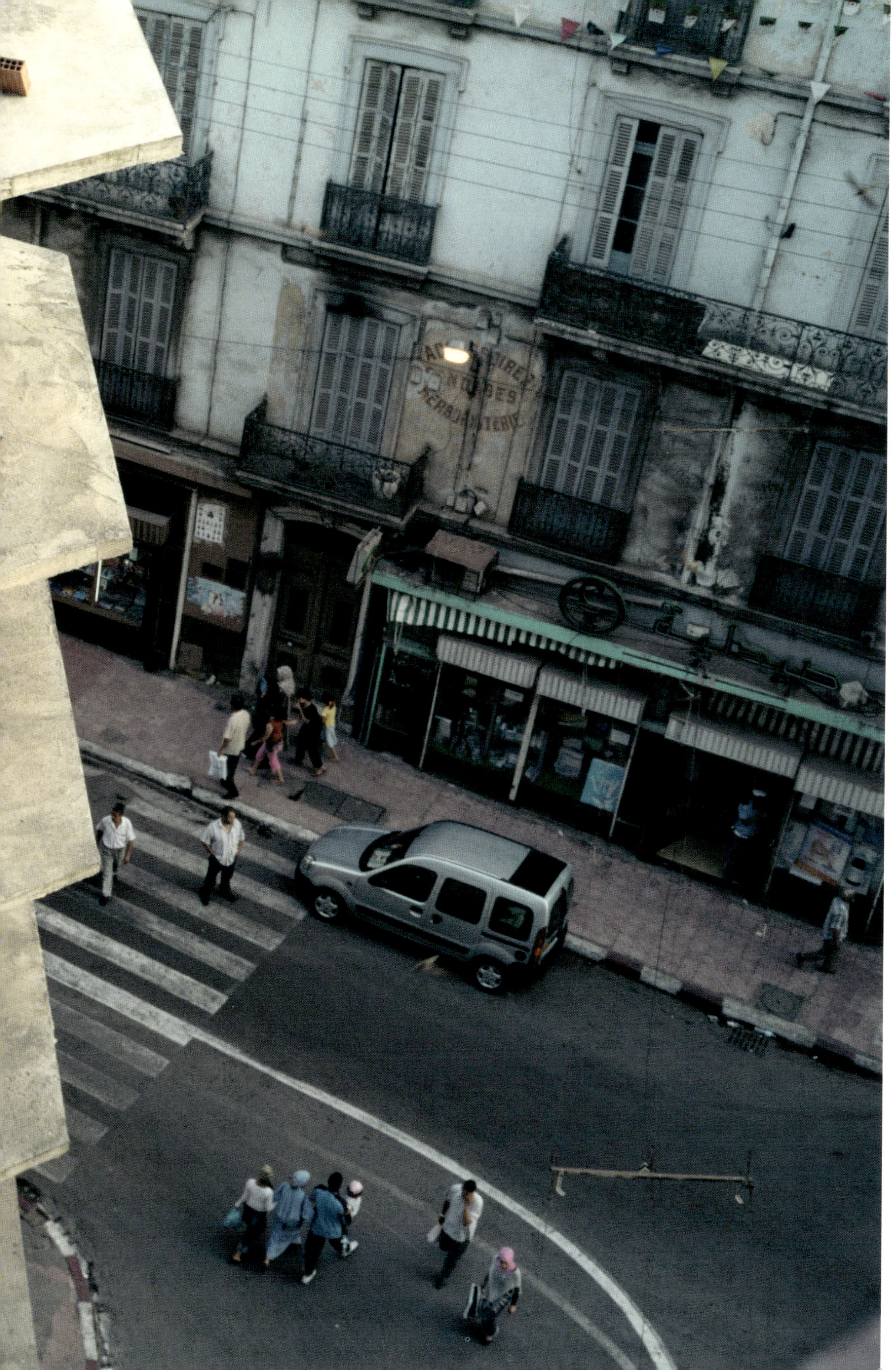

245.

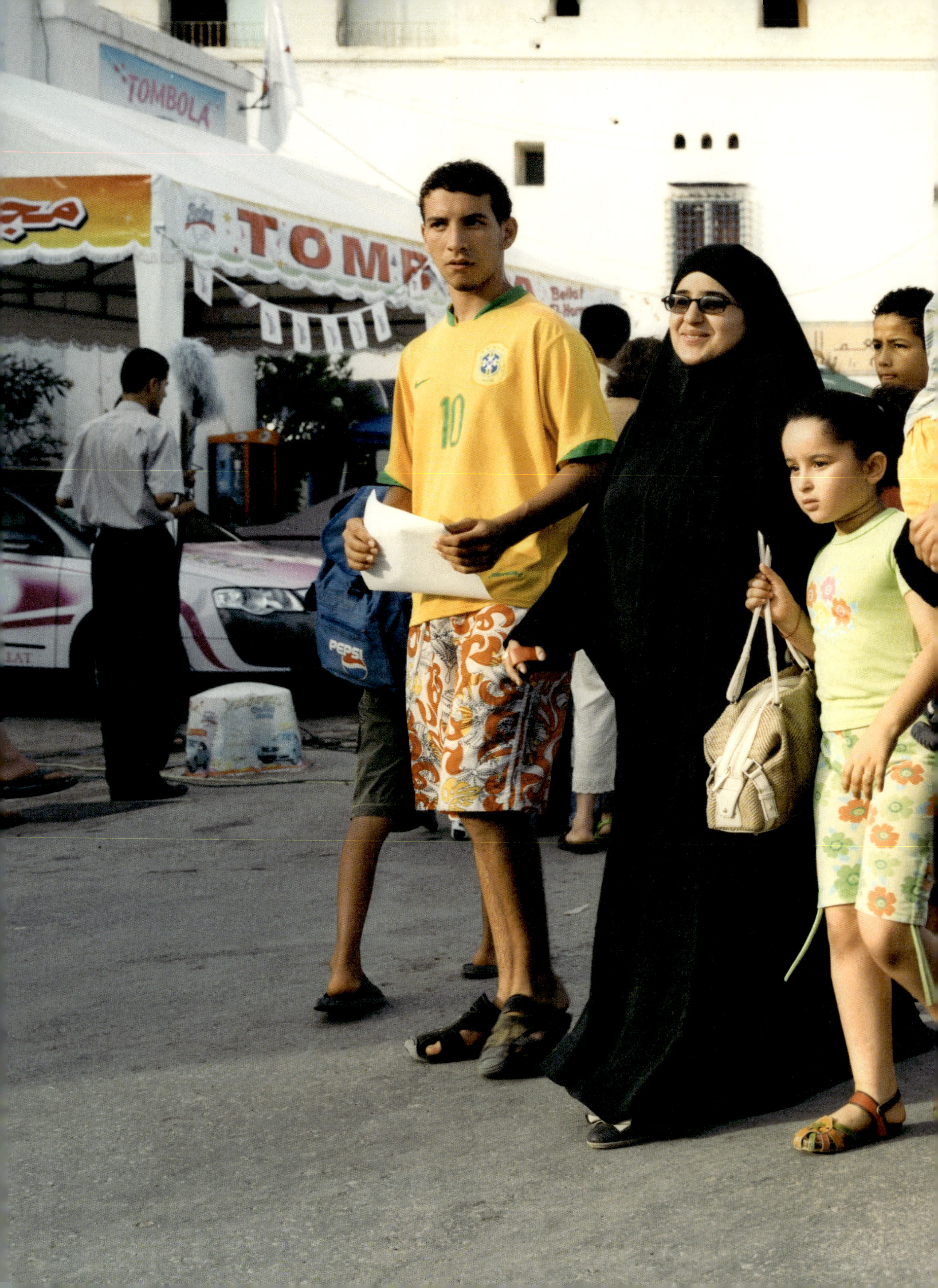

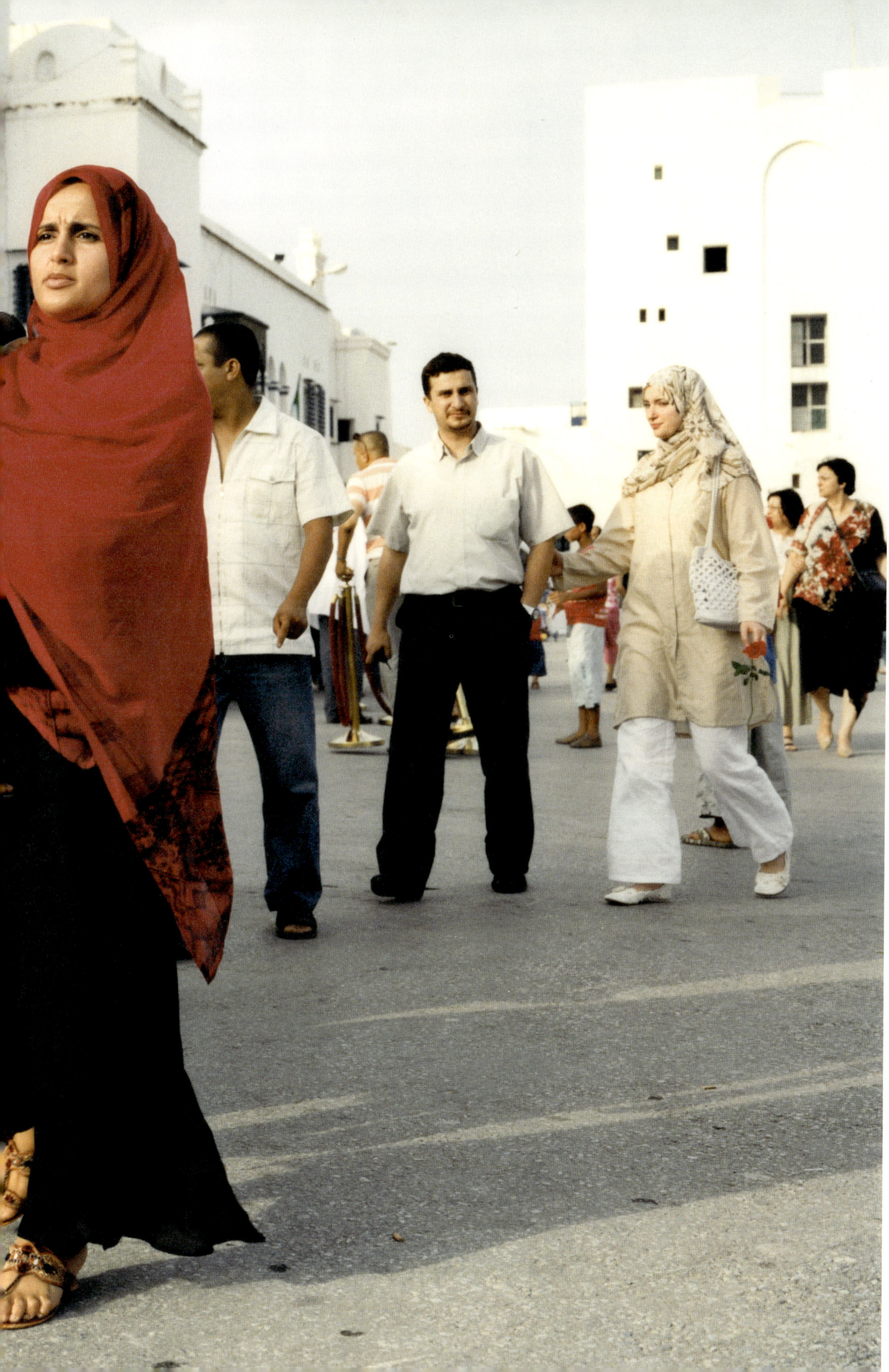

247.

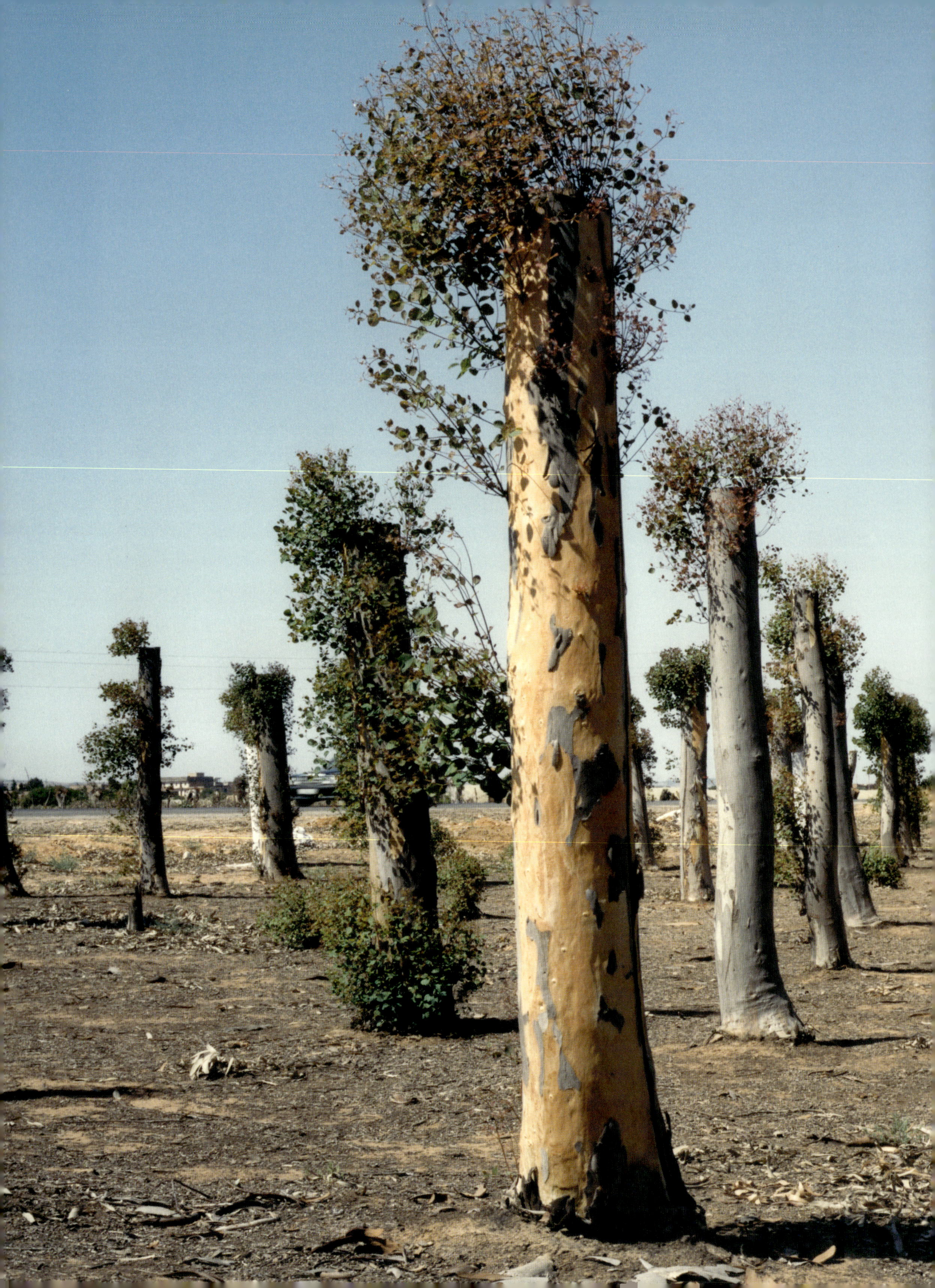

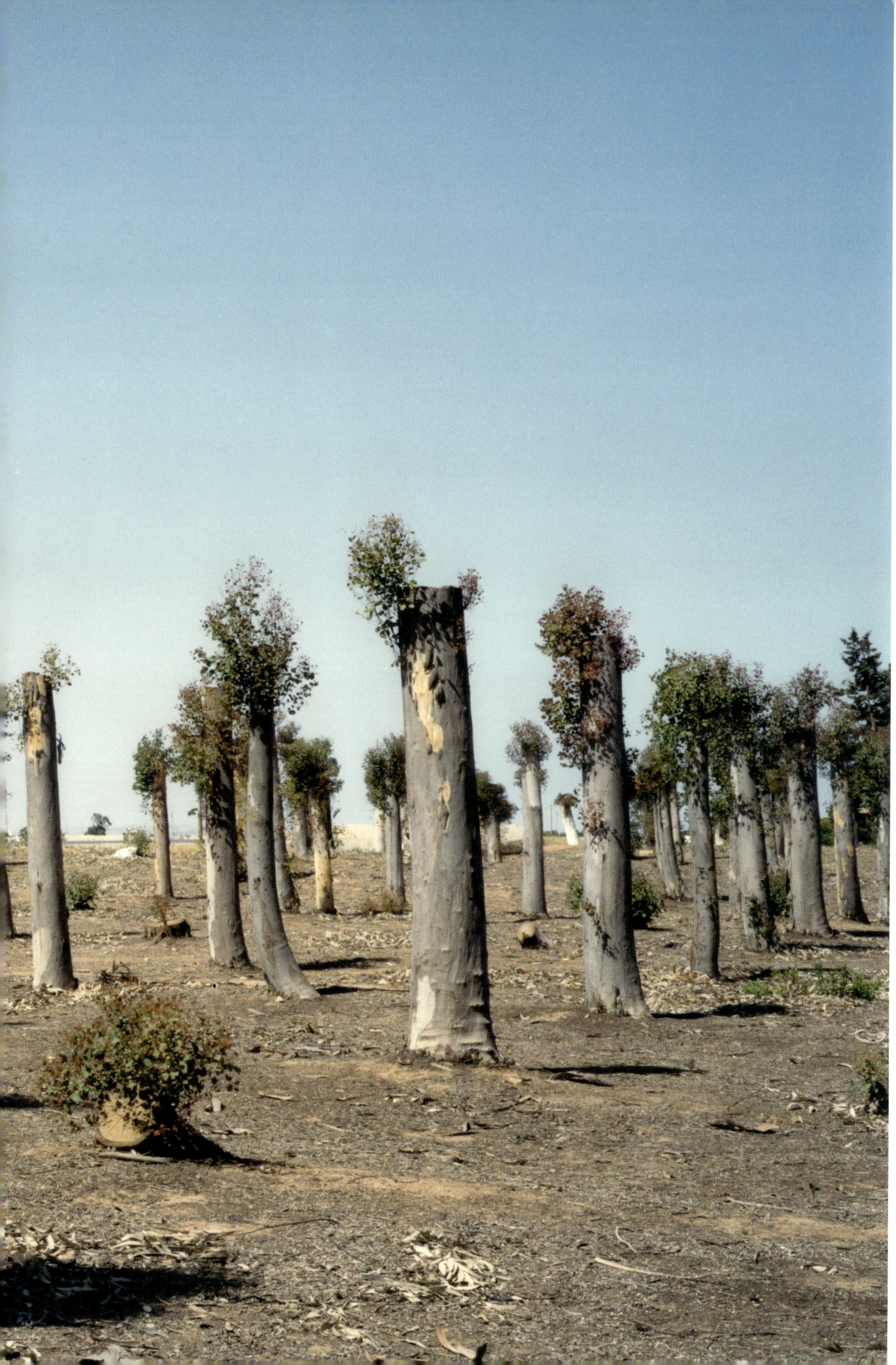

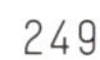

249.

250.

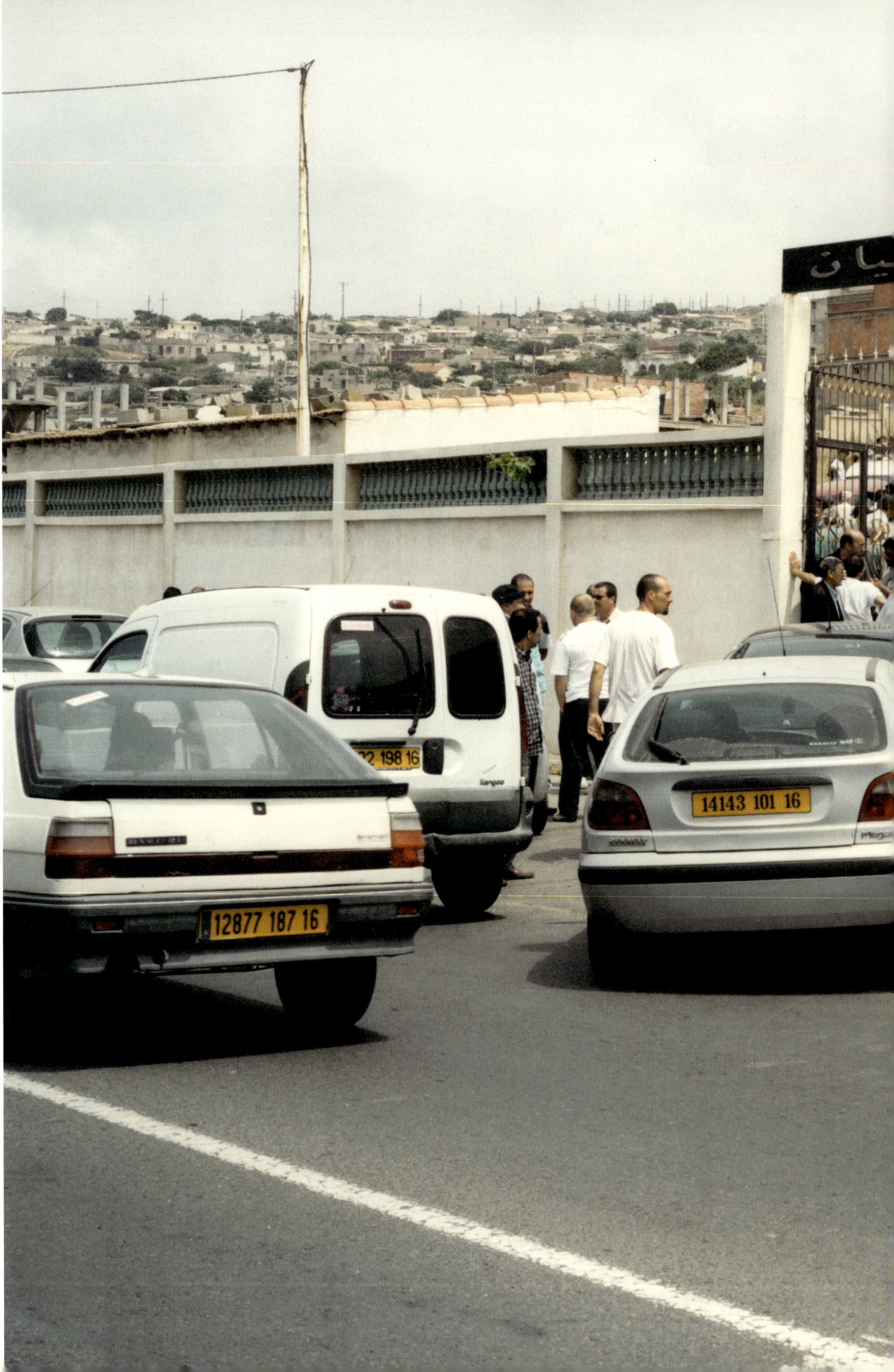

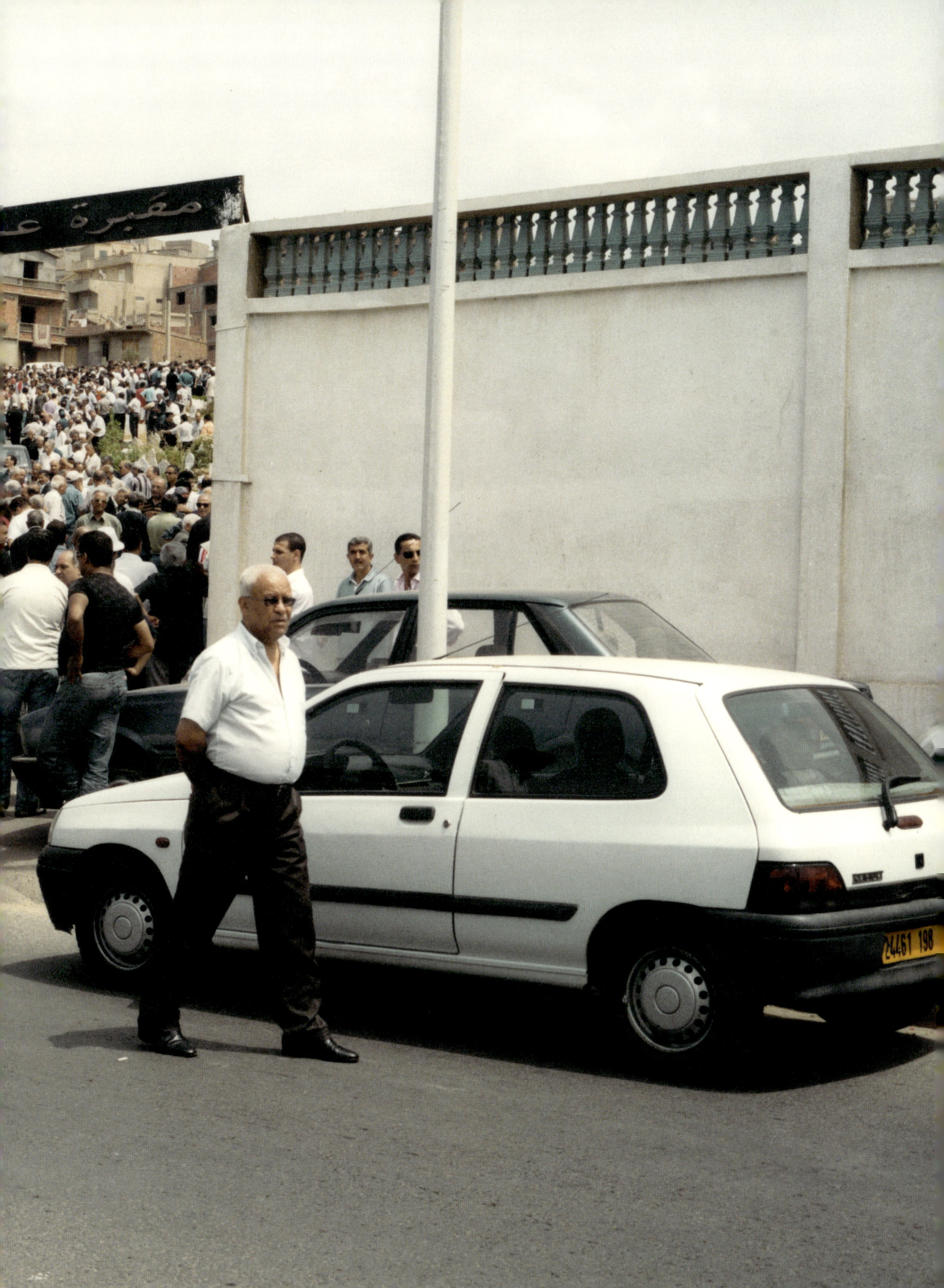

مقبرة ع

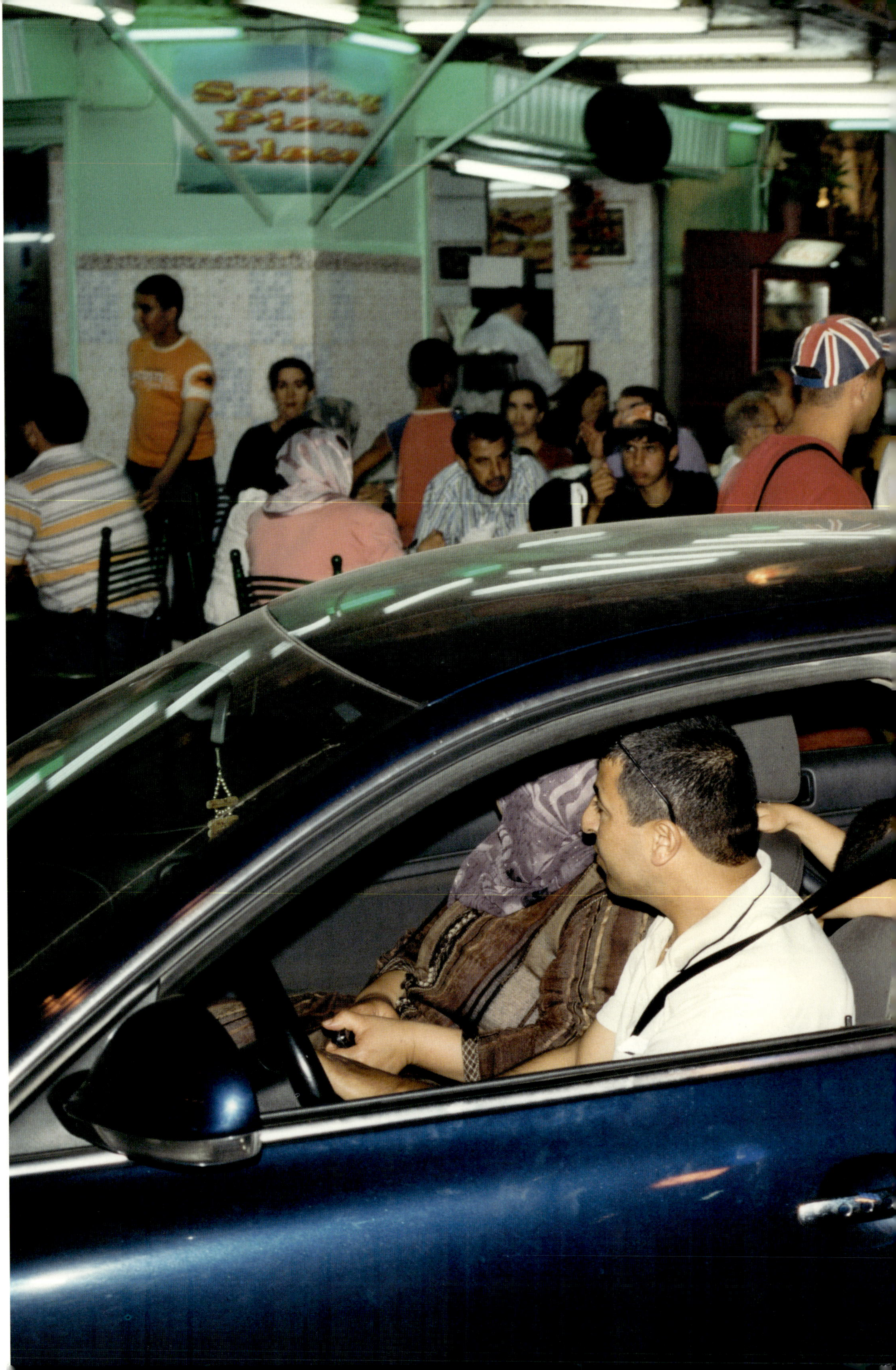

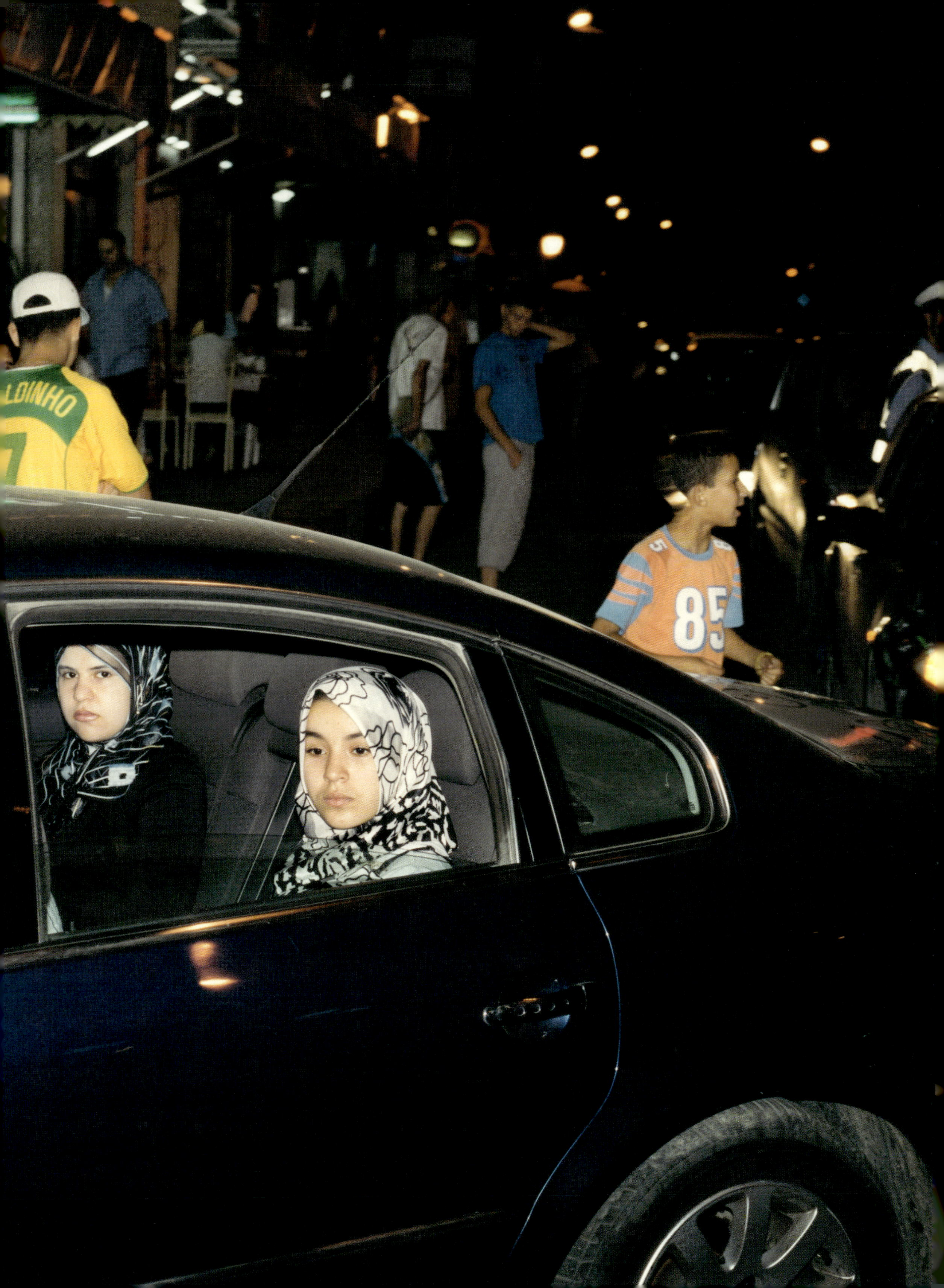

Morocco has the lowest gross domestic product (GDP) per person in the Mediterranean. It is closely followed by Syria, Albania and Egypt. Unemployment is high (19.3%) and, at 48.3%, illiteracy is the highest of all the Mediterranean countries.

The Mediterranean Sea is the lifeline that connects the country with Europe, its trading partner and most important export market. One way to ignite the national economy is by attracting the millions of potential tourists living in Europe. This is starting to produce results: by 2010, Morocco hopes to draw 10 million tourists a year. Another strategy to help the country out of the doldrums is economic reform that would clear the way for foreign investment.

One of Morocco's most important sources of income, however, is the money that the two million Moroccan emigrants send back to their families. For a decade, Egypt received the largest number of workers' remit-tances on the African continent. It was overtaken by Morocco in 2001, where workers' remittances make up around 8% of GDP, an extremely high amount. Many Moroccans working abroad also invest in their country by buying second homes and spending their summers there. This annual flow of money to North Africa amounts to more than development aid and foreign investment combined. In this way, the northern European countries indirectly contribute to the economies of the countries on the southern side of the Mediterranean.

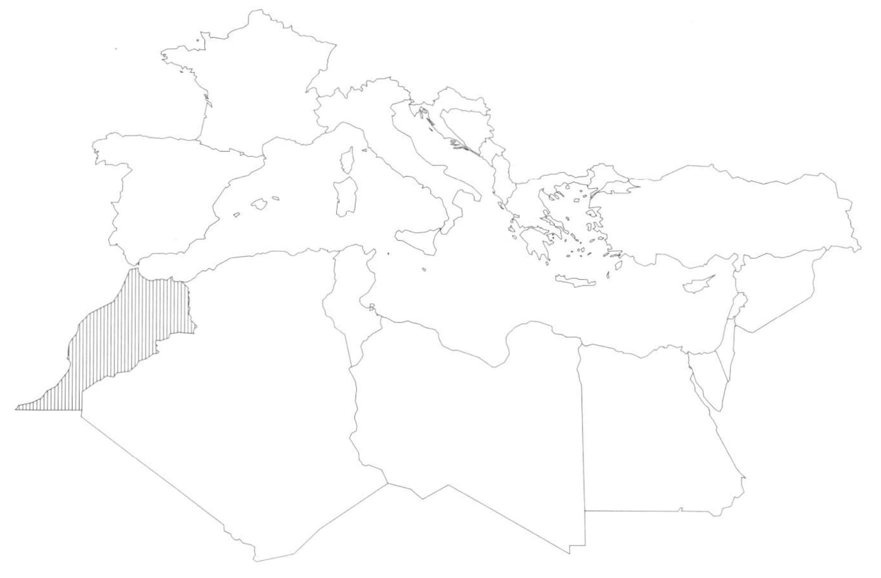

GDP PER CAPITA
IN EURO

GIBRALTAR	26,007.63	
SPAIN	22,943.90	
FRANCE	23,011.98	
ITALY	21,105.66	
CROATIA	10,552.83	
ALBANIA	3,744.55	
GREECE	20,765.25	
CYPRUS	18,450.44	
TURKEY	6,399.78	
SYRIA	3,063.73	
LEBANON	7,080.61	
ISRAEL	19,607.84	
W.B. & GAZA	NA	
EGYPT	3,676.47	
LIBYA	8,918.85	
TUNISIA	5,106.21	
ALGERIA	5,514.71	
MOROCCO	2,587.15	

SOURCE : THE CIA WORLD FACTBOOK

* : IN THE TURKISH REPUBLIC OF NORTHERN CYPRUS THE GDP PER CAPITA IS 4,857.71

257. SAIDA
A Spanish real-estate developer looking to make his fortune in Morocco. He is focusing predominantly on European Moroccans. In a protected dune area, a complex is currently being built, which includes 3,500 houses, restaurants, schools and hotels.

259. SAIDA
At the beginning of the summer holidays many European Moroccans return to the country in which their parents were born. They visit their families and then relax on the beach. They are very proud of Morocco, but at the same time are aware that it is dirty, corrupt and chaotic.

260. THE AREA AROUND OUJDA
Morocco's economy and infrastructure are not fantastic, particularly in the Rif Mountains. This has long been an extremely poor and rebellious area. Second homes and money from Europe sustain the area.

262. SAIDA
A few years ago, the locals had had enough of the returning Moroccans' lack of morals. Nearly a thousand religious men dressed in djellabas came onto the beach, knelt down and began to pray. This is our beach, was the message.

264. MARTIL
The showroom of a French real-estate and investment company. A day later, the place was filled with Moroccans from Europe who were considering investing in second homes. For native Moroccans, the European Moroccans are no different from any other foreigner.

267. SAIDA
These young men and women hardly ever appear on the beaches in Europe; but in north Morocco it is one big parade of suntanned bodies, BMWs and Mercedes. These four boys spoke Dutch with an Amsterdam accent.

268. SEPARATION FENCE BETWEEN THE SPANISH ENCLAVE OF CEUTA AND MOROCCO
The fence is meant to keep illegal immigrants out. Even so, there is a camp in Ceuta holding several hundreds of people. Spain has the right to send Moroccans and Algerians back home immediately. If the camp gets too full, other refugees have a chance of being put on the boat to Spain.

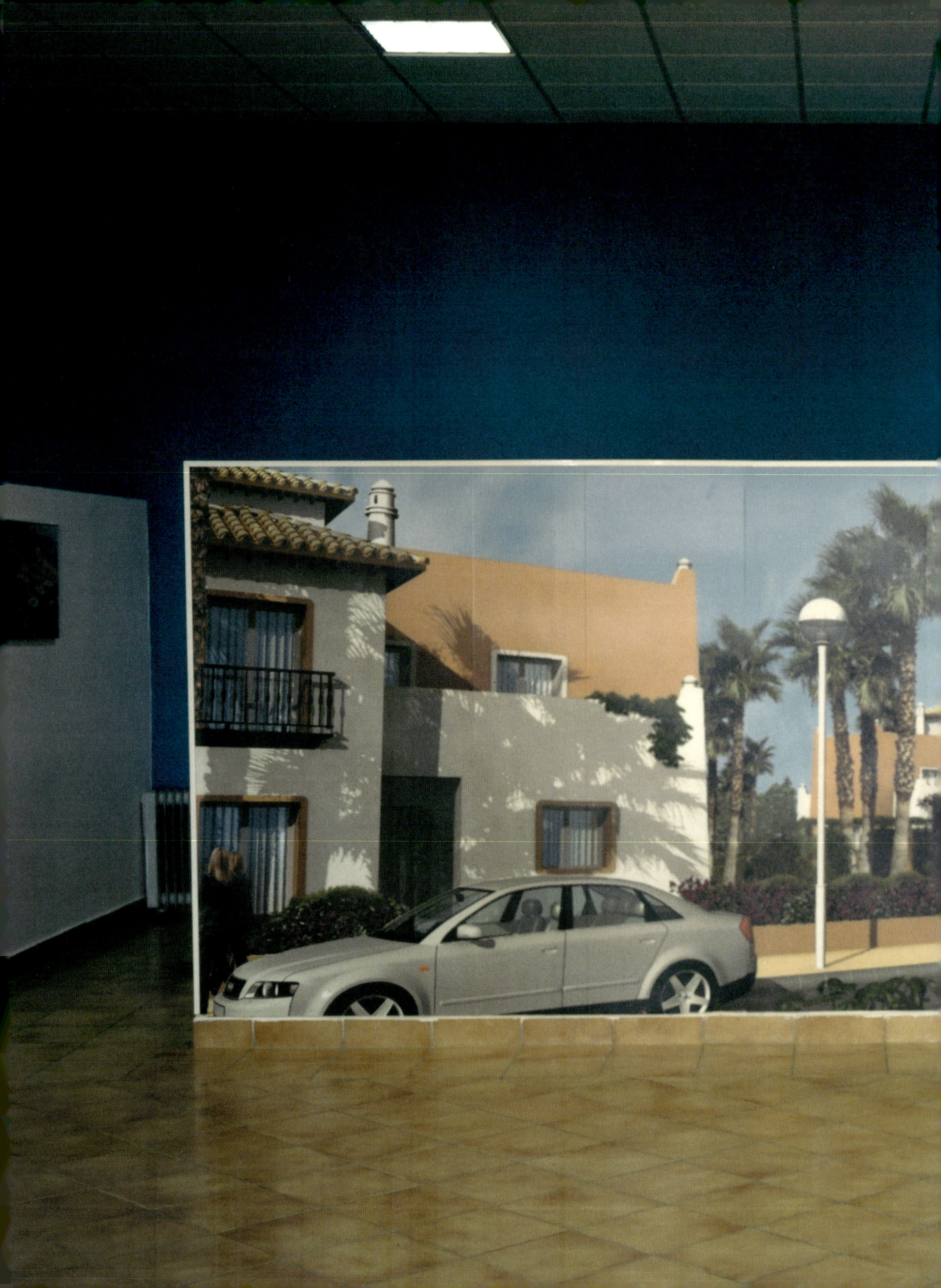

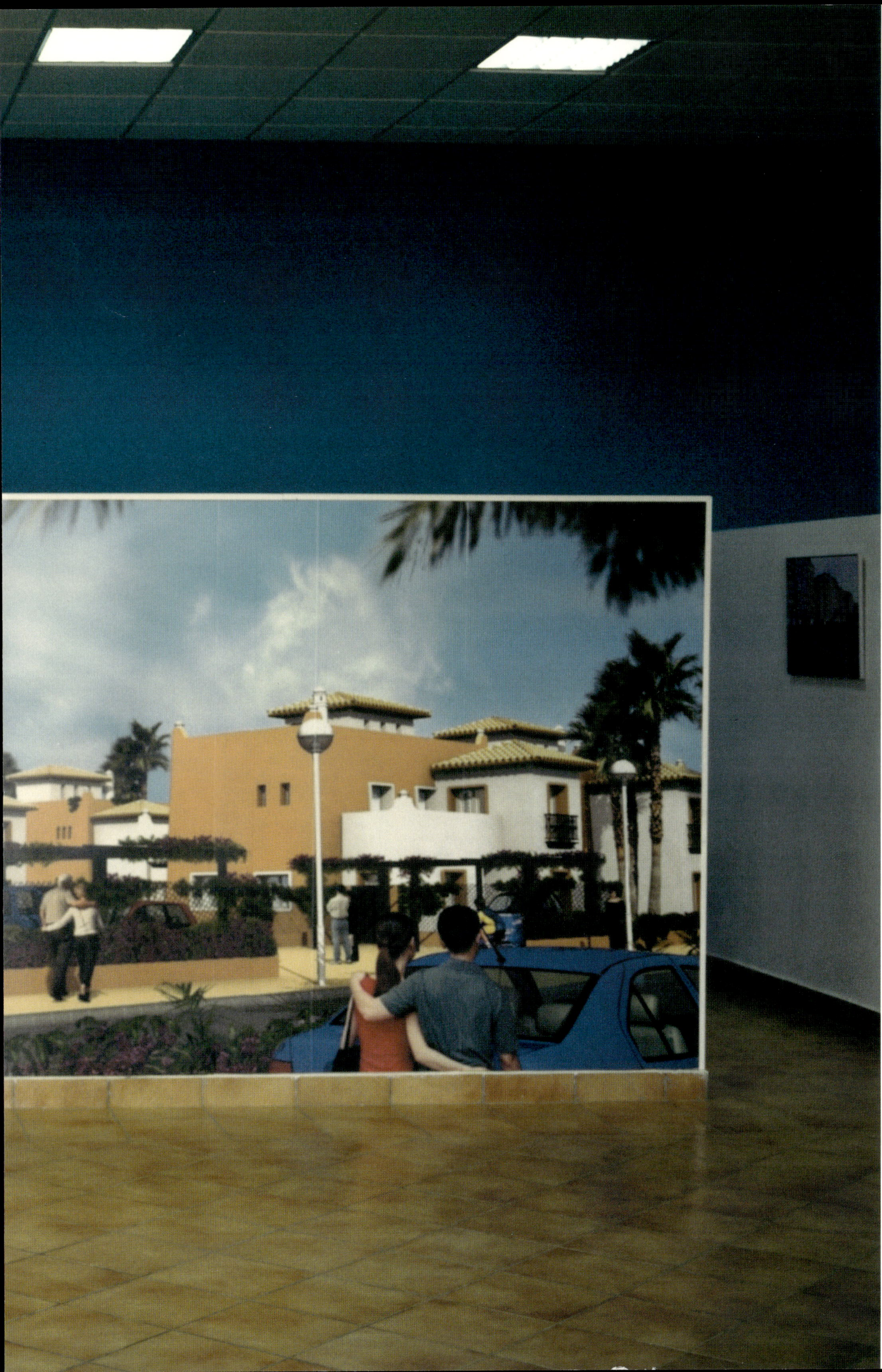

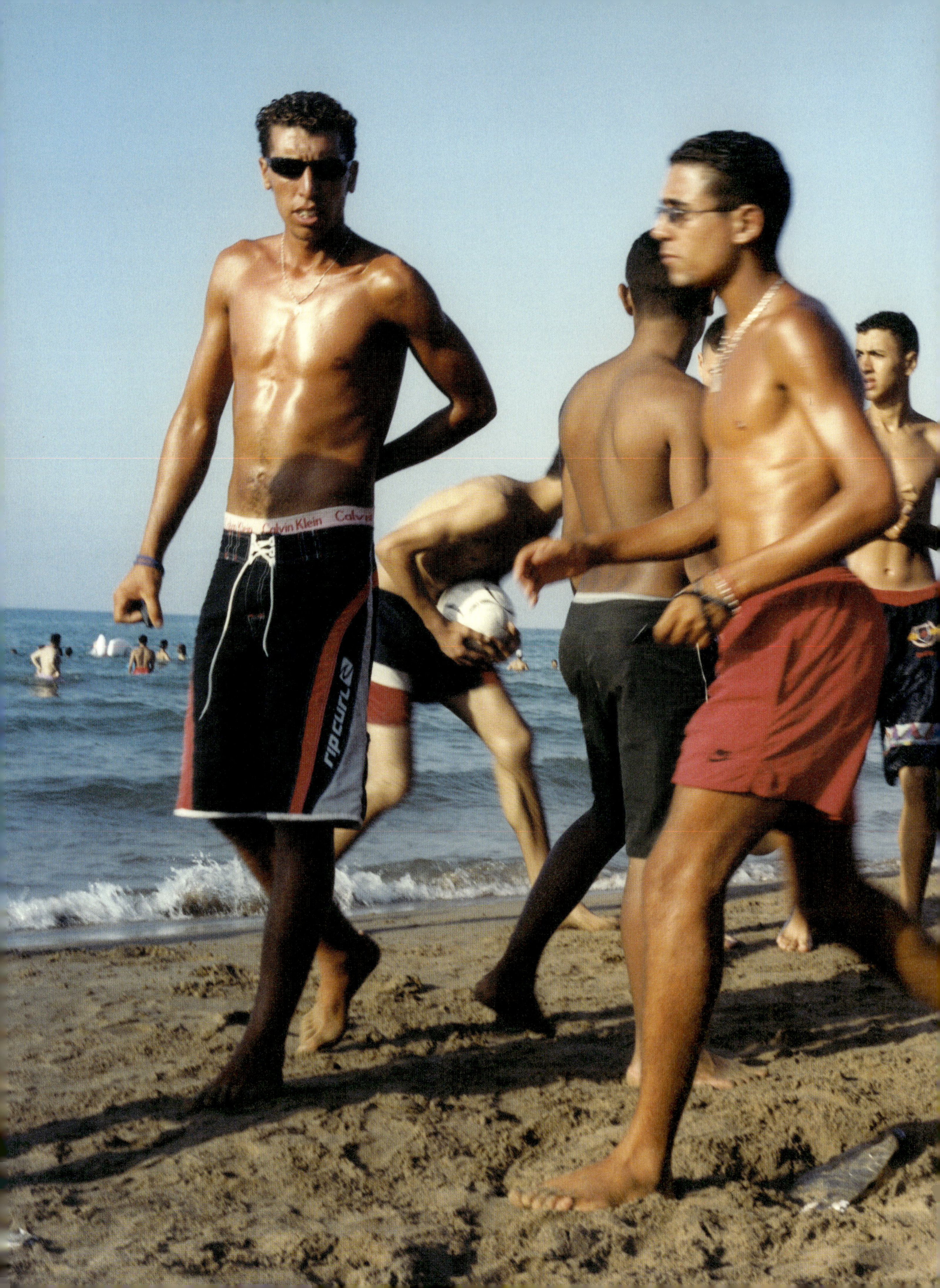

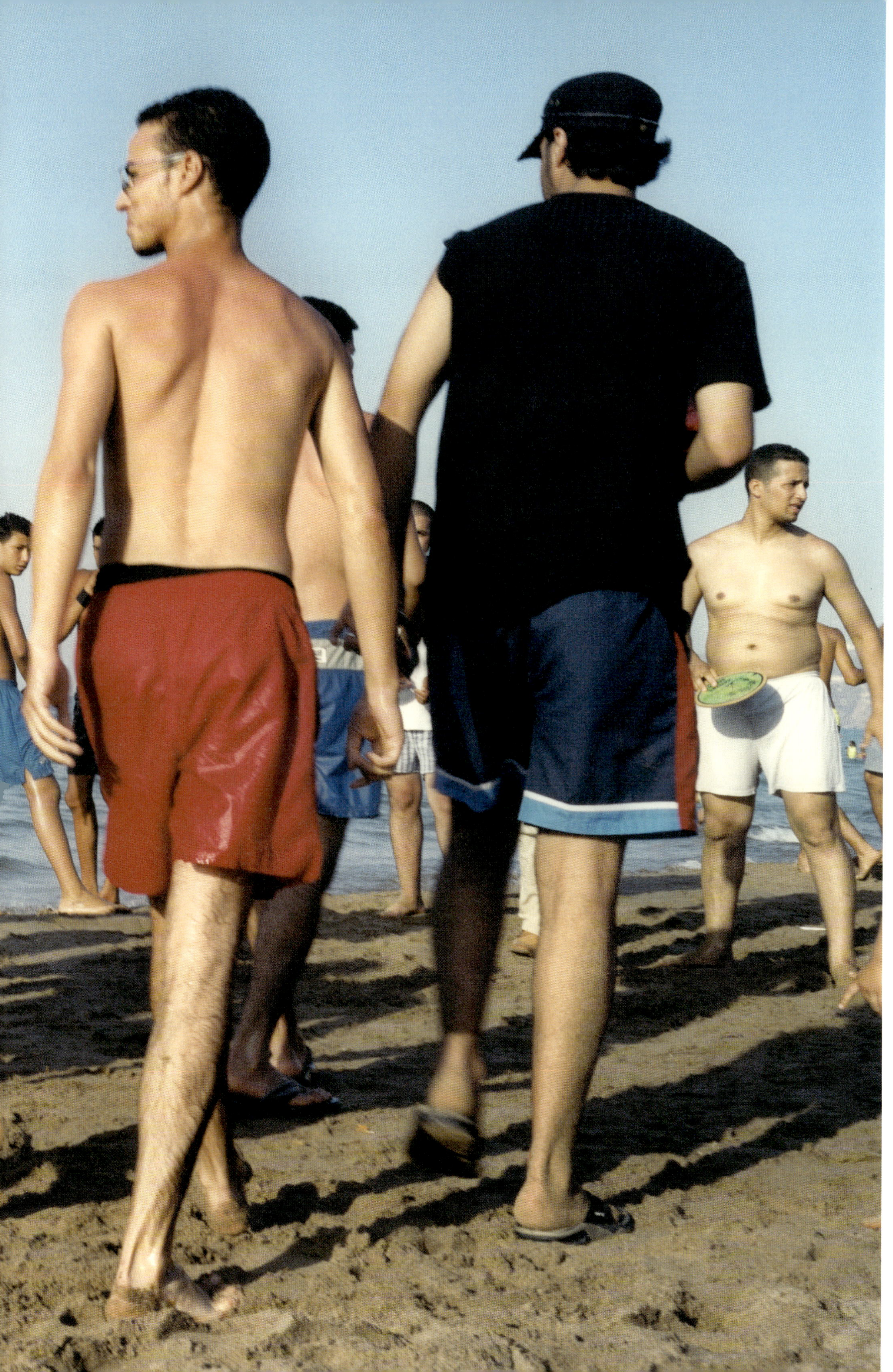

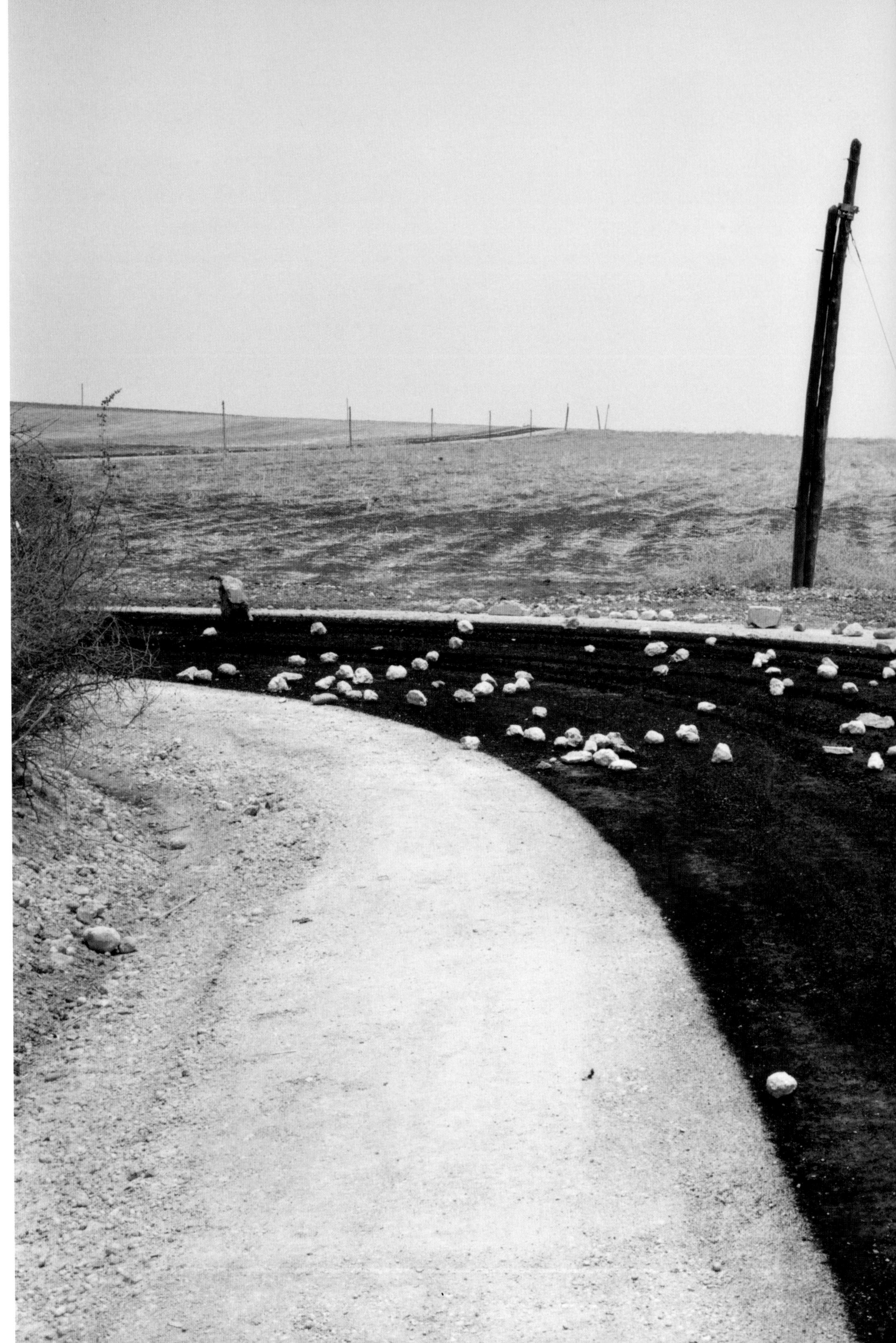

260.

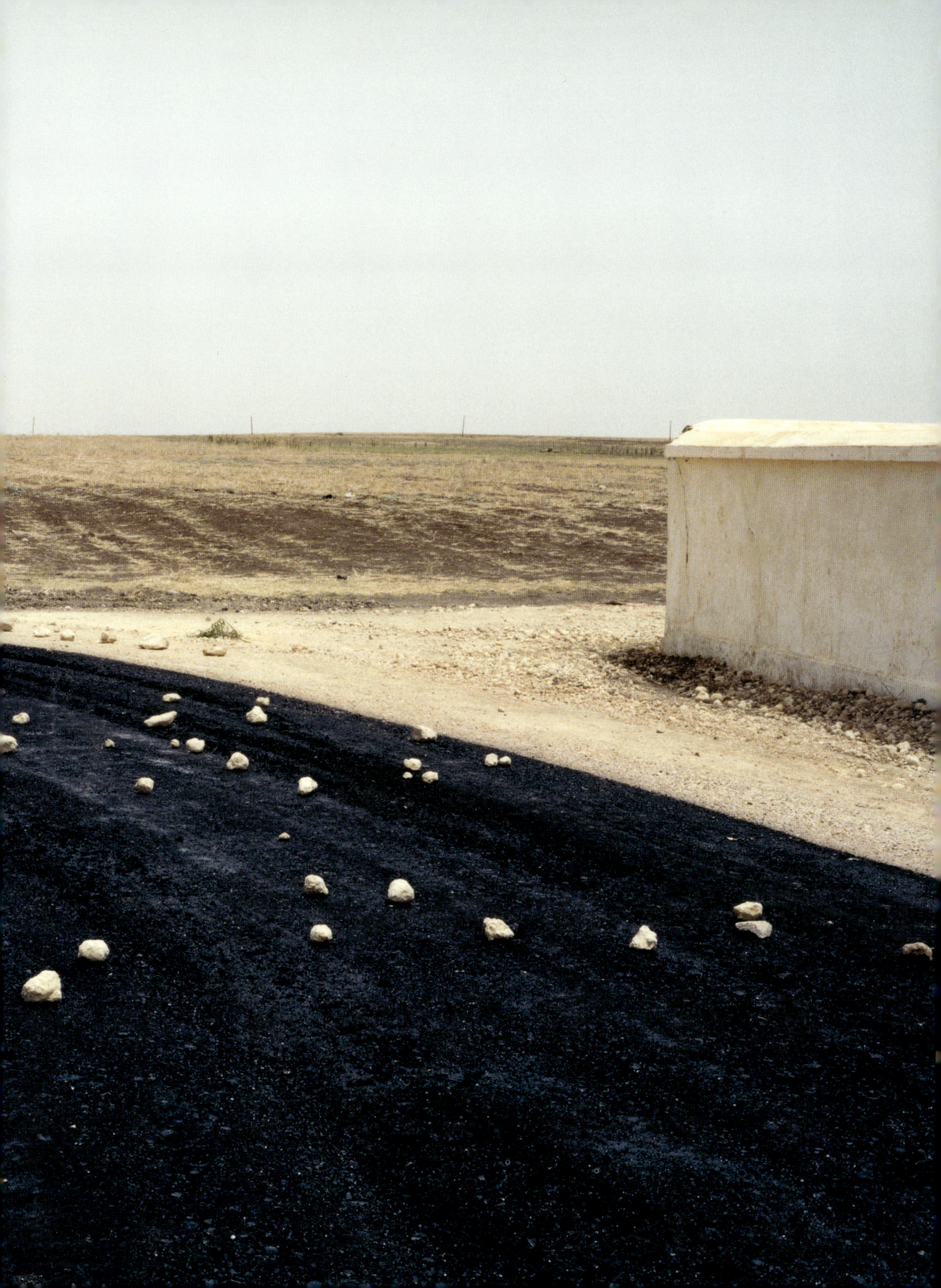

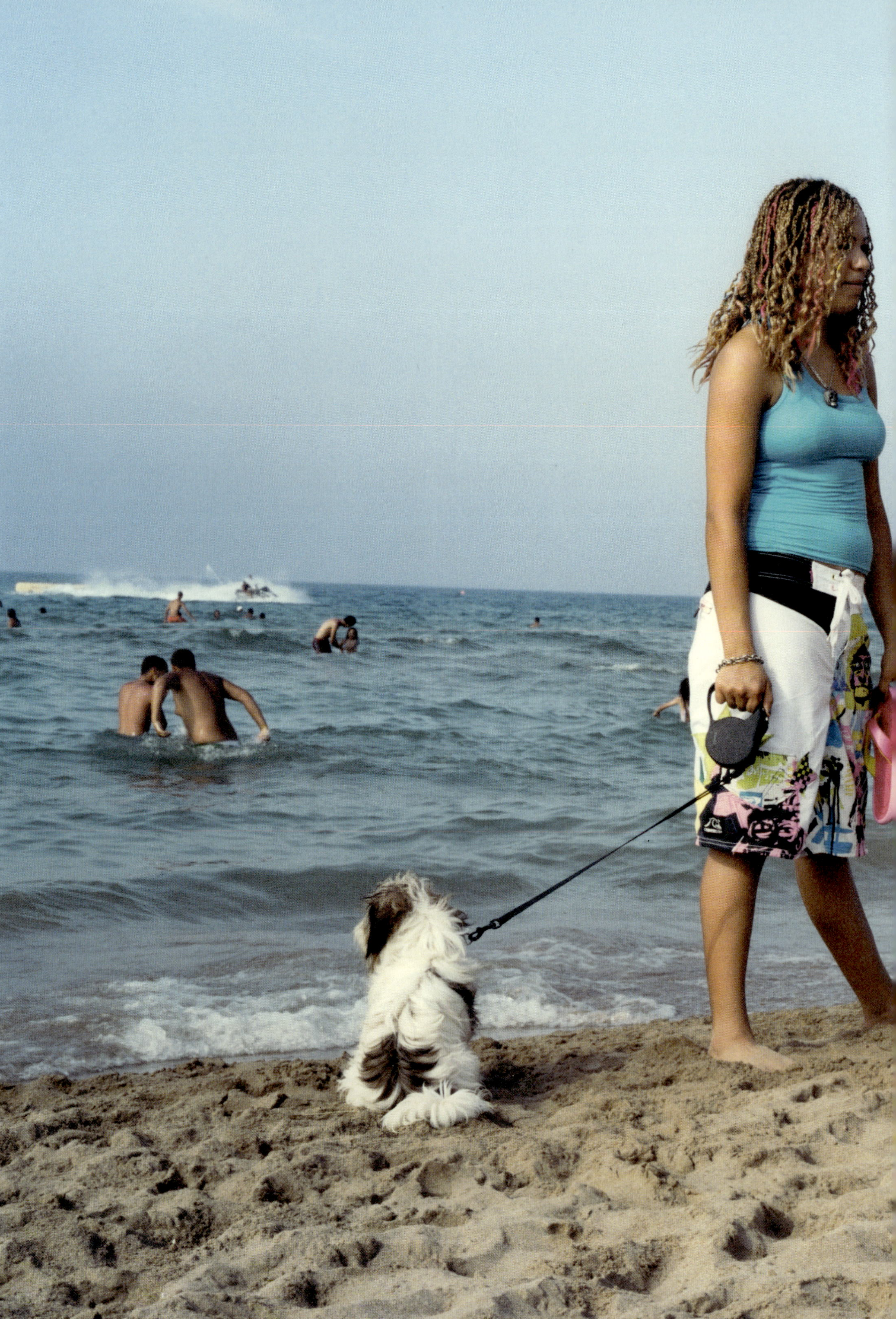

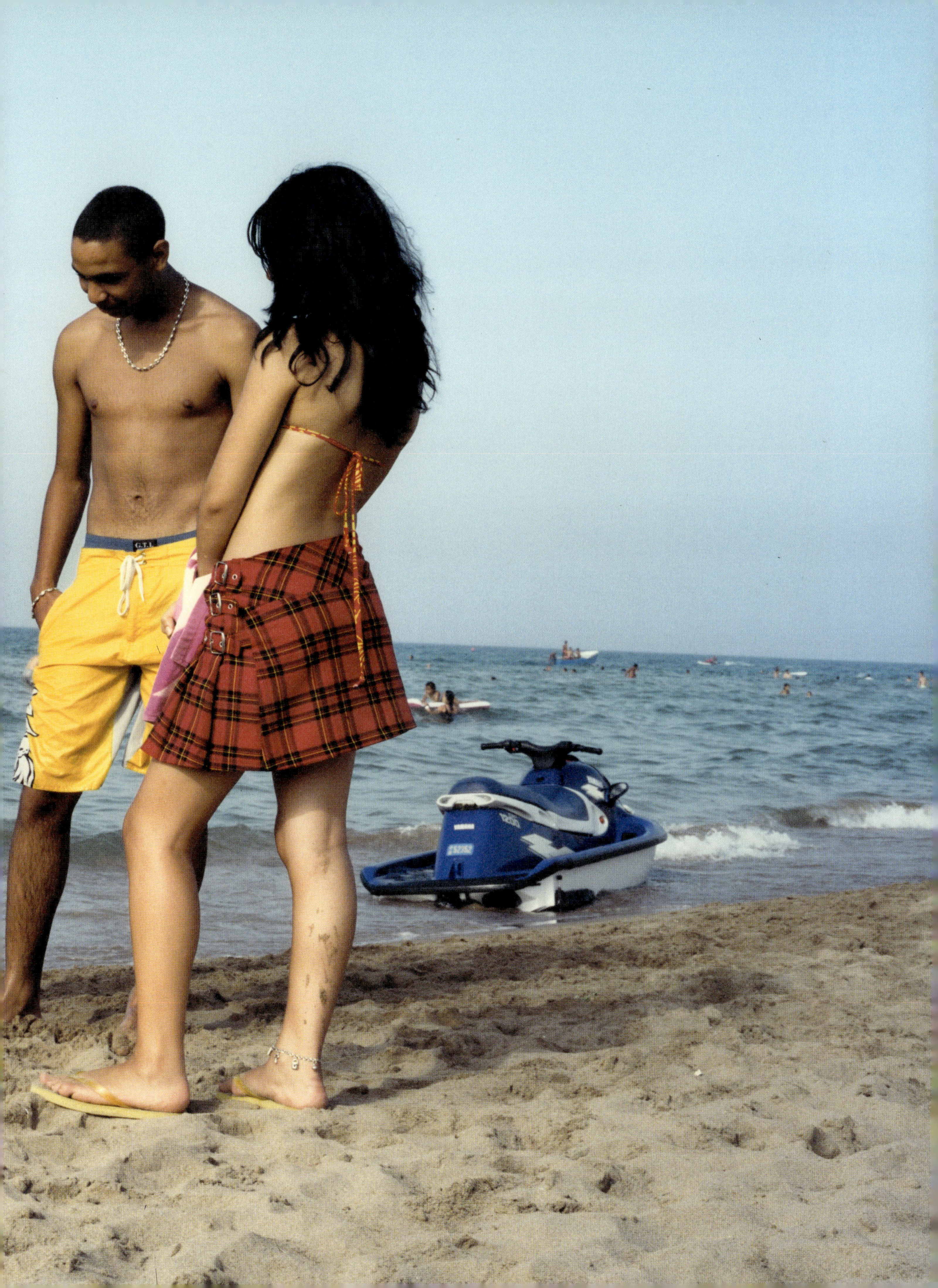

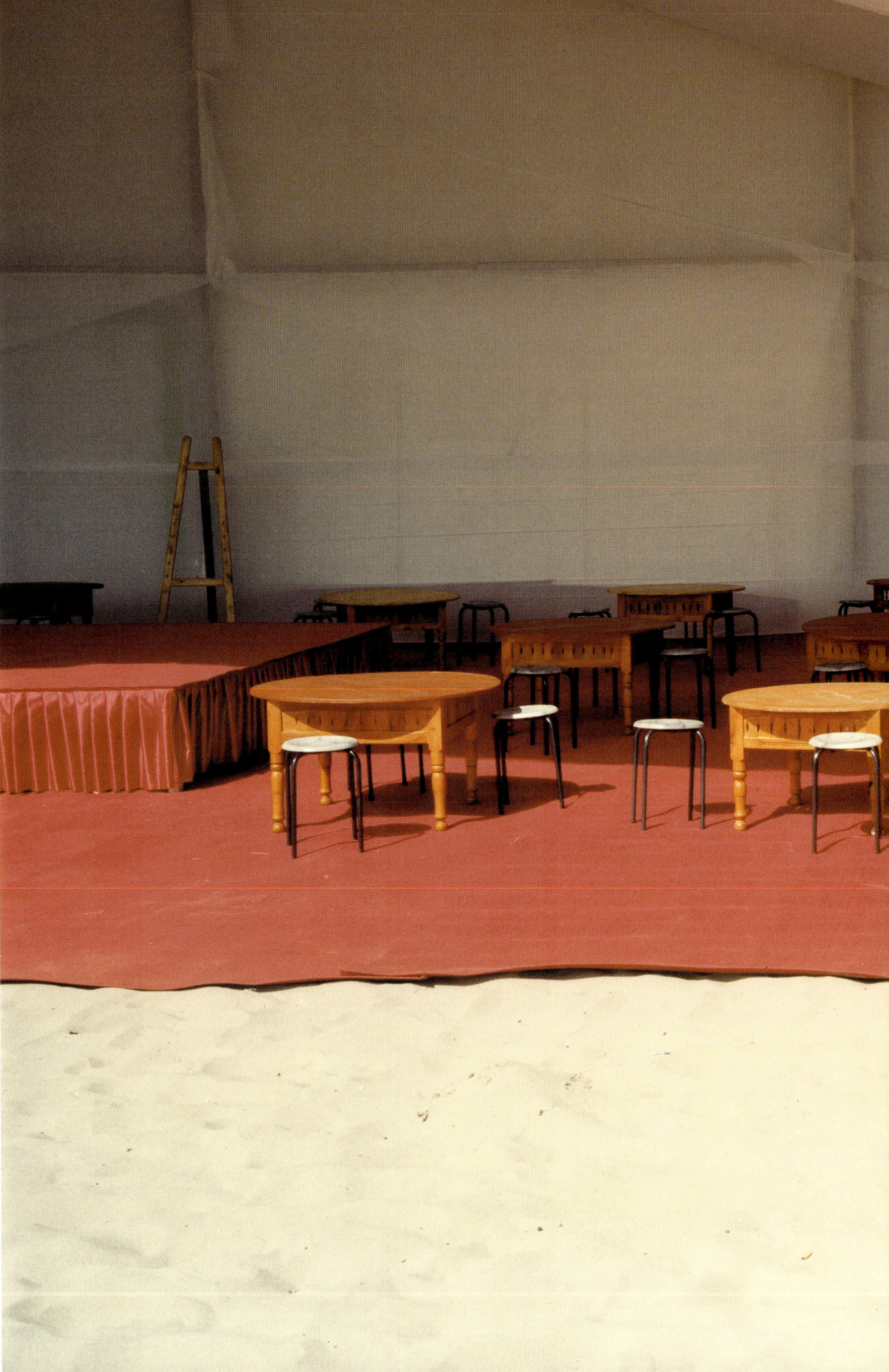

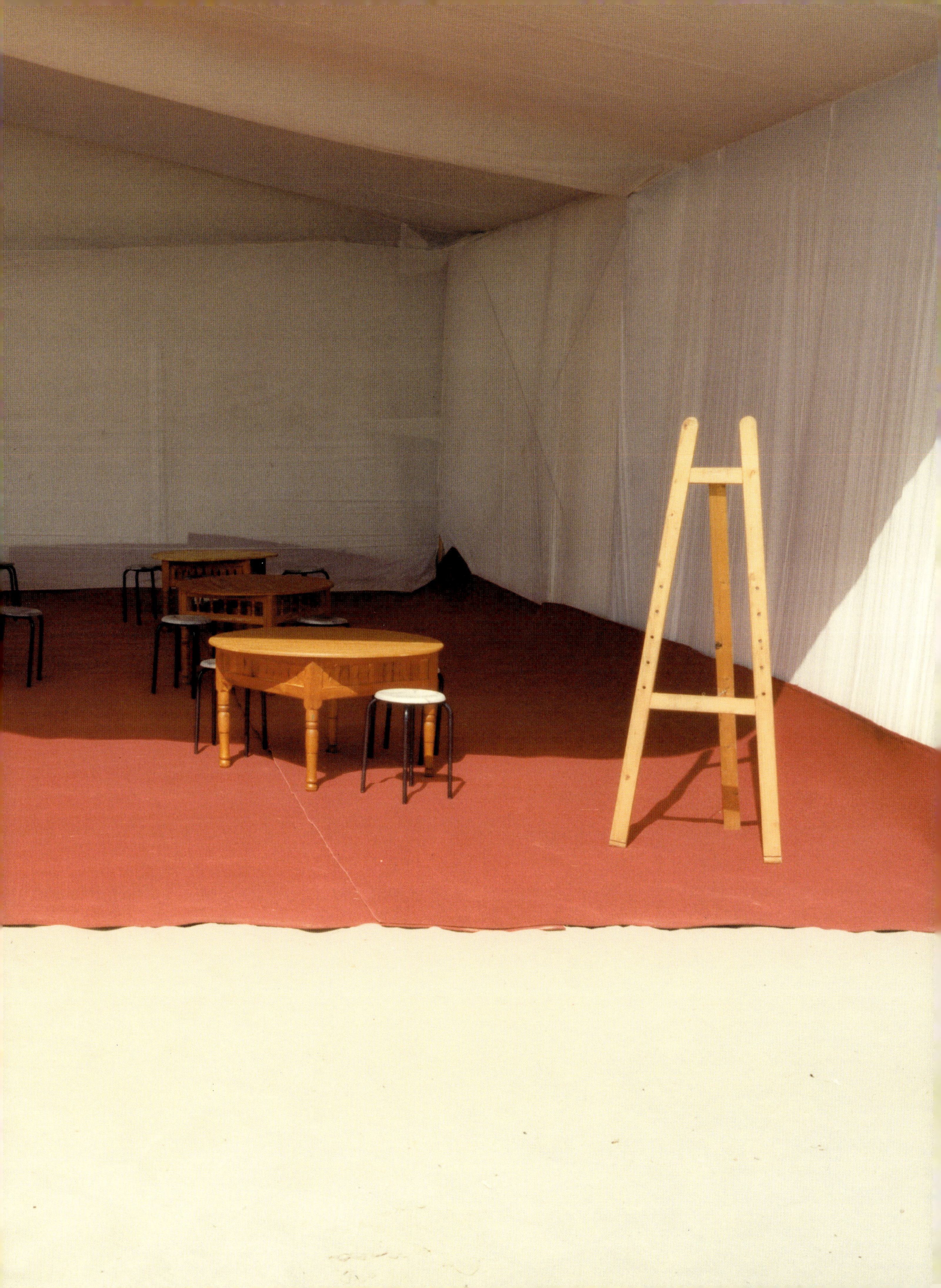

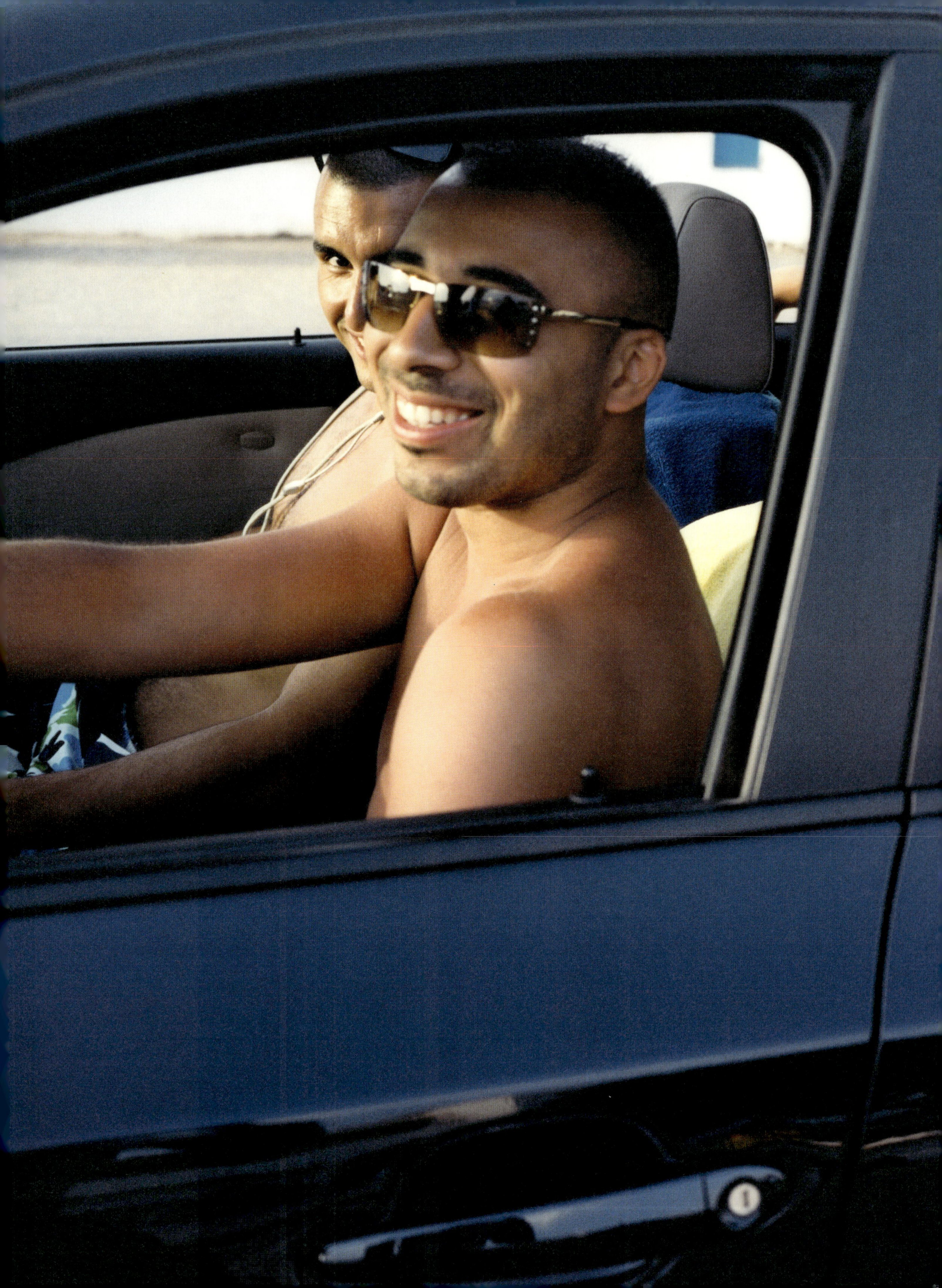

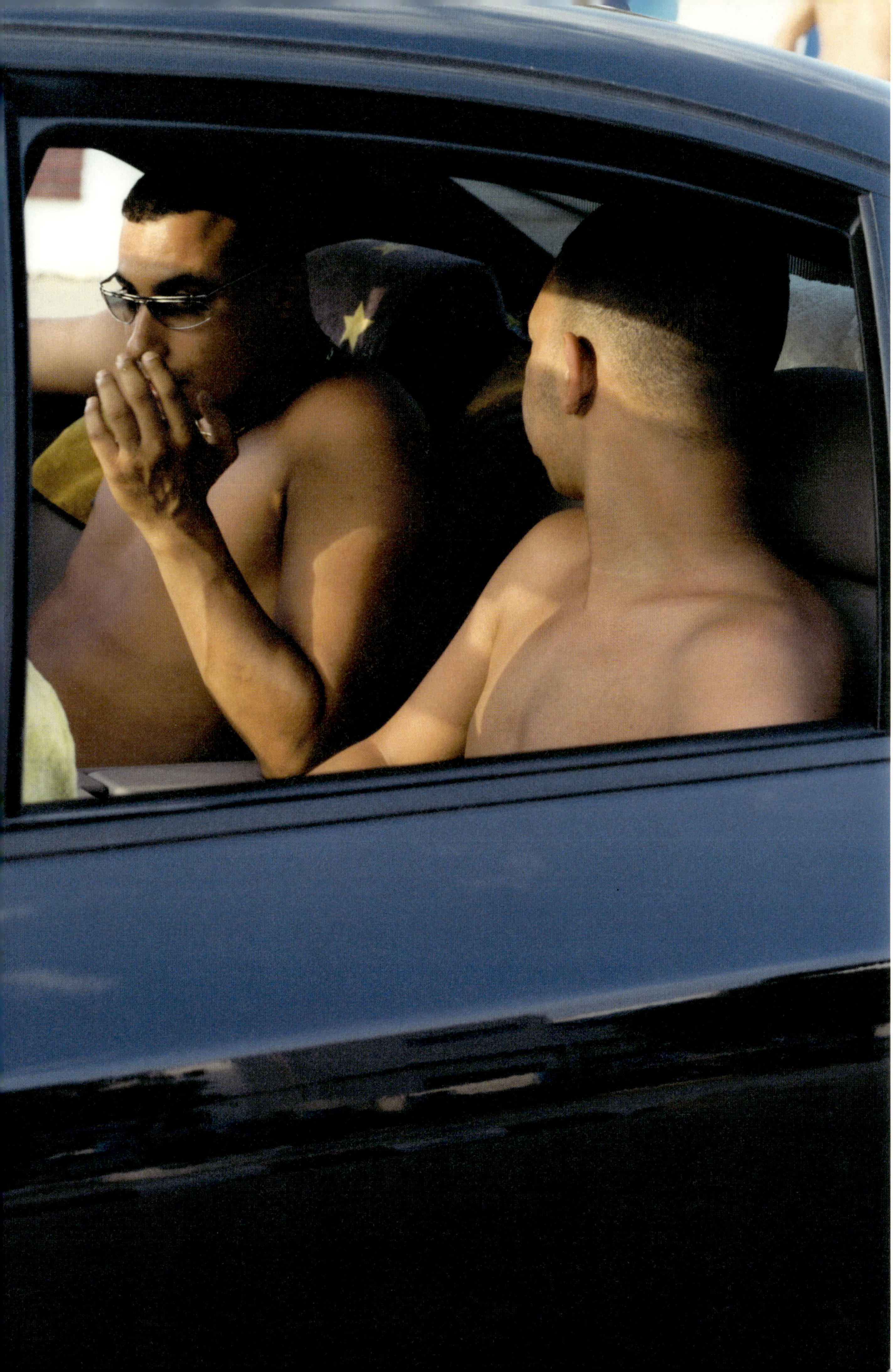

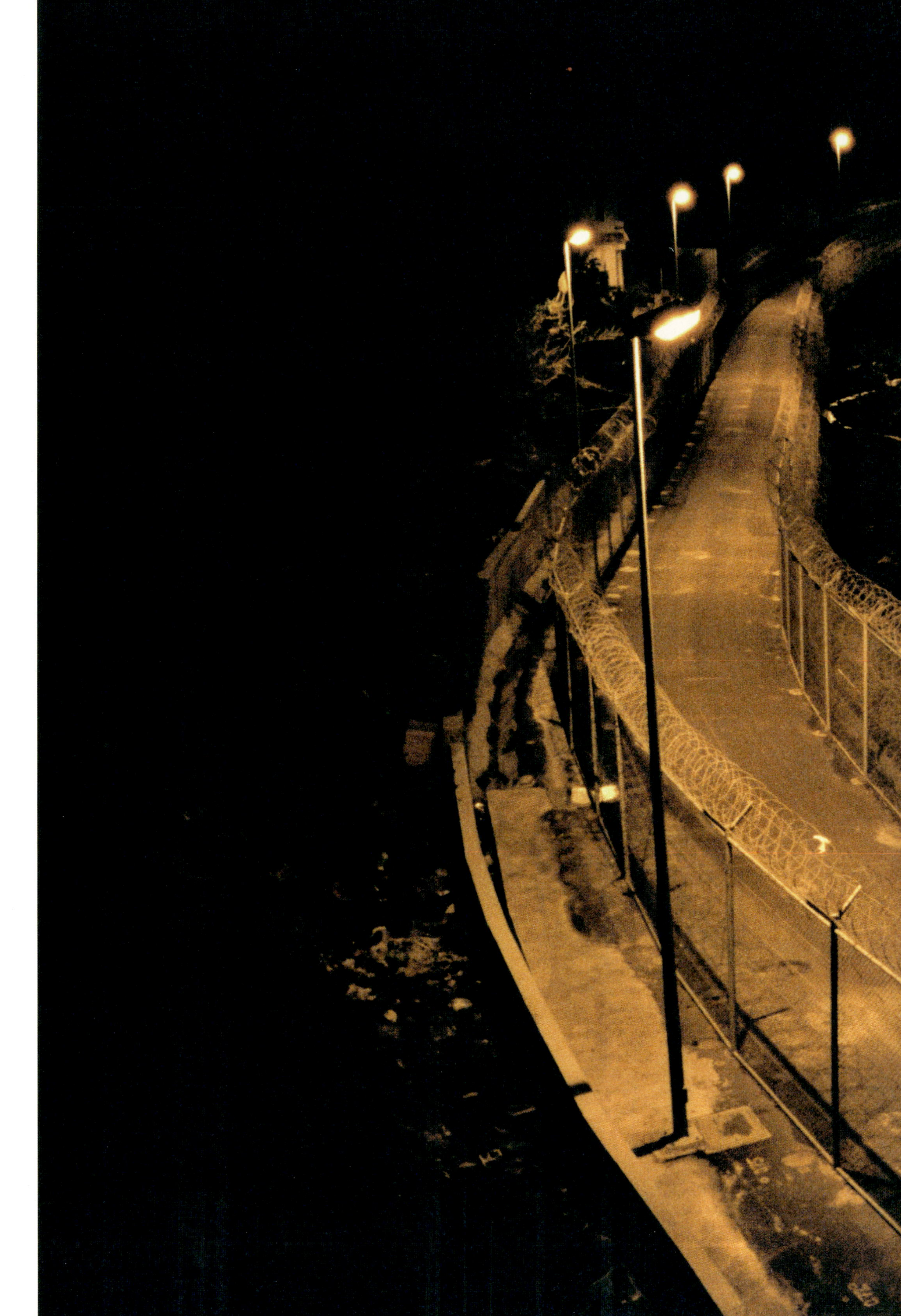

268.

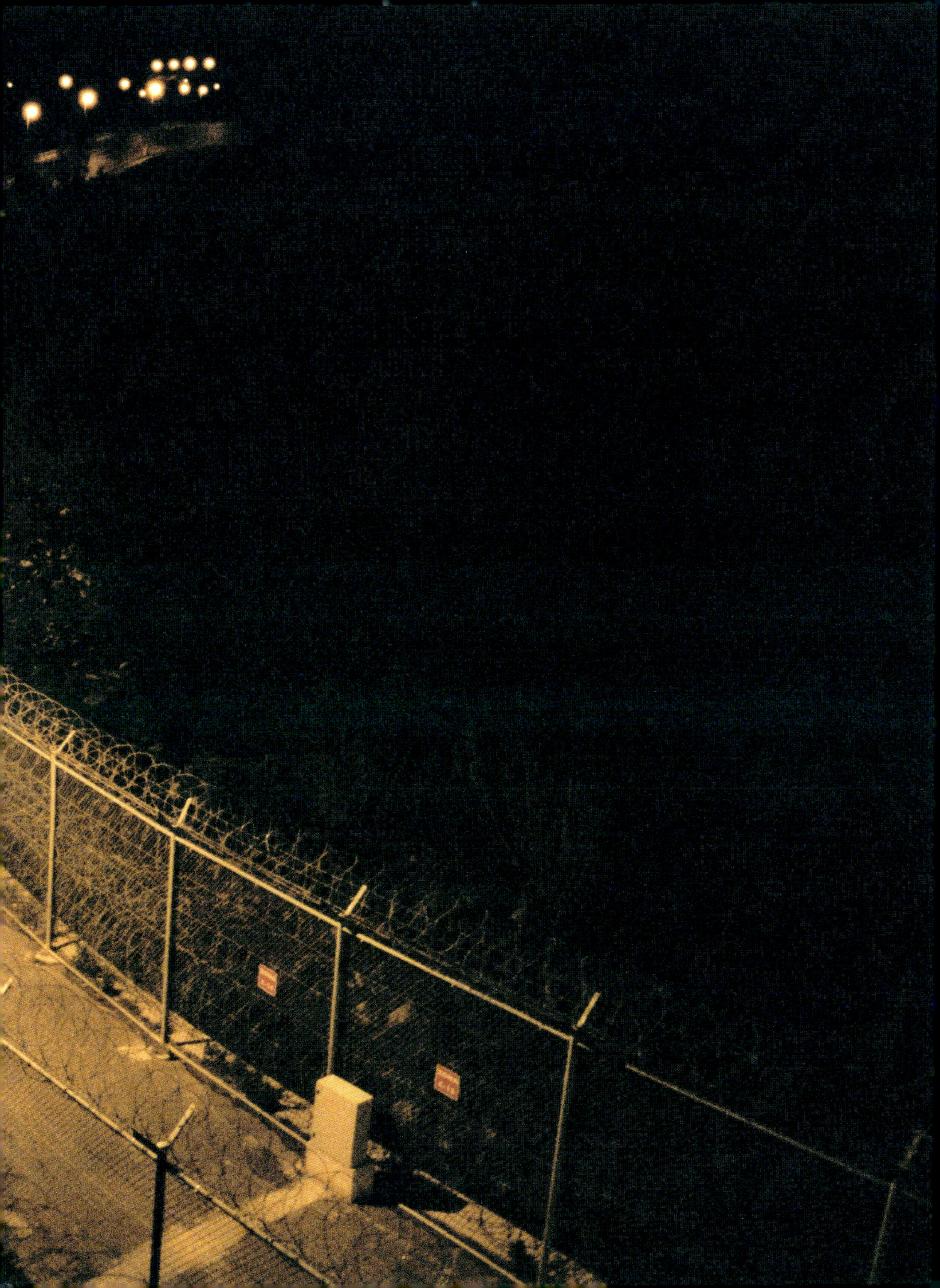

Ad van Denderen (b. 1943) has worked as a photographer for *Vrij Nederland, Stern, NRC Handelsblad, GEO*, and *The Independent magazine*, among others.

He has been awarded a number of prestigious prizes, including the Visa d'Or at the international photo festival Visa pour l'Image in Perpignan in 2001 and the oeuvre prize of The Netherlands Foundation for Visual Arts (Fonds BKVB) in 2007/2008.

Go No Go, his book on migration in Europe, based on 13 years of work, was published in 2003. Earlier publications include a book on Palestine (*Peace in The Holy Land*) in 1997 and *Welkom in Suid-Afrika*, a book about apartheid in 1991. *So Blue, So Blue – Edges of the Mediterranean* was shot between 2003 and 2008.

His work can be found in numerous collections, such as the Stedelijk Museum Amsterdam, The National Museum of Photography Film and Television, Bradford (UK) and the Centre National de l'Audiovisuel (Luxemburg).

His work was exhibited widely in group and solo shows, internationally. *Go No Go* was shown at FOAM and Imagine IC, Amsterdam, the Kunsthalle Wien (Vienna, Austria), La Criée (Rennes, France) and other venues. The project was developed into an audiovisual piece on DVD for Paradox by filmmaker Boris Gerrets and shown at various locations and festivals. It premiered at a special migration meeting of the European Parliament in 2004.

Ad van Denderen is a member of Vu Agency, Paris.

WWW.SOBLUESOBLUE.NL

THANKS TO:
HANS VAN BLOMMESTEIN, LAURA STARINK, ARJEN RIBBENS,
PAUL STEENHUIS, CHRISTIAN CAUJOLLE, FRANK PENDERS,
JENNY SMETS, URS STAHL, MIRA MATIC, BOUDEWIJN RIDDER,
RUUD VISSCHEDIJK, YVO ZIJLSTRA, HUGO GALLEGO SÁNCHEZ,
MISHA VAN DENDEREN, HENK GROOTHUIS, MIA RAMONDT, ROGIER
CREMER, DUBRAVKA UGRESIC, LUTZ FISHMAN, ERIC VISSER,
RUTH EICHHORN, ZIJA SHINI AND FAMILY, INGEBORG BEUGEL,
JOOST KLARENBEEK, JESSICA LUTZ, HANS VAN DER MEER, ABDUL
AND MUSTAFA, NORA BENS, PEP BONET, PAOLO PELLEGRIN,
ROSITA STEENBEEK, XANDRA SCHUTTE, MICHAEL ZEEMAN, HAN
SINGELS, PAUL SCHEFFER, THOMAS DOUBLIEZ, ALMA VERBUNT,
ALI SALMI, NIKOLINA MADUNIC AND FAMILY, ABDELKADER
BENSALAH, DUTCH EMBASSY IN BEIRUT, GILLES BESCHOOR PLUG,
AHMED RACHEDI, PACO OLIVA, MICHAEL WINDIG, MAJDA
ALFSAGA, ABDULATIF CHALED, HERMAN ABBES, ANTHONY
WOUTERS.

SPECIAL THANKS TO:
MICHAEL MACK, HANS AARSMAÑ, BAS VROEGE, RINEKE DIJKSTRA
AND MARGALITH KLEIJWEGT.

SO BLUE, SO BLUE WAS MADE POSSIBLE BY:
STICHTING FONDS ANNA CORNELIS, AMSTERDAM
EYES ON MEDIA, AMSTERDAM

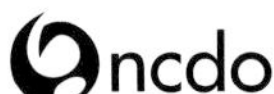

NCDO (DE NATIONALE COMMISSIE VOOR INTERNATIONALE
SAMENWERKING EN DUURZAME ONTWIKKELING), AMSTERDAM

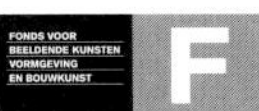

FONDS VOOR BEELDENDE KUNSTEN, VORMGEVING EN BOUWKUNST,
AMSTERDAM

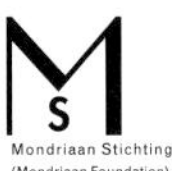

MONDRIAAN STICHTING, AMSTERDAM

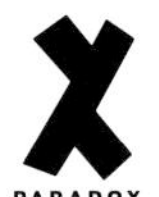

PARADOX, EDAM

FIRST EDITION 2008

© 2008 AD VAN DENDEREN FOR THE IMAGES
© 2008 THE WRITERS FOR THE TEXTS
© 2008 STEIDL MACK FOR THIS EDITION

ALL RIGHTS RESERVED. NO PART OF THIS PUBLICATION MAY BE
REPRODUCED OR TRANSMITTED IN ANY FORM OR BY ANY MEANS,
ELECTRONIC OR MECHANICAL, INCLUDING PHOTOCOPY,
RECORDING OR ANY OTHER STORAGE AND RETRIEVAL SYSTEM,
WITHOUT PRIOR PERMISSION IN WRITING FROM THE PUBLISHER.

PHOTOGRAPHY: AD VAN DENDEREN
PICTURE EDITOR: HANS AARSMAN
TEXTS: FRITS GIERSTBERG, PROSPEKTOR
(ARNOLD VAN BRUGGEN, EEFJE BLANKEVOORT, TOMAS KAAN)
RESEARCH: KAREN LÜTHKE, PROSPEKTOR, INSTITUT EUROPEU
DE LA MEDITERRÀNIA, BARCELONA
TRANSLATOR: CECILY LAYZELL
EDITORS: MICHAEL MACK, BAS VROEGE
ASSISTANT EDITORS: JOBY ELLIS, JOHAN NIEUWENHUIZE
BOOK DESIGN: KUMMER & HERRMAN, UTRECHT
SCANNING: STEIDL'S DIGITAL DARKROOM
PRODUCTION: PARADOX, EDAM, WWW.PARADOX.NL
PRINTING: STEIDL, GÖTTINGEN

STEIDL MACK
DÜSTERE STR. 4
D-37073 GÖTTINGEN
PHONE +49 551-49 60 60
FAX +49 551-49 60 649
E-MAIL: MAIL@STEIDLVILLE.COM
WWW.STEIDLVILLE.COM

ISBN 978-3-86521-734-9

PRINTED IN GERMANY